COMMON LISP
PROGRAMMING
FOR
ARTIFICIAL
INTELLIGENCE

INTERNATIONAL COMPUTER SCIENCE SERIES

Consulting editors **A D McGettrick** University of Strathclyde

J van Leeuwen University of Utrecht

SELECTED TITLES IN THE SERIES

Introduction to Expert Systems *P Jackson*

PROLOG *F Giannesini, H Kanoui, R Pasero and M van Caneghem*

PROLOG Programming for Artificial Intelligence *I Bratko*

POP–11 Programming for Artificial Intelligence *A M Burton and N R Shadbolt*

Parallel Programming *R H Perrott*

Logic Programming and Knowledge Engineering *T Amble*

Functional Programming *A J Field and P G Harrison*

Comparative Programming Languages *L B Wilson and R G Clark*

Distributed Systems: Concepts and Design *G Coulouris and J Dollimore*

Software Prototyping, Formal Methods and VDM *S Hekmatpour and D Ince*

C Programming in a UNIX Environment *J Kay and R Kummerfeld*

An Introduction to Functional Programming through Lambda Calculus
   G Michaelson

Clausal Form Logic: An Introduction to the Logic of Computer Reasoning
   T Richards

Software Engineering (3rd Edn) *I Sommerville*

High-Level Languages and their Compilers *D Watson*

Programming in Ada (3rd Edn) *J G P Barnes*

Interactive Computer Graphics: Functional, Procedural and Device-Level
   Methods *P Burger and D Gillies*

Elements of Functional Programming *C Reade*

Software Development with Modula-2 *D Budgen*

Program Derivation: The Development of Programs from Specifications
   R G Dromey

Programming for Artificial Intelligence: Methods, Tools and Applications
   W Kreutzer and B J McKenzie

Object-Oriented Programming with Simula *B Kirkerud*

Semantics of Programming Languages

Prentice Hall International Series in Computer Science

C. A. R. Hoare, Series Editor

BACKHOUSE, R. C., *Program Construction and Verification*
BACKHOUSE, R. C., *Syntax of Programming Languages: Theory and practice*
DEBAKKER, J. W., *Mathematical Theory of Program Correctness*
BARR, M. and WELLS, C., *Category Theory for Computing Science*
BEN-ARI, M., *Principles of Concurrent and Distributed Programming*
BIRD, R. and WADLER, P., *Introduction to Functional Programming*
BJÖRNER, D. and JONES, C. B., *Formal Specification and Software Development*
BORNAT, R., *Programming from First Principles*
BUSTARD, D., ELDER, J. and WELSH, J., *Concurrent Program Structures*
CLARK, K. L. and McCABE, F. G., *Micro-Prolog: Programming in logic*
CROOKES, D., *Introduction to Programming in Prolog*
DROMEY, R. G., *How to Solve it by Computer*
DUNCAN, E., *Microprocessor Programming and Software Development*
ELDER, J., *Construction of Data Processing Software*
ELLIOTT, R. J. and HOARE, C. A. R., (eds.), *Scientific Applications of Multiprocessors*
GOLDSCHLAGER, L. and LISTER, A., *Computer Science: A modern introduction (2nd edn).*
GORDON, M. J. C., *Programming Language Theory and its Implementation*
HAYES, I, (ed) *Specification Case Studies*
HEHNER, E. C. R., *The Logic of Programming*
HENDERSON, P., *Functional Programming: Application and implementation*
HOARE, C. A. R., *Communicating Sequential Processes*
HOARE, C. A. R., and JONES, C. B. (eds), *Essays in Computing Science*
HOARE, C. A. R., and SHEPHERDSON, J. C. (eds), *Mathematical Logic and Programming Languages*
HUGHES, J. G., *Database Technology: A software engineering approach*
INMOS LTD, *Occam 2 Reference Manual*
JACKSON, M. A., *System Development*
JOHNSTON, H., *Learning to Program*
JONES, C. B., *Systematic Software Development using VDM (2nd edn)*
JONES, C. B. and SHAW, R. C. F. (eds), *Case Studies in Systematic Software Development*
JONES, G., *Programming in occam*
JONES, G, and GOLDSMITH, M., *Programming in occam 2*
JOSEPH, M., PRASAD, V. R. and NATARAJAN, N., *A Multiprocessor Operating System*
LEW, A., *Computer Science: A mathematical introduction*
KALDEWAIJ, A., *Programming: The Derivation of Algorithms*
KING, P. J. B., *Computer and Communications Systems Performance Modelling*
MARTIN, J. J., *Data Types and Data Structures*
MEYER, B., *Introduction to the Theory of Programming Languages*
MEYER, B., *Object-oriented Software Construction*
MILNER, R., *Communication and Concurrency*
MORGAN, C., *Programming from Specifications*
PEYTON JONES, S. L., *The Implementation of Functional Programming Languages*
POMBERGER, G., *Software Engineering and Modula-2*
POTTER, B., SINCLAIR, J., TILL, D., *An Introduction to Formal Specification and Z*
REYNOLDS, J. C., *The Craft of Programming*
RYDEHEARD, D. E. and BURSTALL, R. M., *Computational Category Theory*
SLOMAN, M. and KRAMER, J., *Distributed Systems and Computer Networks*
SPIVEY, J. M., *The Z Notation: A reference manual*
TENNENT, R. D., *Principles of Programming Languages*
WATT, D, A., *Programming Language Concepts and Paradigms*
WATT, D. A., WICHMANN, B. A., and FINDLAY, W., *ADA: Language and methodology*
WELSH, J. and ELDER, J., *Introduction to Modula 2*
WELSH, J. and ELDER, J., *Introduction to Pascal (3rd edn)*
WELSH, J. ELDER, J. and BUSTARD, D., *Sequential Program Structures*
WELSH, J. and HAY, A., *A Model Implementation of Standard Pascal*
WELSH, J. and McKEAG, M., *Structured System Programming*
WIKSTRÖM, Å., *Functional Programming using Standard ML*

Semantics
of
Programming Languages

R. D. Tennent

Queen's University
Kingston, Canada

Prentice Hall
New York   London   Toronto   Sydney   Tokyo   Singapore

First published 1991 by
Prentice Hall International (UK) Ltd
66 Wood Lane End, Hemel Hempstead
Hertfordshire HP2 4RG
A division of
Simon & Schuster International Group

Transferred to digital print on demand 2002
Printed and bound by Antony Rowe Ltd, Eastbourne

Library of Congress Cataloging-in-Publication Data

Tennent, R. D., 1944-
  Semantics of programming languages / R. D. Tennent.
    p.   cm.
  Includes bibliographical references and index.
  ISBN 0-13-805607-2 (cloth) : — ISBN 0-13-805599-8 (pbk.)

  1. Programming languages (Electronic computers) — Semantics.
I. Title.
QA76.7.T473 1990
005.13--dc20   90-23067
                                                                   CIP

British Library Cataloguing in Publication Data

Tennent, R. D. 1944-
  Semantics of programming languages.
  1. Computer systems. Programming
  1. Title
  005.1

ISBN 0-13-805607-2
ISBN 0-13-805599-8 pbk

---

1 2 3 4 5   95 94 93 92 91

For Alan and Jenny

Contents

Glossary of Notation   xi

List of Tables   xv

Foreword by John C. Reynolds   xvii

Preface   xix

I Introduction   1

1 Semantics   3
   1.1 An Example: Binary Numerals   4
   1.2 Discussion   7
      1.2.1 Compositionality   7
      1.2.2 Full Abstraction   9
      1.2.3 Formality   10
      1.2.4 Comprehensibility   10
   1.3 Overview   12
   Exercises   13
   Bibliographic Notes   13

2 Mathematical Preliminaries   15
   2.1 Natural Deduction   15
   2.2 Functions   19
   2.3 Partial Functions   21
   2.4 Natural Numbers   22
   2.5 Products of Sets   22
   2.6 Sums of Sets   23

2.7 Binary Relations   23
2.8 Partially-Ordered Sets   24
Exercises   25
Bibliographic Notes   27

II Basic Concepts   29

3 A Simple Imperative Language   31
3.1 Expressions and Commands   32
    3.1.1 Syntax   32
    3.1.2 Semantics   34
3.2 Assignment Commands   36
3.3 Indefinite Iterations   38
3.4 Programs   41
3.5 Operational Semantics   42
3.6 Programming Logic   46
    3.6.1 Syntax and Semantics   47
    3.6.2 Rules and Axioms   48
    3.6.3 Soundness   51
3.7 Non-Determinism   53
Exercises   55
Bibliographic Notes   57

4 A Simple Applicative Language   59
4.1 Definitions and Function Applications   60
4.2 Function Definitions   66
4.3 Defined Notation   67
4.4 Elementary Properties   70
4.5 Programming Logic   73
    4.5.1 Syntax and Semantics   74
    4.5.2 Substitution   75
    4.5.3 Rules and Axioms   79
Exercises   82
Bibliographic Notes   85

5 Recursion and Domain Theory   86
5.1 Recursive Definitions   86
5.2 Computational Domains   88
5.3 Continuous Functions   92
5.4 Domain-Theoretic Semantics   96
5.5 Operational Semantics   103
5.6 Programming Logic   105
    5.6.1 Syntax and Semantics   105

		5.6.2 Rules and Axioms	105
	5.7	Full Abstraction	108
		Exercises	109
		Bibliographic Notes	111

III   An Algol-Like Language 113

6   An Algol-Like Language I   **115**

	6.1	Syntax	116
	6.2	Semantics	119
	6.3	Call by Value	123
	6.4	Programming Logic	127
		6.4.1 Syntax and Semantics	127
		6.4.2 Axioms and Derived Rules	128
		Exercises	132
		Bibliographic Notes	134

7   An Algol-Like Language II   **135**

	7.1	Coercions	135
	7.2	Local Variables	143
	7.3	Product Types and Arrays	145
	7.4	Acceptors	148
	7.5	Jumps	151
		7.5.1 Completions	151
		7.5.2 Programming Logic	155
	7.6	Block Expressions	156
		Exercises	158
		Bibliographic Notes	159

IV   Advanced Techniques 161

8   An Introduction to Category Theory   **163**

	8.1	Categories	164
	8.2	Special Objects and Morphisms	167
	8.3	Functors and Natural Transformations	171
		Exercises	176
		Bibliographic Notes	176

9   Possible Worlds   **177**

	9.1	Functor-Category Semantics	177
	9.2	Semantic-Domain Functors	179
	9.3	Semantic Valuations	183

9.4	Semantics of Local Variables	186
9.5	Specifications	189
9.6	Non-Interference Specifications	191
9.7	Semantics of Block Expressions	196
	Exercises	198
	Bibliographic Notes	199

10 Recursively-Defined Domains **200**

10.1	Examples	200
10.2	Embeddings of Domains	204
10.3	Least Fixed Points of Functors	208
10.4	Applications	215
	10.4.1 Intermediate Output	215
	10.4.2 Lists	216
	10.4.3 Untyped Procedures	218
	Exercises	219
	Bibliographic Notes	219

Bibliography **221**

Index **233**

Glossary of Notation

θ	a phrase type	4
$[\![\theta]\!]$	the domain of phrase meanings of type θ	4
$X\!:\!\theta$	X is a well-formed phrase of phrase type θ	5
$[\theta]$	the set of well-formed phrases of type θ	6
$[\![X]\!]_\theta$	the meaning of phrase X of type θ	6
$X \equiv_\theta X'$	X and X' of type θ are semantically equivalent	8
Z	a specification	15
Σ	a finite set of specifications	16
$\Sigma \vdash Z$	Z holds whenever all elements of Σ do	16
$\Sigma' \vdash \Sigma$	$\Sigma \subseteq \Sigma'$	18
dom f	the domain of function f	19
codom f	the co-domain of function f	19
graph f	the graph of function f	19
$f\!:\!A \rightarrow B$	f is a function from A to B	19
id_A	the identity function on A	20
$(f \mid a \mapsto b)$	the function like f except that a is mapped to b	20
$f \,;\, g$	the composite of functions f and g	20
$f\!:\!A \rightharpoonup B$	f is a partial function from A to B	21
N	the set of natural numbers	22
f^n	the n-th iterate of function f	22
ω	the ordered set of natural numbers	22
$A_0 \times A_1$	the Cartesian product of sets A_0 and A_1	22
$\prod_{i \in I} A_i$	the generalized product of sets	22
A^n	the set of all n-tuples over set A	23
A^ω	the set of all infinite sequences over set A	23
$A^{\omega \times \omega}$	the set of all infinite matrices over set A	23
$I \rightarrow A$	the set of all functions from I to A	23
$A_0 + A_1$	the sum (or disjoint union) of sets A_0 and A_1	23
$\sum_{i \in I} A_i$	the generalized sum of sets	23
A^*	the set of all finite tuples over set A	23

$a\,R\,a'$	a is related by R to a'	23
$[a]_R$	the R-equivalence class of a	24
A/R	the set of R-equivalence classes	24
R^*	the reflexive and transitive closure of relation R	24
$\sqsubseteq$	a partial order	24
$|D|$	the carrier (or set underlying) poset D	25
$\sqsubseteq_D$	the partial order of poset D	25
$d \in D$	d is an element of the set underlying poset D	25
$\perp_D$	the bottom (or least element) of poset D	25
$\mathrm{lub}\,S, \bigsqcup S$	the least upper bound of S	25
$a \sqcup b$	the least upper bound of $\{a,b\}$	25
$\bigsqcup_{i \in I} s_i$	the least upper bound of $\{\ldots, s_i, \ldots\}$	25
D^ω	the set of all ascending ω-chains over poset D	25
τ	a data type	32
C	a command phrase	32
B	a Boolean expression	32
N	a numerical expression	32
$[\![\tau]\!]$	the set of values of type τ	34
S	the set of computational states	34
s	a computational state	35
ι	an identifier	37
π_0	the assignment of types to pre-defined identifiers	37
$[\tau]$	the set of pre-defined τ-valued variable identifiers	37
g_0	the mapping of inputs to initial states	42
k_0	the mapping of final states to outputs	42
(C, s)	a machine configuration	43
$(C, s) \triangleright (C', s')$	(C, s) reduces in one step to (C', s')	43
$C \overset{s}{\triangleright} C'$	(C, s) reduces in one step to (C', s)	43
$\{\!\!\{X\}\!\!\}$	operational valuation of phrase X	43
$[P](\iota \mapsto E)$	result of substituting E for ι in P	48
π	an assignment of phrase-types to identifiers	61
$\pi \vdash X \!:\! \theta$	X is a phrase of type θ in π	61
$\pi(\iota)$	the type of ι in π	63
u	an environment, mapping identifiers to meanings	64
$[\![\pi]\!]$	the π-compatible environments	64
$[\theta]_\pi$	the set of phrases of type θ in π	64
$[\![X]\!]_{\pi\theta}$	the semantics of phrase X of type θ in π	64
u_0	the assignment of meanings to pre-defined identifiers	64
$\pi' \vdash \pi$	π' is an extension of π	71
$[\![\pi' \vdash \pi]\!]$	environment-restriction map	72
$free(X)$	the set of free identifiers in phrase X	72
σ	an assignment of phrases to identifiers	76
$free(\sigma)$	$\bigcup_{\iota \in \mathrm{dom}\,\sigma} free(\sigma(\iota))$	76

$[X]\sigma$	apply the substitution specified by σ to phrase X	76
$[\pi_0]_{\pi_1}$	the set of type-preserving substitutions from π_0 to π_1	77
$\ddot{A}$	the discretely-ordered domain with carrier A	89
$D \times E$	the product of domains D and E	89
$D + E$	the sum of domains D and E	90
$D_\perp$	the domain obtained by "lifting" domain D	90
$A \to D$	the domain of functions from set A to D	91
$A \rightharpoonup D$	the domain of partial functions from set A to D	91
$D \to E$	the domain of continuous functions from D to E	95
$D \rightharpoonup E$	the continuous partial functions from D to E	95
$X \rhd_\theta X'$	$X \in [\theta]_{\pi_0}$ reduces in one step to X'	103
$m \,\|\theta\|\, X$	$m \sqsubseteq \{\!X\!\}$ in $[\![\theta]\!]$	103
$\mathcal{E}[\![\theta]\!]$	the domain of expressible meanings of phrase type θ	125
$\theta \vdash \theta'$	θ coerces to θ'	136
$\theta \simeq \theta'$	$\theta \vdash \theta'$ and $\theta' \vdash \theta$	136
$[\![\theta \vdash \theta']\!]$	the conversion function from $[\![\theta]\!]$ to $[\![\theta']\!]$	136
$\langle X \rangle \pi$	a least type of X in π	138
$[\![\pi' \vdash \pi]\!]$	the component-wise conversion of environments	140
dom f	the domain object for morphism f	164
codom f	the co-domain object for morphism f	164
$f : x \to y$	f is a morphism from x to y	164
id_x	the identity morphism on x	164
$f \,;\, g$	the composite of morphisms f and g	164
$\mathbf{C}$	a category	164
$\mathbf{S}$	the category of sets and functions	164
$\mathbf{D}$	the category of domains and continuous functions	164
$\mathbf{C}^{\mathrm{op}}$	the category opposite to $\mathbf{C}$	165
$\mathbf{C}_0 \times \mathbf{C}_1$	the product of categories $\mathbf{C}_0$ and $\mathbf{C}_1$	166
$\mathbf{C}^{\to}$	the category of arrows of category $\mathbf{C}$	166
$c \cong c'$	the objects c and c' are isomorphic	167
$c_0 \times c_1$	a product of objects c_0 and c_1	168
π_i	a projection morphism from a product object	168
$f_0 \times f_1$	the product of morphisms f_0 and f_1	169
$c_0 + c_1$	a sum of objects c_0 and c_1	169
ι_i	an injection morphism into a sum object	169
$f_0 + f_1$	the sum of morphisms f_0 and f_1	170
$c \Rightarrow d$	an exponentiation of objects c and d	170
η	the evaluation morphism for an exponential object	170
$f \to g$	the exponentiation of morphisms f and g	171
$F : \mathbf{C} \to \mathbf{C}'$	F is a functor from $\mathbf{C}$ to $\mathbf{C}'$	171
Θ	the category of phrase types	172
$\mathbf{D}_\perp$	the category of domains with least elements	172
$\mathrm{id}_{\mathbf{C}}$	the identity functor on category $\mathbf{C}$	172

$\eta\colon F \xrightarrow{\cdot} G$	η is a natural transformation from F to G	173
$\mathbf{\Pi}$	the category of phrase-type assignments	174
id_F	the identity natural transformation on functor F	174
$\eta \mathbin{;} \tau$	the composite of natural transformations η and τ	175
$\mathbf{C} \Rightarrow \mathbf{C}'$	the category of functors from $\mathbf{C}$ to $\mathbf{C}'$	175
$\mathbf{2}$	the category with morphism $0 \to 1$	175
$\mathbf{W}$	a category of possible worlds	178
$\times V$	a state-set expansion morphism in $\mathbf{W}$	187
$\lceil W$	a state-set restriction morphism in $\mathbf{W}$	194
$\lceil Q$	a state-change restriction morphism in $\mathbf{W}$	194
$+D$	an answer-domain adjunction morphism in $\mathbf{W}$	196
f^P	the projection corresponding to an embedding f	204
$f\colon D \lhd E$	f is an embedding of D into E	204
$\mathbf{D}^E$	the category of domains and embeddings	204
$\eta\colon \Delta \to D$	η is a cone with vertex D for Δ	206
$f \xrightarrow{E} g$	partial exponentiation of embeddings f and g	212
$f \xrightarrow{E} g$	total exponentiation of embeddings f and g	214

List of Tables

1.1	Syntax of binary numerals.	6
1.2	Semantic equations for binary numerals.	7
2.1	Syntax of specifications.	16
2.2	Semantic equations for specifications.	17
2.3	Natural-deduction rules for propositional logic.	17
3.1	Syntax of the imperative language.	33
3.2	Semantic equations for the imperative language.	35
3.3	Command equivalences.	36
3.4	Operational semantics of the imperative language.	44
3.5	Trace of a computation.	45
4.1	Syntax of the applicative language.	62
5.1	Operational semantics of the applicative language.	104
5.2	A derivation of Park's Theorem in LCF.	108
7.1	A class of counter objects.	146
7.2	An array declarator.	148
7.3	Continuation semantics.	152
9.1	Semantic-domain functors.	182
9.2	Semantic equations.	183
9.3	Semantics of specifications.	190

Foreword

Why is it so hard to design a good programming language? Naively, one might expect that a straightforward extension of the conventional notation of science and mathematics should provide a completely adequate programming language. But the history of language design has destroyed this illusion.

We do have languages that can be fairly called clean and uniform, most notably the simple imperative language and various forms of the lambda calculus. For these languages we can give elegant semantics and simple logics for proving that programs meet their specifications. Moreover, for programs within their limited domains of discourse, these languages are natural vehicles of expression; they rarely lead the programmer into a misunderstanding of what he has written.

However, so-called practical languages invariably have horrendously complex semantics and proof methods, with subtle complications that are a rich source of programming errors. With such languages, programmers spend as much time fighting the language as solving their real problems, practical program verification is impossible, and trustworthy programs are unattainable. A telling symptom of this state of affairs is the existence of "wizards," programmers whose primary expertise is understanding the anomalies of a particular language or system.

The truth of the matter is that putting languages together is a very tricky business. When one attempts to combine language concepts, unexpected and counterintuitive interactions arise. At this point, even the most experienced designer's intuition must be buttressed by a rigorous definition of what the language means.

Of course, this is what programming-language semantics is all about. Over the last quarter century, a group of mathematicians, logicians, and theoretical computer scientists have devised an impressive array of definitional techniques, and demonstrated that these techniques suffice to describe the most complicated programming languages. In doing so, however, they have revealed just how complicated these languages really are; their definitions are immense formal handbooks for the ultimate wizards.

The hitch is that defining a language *a posteriori*, i.e. after its design has been frozen by the existence of implementations and users, can hardly improve it. To create a good programming language, semantics must be used *a priori*, as a design tool that embodies and extends the intuitive notion of uniformity.

That is the subject of this book. Bob Tennent begins with a thorough exposition of the semantics and proof systems of the simple imperative language and the simply typed lambda calculus. Then he examines how these languages, along with their semantics and proof systems, can be combined in a way that basically follows the design of ALGOL 60. At this point he demonstrates dramatically how a clear understanding of the underlying theory of a language can guide the details of its design.

Reading through the manuscript, I am particularly impressed by the avoidance of unnecessary (but only unnecessary) mathematics. The author has done a fine job of making the subject as accessible as possible without sacrificing rigor or clarity. To do so, however, he has largely limited his exposition to what is needed to show a realistic application of semantic techniques.

Thus this is not a comprehensive treatise on the whole of semantics. In particular, much more can be said about call by value, continuations, and especially type systems. Moreover, the reader should not infer that Algol-like languages are generally accepted as the probable mainstream of future language development. Strong cases can also be made for Scheme-like languages and for purely functional languages.

But such matters are for other books. Here one has a rigorous but accessible demonstration of why semantics is vital to the future of programming-language design.

John C. Reynolds
3 September 1990

Preface

This book is intended to provide for beginning graduate students a concise survey of the most important and fundamental work on semantics of "conventional" programming languages, together with the necessary background material from logic, type theory, domain theory, and category theory. The prerequisites are: some experience with high-level programming languages, preferably including a modern "functional" language such as SCHEME or ML, and elementary discrete mathematics, especially propositional and predicate logic, and partially-ordered sets. Chapter 2 summarizes the conventional mathematical and logical material assumed in the rest of the book.

The book is not intended for general undergraduate use; however, the material should not be inaccessible to undergraduates with some interest in the subject, provided they have sufficient mathematical maturity. If the book is being used as a text and the students are lacking in this respect, it will be necessary to adopt a relatively slow pace of presentation and to skim over or omit some of the more difficult topics (which are generally in the concluding sections of chapters) and Part IV.

All of the three major approaches to semantics – denotational, operational, and axiomatic – and the relations between them are discussed. The standard denotational-semantic concepts (states, environments, continuations, domain equations) are presented, and also *possible worlds*, an important technique in logic that has recently been applied to describing programming languages. Concurrency is not discussed.

The necessary elementary domain theory (complete partial orders, continuous functions, fixed points, inverse limits) is presented, but more advanced topics such as bounded-completeness, algebraicity, powerdomains, information systems, universal domains, and effectiveness are not discussed. To allow the reader to become comfortable with semantic methods using familiar mathematical tools, I defer explicit introduction of domain-theoretic concepts by using partial functions on sets of states to interpret a simple imperative language and conventional set-theoretic functions to interpret a simple functional language without recursion. The use of possibly "bottom-less" domains allows a nice continuity between the set-theoretic and domain-theoretic constructions, particularly in the solution of recursive domain equations.

The presentation of denotational-semantic methods is unconventional in some other respects. In their pioneering papers, it was convenient for Dana Scott and Christopher Strachey to demonstrate their new techniques on typeless or dynamically-typed languages. Most workers in the field (including this author) went on to use virtually the same techniques on statically-typed languages. But this style of semantics is cumbersome and unrealistic because of the unnecessary type-checking and branching on types that appears in the semantic equations.

The presentation here uses minor variants of the traditional techniques in order to deal more satisfactorily with statically-typed languages. For example, Boolean and numerical expressions are distinguished syntactically, and there are separate domains of expressible values for each of these types of expressions, rather than a single domain of *all* expressible values. Although the syntactic descriptions must be slightly more complex to make the appropriate type distinctions, the semantic descriptions are much simpler and more realistic and precise. Inference rules in natural-deduction style are used to specify non-context-free type and scope constraints on the syntax.

Modern research on semantics, domain theory and type theory is increasingly dependent on category-theoretical terminology, concepts, and techniques. Chapter 8 is a short introduction to some elementary concepts of category theory, and these are used to give elegant presentations of inverse-limit construction and possible-world semantics.

The style of *operational* semantics discussed is the "structured" form of reduction system popularized by Robin Milner and Gordon Plotkin. The operational descriptions presented are proved functionally equivalent (at the level of complete programs) to the denotational ones. The concept of full abstraction is defined but discussed only briefly.

The *axiomatic* systems presented are: fragments of propositional and predicate logic; Floyd–Hoare logic for a simple imperative language; simply-typed lambda calculus and Dana Scott's "Logic for Computable Functions" for an applicative language; and John Reynolds's "Specification Logic" for an Algol-like language. Only small examples of these systems in actual use are presented, but each is given a denotational interpretation and shown to be sound.

A detailed study of the subject of *completeness* of programming logics is beyond the scope of an introductory text. Some readers may be surprised that I do not even discuss Stephen Cook's notion of relative completeness. The reason is that researchers are increasingly questioning the robustness of this notion. The well-known result of Ed Clarke (that an Algol-like language cannot have a sound and Cook-complete Hoare-style logic) has been regarded by some as justification for restricting the power of Algol-like languages; however, the result may turn out to be just further evidence of the inappropriateness of the criterion.

To give examples, I have chosen to focus attention on a *single* ALGOL 60-like language and two important fragments of it: the simple imperative language of **while** programs, and a "sugared" version of the applicative language that Gordon Plotkin termed PCF; i.e., the simply-typed lambda notation augmented by conditionals, recursion, and arithmetic. This approach emphasizes call-by-name, statically-typed, and deterministic languages, but there is also some brief discussion of the semantics of call-by-value, dynamically-typed, and indeterminate languages. Although ALGOL 60-like languages are relatively unfamiliar these days, their *semantic* elegance, as revealed to us by John Reynolds, is, in my view, compelling.

Some of the material in this book was written for the chapter on "Denotational Semantics" in Volume II of the *Handbook of Logic in Computer Science*, edited by S. Abramsky, D. M. Gabbay, and T. S. E. Maibaum, to be published by Oxford University Press.

I am very grateful to John Reynolds for writing a foreword and to everyone who gave me comments on draft versions of (parts of) this material, especially David Andrews, Ellen Atack, David Barnard, Ian Carmichael, Gwen Clarke, Laurie Hendren, Tony Hoare, Peter O'Hearn, Andy Pitts, John Reynolds, Edmund Robinson, David Schmidt, Allen Stoughton, Kevin Tobin, and Chris Wadsworth. The remaining omissions, obscurities and errors are my responsibility.

R.D.T.

PART I

Introduction

Chapter 1

Semantics

Semantics is a strange kind of applied mathematics; it seeks profound definitions rather than difficult theorems. The mathematical concepts which are relevant are immediately relevant. Without any long chains of reasoning, the application of such concepts directly reveals regularity in linguistic behaviour, and strengthens and objectifies our intuitions of simplicity and uniformity.

J. C. Reynolds (1980)

Designers, implementers, and serious users of a programming language need a complete and accurate understanding of the *semantics* (the intended meaning) as well as the *syntax* (the form) of every construct of that language. For the *syntactic* aspects of programming languages, there is a well-developed and widely-known mathematical theory of formal languages which supports accurate description of (the context-free aspects of) the syntax of programming languages, and correct implementation of scanners and parsers. But the *semantic* descriptions in reference manuals and language standards are almost always inadequate because they are based primarily on implementation techniques and intuition.

A rigorous mathematical theory of the semantics of programming languages is needed to support correct description and implementation of their meanings, systematic development and verification of programs, analysis of existing programming languages, and design of new languages that are simpler and more regular. This theory and its applications are the subjects of this book.

1.1   An Example: Binary Numerals

*It may seem that the equations are circular or even vacuous in content.
Such a conclusion is wrong, however, because there is an easily appreciated
point to the definition: namely, the explication of the* positional notation.

D. Scott and C. Strachey (1971)

In this section we present a description of the syntax and semantics of the
"language" of binary numerals; i.e., positional representation of natural
numbers, using base 2. For example, 1101 is a binary numeral and it
denotes the natural number thirteen. This will allow us to introduce some
of our notational conventions and to discuss various issues in a relatively
simple context.

The first step is to specify the (names of the) *phrase types* for the language, as follows:

bin   binary-number phrases

nat   natural-number phrases.

There are two types of phrases, and they will denote binary numbers (0 or
1), and general natural numbers (such as 13), respectively. This is specified
more precisely by defining the *domains of interpretation* or sets of possible
meanings for the two phrase types:

$$[\![\mathbf{bin}]\!] = \{0,1\}$$
$$[\![\mathbf{nat}]\!] = \{0,1,2,\ldots\}$$

For any phrase type θ, $[\![\theta]\!]$ will always denote the corresponding domain of
interpretation. Notice that $[\![\mathbf{bin}]\!]$, the set of binary numbers, is a subset of
$[\![\mathbf{nat}]\!]$, the set of all natural numbers.

Next, we specify the *syntax* of the language of binary numerals. It is
conventional in computer science to use a notation known as BNF (Backus–
Naur Formalism) to describe syntax formally, as in the following:

$$\langle\mathbf{bin}\rangle ::= 0 \mid 1$$
$$\langle\mathbf{nat}\rangle ::= \langle\mathbf{bin}\rangle \mid \langle\mathbf{nat}\rangle\langle\mathbf{bin}\rangle$$

Intuitively, this states that

(i)   0 is a binary-number phrase;

(ii)   1 is a binary-number phrase;

(iii) if B is any binary-number phrase then B is also a natural-number
       phrase;

(iv)   if N is any natural-number phrase and B is any binary-number phrase
       then NB is a natural-number phrase;

and there are no other binary-number or natural-number phrases.

For more complex languages, BNF and similar context-free formalisms are inadequate, and in this book we will use another meta-notation to describe syntax: formal systems of axioms and inference rules for formulas of the form $X: \theta$, interpreted as asserting that X is a well-formed phrase of type θ. A description of the syntax of binary numerals in this notation is given in Table 1.1.

The first two rules have an empty set of premisses above the horizontal line, and so are *axioms*. The remaining rules have one or two premisses, and are *inference rules*. The symbols B and N used in the rules are termed *syntactic meta-variables*. In our meta-language (i.e., the language in which the description is written), they stand for arbitrary binary-number and natural-number phrases, respectively, of the object language (i.e., the language being defined). The premisses of the rules (above the horizontal line) have the form $X: \theta$ where X is a syntactic meta-variable and θ is its phrase type. The conclusions of rules are arbitrary syntactic phrases, but the meta-variables in the conclusion of each rule are those whose types are defined in the premisses of the rule, so that the general form of an inference rule is

$$\frac{\cdots X_i: \theta_i \cdots}{\cdots X_i \cdots : \theta}$$

Here is a simple derivation using the formal system of Table 1.1:

$$\frac{\dfrac{\dfrac{1: \mathbf{bin}}{1: \mathbf{nat}} \quad 1: \mathbf{bin}}{11: \mathbf{nat}} \quad 0: \mathbf{bin}}{\dfrac{110: \mathbf{nat}}{1101: \mathbf{nat}} \quad 1: \mathbf{bin}}$$

The derivation defines the "phrase structure" of the numeral 1101.

Finally, we complete the semantic description by defining the following *valuation functions*:

$$[\![\cdot]\!]_{\mathbf{bin}}: [\mathbf{bin}] \rightarrow [\![\mathbf{bin}]\!]$$
$$[\![\cdot]\!]_{\mathbf{nat}}: [\mathbf{nat}] \rightarrow [\![\mathbf{nat}]\!],$$

where, for any phrase type θ, $[\theta]$ denotes the set of all well-formed phrases of type θ. These functions will map syntactically well-formed phrases to their intended meanings in the appropriate domain of interpretation. That is, for any phrase $X \in [\theta]$, $[\![X]\!]_\theta \in [\![\theta]\!]$ is the intended meaning of X; for example, we want $[\![1101]\!]_{\mathbf{nat}} = 13$. It is appropriate that the semantics be given by *functions*: we want *every* well-formed phrase to have a *unique* meaning.

The type subscript on phrase-valuation brackets will often be omitted when the type is obvious from the phrase itself or from the context. In

Zero:

$$\overline{0: \mathbf{bin}}$$

One:

$$\overline{1: \mathbf{bin}}$$

Primitive Numeral:

$$\frac{B: \mathbf{bin}}{B: \mathbf{nat}}$$

Composite Numeral:

$$\frac{N: \mathbf{nat} \quad B: \mathbf{bin}}{NB: \mathbf{nat}}$$

Table 1.1 Syntax of binary numerals.

many presentations, valuation functions are written $\mathcal{B}[\![\cdot]\!]$, $\mathcal{N}[\![\cdot]\!]$, and so on, where here the double brackets help separate the language being defined from the meta-language. Other authors provide the typing information *within* the brackets, as in $[\![N: \mathbf{nat}]\!]$.

The valuation functions for our language can be defined by the *semantic equations* in Table 1.2; for example,

$$\begin{aligned}
[\![1101]\!]_{\mathbf{nat}} &= 2 \times [\![110]\!]_{\mathbf{nat}} + 1 \\
&= 2 \times (2 \times [\![11]\!]_{\mathbf{nat}} + 0) + 1 \\
&= 2 \times (2 \times (2 \times [\![1]\!]_{\mathbf{nat}} + 1) + 0) + 1 \\
&= 2 \times (2 \times (2 \times 1 + 1) + 0) + 1 \\
&= 13.
\end{aligned}$$

Notice that there is a semantic equation for each rule in the syntax, and that the syntactic meta-variables in each equation are those of the corresponding syntax rule. It is not entirely obvious that these equations properly define mathematical functions. This is clear for $[\![\cdot]\!]_{\mathbf{bin}}$, but notice that $[\![\cdot]\!]_{\mathbf{nat}}$ appears on *both* sides of the last of the equations! However, the use on the right-hand side is on a *sub*-phrase N of the phrase NB on the left-hand side, and so $[\![N]\!]_{\mathbf{nat}}$ is *uniquely* defined for *every* binary numeral N because the (unique) syntactic derivation for any binary numeral is of finite length.

A skeptical reader might also question whether an equation such as $[\![0]\!]_{\mathbf{bin}} = 0$ has any content. Despite appearances, it is not circular. The 0 on the left-hand side is a phrase in the *object language*; it is part of the notation chosen by the designer of that language. The 0 on the right-hand side represents the natural number zero in the *meta-language*, the language used to communicate the syntactic and semantic descriptions. We could,

$$[\![0]\!]_{\mathbf{bin}} = 0$$
$$[\![1]\!]_{\mathbf{bin}} = 1$$
$$[\![B]\!]_{\mathbf{nat}} = [\![B]\!]_{\mathbf{bin}}$$
$$[\![NB]\!]_{\mathbf{nat}} = 2 \times [\![N]\!]_{\mathbf{nat}} + [\![B]\!]_{\mathbf{bin}}$$

Table 1.2 Semantic equations for binary numerals.

if we chose to, adopt any other acceptable meta-linguistic representation of the natural number zero without significantly changing the semantic valuation; but we could not change the 0 in the object language without thereby changing the language we were attempting to describe.

The equation $[\![0]\!]_{\mathbf{bin}} = 0$ simply states that the object-language symbol 0 denotes the natural number zero. This is just one part of a description that, as a whole, is definitely non-trivial: it explicates the *linguistic* concept of positional notation in terms of the *mathematical* operations of multiplication and addition of natural numbers, which are independent of any specific representation of the natural numbers.

1.2 Discussion

In this section we discuss several criteria for evaluating semantic descriptions: compositionality, full abstraction, formality, and comprehensibility.

1.2.1 Compositionality

The meaning of a sentence must remain unchanged when a part of the sentence is replaced by an expression having the same meaning.

G. Frege (1892)

The semantic description of binary numerals in Section 1.1 has the property that

the meaning of every composite phrase is expressed as a function of the meanings of its immediate sub-phrases,

as in

$$[\![NB]\!]_{\mathbf{nat}} = \cdots [\![N]\!]_{\mathbf{nat}} \cdots [\![B]\!]_{\mathbf{bin}} \cdots .$$

This property is termed *compositionality*.

If X and X' are well-formed phrases of some type θ, we say that X and X' are *semantically equivalent* and write $X \equiv_\theta X'$ when $[\![X]\!]_\theta = [\![X']\!]_\theta$. An important benefit of compositionality is that replacing any component of a program by a semantically-equivalent phrase yields a program that is semantically equivalent to the original; that is, $X \equiv_\theta X'$ implies that, for every program context $\cdots\_\cdots$ (of type θ', say) in which phrases of type θ may be used,

$$\cdots X \cdots \equiv_{\theta'} \cdots X' \cdots .$$

For example, it is evident from the semantics of the preceding section that $0B \equiv_{\textbf{nat}} B$ for all B: **bin**, and this means that *any* numeral with a "leading zero" can be simplified to a semantically-equivalent numeral without that leading zero. This illustrates how semantic equivalences of programming-language constructs can be used to justify optimizing code transformations by compilers.

A technical benefit of compositionality is that it allows properties of valuations to be proved by *structural induction*, that is, induction on the syntactic complexity of linguistic phrases: a property is proved

(i)   for each of the syntactic primitives (the basis), and

(ii) for each of the composite constructs, on the assumption (the inductive hypothesis) that its immediate constituents have the property.

The conclusion is that all phrases have the property.

For example, consider the "successor" operation $'$ on binary numerals defined as follows:

$$0' = 1$$
$$1' = 10$$
$$N0' = N1$$
$$N1' = N'0$$

We use structural induction to prove the correctness of this definition.

Proposition 1.1   *For all* $N \in [\textbf{nat}]$, $[\![N']\!] = [\![N]\!] + 1$.

Proof. Cases 0, 1, and $N0$ are immediate; for numerals of the form $N1$:

$$
\begin{aligned}
[\![N1']\!] &= [\![N'0]\!] &&\text{(by the definition of $'$)} \\
&= 2 \times [\![N']\!] &&\text{(by the definition of $[\![\cdot]\!]$)} \\
&= 2 \times ([\![N]\!] + 1) &&\text{(by induction)} \\
&= 2 \times [\![N]\!] + 2 &&\text{(by arithmetic)} \\
&= [\![N1]\!] + 1 &&\text{(by the definition of $[\![\cdot]\!]$).}
\end{aligned}
$$

We conclude that, for *all* $N \in [\textbf{nat}]$, $[\![N']\!] = [\![N]\!] + 1$. $\square$

It is generally thought that compositionality also has conceptual benefits, particularly to a language designer: each feature of a language can be considered and evaluated in relative isolation from other linguistic elements, and the semantic interpretation is *structured* by the syntax of the language.

The compositional style of semantic description we have been discussing is known as the *denotational* approach to semantics because of its emphasis on the abstract mathematical meaning denoted by *each* syntactic phrase. The approach was first used by logicians to interpret languages such as first-order predicate logic. In this book, the term "semantics" (without further qualification) is to be interpreted in the logician's sense of *denotational* (i.e., compositional) semantics.

As an example of a semantical treatment that is *not* compositional, consider the equation

$$[\![\text{while } E \text{ do } C]\!] \quad = \quad [\![\text{if } E \text{ then } (C \, ; \text{while } E \text{ do } C)]\!],$$

which asserts that the interpretation of **while** E **do** C is to be that of a more complex command form. Although one might want this equation to be *true* of the meanings, it is not a *compositional* interpretation of the **while** loop, because the phrase on the right-hand side is not a proper sub-phrase of that on the left. Even if the equation were simplified by using compositional interpretations of **if** and ; to something of the form

$$[\![\text{while } E \text{ do } C]\!] \quad = \quad \cdots [\![E]\!] \cdots [\![C]\!] \cdots [\![\text{while } E \text{ do } C]\!] \cdots,$$

the interpretation would not be compositional; however, we will see that such an equation can be *solved*, and the solution used to give a compositional interpretation of the **while** loop.

As another example, consider interpreting procedure definitions in terms of the *text* of the definition or a translation of it, as is done by a compiler or interpreter. The valuation for procedure *calls* must then be expressed in terms of the meaning of that text; however, the text defining the procedure is not usually a sub-phrase of the call, so this would not be a compositional interpretation.

1.2.2 Full Abstraction

Compositionality can always be achieved in a completely trivial way by defining $[\![X]\!]_\theta = X$ for all phrases X that are not complete programs; that is, every phrase that is not a complete program denotes itself! In fact, the valuation for binary-number phrases in Section 1.1 is essentially like this. Usually, however, such a trivial semantics makes too many distinctions between phrases. A "good" semantic definition should map abstractly equivalent phrases to the *same* semantic meaning. When an interpretation unnecessarily distinguishes phrase meanings, it is described as being "too operational" or "too concrete."

Ideally, a semantic interpretation is *fully* abstract; that is to say, it does not distinguish phrases semantically unless there exist program contexts for those phrases that allow the differences to be observed. More formally: a semantic valuation is termed *fully abstract* if and only if, for all phrase types θ and $P, P' \in [\theta]$, if $\cdots P \cdots \equiv_{\theta'} \cdots P' \cdots$ for every program context $\cdots \_\_ \cdots$ in which a phrase of type θ may be used, then $P \equiv_\theta P'$. This is the converse of the substitutivity principle for compositional valuations discussed in Section 1.2.1.

It is easy to see that the semantic interpretation of binary numerals in Section 1.1 is fully abstract as well as compositional. There exist **nat** contexts that require that the values of the two phrases of type **bin** be distinct; for example, $[\![10]\!] \neq [\![11]\!]$, and so 1__ is such a context. Unfortunately, full abstraction can be very difficult or impossible to achieve for more complex languages.

The practical significance of full abstraction is as follows: if the semantics unnecessarily distinguishes the meanings of phrases P and P', an axiom asserting the equivalence of P and P' could not be validated by the semantics, and an axiom asserting that P and P' are *not* equivalent might incorrectly be regarded as sound.

1.2.3   Formality

Mathematical rigor should not be confused with *formality*, which is certainly not sufficient (and usually not even necessary) for rigor. For example, a compiler is a completely formal description of a programming language; but by itself such a description does *not* support mathematical reasoning about the semantics of the language. For most purposes it is actually preferable to use relatively *informal* descriptions, provided these are based on a rigorous theoretical analysis, just as mathematicians normally present rigorous mathematics in an informal style.

A fully formalized description language may be necessary for some applications. For example, formal semantic descriptions might be used as input to a system for generating language implementations or for other kinds of automatic analysis, just as formal syntactic descriptions are now routinely used as input to generators of scanners and parsers. Formalizing a description language may also be necessary if one wishes to discuss properties of some class of semantic descriptions.

1.2.4   Comprehensibility

Ideally, rigorous denotational-semantic descriptions of programming languages would be comprehensible to every programmer, implementer, and language designer; but it has become apparent that the necessary mathematics is too challenging for this goal to be achievable. This is not just a question of improving the meta-language: semantic description is essentially a conceptual exercise, not a notational one. A comparable situation is that engineers rarely understand the foundational constructions of the set of real numbers using Cauchy sequences or Dedekind cuts.

Fortunately, it is *not* essential that programmers and implementers understand rigorous semantics directly. Other styles of description can be used to express the aspects of programming-language semantics that are relevant to programmers and implementers.

- Implementers can benefit from semantic descriptions that specify how programs are executed using a particular style of implementation on some appropriately idealized or abstract computer. This is termed *operational* semantics because it describes *how* programs are executed rather than just *what* the results of the executions should be.

  However, operational descriptions, like implementations, are often very intricate and the concepts underlying the linguistic features can be so obscured by representational detail that the *correctness* of the description may be in doubt. By using a denotational description of a language as a representation-independent standard, it is possible to verify the correctness of operational descriptions.

- Programmers can benefit from formal systems of axioms and rules for developing, transforming, and verifying programs. Such formal systems can be thought of as being *implicit* descriptions of the semantics of the programming language, and this has come to be known as the *axiomatic* approach to semantics.

  However, it is important that such a formal system be *sound*; i.e., that every formula that can be derived in the formal system be true in the intended interpretation. It has happened that "axiomatic definitions" of programming languages subsequently turned out to be incorrect or even inconsistent. The converse question of *completeness* is also of theoretical interest: is *every* true formula derivable in the formal system?

  Such questions can be addressed by using the denotational semantics of the programming language to interpret the formulas and then studying the soundness and completeness of the formal system in the same way that logicians study such questions for formal mathematical theories.

- Descriptions of programming-language semantics suitable for use in reference manuals and language standards must be expressed fairly informally. However, it is very difficult to achieve both accuracy and readability in such descriptions. A rigorous semantic analysis can be of assistance to the author of an informal semantic description by suggesting concepts with which to express the description, and by providing a reference that can help to ensure that no errors or unintended omissions are being made.

Denotational-semantic descriptions should therefore not be judged by their comprehensibility to programmers and implementers, but rather by the extent to which they provide rigorous support for techniques usable by them.

In summary, denotational, operational, axiomatic, and informal approaches to semantics are *all* useful in various ways and complement each other; all of them will be discussed in this book. A good design criterion for a programming language is that it should be elegantly describable in *each* of these styles of semantic description. Such a language should be simple to use, simple to reason about, and simple to implement.

1.3   Overview

The aim of this book is to give a coherent introduction to the semantical concepts and mathematical techniques needed to describe the semantics of conventional high-level programming languages, and to apply such descriptions to

- verifying the correctness of operational descriptions;
- demonstrating the soundness of axiomatic descriptions; and
- analyzing and designing programming languages.

The order of presentation will be as follows. Chapter 2 will summarize the mathematical notation and concepts assumed in the rest of the book. We will begin our treatment of the semantics of programming languages in Chapters 3 and 4 by studying two "mini-languages":

- a simple algorithmic language with expressions, assignments to simple variables, conditionals, and loops; and
- a simple "functional" language with local definitions of identifiers for simple values and functions.

In Chapter 5, we will add recursive definitions to the functional language and treat the semantics using a mathematical theory of partially-ordered computational domains. For each of these languages, we will present an operational and an axiomatic description as well as a denotational one, and show how to verify the appropriate correctness and soundness properties.

Chapter 6 will begin the treatment of an ALGOL 60-like "procedural" language by showing how the "core" of the language can be obtained by *combining* (the syntax and the semantics of) the two mini-languages of the preceding chapters. In Chapter 7, we will add a variety of linguistic features to this core, and discuss the semantic methods appropriate to each extension.

Chapter 8 will introduce some elementary concepts of the branch of mathematics called category theory, and in Chapters 9 and 10, these concepts will be used to present some advanced semantic methods.

Exercises

1.1 Suppose that the last syntax rule for the language of binary numerals in Section 1.1 were changed to

$$\frac{N:\textbf{nat} \quad B:\textbf{bin}}{BN:\textbf{nat}}$$

Define *denotational* semantics for binary numerals using this syntactic description. Hint: the meaning of a binary numeral must now be an ordered pair of the form (n, l) where n is its numerical value (which should be as before) and l is its length.

1.2 Describe the syntax and denotational semantics of "reduced" binary numerals (i.e., without unnecessary leading zeroes); for example, the numeral 001101 is not reduced, but 1101 and 0 are. Hint: use a phrase type **pos** (positive numbers) with $[\![\textbf{pos}]\!] = \{1, 2, 3, \ldots\}$.

1.3 Describe the syntax and denotational semantics of binary numerals with fractions (e.g., 101.1011, which denotes 5.6875). You may assume that Q denotes the set of all rational numbers.

1.4 (a) Define the syntax and semantics of the language of *octal* (base 8) numerals.

 (b) Define a function that maps octal numerals to equivalent binary numerals, and verify the correctness of the definition.

1.5 Define an operation $\oplus$ on binary numerals such that

$$[\![N_0 \oplus N_1]\!] = [\![N_0]\!] + [\![N_1]\!]$$

and verify the correctness of the definition.

1.6 Describe the syntax and denotational semantics of Roman numerals.

Bibliographic Notes

The denotational approach to semantics may be traced back to [Fre92, Car56, Tar56]. The feasibility of describing *programming* languages compositionally was first demonstrated by D. Scott and C. Strachey [SS71, Sco72a, Str72]. [Sto77, Gor79, Sch86, MA86] are textbooks on the denotational approach to describing the semantics of programming languages and its applications. [Ten81] analyzes programming languages using denotational-semantic concepts, and discusses language-design methods suggested by the denotational analysis. For further discussion of compositionality, see [Jan86]. The concept of full abstraction was introduced in [Mil75].

The comparison of rigorous semantics with foundational studies of real numbers is due to D. Scott (quoted in [MC88]). [Lan64, LW69] are descriptions of two early operational approaches to semantics. [Rey72, Plo81, Kah88] discuss properties of and relations between various operational approaches. The axiomatic approach to semantics has its origins in [Flo67, Hoa69]. The success of the approach as a method of specifying semantics is assessed in [Sch74, GM81, BTT82, MH82, Lei85b, Mey86]. The view that the various approaches to semantics should be regarded as *complementary* seems to have been first stated in [HL74]. [MS76, dB⁺80a, LS84] discuss operational, denotational, and axiomatic approaches and the relations between them.

Chapter 2

Mathematical Preliminaries

This chapter surveys the logical and mathematical notation and concepts that are assumed in the rest of the book.

2.1 Natural Deduction

In this section, we discuss the *natural-deduction* presentation of a fragment (technically, the negative fragment) of intuitionistic propositional logic.

We first present the syntax, using the same style of description as was used for the language of binary numerals in Section 1.1. For reasons that will become evident in subsequent chapters, we term the formulas *specifications*. We use **spec** as the phrase type for specifications and Z as a meta-variable ranging over [**spec**]. Then, a syntax for specification formulas, apart from the *atomic* formulas which we leave unspecified for now, is described in Table 2.1. We have bracketing, conjunction (&) and implication ($\Rightarrow$) of formulas, and an always-false formula (**absurd**); the latter is primarily used to express *negation*: $\neg Z$ can be defined to be $Z \Rightarrow$ **absurd**.

In fact, these syntax rules describe only an *abstract* syntax for specification formulas; i.e., a syntax that specifies *what* the sets of phrase structures (derivations) are, but does not determine certain aspects of *how* these phrase structures are represented as linear strings, such as operator precedence and associativity. Technically, the abstract syntax is *syntactically ambiguous*, in that some strings would be assigned more than one phrase structure; for example, if Z_0, Z_1, and Z_2 are atomic specifications, there are *two* derivations of $Z_0 \Rightarrow Z_1 \Rightarrow Z_2$: **spec** from Z_0: **spec**, Z_1: **spec**, and Z_2: **spec**.

At first sight this might seem to be a serious problem, leading to ambiguity of the semantic interpretation. But because each well-formed phrase

15

Bracketing:

$$\frac{Z \colon \textbf{spec}}{(Z) \colon \textbf{spec}}$$

Conjunction:

$$\frac{Z_0 \colon \textbf{spec} \quad Z_1 \colon \textbf{spec}}{Z_0 \ \& \ Z_1 \colon \textbf{spec}}$$

Implication:

$$\frac{Z_0 \colon \textbf{spec} \quad Z_1 \colon \textbf{spec}}{Z_0 \Rightarrow Z_1 \colon \textbf{spec}}$$

Absurdity:

$$\frac{}{\textbf{absurd} \colon \textbf{spec}}$$

Table 2.1 Syntax of specifications.

is the conclusion of exactly *one* rule and valuation functions are defined compositionally, each *derivation* allowed by the syntax will have an unambiguous meaning, and this is adequate for our purposes. For actual use of (linearized strings of) the language, it would be necessary to define a more refined (or "concrete") syntax that unambiguously specified a unique derivation for every well-formed string. To give concrete examples in this text, we will simply adopt informal conventions or use parentheses to indicate syntactic structure. For specifications, we assume that & binds more tightly than $\Rightarrow$, and that $\Rightarrow$ associates to the right, so that $Z_0 \Rightarrow Z_1 \ \& \ Z_2 \Rightarrow Z_3$ is to be regarded as having the same phrase structure as $Z_0 \Rightarrow \big((Z_1 \ \& \ Z_2) \Rightarrow Z_3\big)$.

To define a semantic interpretation for specifications, we first define the domain of interpretation as follows: $[\![\textbf{spec}]\!] = \{true, false\}$; then the semantic equations of Table 2.2 define a valuation

$$[\![\cdot]\!] \colon [\textbf{spec}] \to [\![\textbf{spec}]\!]$$

for specifications (strictly, for *derivations* of specifications). A specification formula Z is termed *valid* if and only if $[\![Z]\!] = true$.

We will also use constructs called *sequents*, which intuitively are specifications subject to *assumptions*. A sequent has the form $\Sigma \vdash Z$ where Z is a formula and Σ is a finite set of "assumption" formulas; a sequent $\{Z_1, Z_2, \ldots, Z_n\} \vdash Z$ is valid if and only if $[\![Z]\!] = true$ whenever $[\![Z_i]\!] = true$ for every $i = 1, 2, \ldots, n$.

We now present a formal system for deriving valid sequents; the system is in a form known as *natural deduction*. The inference rules are given in

$$[\![(Z)]\!] = [\![Z]\!]$$

$$[\![Z_0 \ \& \ Z_1]\!] = \begin{cases} \textit{true}, & \text{if } [\![Z_0]\!] = \textit{true} \text{ and } [\![Z_1]\!] = \textit{true} \\ \textit{false}, & \text{otherwise} \end{cases}$$

$$[\![Z_0 \Rightarrow Z_1]\!] = \begin{cases} \textit{false}, & \text{if } [\![Z_0]\!] = \textit{true} \text{ and } [\![Z_1]\!] = \textit{false} \\ \textit{true}, & \text{otherwise} \end{cases}$$

$$[\![\textbf{absurd}]\!] = \textit{false}$$

Table 2.2 Semantic equations for specifications.

&-*Introduction*:

$$\frac{Z_0 \quad Z_1}{Z_0 \ \& \ Z_1}$$

&-*Elimination*:

$$\frac{Z_0 \ \& \ Z_1}{Z_i} \quad (i = 0, 1)$$

$\Rightarrow$-*Introduction*:

$$\begin{array}{c} [Z_0] \\ \vdots \\ Z_1 \\ \hline Z_0 \Rightarrow Z_1 \end{array}$$

$\Rightarrow$-*Elimination*:

$$\frac{Z_0 \quad Z_0 \Rightarrow Z_1}{Z_1}$$

absurd-*Elimination*:

$$\frac{\textbf{absurd}}{Z}$$

Table 2.3 Natural-deduction rules for propositional logic.

Table 2.3. As in a conventional formal system, a rule like &-Introduction specifies the derivability of any formula of the form $Z_0 \ \& \ Z_1$ from the derivability of both Z_0 and Z_1; but in a natural-deduction framework, such rules also specify the derivability of *sequents*. In particular, the derivability of $\Sigma \vdash Z$ when $Z \in \Sigma$ is implicit in the natural-deduction framework. The natural-deduction rule of &-Introduction should be regarded as an *abbrevi-*

ation of the conventional rule

$$\frac{\Sigma \vdash Z_0 \quad \Sigma \vdash Z_1}{\Sigma \vdash Z_0 \ \& \ Z_1}$$

In practice, the Σ here would be the union of whatever assumptions are needed to derive Z_0 and Z_1 (other than axioms and "cancelled" assumptions; see below). We write $\Sigma' \vdash \Sigma$ when $\Sigma \subseteq \Sigma'$; the "structural rule"

$$\frac{\Sigma \vdash Z}{\Sigma' \vdash Z} \quad \text{when } \Sigma' \vdash \Sigma$$

is also implicit in the natural-deduction framework.

All of the other rules in Table 2.3 are to be interpreted in the same way as &-Introduction, except that $\Rightarrow$-Introduction has a special form that allows an assumption to be *cancelled*. It should be regarded as an abbreviation of the following conventional rule:

$$\frac{\Sigma \cup \{Z_0\} \vdash Z_1}{\Sigma \vdash Z_0 \Rightarrow Z_1}$$

Formula Z_0, which can be used as an additional assumption in deriving Z_1, is said to be *cancelled* or *discharged* by incorporating it into the implication formula $Z_0 \Rightarrow Z_1$. Readers familiar with the "deduction theorem" in mathematical logic will recognize that the rule of $\Rightarrow$-Introduction is essentially the same principle, incorporated into the formal system itself. The main advantage of the natural-deduction form of inference rule is that any assumptions that are left unchanged by the inference step can remain implicit in the presentation of the rule.

The following is an example of a formal proof using this system. The proof has the form of a tree with the leaves at the top being assumptions ($Z_0 \ \& \ Z_1$ and $Z_0 \Rightarrow Z_1 \Rightarrow Z_2$), the root at the bottom being the conclusion (Z_2), and the internal nodes being instances of inference rules &-Elimination (&-E) or $\Rightarrow$-Elimination ($\Rightarrow$-E):

$$\cfrac{\cfrac{Z_0 \ \& \ Z_1}{Z_1} \ (\&\text{-E}) \qquad \cfrac{\cfrac{Z_0 \ \& \ Z_1}{Z_0} \ (\&\text{-E}) \qquad Z_0 \Rightarrow Z_1 \Rightarrow Z_2}{Z_1 \Rightarrow Z_2} \ (\Rightarrow\text{-E})}{Z_2} \ (\Rightarrow\text{-E})$$

We can now apply the rule of $\Rightarrow$-Introduction ($\Rightarrow$-I) at the bottom to discharge two occurrences of assumption $Z_0 \ \& \ Z_1$:

$$\cfrac{\cfrac{\cfrac{[Z_0 \ \& \ Z_1]}{Z_1} \ (\&\text{-E}) \qquad \cfrac{\cfrac{[Z_0 \ \& \ Z_1]}{Z_0} \ (\&\text{-E}) \qquad Z_0 \Rightarrow Z_1 \Rightarrow Z_2}{Z_1 \Rightarrow Z_2} \ (\Rightarrow\text{-E})}{Z_2} \ (\Rightarrow\text{-E})}{Z_0 \ \& \ Z_1 \Rightarrow Z_2} \ (\Rightarrow\text{-I})$$

Square brackets $[\cdots]$ are used to indicate cancelled assumptions. The sequent derived is

$$\{Z_0 \Rightarrow Z_1 \Rightarrow Z_2\} \vdash Z_0 \,\&\, Z_1 \Rightarrow Z_2,$$

because $Z_0 \Rightarrow Z_1 \Rightarrow Z_2$ is the only uncancelled assumption. A further use of $\Rightarrow$-Introduction would yield a sequent with an empty set of assumptions.

As a second example, the following derivation shows that a use of $\Rightarrow$-Introduction is allowed to cancel *zero* occurences of an assumption:

$$\frac{Z_1}{Z_0 \Rightarrow Z_1} \ (\Rightarrow\text{-I})$$

Here the formula Z_0 is, in principle, cancelled, but there are no occurrences of it as an assumption. Another use of $\Rightarrow$-Introduction would then cancel the occurrence of Z_1 as an assumption and yield a proof of the tautology $Z_1 \Rightarrow Z_0 \Rightarrow Z_1$.

It can easily be verified that each of the inference rules in Table 2.3 preserves validity of sequents. For example, we will show that $\Sigma \vdash Z_0 \Rightarrow Z_1$ is valid whenever $\Sigma \cup \{Z_0\} \vdash Z_1$ is valid. Assume that $[\![Z]\!] = true$ for every $Z \in \Sigma$; we must prove that $[\![Z_0 \Rightarrow Z_1]\!] = true$. Assume that $[\![Z_0]\!] = true$; we now must show that $[\![Z_1]\!] = true$, and this follows from the validity of $\Sigma \cup \{Z_0\} \vdash Z_1$ because, for every $Z' \in (\Sigma \cup \{Z_0\})$, we have that $[\![Z']\!] = true$.

2.2 Functions

Let A and B be sets; a *function* from A to B is any correspondence f that maps every $a \in A$ to some unique $f(a) \in B$. We use the following notation and terminology:

- dom $f = A$ (the *domain* of f);
- codom $f = B$ (the *co-domain* of f);
- graph $f = \{(a,b) \in A \times B \mid b = f(a)\}$ (the *graph* of f).

We also use $f\colon A \longrightarrow B$ to indicate that f is a function with dom $f = A$ and codom $f = B$. When the argument to a function can be expressed by a single symbol, the parentheses around it might be omitted; for example, we can write fi instead of $f(i)$. The co-domain of a function f is sometimes called its "range," but this term is also used for the image set

$$\{b \in \text{codom } f \mid f(a) = b \text{ for some } a \in \text{dom } f\},$$

which may be a proper subset of the co-domain. Functions f and g are regarded as being equal if

- dom $f = $ dom g,

- codom f = codom g, and
- graph f = graph g.

The following re-statement is referred to as the *principle of extensionality*; for $f, g: A \rightarrow B$,

$$\text{if } f(a) = g(a) \text{ for all } a \in A \text{ then } f = g.$$

A function $f: A \rightarrow B$ is *injective* or *one-to-one* if $f(a) = f(a')$ implies $a = a'$, and *surjective* or *onto* if, for every $b \in B$, there exists an $a \in A$ such that $f(a) = b$.

A function f is a *constant* function if, for some $b \in$ codom f, $f(a) = b$ for every $a \in$ dom f. The *identity* function on a set A is the function $\text{id}_A: A \rightarrow A$ such that $\text{id}_A(a) = a$, for every $a \in A$. Let f be a function; for any a and b, $(f \mid a \mapsto b)$ will denote the "perturbed" function f' with

- dom f' = dom $f \cup \{a\}$,
- codom f' = codom $f \cup \{b\}$,
- $f'(a) = b$, and
- $f'(a') = f(a')$ for every $a' \in$ dom f such that $a' \neq a$.

We use $(f \mid a_1 \mapsto b_1 \mid a_2 \mapsto b_2 \mid \cdots \mid a_n \mapsto b_n)$ as an abbreviation for

$$\left(\cdots \left((f \mid a_1 \mapsto b_1) \mid a_2 \mapsto b_2 \right) \cdots \mid a_n \mapsto b_n \right).$$

Let f and g be functions with dom g = codom f; their *composite*, denoted $f \, ; g$ (or $g \cdot f$), is the function defined by

- dom$(f \, ; g)$ = dom f,
- codom$(f \, ; g)$ = codom g, and
- $(f \, ; g)(x) = g\big(f(x)\big)$ for every $x \in$ dom f.

Let $f: A \rightarrow B$, $g: B \rightarrow C$, $f': A \rightarrow B'$, and $g': B' \rightarrow C$ be functions; the diagram

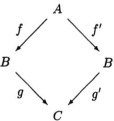

is said to *commute* if the two "paths" from A to C are equivalent (i.e., $f; g = f'; g'$), and similarly for more complex diagrams of sets and functions.

Let f be a function and S be a subset of dom f; the *restriction* of f to S is the function f' with

- dom f' = S,

- codom $f' =$ codom f, and

- $f'(s) = f(s)$ for every $s \in S$.

A function f' is termed an *extension* of a function f if

- dom $f \subseteq$ dom f',

- codom $f \subseteq$ codom f', and

- graph $f \subseteq$ graph f'.

2.3 Partial Functions

Let A and B be sets; a *partial function* from A to B is any correspondence f that maps elements $a \in A$ to unique $f(a) \in B$, without the requirement that *all* elements of A are so mapped: $f(a)$ can be *undefined* for some (or all or no) elements a of A. For example, there is a partial function from A to B that has the empty set as its graph; it is undefined for *every* element of A. We use $f: A \longrightarrow B$ to indicate that f is a partial function with dom $f = A$ and codom $f = B$. The notations dom f, codom f, graph f, id_A, $(f \mid a \mapsto b)$, and $f ; g$, and the terminology of domain, co-domain, graph, composite, commuting diagram, perturbation, restriction, and extension can be used for partial functions as well as conventional (total) functions. For example, if f and g are partial functions with dom $g =$ codom f, their *composite*, denoted $f ; g$ (or $g \cdot f$), is the partial function defined by

- $\mathrm{dom}(f ; g) = \mathrm{dom}\, f$,

- $\mathrm{codom}(f ; g) = \mathrm{codom}\, g$,

and, for every $x \in$ dom f,

$$(f ; g)(x) = \begin{cases} \text{undefined,} & \text{if } f(x) \text{ is undefined} \\ g(f(x)), & \text{otherwise.} \end{cases}$$

Note that $(f ; g)(x)$ is undefined when $f(x)$ is undefined, even if g is a constant function. For the same reason, $f(x)$ must be *defined* if $(f ; g)(x)$ is defined.

The set

$$\{x \in \mathrm{dom}\, f \mid f(x) \text{ is defined}\}$$

is sometimes termed the "domain (of definition)" of partial function f, but we will not use this terminology.

2.4   Natural Numbers

The set N of *natural numbers* can be described as the set generated by
picking an initial "zero" element, 0, and applying a "successor" operation,
σ, arbitrarily many times, subject to the constraints that $0 \neq \sigma(n)$ for any
$n \in N$, and σ is injective ("one-to-one"). Furthermore, for any $S \subseteq N$, if

(i) $0 \in S$, and

(ii) for every $n \in S$, $\sigma(n) \in S$,

then $S = N$. This justifies the method of *mathematical induction*: a property is proved:

(i)   for 0 (the basis), and

(ii) for any successor number $\sigma(n)$ on the assumption (the inductive hy-
      pothesis) that its predecessor n has the property.

The conclusion is that *every* natural number has the property.

    If A is a set, the *iterates* of $f: A \rightarrow A$ are the functions $f^n: A \rightarrow A$ for
$n \in N$ defined as follows:

(i) $f^0 = \mathrm{id}_A$, and

(ii) $f^{\sigma(n)} = f^n \, ; f$.

The iterates of a *partial* function on a set can be similarly defined.

    When we wish to emphasize that the set of natural numbers is *ordered*
(in the usual way), we denote it by ω (the Greek letter *omega*).

2.5   Products of Sets

The (Cartesian) *product* $A_0 \times A_1$ of sets A_0 and A_1 can be defined as follows:

$$A_0 \times A_1 = \left\{ f: \{0,1\} \rightarrow (A_0 \cup A_1) \mid f(0) \in A_0 \text{ and } f(1) \in A_1 \right\}$$

That is, the elements of $A_0 \times A_1$ are *functions* f such that $f(i) \in A_i$. We
will sometimes use the notation f_i as an alternative to $f(i)$. This approach
to set products is convenient because it can be generalized by considering
index sets other than $\{0,1\}$. If I is *any* set and A_i is a set for every $i \in I$,

$$\prod_{i \in I} A_i \;\; = \;\; \left\{ f: I \rightarrow \bigcup_{i \in I} A_i \;\middle|\; f(i) \in A_i \text{ for all } i \in I \right\}$$

The functions f can be thought of as (finite or infinite) tuples with one
component from A_i for every $i \in I$.

    Here are some important special cases of this concept:

- $A_0 \times A_1 \times \cdots \times A_{n-1} = \prod_{i \in \{0,1,2,\ldots,n-1\}} A_i$ (the Cartesian product of the A_i);
- $A^n = \prod_{i \in \{0,1,2,\ldots,n-1\}} A$ (the set of all n-tuples of elements of A);
- $A^\omega = \prod_{i \in \omega} A$ (the set of all countably-infinite sequences a of elements of A, with components denoted by $a(i)$ or a_i, for $i \in \omega$);
- $A^{\omega \times \omega} = \prod_{i \in \omega \times \omega} A$ (the set of all countably-infinite two-dimensional matrices a of elements of A, with components denoted by $a(i,j)$ or a_{ij}, for $i, j \in \omega$);
- $I \to A = A^I = \prod_{i \in I} A$ (the set of all functions f with dom $f = I$ and codom $f = A$).

2.6 Sums of Sets

The *sum* (or disjoint union) $A_0 + A_1$ of sets A_0 and A_1 can be defined as follows:

$$A_0 + A_1 = \{(0, a_0) \mid a_0 \in A_0\} \cup \{(1, a_1) \mid a_1 \in A_1\}$$

The "tags" 0 and 1 are used to distinguish whether an element of the sum originated from A_0 or A_1, respectively, in case these sets have elements in common. When A_0 and A_1 are *disjoint* (i.e., $A_0 \cap A_1 = \emptyset$), the tags are not needed, and we can informally pretend they aren't there. The concept of set sums can also be generalized; if I is any set and A_i is a set for every $i \in I$,

$$\sum_{i \in I} A_i = \bigcup_{i \in I} \{(i, a_i) \mid a_i \in A_i\}$$

For example, for any set A we can define $A^* = \sum_{i \in \omega} A^i$, the set of all (finite) sequences with components from A.

2.7 Binary Relations

A *binary relation* on a set A is any subset R of $A \times A$, and we write $a\,R\,a'$ to specify that $(a, a') \in R$. A binary relation R on A is

- *reflexive* if $a\,R\,a$, for all $a \in A$;
- *transitive* if $a\,R\,a'$ and $a'\,R\,a''$ imply $a\,R\,a''$, for all $a, a', a'' \in A$;
- *symmetric* if $a\,R\,a'$ implies $a'\,R\,a$, for all $a, a' \in A$; and
- *anti-symmetric* if $a\,R\,a'$ and $a'\,R\,a$ imply $a = a'$, for all $a, a' \in A$.

A reflexive and transitive binary relation is termed a *pre-order* (or "quasi-order"). A symmetric pre-order is termed an *equivalence relation* and an anti-symmetric pre-order is termed a *partial order*.

If R is a pre-order and $a\,R\,a'$ or $a'\,R\,a$, a and a' are said to be *comparable*, and *incomparable* otherwise. If $a\,R\,a'$ only when $a = a'$, R is termed the *discrete* pre-order on A.

If R is an equivalence relation on A and $a \in A$, we write $[a]_R$ for the R-equivalence class of a:

$$[a]_R = \{a' \in A \mid a'Ra\},$$

and A/R for the set of R-equivalence classes:

$$A/R = \{[a]_R \mid a \in A\}.$$

If $R \subseteq A \times A$, we use R^* to denote the binary relation on A defined as follows: $a\,R^*\,a'$ just if, for some $n \in \{0, 1, 2, \ldots\}$, $a = a_0$, $a' = a_n$, and $a_{i-1}\,R\,a_i$ for every $i = 1, 2, \ldots, n$. This is the smallest (with respect to the subset ordering) reflexive and transitive binary relation on A that includes R.

2.8   Partially-Ordered Sets

A pair $(A, \sqsubseteq)$ consisting of a set A and a partial ordering $\sqsubseteq$ on A is termed a *partially-ordered set*, or *poset*. Let $(A, \sqsubseteq)$ be a poset; then

- $a \in A$ is a *minimal* element of the poset if there is no $a' \in A$ such that $a' \sqsubseteq a$ and $a' \neq a$;

- $a \in A$ is the *least* element of the poset if $a \sqsubseteq a'$ for every $a' \in A$;

- $a \in A$ is an *upper bound* of $S \subseteq A$ if $s \sqsubseteq a$ for every $s \in S$;

- $a \in A$ is the *least upper bound* or *join* or *limit* of $S \subseteq A$ if it is an upper bound of S and, for all $a' \in A$ that are upper bounds of S, $a \sqsubseteq a'$;

- $a \in A^\omega$ is an *ascending ω-chain* (hereafter abbreviated to just *chain*) in A if, for $i, j \in \omega$, $a_i \sqsubseteq a_j$ when $i \leq j$.

The concepts of *maximal* and *greatest* elements of posets, and *lower bounds* and *greatest lower bounds* (*meets*) of subsets of posets can be defined dually.

Let $(A, \sqsubseteq)$ be a poset. An element $a \in A$ is said to *immediately precede* $a' \in A$ if $a \sqsubseteq a'$ and there is no $a'' \in A$ such that $a \sqsubseteq a'' \sqsubseteq a'$. A diagram of (the graph of) the immediately-precedes relation for a poset is termed a *Hasse diagram* of the poset; such diagrams are often used to present posets pictorially. For example, the following is the Hasse diagram of the set of all subsets of $\{0, 1, 2\}$, ordered by the subset relation.

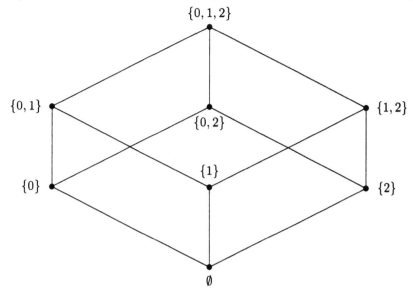

Notice that there is no (direct) edge between, say, $\{0\}$ and $\{0,1,2\}$.

Let D be a poset; we use the following notation:

- $|D|$ for the underlying set (or carrier) of D;
- $\sqsubseteq_D$ for the partial order of D;
- $d \in D$ as an abbreviation for $d \in |D|$;
- $\perp_D$ ("bottom" of D) for the least element of D, if it exists;
- $\mathrm{lub}\, S$ or $\bigsqcup S$ for the least upper bound of $S \subseteq |D|$, if it exists;
- $a \sqcup b$ for $\bigsqcup \{a, b\}$ and $\bigsqcup_{i \in I} s_i$ for $\bigsqcup \{s_i \mid i \in I\}$, if these exist;
- D^ω for the set of all chains in $|D|^\omega$.

Exercises

2.1   Use the semantics of specifications to prove that each of the rules of Table 2.3 preserves validity of sequents.

2.2   Prove that composition is an associative operation on (total or partial) functions.

2.3   What is wrong with the following "proof" that all horses are the same color?

> The proof is by mathematical induction on n, the number of horses being considered.
>
> (a) The basis, for $n = 1$, is trivial.

(b) For the induction step, assume that all of the horses in every set of n horses are the same color, and consider any set $H = \{h_0, h_1, \ldots, h_n\}$ of $n + 1$ horses. If one horse, say h_0, is removed from H, the remaining n elements $h_1, h_2, \ldots, h_n$ are the same color by the induction hypothesis; but if another horse, say h_n, is removed, the remaining n horses $h_0, h_1, \ldots, h_{n-1}$ are also the same color by induction. Because the two subsets have elements $h_1, h_2, \ldots, h_{n-1}$ in common, the $n + 1$ horses of H are the same color.

(c) By mathematical induction, any finite set of horses are the same color, and so if there are m horses, all of them are the same color.

2.4 Which of the following statements are correct?

(a) If $A_i = \emptyset$ (the empty set) for any $i \in I$, $\prod_{i \in I} A_i = \emptyset$.

(b) $\prod_{i \in \emptyset} \emptyset$ is a one-element set.

2.5 For any set A, let $\#A$ be the cardinality (number of elements) of A; express $\#(A_0 \times A_1)$, $\#(A_0 + A_1)$, $\#\left(\prod_{i \in I} A_i\right)$, $\#\left(\sum_{i \in I} A_i\right)$, and $\#(A_0 \to A_1)$ in terms of the cardinalities of the A_i.

2.6 (a) Let $\sqsubseteq$ be a partial order on a set A; prove that the binary relation $\sqsubset$ defined by $a \sqsubset a'$ if and only if $a \sqsubseteq a'$ and $a \neq a'$ is irreflexive and transitive.

(b) Let $\sqsubset$ be an irreflexive and transitive relation on a set A; prove that the binary relation $\sqsubseteq$ defined by $a \sqsubseteq a'$ if and only if $a \sqsubset a'$ or $a = a'$ is a partial order on A.

2.7 For any set A, which pre-order on A is both an equivalence relation and a partial order?

2.8 For each of the following cases, define a set and a relation on that set that is

(a) reflexive and symmetric, but not transitive;

(b) reflexive and transitive, but not symmetric;

(c) transitive and symmetric, but not reflexive.

2.9 Prove that, if it exists, the least upper bound of a subset of a poset is unique.

2.10 Draw the Hasse diagram of a partially-ordered set with two minimal elements but no least element.

2.11 Draw the Hasse diagram of a partially-ordered set with a pair of elements having two common upper bounds but no least upper bound.

2.12 A pair $(A, \sqsubseteq)$ consisting of a set A and a pre-ordering $\sqsubseteq$ on A is termed a *pre-ordered set*. Which of the concepts defined for partially-ordered sets in Section 2.8 can be generalized to pre-ordered sets?

Bibliographic Notes

For more discussion of natural deduction, see [Pra65, vD83]. The remaining material in this chapter is fairly standard and can be found in many textbooks on discrete mathematics; a good one is [PY73].

PART II

Basic Concepts

Chapter 3

A Simple Imperative Language

Computer oriented languages differ from their mathematical counterparts by virtue of their dynamic character. An expression does not generally possess one uniquely determined value of the expected sort, but rather the value depends upon the state of the system at the time of initialization of evaluation.

D. S. Scott and C. Strachey (1971)

In this chapter, we discuss a programming language consisting of *expressions* and *commands*, also known as "statements" (i.e., imperative statements). The key semantic notion is that of the *state* (of the variables of the computation). In general, the value of an expression depends on the current state; the computing device changes the state when it *executes* a command. The course of the computation is determined by *control structures* such as conditional and iterative commands. Languages that support this style of programming are described as being *imperative*.

The imperative language we consider in this chapter is "simple" in that there are no jumps, procedures, local declarations, data structures, or modules; but all of these features will be considered in subsequent chapters. We will define an abstract syntax, a denotational-semantic interpretation, an operational semantics, and an axiomatic semantics for the language, and verify the correctness of the latter two using the denotational semantics. We will also briefly consider the semantics of a version of the language with *non-deterministic* control structures in Section 3.7; this can be skipped without loss of continuity.

3.1 Expressions and Commands

3.1.1 Syntax

The types for our initial language fragment are determined by the following
BNF-like productions:

$$\tau ::= \mathbf{bool} \mid \mathbf{nat} \qquad \text{data types}$$

$$\theta ::= \mathbf{exp}[\tau] \mid \mathbf{comm} \quad \text{phrase types;}$$

that is, τ and θ are meta-variables ranging over the sets $\{\mathbf{bool}, \mathbf{nat}\}$ and
$\{\mathbf{exp}[\mathbf{bool}], \mathbf{exp}[\mathbf{nat}], \mathbf{comm}\}$, respectively. The data types represent the
sets of Boolean (truth) values and natural numbers, respectively. Additional
data types (**int**, **real**, **char**, ...) can be treated analogously. The phrase
types are as follows: expressions for each of the data types, and commands.

The abstract syntax of the language fragment is defined by the inference
rules of Table 3.1. We use C, B, and N as syntactic meta-variables ranging over the commands, Boolean expressions, and numerical expressions,
respectively.

There are two "generic" constructions, bracketing and conditional selection, which are applicable with all of the phrase types. For example, the
Conditional Rule may be regarded as an abbreviation for the following three
rules:

$$\frac{B \colon \mathbf{exp}[\mathbf{bool}] \quad B_0 \colon \mathbf{exp}[\mathbf{bool}] \quad B_1 \colon \mathbf{exp}[\mathbf{bool}]}{\mathbf{if}\ B\ \mathbf{then}\ B_0\ \mathbf{else}\ B_1 \colon \mathbf{exp}[\mathbf{bool}]}$$

$$\frac{B \colon \mathbf{exp}[\mathbf{bool}] \quad N_0 \colon \mathbf{exp}[\mathbf{nat}] \quad N_1 \colon \mathbf{exp}[\mathbf{nat}]}{\mathbf{if}\ B\ \mathbf{then}\ N_0\ \mathbf{else}\ N_1 \colon \mathbf{exp}[\mathbf{nat}]}$$

$$\frac{B \colon \mathbf{exp}[\mathbf{bool}] \quad C_0 \colon \mathbf{comm} \quad C_1 \colon \mathbf{comm}}{\mathbf{if}\ B\ \mathbf{then}\ C_0\ \mathbf{else}\ C_1 \colon \mathbf{comm}}$$

The first two forms are conditional *expressions*, and the third is the more
familiar conditional *command*. Note that in each case the two "arms" must
have the same phrase type.

The remaining numerical expressions are: a constant and a unary operation on a numerical operand. The remaining Boolean expressions are: a
constant, unary and binary operations on Boolean operands, an ordering
predicate on numerical operands, and equality predicates for all data types.
Additional constants (**false**, $1, 2, \ldots$), predicates ($\neq, \leq, >, \ldots$), and operators (**or**, $\supset, +, \times, \ldots$) can be treated analogously, and will be used freely
whenever convenient.

The remaining commands are: a null command (which has no effect),
sequential composition, and a loop. The loop form **for** N **do** C is executed
by evaluating the numerical expression N and then executing the body C

Bracketing:

$$\frac{X\colon\theta}{(X)\colon\theta}$$

Conditional:

$$\frac{B\colon \mathbf{exp[bool]} \quad X_0\colon\theta \quad X_1\colon\theta}{\mathbf{if}\ B\ \mathbf{then}\ X_0\ \mathbf{else}\ X_1\colon\theta}$$

Zero:

$$\overline{0\colon \mathbf{exp[nat]}}$$

Successor:

$$\frac{N\colon \mathbf{exp[nat]}}{\mathbf{succ}\ N\colon \mathbf{exp[nat]}}$$

Truth:

$$\overline{\mathbf{true}\colon \mathbf{exp[bool]}}$$

Negation:

$$\frac{B\colon \mathbf{exp[bool]}}{\mathbf{not}\ B\colon \mathbf{exp[bool]}}$$

Conjunction:

$$\frac{B_0\colon \mathbf{exp[bool]} \quad B_1\colon \mathbf{exp[bool]}}{B_0\ \mathbf{and}\ B_1\colon \mathbf{exp[bool]}}$$

Ordering:

$$\frac{N_0\colon \mathbf{exp[nat]} \quad N_1\colon \mathbf{exp[nat]}}{N_0 < N_1\colon \mathbf{exp[bool]}}$$

Equality:

$$\frac{E_0\colon \mathbf{exp[\tau]} \quad E_1\colon \mathbf{exp[\tau]}}{E_0 = E_1\colon \mathbf{exp[bool]}}$$

Null:

$$\overline{\mathbf{skip}\colon \mathbf{comm}}$$

Sequencing:

$$\frac{C_0\colon \mathbf{comm} \quad C_1\colon \mathbf{comm}}{C_0\ ;\ C_1\colon \mathbf{comm}}$$

Definite Iteration:

$$\frac{N\colon \mathbf{exp[nat]} \quad C\colon \mathbf{comm}}{\mathbf{for}\ N\ \mathbf{do}\ C\colon \mathbf{comm}}$$

Table 3.1 Syntax of the imperative language.

that number of times. It is termed a "definite" iteration because the number of repetitions is determined before they begin. The construction

$$\textbf{if } B \textbf{ then } C$$

will be regarded as an abbreviation for

$$\textbf{if } B \textbf{ then } C \textbf{ else skip}$$

when C: **comm**. Initially, we do not provide any state-changing commands; the most important of these, *assignments*, will be considered in the next section.

3.1.2 Semantics

Each data-type name τ denotes a non-empty set $[\![\tau]\!]$ of values possible for some kind of expression:

$$[\![\textbf{bool}]\!] = \{true, false\} \quad \text{truth values}$$
$$[\![\textbf{nat}]\!] = \{0, 1, 2, \ldots\} \quad \text{natural numbers}$$

The sets of possible meanings for expression and command phrases are then defined as follows: if S is a set of states,

$$[\![\textbf{exp}[\tau]]\!] = S \rightarrow [\![\tau]\!]$$
$$[\![\textbf{comm}]\!] = S \rightarrow S,$$

where, for any sets A and B, $A \rightarrow B$ denotes the set of all functions from A to B. The meaning of an expression is the function that, for any state, yields the value of the expression relative to that state, and the meaning of a command is some state transformation. The set of states, S, may be left unspecified for now. These domains reflect our (current) assumptions that an expression has a value at every state, that expression evaluations never change the state, and that command executions always terminate normally.

The use of input-to-output functions as command and expression meanings allows us to abstract away from certain "operational" aspects of program execution. For example, the command **if** $N = N$ **then** C is semantically equivalent to C, despite the difference in their computational behavior (in a straightforward implementation). This is only possible because there is no way to observe "intermediate" execution states.

We must now define semantic valuation functions

$$[\![\cdot]\!]_{\textbf{exp}[\tau]} \colon [\textbf{exp}[\tau]] \rightarrow [\![\textbf{exp}[\tau]]\!]$$
$$[\![\cdot]\!]_{\textbf{comm}} \colon [\textbf{comm}] \rightarrow [\![\textbf{comm}]\!]$$

$[\![(X)]\!] = [\![X]\!]$

$[\![\text{if } B \text{ then } X_0 \text{ else } X_1]\!]s = \begin{cases} [\![X_0]\!]s, & \text{if } [\![B]\!]s = true \\ [\![X_1]\!]s, & \text{if } [\![B]\!]s = false \end{cases}$

$[\![\text{true}]\!]s = true$

$[\![\text{not } B]\!]s = \begin{cases} true, & \text{if } [\![B]\!]s = false \\ false, & \text{if } [\![B]\!]s = true \end{cases}$

$[\![B_0 \text{ and } B_1]\!]s = \begin{cases} true, & \text{if } [\![B_0]\!]s = true \text{ and } [\![B_1]\!]s = true \\ false, & \text{otherwise} \end{cases}$

$[\![N_0 < N_1]\!]s = ([\![N_0]\!]s < [\![N_1]\!]s)$

$[\![E_0 = E_1]\!]s = ([\![E_0]\!]s = [\![E_1]\!]s)$

$[\![0]\!]s = 0$

$[\![\text{succ } N]\!]s = ([\![N]\!]s) + 1$

$[\![\text{skip}]\!]s = s$

$[\![C_0 \,;\, C_1]\!]s = [\![C_1]\!]([\![C_0]\!]s)$

$[\![\text{for } N \text{ do } C]\!]s = [\![C]\!]^n(s), \text{ where } n = [\![N]\!]s$

Table 3.2 Semantic equations for the imperative language.

where $[\theta]$ is, as before, the set of well-formed phrases of type θ. A semantic equation for each rule in the syntax is given in Table 3.2. Further constants, predicates and operators would be treated analogously. The semantic meta-variable s ranges over the set of states S.

The interpretation of bracketing ensures that brackets only define syntactic structure. The interpretation of the expressions is straightforward: the state argument is inherited by sub-expressions (and will be available to state-dependent forms of expression when these are added), and each feature of the object language is interpreted by the corresponding mathematical concept.

The null command has no effect on the state, and sequencing is interpreted as composition of state-transforming functions. These interpretations can be expressed more directly as follows:

$$[\![\text{skip}]\!] = id_S$$
$$[\![C_0 \,;\, C_1]\!] = [\![C_0]\!] \,;\, [\![C_1]\!]$$

The use of ; on both sides of the latter equation is merely a convenience; the semantics would be the same if we were to write

$$[\![C_0 \,;\, C_1]\!] = [\![C_1]\!] \cdot [\![C_0]\!]$$

$$C\,;\mathbf{skip} \equiv_{\mathbf{comm}} C \equiv_{\mathbf{comm}} \mathbf{skip}\,;C$$

$$(C_0\,;C_1)\,;C_2 \equiv_{\mathbf{comm}} C_0\,;(C_1\,;C_2)$$

$$\mathbf{if\ true\ then}\ C_0\ \mathbf{else}\ C_1 \equiv_{\mathbf{comm}} C_0$$

$$\mathbf{if\ false\ then}\ C_0\ \mathbf{else}\ C_1 \equiv_{\mathbf{comm}} C_1$$

$$(\mathbf{if}\ B\ \mathbf{then}\ C_0\ \mathbf{else}\ C_1)\,;C_2 \equiv_{\mathbf{comm}} \mathbf{if}\ B\ \mathbf{then}\ (C_0\,;C_2)\ \mathbf{else}\ (C_1\,;C_2)$$

$$\mathbf{for}\ 0\ \mathbf{do}\ C \equiv_{\mathbf{comm}} \mathbf{skip}$$

$$\mathbf{for\ succ}\ N\ \mathbf{do}\ C \equiv_{\mathbf{comm}} (\mathbf{for}\ N\ \mathbf{do}\ C)\,;C$$

$$\mathbf{for}\ N\ \mathbf{do\ skip} \equiv_{\mathbf{comm}} \mathbf{skip}$$

Table 3.3 Command equivalences.

The loop form **for** N **do** C is interpreted as an iteration of the state transformation denoted by C; notice that changes to the state in C do not affect the number of iterations, which is determined by evaluating N in the initial state.

The command equivalences in Table 3.3 are easily validated using the semantic valuation. For example,

$$[\![(C_0\,;C_1)\,;C_2]\!]s = [\![C_2]\!]\big([\![C_1]\!]([\![C_0]\!]s)\big) = [\![C_0\,;(C_1\,;C_2)]\!]s$$

for every $s \in S$, and so $(C_0\,;C_1)\,;C_2 \equiv_{\mathbf{comm}} C_0\,;(C_1\,;C_2)$. In fact, it can be proved by a structural induction over all forms of command in the language that *every* command is, for now, equivalent to **skip**; however, all of the equivalences listed will remain valid when state-changing assignment commands are added in the next section.

3.2   Assignment Commands

We are faced with the problem of variables which actually vary.
C. Strachey (1967)

The most glaring omissions from the language fragment described in the preceding section are ways to access and change the computational state. We therefore assume a set of *variable-identifiers*, ranged over by meta-variable ι (the Greek letter *iota*), and a type-assigning function π_0 from these to data types; the lexical rules for variable-identifiers need not concern us. We use dom π_0 to denote the domain of π_0, that is to say, the set of all variable-identifiers, and, for every data type τ,

$$[\tau] = \{\iota \in \operatorname{dom} \pi_0 \mid \pi_0(\iota) = \tau\};$$

i.e., the set of τ-valued variable-identifiers. This notation should not be confused with $[\theta]$ for *phrase* types θ.

We now augment the syntactic rules for our language as follows:

Variable-Identifier:

$$\frac{}{\iota: \mathbf{exp}[\tau]} \quad \text{when } \iota \in [\tau]$$

Assignment:

$$\frac{E: \mathbf{exp}[\tau]}{\iota := E: \mathbf{comm}} \quad \text{when } \iota \in [\tau]$$

The variable-identifier form of expression and the assignment command allow named components of the computational state to be, respectively, accessed and updated.

The following is an example of a code fragment in this language; it has the effect of decrementing (if possible) the value of $n \in [\mathbf{nat}]$ (using additional variables $i, j \in [\mathbf{nat}]$):

$$
\begin{aligned}
&i := 0 \,; j := 0; \\
&(\textbf{for } n \textbf{ do} \\
&\quad (\textbf{if } i > 0 \textbf{ then} \\
&\qquad j := \mathbf{succ}\, j); \\
&\quad i := \mathbf{succ}\, i); \\
&n := j
\end{aligned}
$$

We assume that the "syntactic scopes" of all control structures such as **if** and **for** extend as far to the right as possible; for example, assignment $i := \mathbf{succ}\, i$ in the above is within the body of the **for** loop, which should in any case be clear from the indentation.

To describe the semantics of assignment commands and variables used as expressions, we define an appropriate set of states as follows:

$$S = \prod_{\iota \in \operatorname{dom} \pi_0} [\![\pi_0(\iota)]\!].$$

That is, S is the set of all functions s from variable-identifiers to values such that, for every variable-identifier $\iota \in [\tau]$, $s(\iota) \in [\![\tau]\!]$. Then, the semantic equations are as follows:

$$[\![\iota]\!]s = s(\iota)$$
$$[\![\iota := E]\!]s = \big(s \mid \iota \mapsto [\![E]\!]s\big),$$

where $\big(s \mid \iota \mapsto [\![E]\!]s\big)$ is the state s' such that $s'(\iota) = [\![E]\!]s$ and, for all variable-identifiers $\iota' \neq \iota$, $s'(\iota') = s(\iota')$. Informally: the value of a variable-identifier at some state is the value in that component of the state, and the effect of executing an assignment in some state is to produce a "new" state that is identical except that the value in the component for the variable-identifier is replaced by the value of the right-hand side expression at the "old" state.

The following is an example of a command equivalence that can be validated using the valuation for assignment:

$$\iota := (\textbf{if } B \textbf{ then } E_0 \textbf{ else } E_1) \ \equiv_{\textbf{comm}} \ \textbf{if } B \textbf{ then } (\iota := E_0) \textbf{ else } (\iota := E_1)$$

where $\iota \in [\tau]$, $B \colon \textbf{exp[bool]}$, and $E_0, E_1 \colon \textbf{exp}[\tau]$, and of course all of the equivalences listed in Table 3.3 remain valid.

3.3   Indefinite Iterations

The **for** loop is often inconvenient or inefficient because the number of iterations is determined before the iteration begins. So, let us replace the **for** loop by the following:

Indefinite Iteration:

$$\frac{B \colon \textbf{exp[bool]} \quad C \colon \textbf{comm}}{\textbf{while } B \textbf{ do } C \colon \textbf{comm}}$$

Expression B is evaluated and command C is executed repeatedly, in alternation, until the value of B becomes *false*.

Unfortunately, it is possible that the value *never* becomes *false*, and then the execution does not terminate. We therefore re-define the set of command meanings as follows:

$$[\![\textbf{comm}]\!] = S \rightharpoonup S;$$

i.e., the set of all *partial* functions on S. The intention is that $[\![C]\!]s$ is to be undefined if and only if execution of command C from initial state s fails to terminate. No changes to the semantic equations of Sections 3.1 and 3.2 are needed if we view the semi-colon as denoting composition of *partial* functions, and similarly for c^n.

It is convenient to introduce also the following form of command:

Divergence:

$$\frac{}{\textbf{diverge} \colon \textbf{comm}}$$

This command is intended to always fail to terminate, regardless of what the computational state is initially; i.e., $[\![\mathbf{diverge}]\!]s$ is undefined for every $s \in S$. The **diverge** command is obviously useless in practice; however, it will be useful in formulating the semantics of the **while** loop.

We may now treat the semantics of the **while** loop. We want an interpretation for which the following semantic equivalence holds:

$$\text{while } B \text{ do } C \equiv_{\text{comm}} \text{if } B \text{ then } (C \,;\, \text{while } B \text{ do } C). \qquad (3.1)$$

This means that we must obtain an interpretation such that

$$[\![\text{while } B \text{ do } C]\!] = [\![\text{if } B \text{ then } (C \,;\, \text{while } B \text{ do } C)]\!].$$

If we let c stand for the (currently unknown) meaning of **while** B **do** C and simplify the right-hand side using the known valuations for **if** and ;, we get an *equation* of the form

$$c = \cdots [\![B]\!] \cdots [\![C]\!] \cdots c \cdots$$

such that a solution for c, the indeterminate of the equation, would be the desired interpretation of the **while** loop. But how can we solve this equation?

Consider the sequence of commands C_i for $i \in N$, defined inductively as follows:

$$C_0 = \mathbf{diverge}$$
$$C_{i+1} = \text{if } B \text{ then } (C \,;\, C_i)$$

The right-hand side of the definition of C_{i+1} is obtained from the right-hand side of (3.1) by replacing **while** B **do** C by C_i. The meaning of each of the C_i is an *approximation* to the desired meaning of the **while** loop in the sense that, *if* C_i terminates for some initial state, then so does **while** B **do** C, and the final states will be the same; furthermore, as i increases, the approximations can only improve in the sense that terminating states (rather than non-termination) can be obtained after longer computations. The C_i can be thought of as specifying the effect obtained by executing the loop using an implementation that works correctly provided the loop terminates in fewer than i iterations, but self-destructs otherwise.

These syntactic considerations motivate the following semantic construction. Let c_0 be the partial function on S that is everywhere undefined; that is, c_0 has the empty set as its graph. Then, for $i \in N$, let

$$c_{i+1}(s) = \begin{cases} ([\![C]\!] \,;\, c_i)(s), & \text{if } [\![B]\!]s = \textit{true} \\ s, & \text{if } [\![B]\!]s = \textit{false.} \end{cases}$$

It is clear that, for every $i \in N$, $c_i = [\![C_i]\!]$. Furthermore, it can be shown by mathematical induction that graph $c_i \subseteq$ graph c_{i+1} for every $i \in N$; this allows us to define the partial function c_∞ on S whose graph is the *union* of the graphs for all the c_i:

$$\text{graph } c_\infty \ = \ \bigcup_{i \in N} \text{graph } c_i.$$

Then we define $[\![\textbf{while } B \textbf{ do } C]\!]$ to be c_∞. Note that this interpretation of the **while** loop is compositional, because $[\![\textbf{while } B \textbf{ do } C]\!]$ is defined in terms of $[\![B]\!]$ and $[\![C]\!]$ only, albeit in a more complex manner than usual.

For example, suppose we add a decrementation operator **pred** to the language, and consider the following **while** loop:

$$\textbf{while } n > 0 \textbf{ do } n := \textbf{pred } n; \tag{3.2}$$

then

$$C_0 = \textbf{diverge}$$
$$C_1 = \ \textbf{if } n > 0 \textbf{ then}$$
$$\qquad n := \textbf{pred } n;$$
$$\qquad \textbf{diverge}$$
$$C_2 = \ \textbf{if } n > 0 \textbf{ then}$$
$$\qquad n := \textbf{pred } n;$$
$$\qquad \textbf{if } n > 0 \textbf{ then}$$
$$\qquad\qquad n := \textbf{pred } n;$$
$$\qquad\qquad \textbf{diverge}$$

and so on. The partial functions $c_i = [\![C_i]\!]$ are as follows:

$c_0(s)$ is undefined for every $s \in S$

$$c_1(s) \ = \ \begin{cases} \text{undefined,} & \text{if } [\![n]\!]s \geq 1 \\ s, & \text{if } [\![n]\!]s = 0 \end{cases}$$

$$c_2(s) \ = \ \begin{cases} ([\![n := \textbf{pred } n]\!] \, ; c_1)(s), & \text{if } [\![n]\!]s > 0 \\ s, & \text{if } [\![n]\!]s = 0 \end{cases}$$

$$\quad = \ \begin{cases} \text{undefined,} & \text{if } [\![n]\!]s \geq 2 \\ (s \mid n \mapsto 0), & \text{if } [\![n]\!]s < 2 \end{cases}$$

$$\vdots$$

$$c_i(s) \ = \ \begin{cases} \text{undefined,} & \text{if } [\![n]\!]s \geq i \\ (s \mid n \mapsto 0), & \text{if } [\![n]\!]s < i \end{cases}$$

$$\vdots$$

The meaning of (3.2) is then the function c_∞ whose graph is the union of the graphs of all the c_i; i.e., $c_\infty(s) = (s \mid n \mapsto 0)$ for all $s \in S$. Hence, (3.2) is semantically equivalent to $n := 0$. Note that c_∞ in this example is actually a *total* function (defined for every possible argument), but every c_i for $i \in N$ is strictly partial (undefined for some arguments).

The following proposition shows that in general our interpretation of the **while** loop satisfies equivalence 3.1:

Proposition 3.1   *For any* B: **exp[bool]** *and* C: **comm**,

$$[\![\text{while } B \text{ do } C]\!] \;=\; [\![\text{if } B \text{ then } (C \,;\, \text{while } B \text{ do } C)]\!].$$

Proof. Consider any $s \in S$; we will show that

$$[\![\text{while } B \text{ do } C]\!]s = c_\infty(s) \qquad (3.3)$$

and

$$[\![\text{if } B \text{ then } (C \,;\, \text{while } B \text{ do } C)]\!]s$$
$$= \begin{cases} ([\![C]\!] \,;\, c_\infty)(s), & \text{if } [\![B]\!]s = true \\ s, & \text{if } [\![B]\!]s = false \end{cases} \qquad (3.4)$$

are either both undefined or both defined and equal, where c_∞ is as defined above. Either

- (3.3) is undefined

$$\iff \quad c_i(s) \text{ is undefined for every } i \in N$$
$$\iff \quad [\![B]\!]s = true \text{ and either } [\![C]\!]s \text{ is undefined}$$
$$\quad\quad \text{or } c_{i-1}\big([\![C]\!]s\big) \text{ is undefined for every } i > 0$$
$$\iff \quad (3.4) \text{ is undefined;}$$

  or

- (3.3) is defined and equal to $s' \in S$

$$\iff \quad c_i(s) = s' \text{ for some } i > 0$$
$$\iff \quad ([\![B]\!]s = false \text{ and } s = s')$$
$$\quad\quad \text{or } ([\![B]\!]s = true \text{ and } s' = c_{i-1}([\![C]\!]s) \text{ for some } i > 0)$$
$$\iff \quad (3.4) \text{ is defined and equal to } s'. \quad \square$$

Other looping control structures, such as **repeat** C **until** B, can be treated analogously; however, "jumps," such as multi-level exits and the **goto**, require more complex techniques, to be discussed in Chapter 7. The limit construction described in this section will be generalized to treat recursive definitions in Chapter 5.

3.4   Programs

We can introduce a type name **prog** for (complete) programs, and define

$$[\![\text{prog}]\!] = I \to O$$

for appropriate sets I and O of *inputs* and *outputs*, respectively. To avoid having to deal with the intricacies of input and output operations, we will regard any command by itself as a complete program, as follows,

Program:

$$\frac{C\colon \mathbf{comm}}{C\colon \mathbf{prog}}$$

and assume the existence of (partial) functions

$$g_0\colon I \rightharpoonup S$$
$$k_0\colon S \rightharpoonup O$$

that map inputs to (initial) states, and (final) states to outputs in some standard way; then

$$[\![C]\!]_{\mathbf{prog}} = g_0 \; ; [\![C]\!]_{\mathbf{comm}} \; ; k_0.$$

For example, suppose that

- input and output consist of single natural numbers;
- the input is made available to the program as the initial value of a variable *in*, and all other variables are initialized to standard initial values v_τ for each data type τ (such as $v_{\mathbf{bool}} = \mathit{false}$ and $v_{\mathbf{nat}} = 0$); and
- the output is produced from the final value of a variable *out*.

Then we can define

- $I = O = N$;
- $g_0(n) = (s_0 \mid in \mapsto n)$ where $s_0(\iota) = v_\tau$ when $\iota \in [\tau]$; and
- $k_0(s) = s(out)$.

As a second example, if programs are executed only to produce an indication that they have terminated, we would take I and O to be singleton sets, say $\{*\}$, with $g_0(*) = s_0$ and $k_0(s) = *$ for every $s \in S$. Then, there are exactly two program meanings: the identity function, signifying program termination, and the undefined function, signifying non-termination. Note that the meaning of non-terminating programs "approximates" the meaning of terminating ones, in that the graph of the undefined function is a subset of the graph of the identity function.

3.5   Operational Semantics

Unless there is a prior, generally-accepted mathematical definition of a language at hand, who is to say whether a proposed implementation is correct?
                                                                    D. S. Scott (1969)

In this section, we present an *operational* semantics for our simple imperative language. The style of implementation formalized is not very realistic, but our aim is not to discuss implementation techniques in any detail, but rather to clarify the differences between operational and denotational descriptions, and to demonstrate how the latter can be used to verify the correctness of the former. We simplify the presentation by interpreting only the commands operationally, using the denotational semantics for the expressions.

We will obtain an operational semantics for the commands by defining a binary relation $\triangleright$ on "machine configurations" of the form (C, s), where command C is the *program* component, and state $s \in S$ is the *data* component. (The use of abstract states in the operational configurations simplifies the presentation, but it would be better if configurations were *finitary*; in fact, any program in this language can use only a syntactically-determinable finite set of variables. Also, the data component should really contain *representations* of truth values and numbers, rather than the abstract values themselves, but we will ignore this technicality.) The relationship $(C, s) \triangleright (C', s')$ should hold just when this change of configuration is a single computational step.

The $\triangleright$ relation is defined to be the smallest (with respect to the subset ordering) binary relation on configurations satisfying the axioms and rules of Table 3.4, where $C \overset{s}{\triangleright} C'$ abbreviates $(C, s) \triangleright (C', s)$. The treatment of command sequencing can be explained intuitively as follows: $C_0 \,;\, C_1$ is executed by trying to reduce C_0 (possibly in several steps) to **skip**, which is irreducible, and then reducing C_1. Table 3.5 is a (partial) "trace" of a computation according to this operational interpretation; s is any state.

The primary focus of the operational semantics is the notion of a single computational step (in a particular style of implementation); however, it is possible to *derive* the input-to-output behavior of complete programs. It is easy to verify by structural induction that the $\triangleright$ relation is functional; i.e., $(C, s) \triangleright (C', s')$ and $(C, s) \triangleright (C'', s'')$ imply $(C', s') = (C'', s'')$. This means that we can define a valuation $\{\cdot\}$ on commands as follows: for any $s \in S$,

$$\{C\}s \;=\; \begin{cases} s', & \text{if } (C, s) \triangleright^* (\textbf{skip}, s') \\ \text{undefined}, & \text{otherwise}, \end{cases}$$

where $\triangleright^*$ is the reflexive and transitive closure (Section 2.7) of $\triangleright$.

We now show that this valuation is equal to the denotational valuation.

Proposition 3.2 *For all commands C, $\{C\} = [\![C]\!]$.*

Proof. We first show that $\text{graph}\{C\} \subseteq \text{graph}[\![C]\!]$. It can be directly verified that each of axioms 3.5 to 3.11 of the definition of $\triangleright$ in Table 3.4 has the following property:

$$[\![C]\!]s = [\![C']\!]s' \text{ when } (C, s) \triangleright (C', s');$$

$$\frac{}{(C) \; \overset{s}{\triangleright} \; C} \tag{3.5}$$

$$\frac{}{(\iota := E, s) \; \triangleright \; (\mathbf{skip}, (s \mid \iota \mapsto [\![E]\!]s))} \tag{3.6}$$

$$\frac{}{\mathbf{while} \; B \; \mathbf{do} \; C \; \overset{s}{\triangleright} \; \mathbf{if} \; B \; \mathbf{then} \; C \; ; \mathbf{while} \; B \; \mathbf{do} \; C} \tag{3.7}$$

$$\frac{[\![B]\!]s = \mathit{true}}{\mathbf{if} \; B \; \mathbf{then} \; C_1 \; \mathbf{else} \; C_2 \; \overset{s}{\triangleright} \; C_1} \tag{3.8}$$

$$\frac{[\![B]\!]s = \mathit{false}}{\mathbf{if} \; B \; \mathbf{then} \; C_1 \; \mathbf{else} \; C_2 \; \overset{s}{\triangleright} \; C_2} \tag{3.9}$$

$$\frac{}{\mathbf{diverge} \; \overset{s}{\triangleright} \; \mathbf{diverge}} \tag{3.10}$$

$$\frac{}{\mathbf{skip} \; ; C \; \overset{s}{\triangleright} \; C} \tag{3.11}$$

$$\frac{(C_0, s) \; \triangleright \; (C_0', s')}{(C_0 \; ; C_1, s) \; \triangleright \; (C_0' \; ; C_1, s')} \tag{3.12}$$

Table 3.4 Operational semantics of the imperative language.

furthermore, $[\![C_0 ; C_1]\!]s = [\![C_0' ; C_1]\!]s'$ when $[\![C_0]\!]s = [\![C_0']\!]s'$, so that rule 3.12 preserves this property. But $(C, s) \; \triangleright^* \; (\mathbf{skip}, s')$ when $\{C\}s = s'$, and so we conclude that $[\![C]\!]s = [\![\mathbf{skip}]\!]s' = s'$.

In the other direction, $\mathrm{graph}[\![C]\!] \subseteq \mathrm{graph}\{C\}$ can be proved by structural induction on C. We discuss the **while** case in detail.

Suppose

$$C = \mathbf{while} \; B \; \mathbf{do} \; C';$$

the structural-induction hypothesis is that, for all $s_0, s_1 \in S$, if $[\![C']\!]s_0 = s_1$ then $(C', s_0) \; \triangleright^* \; (\mathbf{skip}, s_1)$. Let commands C_i for $i \in N$ be the approximations to **while** B **do** C' defined in Section 3.3. We can show by mathematical induction that, for every $i \in N$, $\mathrm{graph}[\![C_i]\!] \subseteq \mathrm{graph}\{\mathbf{while} \; B \; \mathbf{do} \; C'\}$.

$\left(\textbf{while } n > 0 \textbf{ do } n := \textbf{pred } n, (s \mid n \mapsto 2)\right)$
$\triangleright$ (by (3.7))
$\left(\textbf{if } n > 0 \textbf{ then } (n := \textbf{pred } n \,; \textbf{ while } n > 0 \textbf{ do } n := \textbf{pred } n), (s \mid n \mapsto 2)\right)$
$\triangleright$ (by (3.8))
$\left((n := \textbf{pred } n \,; \textbf{ while } n > 0 \textbf{ do } n := \textbf{pred } n), (s \mid n \mapsto 2)\right)$
$\triangleright$ (by (3.5))
$\left(n := \textbf{pred } n \,; \textbf{ while } n > 0 \textbf{ do } n := \textbf{pred } n, (s \mid n \mapsto 2)\right)$
$\triangleright$ (by (3.6), (3.12))
$\left(\textbf{skip} \,; \textbf{ while } n > 0 \textbf{ do } n := \textbf{pred } n, (s \mid n \mapsto 1)\right)$
$\triangleright$ (by (3.11))
$\left(\textbf{while } n > 0 \textbf{ do } n := \textbf{pred } n, (s \mid n \mapsto 1)\right)$
$\triangleright^*$ (as above)
$\left(\textbf{while } n > 0 \textbf{ do } n := \textbf{pred } n, (s \mid n \mapsto 0)\right)$
$\triangleright$ (by (3.7))
$\left(\textbf{if } n > 0 \textbf{ then } (n := \textbf{pred } n \,; \textbf{ while } n > 0 \textbf{ do } n := \textbf{pred } n), (s \mid n \mapsto 0)\right)$
$\triangleright$ (by (3.9) and the definition of **if** B **then** C)
$\left(\textbf{skip}, (s \mid n \mapsto 0)\right)$

Table 3.5 Trace of a computation.

The basis case is trivial because $C_0 = \textbf{diverge}$. For

$$C_{i+1} = \textbf{if } B \textbf{ then } (C' \,; C_i),$$

the mathematical-induction hypothesis is that, for all $s_0, s_1 \in S$, if $\llbracket C_i \rrbracket s_0 = s_1$ then $(\textbf{while } B \textbf{ do } C', s_0) \triangleright^* (\textbf{skip}, s_1)$. Now, assume that $\llbracket C_{i+1} \rrbracket s = s'$.

If $\llbracket B \rrbracket s = \textit{false}$, then $s' = s$ and $(\textbf{while } B \textbf{ do } C', s) \triangleright^* (\textbf{skip}, s')$. On the other hand, if $\llbracket B \rrbracket s = \textit{true}$, let $s'' = \llbracket C' \rrbracket s$, so that $\llbracket C_i \rrbracket s'' = s'$; then

$(\textbf{while } B \textbf{ do } C', s)$
$\quad \triangleright \quad (\textbf{if } B \textbf{ then } (C' \,; \textbf{while } B \textbf{ do } C'), s) \quad$ (by (3.7))
$\quad \triangleright^* \quad (C' \,; \textbf{while } B \textbf{ do } C', s) \quad$ (by $\llbracket B \rrbracket s = \textit{true}$ and (3.8))
$\quad \triangleright^* \quad (\textbf{skip} \,; \textbf{while } B \textbf{ do } C', s'')$
$\qquad\qquad$ (by $\llbracket C' \rrbracket s = s''$ and the structural-induction hypothesis)
$\quad \triangleright \quad (\textbf{while } B \textbf{ do } C', s'') \quad$ (by (3.11))
$\quad \triangleright^* \quad (\textbf{skip}, s')$
$\qquad\qquad$ (by $\llbracket C_i \rrbracket s'' = s'$ and the mathematical-induction hypothesis).

In both cases, $(C, s) \; \rhd^* \; (\textbf{skip}, s')$, and so $\text{graph}[\![C_{i+1}]\!] \subseteq \text{graph}\{C\}$. By induction on i, $\text{graph}[\![C_i]\!] \subseteq \text{graph}\{C\}$ for every $i \in N$, and since

$$\text{graph}[\![C]\!] \;\; = \;\; \bigcup_{i \in N} \text{graph}[\![C_i]\!],$$

we can conclude that $\text{graph}[\![C]\!] \subseteq \text{graph}\{C\}$.   □

   This kind of result can be interpreted in different ways. Technically, the proposition shows that the operational description for commands defined in this section is functionally equivalent (but clearly not *identical*) to the denotational description given in preceding sections. One view is that a denotational description is conceptually more fundamental than representation-dependent operational interpretations, and so the result shows that the operational description presented is *correct* relative to the more definitive denotational description.

   Other authors take the view that an *operational* description is more fundamental because the effects it specifies are observable; in this view, such a proposition should be interpreted as showing that the denotational valuation is "computationally adequate" in the sense that it is consistent with the operational interpretation (at the level of programs).

   The difference between these views is a philosophical one, and the reader is invited to choose between them.

3.6   Programming Logic

Computer programming is an exact science in that all the properties of a program and all the consequences of executing it in any given environment can, in principle, be found out from the text of the program itself by means of purely deductive reasoning. It is therefore desirable and interesting to elucidate the axioms and rules of inference which underlie our reasoning about computer programs.

                                                            C. A. R. Hoare (1969)

Programming logics are formal systems of axioms and inference rules for reasoning about program meanings, particularly systems that are useful for specifying, developing, transforming, and verifying programs. Sometimes they are termed "axiomatic semantics." In this section we study a system called Floyd–Hoare logic which is widely used for reasoning about simple imperative programs of the kind we have been considering in this chapter. Most readers will have seen some informal use of the methods in programming courses, and several textbooks discuss the techniques in great detail. Our aim here is not to discuss programming methodology, but rather to clarify the differences between denotational and axiomatic descriptions and to demonstrate how semantics can be used to show the *soundness* of a formal system.

3.6.1   Syntax and Semantics

First, we need formulas for making assertions about properties of particular states. We add a new phrase type as follows:

$$\theta ::= \cdots \mid \textbf{assert},$$

and let $[\![\textbf{assert}]\!]$ be $S \rightarrow [\![\textbf{bool}]\!]$, where S is the set of states. Thus, assertions are similar to Boolean expressions; nevertheless, in general it is appropriate to distinguish them. For example, an assertion language may include notations that are not in the programming language (and may even be incomputable in principle), such as universal or existential quantification. For now, however, it is convenient to assume that assertions and Boolean expressions have the *same* syntax and semantics.

Second, we need a class of formulas for specifying properties of the meanings of commands, expressions, assertions, and so on. These are termed *specifications* and we use the phrase type **spec**; however, except when indicated otherwise, **spec** will not be in the range of meta-variable θ. In particular, we do not want "conditional" specifications of the form **if** B **then** Z_0 **else** Z_1 for Z_0, Z_1: **spec** and B: **exp**[bool]. We define $[\![\textbf{spec}]\!]$ to be $\{true, false\}$; note that states play no explicit role here.

The atomic specifications are as follows:

   Hoare Triple:

$$\frac{P:\textbf{assert} \quad C:\textbf{comm} \quad Q:\textbf{assert}}{\{P\}C\{Q\}:\textbf{spec}}$$

Assertions P and Q are termed the *pre-condition* and *post-condition*, respectively, of the Hoare triple $\{P\}C\{Q\}$. Informally, $\{P\}C\{Q\}$ is true just if any terminating execution of C starting with any state satisfying P terminates in a final state satisfying Q. The Hoare triple specifies what command C is intended to do (when it terminates); i.e., achieve Q whenever P is initially true. The Hoare-triple form of specification is termed a *partial-correctness* formula because verification of termination is regarded as a separate obligation that the programmer must fulfil to complete a verification of program correctness.

The semantic equation for the Hoare-triple form of specification is as follows:

$$[\![\{P\}C\{Q\}]\!]$$
$$= \text{for all } s_0, s_1 \in S, \text{ if } [\![P]\!]s_0 \text{ and } [\![C]\!]s_0 = s_1 \text{ then } [\![Q]\!]s_1$$

Although every specification has a truth value that is independent of states, there is here an "implicit" quantification over the set of states S. Notice that C trivially satisfies a Hoare-triple specification when execution of C fails to terminate.

The non-atomic forms of specification formulas are those described in Table 2.1 of Section 2.1; i.e., we allow conjunction (&) and implication ($\Rightarrow$) as propositional connectives, and **absurd** as a propositional constant. The language is essentially a quantifier-free fragment of multi-sorted predicate logic, with the Hoare-triple form of specification as an atomic formula; that is, $\{P\}C\{Q\}$ should be regarded as being a three-place predicate, $H(P, C, Q)$.

For any assertion P, we will use $\{P\}$ as an abbreviation for

$$\{\textbf{true}\}\textbf{skip}\{P\}.$$

$\{P\}$ is termed a *static-assertion* specification because P must hold at *all* states. This complete our presentation of the syntax and semantics of the *language* of Floyd–Hoare logic.

3.6.2   Rules and Axioms

We now outline a *formal system* of axioms and rules for inferring valid specifications. The inference rules are the natural-deduction rules presented in Table 2.3 of Section 2.1. We now present the axioms, starting with axioms for each of the basic forms of command:

$$\{P\}\textbf{skip}\{P\}$$

$$\{\textbf{true}\}\textbf{diverge}\{\textbf{false}\}$$

$$\{[P](\iota \mapsto E)\}\iota := E\{P\}$$

In the axiom scheme for assignments, $[P](\iota \mapsto E)$ denotes the assertion obtained by substituting E for all occurrences of variable-identifier ι in P, and similarly for $[E'](\iota \mapsto E)$ when E' is an expression. The syntax rule for assignments ensures that $E \in [\textbf{exp}[\tau]]$ if $\iota \in [\tau]$, and so the type of the phrase is preserved by the substitution and the resulting phrase is syntactically well-formed; however, the substitution should be regarded as "structural," rather than purely textual; for example, $[a \times b](b \mapsto c + d)$ should yield $a \times (c + d)$, rather than $a \times c + d$. As an example of the axiom scheme for assignment, we have

$$\{\textbf{succ}\, n > 0\}n := \textbf{succ}\, n\{n > 0\}$$

when n is a numerical variable-identifier.

We now present axioms for each of the composite forms of command:

$$\{P\}C\{Q\} \quad \Rightarrow \quad \{P\}(C)\{Q\}$$

$$\{P\}C_0\{Q\} \& \{Q\}C_1\{R\} \quad \Rightarrow \quad \{P\}C_0 ; C_1\{R\}$$

$$\{P \text{ and } B\}C_0\{Q\} \& \{P \text{ and not } B\}C_1\{Q\}$$
$$\Rightarrow \ \{P\}\text{if } B \text{ then } C_0 \text{ else } C_1\{Q\}$$

$$\{P \text{ and } B\}C\{P\} \quad \Rightarrow \quad \{P\}\text{while } B \text{ do } C\{P \text{ and not } B\}$$

Notice that these axioms are *compositional* in the sense that the consequent of each implication is a Hoare-triple specification of a composite command and the precedent is a conjunction of Hoare-triple specifications for its subcommands. The assertion P in the axiom for the **while** loop is known as an *invariant* of the **while** loop, because any execution of the loop body C preserves it, provided that the loop condition B is true before the execution.

To allow reasoning about expressions, we may add an axiom $\{P\}$ for any "mathematical fact" P about any of the data types. For example, **succ** $n > 0$ is a state-independent fact about numerical expressions, and so we can treat the static-assertion specification $\{\text{succ } n > 0\}$ as an axiom.

The connections between assertional and specificational reasoning are dealt with by the following axioms, which are applicable with any command C:

Pre-Condition Strengthening:

$$\{P_0 \supset P_1\} \& \{P_1\}C\{Q\} \quad \Rightarrow \quad \{P_0\}C\{Q\}$$

Post-Condition Weakening:

$$\{Q_0 \supset Q_1\} \& \{P\}C\{Q_0\} \quad \Rightarrow \quad \{P\}C\{Q_1\}$$

Pre-Condition Disjunction:

$$\{P_1\}C\{Q\} \& \cdots \& \{P_n\}C\{Q\}$$
$$\Rightarrow \{P_1 \text{ or } \cdots \text{ or } P_n\}C\{Q\}$$

Post-Condition Conjunction:

$$\{P\}C\{Q_1\} \& \cdots \& \{P\}C\{Q_n\}$$
$$\Rightarrow \{P\}C\{Q_1 \text{ and } \cdots \text{ and } Q_n\}$$

where $\supset$ is the implication connective for *assertions*; i.e.,

$$[\![P \supset Q]\!]s \ = \ \text{if } [\![P]\!]s \text{ then } [\![Q]\!]s.$$

The last two of these axioms apply when n is zero, yielding the following special cases for any command C and assertion P:

$$\{\textbf{false}\}C\{P\}$$

$$\{P\}C\{\textbf{true}\}.$$

We illustrate the system by sketching a proof of the following specification:

$$\{\textbf{true}\}$$
$$sum := a \; ; i := 0;$$
$$(\textbf{while not}(i = b) \textbf{ do}$$
$$sum := \textbf{succ } sum \; ; i := \textbf{succ } i)$$
$$\{sum = a + b\} \tag{3.13}$$

where $+$ is defined by the following "mathematical facts": $a + 0 = a$ and $a + \textbf{succ } i = \textbf{succ}(a + i)$. The key is to find (by heuristic means) an appropriate invariant assertion for the **while** loop. In this case, we just note that the Boolean negation of the loop condition is $i = b$ and generalize post-condition $sum = a + b$ to $sum = a + i$. A formal proof can then be obtained as follows.

1. Verify that the invariant assertion is initially achieved by proving

$$\{\textbf{true}\}sum := a \; ; i := 0\{sum = a + i\},$$

   using the axioms for assignments and sequencing, the mathematical fact $a = a + 0$, and pre-condition strengthening.

2. Verify that the proposed invariant assertion *is* an invariant of the **while** loop by proving

$$\{sum = a + i \textbf{ and not}(i = b)\}$$
$$sum := \textbf{succ } sum \; ; i := \textbf{succ } i$$
$$\{sum = a + i\},$$

   using the axioms for assignments and sequencing, the mathematical fact $\textbf{succ}(a + i) = a + \textbf{succ } i$, and pre-condition strengthening.

3. Use the axioms for sequencing and the **while** loop to prove

$$\{\textbf{true}\}$$
$$sum := a \; ; i := 0;$$
$$(\textbf{while not}(i = b) \textbf{ do}$$
$$sum := \textbf{succ } sum \; ; i := \textbf{succ } i)$$
$$\{sum = a + i \textbf{ and } i = b\}$$

4. Verify that the invariant and the Boolean negation of the loop condition together imply the desired post-condition, as follows,

$$sum = a + i \textbf{ and } i = b \supset sum = a + b,$$

   and then use post-condition weakening to derive (3.13).

Because of the importance of the invariant assertion in such proofs, the following notation is often used in programs to document the appropriate invariant:

$$\{\textbf{invariant}: P\}$$
$$\textbf{while } B \textbf{ do } C$$

It may be thought of as an abbreviation of

$$\{P\}$$
$$(\textbf{while } B \textbf{ do}$$
$$\{P \textbf{ and } B\} \, C \, \{P\})$$
$$\{P \textbf{ and not } B\}$$

Notice that from any axiom of the form

$$Z_1 \,\&\, Z_2 \,\&\cdots\&\, Z_n \;\Rightarrow\; Z$$

we can *derive* the inference rule

$$\frac{Z_1 \quad Z_2 \quad \cdots \quad Z_n}{Z}$$

using the rules of &-Introduction and $\Rightarrow$-Elimination, as follows:

$$\frac{\dfrac{Z_1 \quad Z_2 \quad \cdots \quad Z_n}{Z_1 \,\&\, Z_2 \,\&\cdots\&\, Z_n} \; (\&\text{-I}) \qquad \overline{Z_1 \,\&\, Z_2 \,\&\cdots\&\, Z_n \;\Rightarrow\; Z}}{Z} \; (\Rightarrow\text{-E})$$

Since *all* of the axioms of the system have this form for *atomic* formulas Z_i and Z, it is possible to re-formulate the entire system without the specification connectives $\&$ and $\Rightarrow$; in fact, Floyd–Hoare logic is conventionally presented in this connective-free style. The format adopted here is essential for extending the system to handle procedures.

3.6.3 Soundness

Our aim in this section is to show that that the formal system presented above is *sound*; i.e., that every sequent derivable using it is in fact valid according to the semantic interpretation of the formulas. We know that each of the inference rules *preserves* validity, and so we need only prove that each axiom is valid. For most of the axioms, it is straightforward to show validity using the semantic equations. We will discuss only the assignment axiom and the axiom for the **while** loop in detail.

The validity of the assignment axiom for our simple language follows immediately from the following result.

Proposition 3.3   *If $E_0 \colon \textbf{exp}[\tau_0]$, $E_1 \colon \textbf{exp}[\tau_1]$, and $\iota \in [\tau_1]$, then, for all $s \in S$,*

$$[\![[E_0](\iota \mapsto E_1)]\!](s) \;=\; [\![E_0]\!](s \mid \iota \mapsto [\![E_1]\!]s).$$

Proof. By structural induction over E_0; we discuss a few representative cases in detail. Throughout, s' will denote $\left(s \mid \iota \mapsto [\![E_1]\!]s \right)$.

Case $E_0 = 0$: $[\![0]\!]s = 0 = [\![0]\!]s'$.

Case $E_0 = \mathbf{succ}\, E$:

$$
\begin{aligned}
&[\![[\mathbf{succ}\, E](\iota \mapsto E_1)]\!]s \\
&= \quad [\![\mathbf{succ}\, [E](\iota \mapsto E_1)]\!]s \\
&= \quad [\![[E](\iota \mapsto E_1)]\!]s + 1 \\
&= \quad [\![E]\!]s' + 1 \text{ (using the induction hypothesis)} \\
&= \quad [\![\mathbf{succ}\, E]\!]s'.
\end{aligned}
$$

Case $E_0 = \iota$: $[\![[\iota](\iota \mapsto E_1)]\!]s = [\![E_1]\!]s = s'(\iota) = [\![\iota]\!]s'$.

Case $E_0 = \iota_0 \neq \iota$: $[\![[\iota_0](\iota \mapsto E_1)]\!]s = [\![\iota_0]\!]s = s(\iota_0) = s'(\iota_0)$ (because $\iota_0 \neq \iota$)
$= [\![\iota_0]\!]s'$. □

To validate the axiom $\{[P](\iota \mapsto E)\}\iota := E\{P\}$, consider states s_0 and s_1 such that $[\![[P](\iota \mapsto E)]\!]s_0 = true$ and $[\![\iota := E]\!]s_0 = s_1$; then,

$$
s_1 = \left(s_0 \mid \iota \mapsto [\![E]\!]s_0\right)
$$

by the semantic equation for assignments, and

$$
[\![[P](\iota \mapsto E)]\!]s_0 = [\![P]\!]\left(s_0 \mid \iota \mapsto [\![E]\!]s_0\right)
$$

by the proposition. We conclude that $[\![P]\!]s_1 = true$, as desired.

Note the importance of the fact that the state at which an expression is evaluated is also the state used for evaluating all of its sub-expressions. Also, it is critical that updating the value of a variable-identifier has no effect on the value of any *other* identifier. Unfortunately, most programming languages do not have these properties.

The validity of the **while** axiom follows immediately from the following result.

Proposition 3.4   *If $[\![\{P \text{ and } B\}C\{P\}]\!] = true$, then, for every $i \in N$, $[\![\{P\}C_i\{P \text{ and not } B\}]\!] = true$,*

where $C_0, C_1, \ldots$ are the commands whose meanings approximate that of the loop **while** B **do** C, as defined in Section 3.3.

The proof is by mathematical induction on i. The case $i = 0$ is trivial because $C_0 = \mathbf{diverge}$. Now, assume the result for C_i and consider any $s, s' \in S$ such that $[\![P]\!]s$ and $[\![C_{i+1}]\!]s = c_{i+1}(s) = s'$. If $[\![B]\!]s = false$ then $s = s'$ and hence $[\![P \text{ and not } B]\!]s' = true$. If $[\![B]\!]s = true$, let s'' be $[\![C]\!]s$; then $[\![P]\!]s'' = true$ from the assumption, and hence $[\![P \text{ and not } B]\!]s' = true$ by the induction hypothesis. In both cases we have $[\![P \text{ and not } B]\!]s' = true$. □

To validate the **while** axiom, assume $[\![\{P \text{ and } B\}C\{P\}]\!] = true$ and consider states s_0 and s_1 such that $[\![P]\!]s_0 = true$ and $[\![\mathbf{while}\, B \,\mathbf{do}\, C]\!]s_0 = s_1$; then $[\![C_i]\!]s_0 = s_1$ for some $i \in N$ and so, by the proposition,

$$
[\![P \text{ and not } B]\!]s_1 = true,
$$

as desired. We conclude that the formal system presented is *sound* with respect to the denotational interpretation presented.

Some authors regard an axiomatic description as definitive, and would interpret this result as showing that the denotational semantics provides a concrete model "consistent with" the axioms. However, it must be kept in mind that there are "non-standard" models of the axioms which may be undesirable or even unimplementable; for example, all of the axioms would be validated if, for every command C, $[\![C]\!]s$ were undefined for all $s \in S$!

Ideally, the formal system would be *complete* relative to the *intended* interpretation, in the sense that every valid sequent would be derivable. Completeness considerations are outside the scope of this text; see the references in the Bibliographic Notes.

3.7   Non-Determinism

One inconvenient thing about a purely imperative language is that you have to specify far too much sequencing. For example, if you write an ordinary program to do matrix multiplication, you have to specify the exact sequence in which all of the n^3 multiplications are to be done. Actually, it doesn't matter in what order you do the multiplications so long as you add them together in the right groups. Thus the ordinary sort of imperative language imposes much too much sequencing, which makes it very difficult to rearrange if you want to make things more efficient.

C. Strachey (1966)

The semantic description of a language need not *fully* specify the result of every computation. It is possible and desirable sometimes to allow implementations some flexibility. Language features whose computational results are not fully determined are described as being *non-deterministic*.

There are several motivations for non-determinacy. One is to allow implementors to take advantage of special properties of particular hardware. For example, floating-point arithmetic cannot realistically be fully determined by a language specification because of hardware differences. Another motivation is to allow programmers to make explicit in their programs that there may be several equally acceptable computational paths to a correct result or even several correct results. An important example of non-determinacy arises with concurrent processes when the relative speeds of the processors are not determined.

The following control structures are described in [Dij76]:

Non-Deterministic Selection:

$$\frac{B_j:\textbf{exp[bool]} \quad C_j:\textbf{comm, for } j = 1, 2, \ldots, n}{\textbf{if } B_1 \rightarrow C_1 \mid \cdots \mid B_n \rightarrow C_n \textbf{ fi}:\textbf{comm}}$$

Non-Deterministic Iteration:

$$\frac{B_j: \mathbf{exp[bool]} \quad C_j: \mathbf{comm}, \text{ for } j = 1, 2, \ldots, n}{\mathbf{do}\ B_1 \to C_1 \mid \cdots \mid B_n \to C_n\ \mathbf{od}: \mathbf{comm}}$$

The Boolean expressions are termed "guards." The **if** form is executed by selecting for execution any of the sub-commands C_j whose corresponding guard B_j is *true*. If none are *true*, the execution fails to terminate, and if more than one is *true*, the implementation can arbitrarily select any one of them for execution. For example, the following assigns *true* or *false* to variable b if m is greater than, or less than n, respectively, but can do *either* if $m = n$:

$$\begin{aligned} \mathbf{if} \quad & m \le n \to b := \mathbf{true} \\ \mid \quad & m \ge n \to b := \mathbf{false} \\ \mathbf{fi} \quad & \end{aligned}$$

The **do** form is executed by, repeatedly, selecting for execution any of the C_j whose guard is *true*, but terminating the repetition when all the guards are *false*.

Semantically, we temporarily re-define the domain of command meanings as follows:

$$[\![\mathbf{comm}]\!] = \mathcal{P}(S \times S)$$

where $\mathcal{P}(\cdot)$ is the usual power-set constructor; that is, a command meaning is a binary relation on states. This approach is adequate for treating partial-correctness axioms, but fails to distinguish between a command that, for some initial state, sometimes fails to terminate, and another that has the same set of possible final states but always terminates. More sophisticated approaches to the semantics of non-determinism are beyond the scope of this book.

We begin by re-defining the valuations for the null command and for sequential composition of commands:

$$[\![\mathbf{skip}]\!] = \{(s_0, s_1) \mid s_1 = s_0\}$$
$$[\![C_0\ ;\ C_1]\!] = [\![C_0]\!]\ ;\ [\![C_1]\!]$$

where $c_0\ ;\ c_1 = \{(s_0, s_1) \mid \text{for some } s \in S, (s_0, s) \in c_0 \text{ and } (s, s_1) \in c_1\}$.

The non-deterministic control structures may then be interpreted as follows:

$$[\![\mathbf{if}\ B_1 \to C_1 \mid \cdots \mid B_n \to C_n\ \mathbf{fi}]\!]$$
$$= \{(s_0, s_1) \mid \text{for some } 1 \le j \le n, [\![B_j]\!]s_0 = true \text{ and } (s_0, s_1) \in [\![C_j]\!]\}$$

$$[\![\mathbf{do}\ B_1 \to C_1 \mid \cdots \mid B_n \to C_n\ \mathbf{od}]\!] = \bigcup_{i \in N} c_i$$

where $c_0 = \emptyset$ and

$$c_{i+1} = \{(s_0, s_1) \mid \text{(for some } 1 \le j \le n,$$
$$[\![B_j]\!]s_0 = \textit{true} \text{ and } (s_0, s_1) \in ([\![C_j]\!] ; c_i))$$
$$\text{or, for all } 1 \le j \le n,$$
$$[\![B_j]\!]s_0 = \textit{false} \text{ and } s_1 = s_0\}$$

and the valuation for the Hoare-triple specification becomes

$$[\![\{P\}C\{Q\}]\!] = \text{for all } s_0, s_1 \in S, \text{ if } [\![P]\!]s_0 \text{ and } (s_0, s_1) \in [\![C]\!] \text{ then } [\![Q]\!]s_1.$$

Note that the programmer must ensure that *every* possible result is correct. Devising axioms and operational semantics for the control structures will be left as exercises for the reader.

Exercises

3.1   Prove by structural induction (Section 1.2.1) that, in the language of Section 3.1 (i.e., without assignments), $C \equiv_{\textbf{comm}} \textbf{skip}$ for *all* C: **comm**.

3.2   Verify the equivalences stated in Sections 3.1 and 3.2 (using the semantic valuations).

3.3   Verify the following command equivalences:

(a) **if** B **then** C **else** C $\equiv_{\textbf{comm}}$ C

(b) **if** B **then** C_0 **else** C_1 $\equiv_{\textbf{comm}}$ **if not** B **then** C_1 **else** C_0

(c) **if** B **then** (**if** B **then** C_0 **else** C_1) **else** C_2 $\equiv_{\textbf{comm}}$
     if B **then** C_0 **else** C_2

(d) **if** B **then** C_0 **else** (**if** B **then** C_1 **else** C_2) $\equiv_{\textbf{comm}}$
     if B **then** C_0 **else** C_2

where B: **exp[bool]** and C, C_0, C_1, C_2: **comm**.

3.4   Are commands

$$C_0 ; (\textbf{if } B \textbf{ then } C_1 \textbf{ else } C_2)$$

and

$$\textbf{if } B \textbf{ then } (C_0 ; C_1) \textbf{ else } (C_0 ; C_2)$$

equivalent?

3.5   Are commands

$$\textbf{for succ } N \textbf{ do } C$$

and

$$C ; \textbf{for } N \textbf{ do } C$$

equivalent?

3.6   Verify the following command equivalences:

(a) $\iota_0 := \iota_0 \equiv_{\text{comm}} \textbf{skip}$

(b) $\iota_0 := \iota_1 \ ; \iota_1 := \iota_0 \equiv_{\text{comm}} \iota_0 := \iota_1$

(c) $\iota_0 := \iota_1 \ ; \iota_2 := \iota_0 \equiv_{\text{comm}} \iota_0 := \iota_1 \ ; \iota_2 := \iota_1$

(d) $\iota_0 := \iota_1 \ ; \iota_2 := \iota_1 \equiv_{\text{comm}} \iota_2 := \iota_1 \ ; \iota_0 := \iota_1$

where $\iota_0, \iota_1, \iota_2 \in [\tau]$ for some data type τ.

3.7   (a) Prove that, in Section 3.3, graph $c_i \subseteq$ graph c_{i+1} for all $i \in N$.

(b) In general, the union of the graphs of partial functions need not be the graph of a partial function; but prove that

$$\bigcup_{i \in N} \text{graph } c_i$$

is the graph of a partial function.

3.8   Define the syntax and semantics of the command form

$$\textbf{repeat } C \textbf{ until } B$$

so as to achieve the equivalence

repeat C **until** B $\equiv_{\text{comm}}$ C ; **if not** B **then repeat** C **until** B,

and then verify the following equivalence using induction:

repeat C **until** B $\equiv_{\text{comm}}$ C ; **while not** B **do** C

3.9   Verify the following command equivalences:

(a) C ; **diverge** $\equiv_{\text{comm}}$ **diverge** $\equiv_{\text{comm}}$ **diverge** ; C

(b) **while false do** C $\equiv_{\text{comm}}$ **skip**

(c) **while true do** C $\equiv_{\text{comm}}$ **diverge**

(d) (**while** B **do** C) ; **if** B **then** C_0 **else** C_1 $\equiv_{\text{comm}}$ (**while** B **do** C) ; C_1

where B: **exp[bool]** and C, C_0, C_1: **comm**.

3.10 Derive the following from the axioms of Section 3.6.2:

$$\{P_1\}C\{Q_1\} \ \& \cdots \& \ \{P_n\}C\{Q_n\}$$
$$\Rightarrow \ \{P_1 \textbf{ and} \cdots \textbf{and } P_n\}C\{Q_1 \textbf{ and} \cdots \textbf{and } Q_n\}$$

$$\{P_1\}C\{Q_1\} \ \& \cdots \& \ \{P_n\}C\{Q_n\}$$
$$\Rightarrow \ \{P_1 \textbf{ or} \cdots \textbf{or } P_n\}C\{Q_1 \textbf{ or} \cdots \textbf{or } Q_n\}$$

3.11 Validate the remaining axioms of Section 3.6.2 using the semantic valuations.

3.12 Fill in the missing parts of the proof sketched for Proposition 3.2.

3.13 Give an operational semantics for evaluation of the *expressions* in the language of this chapter and prove the resulting input-to-output behavior equivalent to that specified by the denotational semantics.

3.14 Devise axioms for the non-deterministic control structures of Section 3.7 and validate them using the semantics.

3.15 Extend the operational semantics of Section 3.5 to treat the non-deterministic control structures of Section 3.7. State and prove an appropriate correctness result.

3.16 (a) Prove that, for every $v \in [\![\tau]\!]$, there exists an expression $E_v \in [\mathbf{exp}[\tau]]$ such that $[\![E_v]\!]s = v$ for all $s \in S$.

     (b) Prove by structural induction that, for every expression E, $[\![E]\!]s = [\![E]\!]s'$ whenever s and s' agree on (the finite set of) all identifiers that occur in E.

     (c) Prove by structural induction that, for every command C, if $[\![C]\!]s = s'$ then s and s' agree on all identifiers not occurring in C.

     (d) Prove by structural induction that, for every command C and states s and s', $[\![C]\!]s$ and $[\![C]\!]s'$ agree on all identifiers used in C whenever s and s' do.

     (e) Use the results above to prove that the semantic valuation for the simple imperative language is fully abstract.

Bibliographic Notes

The language discussed in this chapter is generally known in the literature as the language of "**while** programs." The operational semantics presented is based on [Mil76, Plo81]. The programming logic presented is based on [Flo67, Hoa69], but has been re-formulated here as a multi-sorted quantifier-free first-order theory. The role of Floyd–Hoare logic in programming is discussed in [AA78, Rey81a, Bac86], among many others. The first demonstration of the soundness of the system appears to have been [Lau71]. Completeness issues are discussed in [dBM75, Coo78, Wan78, Apt81, BTT82, BT82, Gol82, Cla84, Lei85a, Pas86, LF87, Abr87, Rob87, HG+88, TZ88, Ber91].

More sophisticated approaches to the semantics of non-determinism are presented in [Plo76, Leh76, Smy78, HP79, Plo82, Bac83, Abr83b, Smy83, Abr83a, Win83, Con90].

Many workers in the area of Programming Methodology have adopted an approach to command semantics known as "predicate transformers" [Dij76]. In their view, any explicit mention of computational states is undesirably "operational," and they prefer to treat the denotation of a command as a function that maps any desired post-condition to the weakest pre-condition that ensures that execution of the command terminates in a state satisfying that post-condition. [Plo79] shows that this approach to command meanings is in fact isomorphic to the state-transformation approach, and so there is no substantive difference between them.

Chapter 4

A Simple Applicative Language

There is a fundamental difference between the environment and the state which is the source of many of the confusions and difficulties about programming languages.

C. Strachey (1972)

In the programming language discussed in the preceding chapter, all identifiers are accessible globally and there are no procedures. In this chapter, we consider a language in which:

- there are *local* definitions of identifiers, rather than assignment commands that change the values of global variables;

- the programmer can use and define *functions*; and

- the main "control structure" is function application, rather than sequencing and iteration.

Languages that emphasize "mathematical" features (such as definitions, functions, and recursion) are termed *applicative* or *declarative* or *functional*, in contrast to *imperative* languages, which emphasize "algorithmic" features (such as assignments, loops, and jumps). The language to be described in this chapter is termed "simple" because it does not have recursive definitions; recursion will be considered separately in Chapter 5.

The key semantic concept to be introduced is that of the *environment*, an assignment of phrase meanings to the identifiers that are used in a phrase without being bound there. "Local" environments are created by identifier-binding constructions such as definitions. We will discuss the abstract syntax and denotational semantics of the language and a programming logic; an operational semantics for the language extended by recursive definitions will be given in Chapter 5.

59

4.1   Definitions and Function Applications

The commonplace expressions of arithmetic and algebra have a certain sim-
plicity that most communications to computers lack.

P. J. Landin (1966)

We begin by describing a language fragment consisting of expressions similar
to those of the preceding chapter, function applications, and local-definition
blocks. The local-definition block has the form

let ι **be** P **in** Q

Intuitively, this allows ι to be used in Q as a symbolic name for the meaning
of phrase P. This might be a *re-definition* of identifier ι; but it is not the
same as an *assignment* to a variable, because the scope of the definition
is at most the sub-phrase Q. In implementation terms, the "old" value
of a variable is overwritten by an assignment, but the "old" meaning of a
re-defined identifier must be retained.

For example, the value of

$$
\begin{aligned}
&\textbf{let } n \textbf{ be } 2 \textbf{ in} \\
&\quad (\textbf{let } n \textbf{ be } n + 1 \textbf{ in } n) + n
\end{aligned}
\qquad (4.1)
$$

is 5. The inner definition of n has no effect on the occurrence of n outside
the parentheses. We are assuming that the syntactic scope of **let** extends
as far to the right as possible, so that that occurrence of n is bound by
the *outer* **let**; furthermore, the occurrence of n in the phrase $n + 1$ is also
bound by the outer **let**.

The types for our language are defined as follows:

$$
\tau ::= \textbf{bool} \mid \textbf{nat} \qquad\qquad \text{data types}
$$

$$
\theta ::= \textbf{val}[\tau] \mid \theta \longrightarrow \theta' \mid (\theta) \quad \text{phrase types.}
$$

Phrases having types of the form $\textbf{val}[\tau]$ will be termed *value phrases*. Syntactically, they will be similar to the expressions considered previously. We
have used a different phrase type in order to emphasize the important *se-*
mantic difference between the expressions of the preceding chapter and
value phrases here: the latter are "pure" in that their values are *state-*
independent, that is to say, not subject to change by assignment commands.

A type of the form $\theta \longrightarrow \theta'$ is a *functional* type: θ is the type of arguments
to the functions, and θ' is the type of the results. A functional type $\theta \longrightarrow \theta'$
is termed *higher-order* if θ is a functional type or θ' is higher-order. For
example,

$$
(\textbf{val}[\textbf{nat}] \longrightarrow \textbf{val}[\textbf{bool}]) \longrightarrow \textbf{val}[\textbf{bool}]
$$

is a higher-order type. The function-space type constructor can be used any
(finite) number of times to construct a type, and so the language has an
infinite number of types. We will discuss multi-argument functions later.

The syntax of our language is defined by the inference rules of Table 4.1. Most of the rules are similar to the syntax rules for expressions in Section 3.1, except that types of the form $\mathbf{exp}[\tau]$ have been replaced by types of the form $\mathbf{val}[\tau]$. Whenever convenient, we will use additional constants $(1, \mathbf{false}, \ldots)$ and operators $(+, \times, \ldots)$ in examples.

The rules for applications and local definitions are new *generic* rules, applicable with all phrase types θ and θ'. The syntax for applications allows *any* phrase of a functional type to be applied to *any* actual-parameter phrase whose type is the argument type of the functional type. In many languages, the function part of an application must be an identifier and the actual parameter must be parenthesized; but there are no semantic reasons for these syntactic conventions.

Before discussing the rule for local definitions, we must explain how the syntax rules allow for *uses* of identifiers. In the simple imperative language of Chapter 3, all identifiers were *variable* identifiers and had *global* scope. In the language being considered here, identifiers can be defined to denote meanings of *arbitrary* phrase types and have *local* scopes. Therefore, our syntax must allow for assignments of arbitrary phrase types to (at least) the identifiers that can appear in phrases without being bound there.

This is elegantly achieved by regarding the syntax rules as being *natural-deduction* rules with sequents of the form $\pi \vdash X : \theta$, where π is a *phrase-type assignment*, a finite set of assumptions of the form $\iota : \theta$ for distinct identifiers ι. The sequent $\pi \vdash X : \theta$ asserts that X is a well-formed phrase of type θ *provided* that the identifiers that are used in X without being bound there have the types assigned to them by π. The natural-deduction framework implicitly provides the following syntax axiom, which allows identifiers to be *used* in well-formed phrases: for any phrase-type assignment π, $\pi \vdash \iota : \theta$ when $\iota : \theta$ is in π. For example,

$$\{\ldots, n : \mathbf{val}[\mathbf{nat}], \ldots\} \vdash n : \mathbf{val}[\mathbf{nat}],$$

but not

$$\{\ldots, n : \mathbf{val}[\mathbf{nat}], \ldots\} \vdash n : \mathbf{val}[\mathbf{bool}]$$

nor

$$\{n : \mathbf{val}[\mathbf{nat}]\} \vdash m : \mathbf{val}[\mathbf{nat}].$$

A phrase-type assignment π can be thought of as the mathematical counterpart of some state of the "symbol table" in a compiler.

To allow for *pre-defined* identifiers, we assume an *initial* phrase-type assignment π_0, which specifies the phrase types of these identifiers, and deem E to be well-formed as a *program* (of type τ) if $\pi \vdash E : \mathbf{val}[\tau]$ for some finite subset π of π_0.

All of the syntax rules in Table 4.1 should now be interpreted as natural deduction rules. The Negation rule, for example, specifies that, for any

Bracketing:

$$\frac{X : \theta}{(X) : \theta}$$

Conditional:

$$\frac{B : \textbf{val[bool]} \quad X_0 : \theta \quad X_1 : \theta}{\textbf{if } B \textbf{ then } X_0 \textbf{ else } X_1 : \theta}$$

Zero:

$$\overline{0 : \textbf{val[nat]}}$$

Successor:

$$\frac{N : \textbf{val[nat]}}{\textbf{succ } N : \textbf{val[nat]}}$$

Truth:

$$\overline{\textbf{true} : \textbf{val[bool]}}$$

Negation:

$$\frac{B : \textbf{val[bool]}}{\textbf{not } B : \textbf{val[bool]}}$$

Conjunction:

$$\frac{B_0 : \textbf{val[bool]} \quad B_1 : \textbf{val[bool]}}{B_0 \textbf{ and } B_1 : \textbf{val[bool]}}$$

Ordering:

$$\frac{N_0 : \textbf{val[nat]} \quad N_1 : \textbf{val[nat]}}{N_0 < N_1 : \textbf{val[bool]}}$$

Equality:

$$\frac{E_0 : \textbf{val}[\tau] \quad E_1 : \textbf{val}[\tau]}{E_0 = E_1 : \textbf{val[bool]}}$$

Application:

$$\frac{P : \theta \rightarrow \theta' \quad Q : \theta}{P\,Q : \theta'}$$

Local Definition:

$$[\iota : \theta]$$
$$\vdots$$
$$\frac{P : \theta \qquad Q : \theta'}{\textbf{let } \iota \textbf{ be } P \textbf{ in } Q : \theta'}$$

Table 4.1 Syntax of the applicative language.

phrase-type assignment π, if $\pi \vdash B$: **val**[**bool**], then $\pi \vdash$ **not** B: **val**[**bool**]. For example,

$$\{\ldots, b\text{: }\mathbf{val}[\mathbf{bool}], \ldots\} \vdash \mathbf{not}\ b\text{: }\mathbf{val}[\mathbf{bool}]$$

is derivable using this rule.

The Local-Definition Rule in Table 4.1 can now be explained. It will here be convenient to regard a type assignment π as being a *function* from a finite set of identifiers dom π to phrase types, so that, for all $\iota \in$ dom π, $\pi(\iota)$ is the assumed type of ι. The Local-Definition Rule should be interpreted as stating that, for any π, if $\pi \vdash P$: θ and $(\pi \mid \iota \mapsto \theta) \vdash Q$: θ' then

$$\pi \vdash \mathbf{let}\ \iota\ \mathbf{be}\ P\ \mathbf{in}\ Q\text{:}\,\theta',$$

where $(\pi \mid \iota \mapsto \theta)$ is the phrase-type assignment π' such that dom $\pi' =$ dom $\pi \cup \{\iota\}$, $\pi'(\iota) = \theta$, and $\pi'(\iota') = \pi(\iota')$ for all $\iota' \in$ dom π distinct from ι. This rule allows an identifier to be re-defined, but gives priority to the most-local definition of that identifier, as is conventional in programming languages. Notice also that the rule makes it clear that the scope of the definition includes Q but not P or any other phrase.

As an example of how this logical approach to syntax works, we will develop the syntactic derivation of value phrase (4.1). For this example, we assume additional obvious axioms for the numerical constants 1 and 2, and an additional rule as follows:

Addition:

$$\frac{N_0\text{: }\mathbf{val}[\mathbf{nat}] \quad N_1\text{: }\mathbf{val}[\mathbf{nat}]}{N_0 + N_1\text{: }\mathbf{val}[\mathbf{nat}]}$$

We start with a derivation of the "inner" **let** using the Addition Rule (+) and the Local-Definition Rule (**let**):

$$\cfrac{\cfrac{n\text{: }\mathbf{val}[\mathbf{nat}] \quad \overline{1\text{: }\mathbf{val}[\mathbf{nat}]}}{n + 1\text{: }\mathbf{val}[\mathbf{nat}]}\ (+) \qquad [n\text{: }\mathbf{val}[\mathbf{nat}]]}{\mathbf{let}\ n\ \mathbf{be}\ n + 1\ \mathbf{in}\ n\text{: }\mathbf{val}[\mathbf{nat}]}\ (\mathbf{let})$$

Notice that the assumption n: **val**[**nat**] in the second premiss has been cancelled by using the Local-Definition Rule, but the same assumption in the first premiss is still uncancelled. The next step uses the Addition Rule again as follows:

$$\cfrac{\cfrac{\cfrac{n\text{: }\mathbf{val}[\mathbf{nat}] \quad \overline{1\text{: }\mathbf{val}[\mathbf{nat}]}}{n + 1\text{: }\mathbf{val}[\mathbf{nat}]} \qquad [n\text{: }\mathbf{val}[\mathbf{nat}]]}{\mathbf{let}\ n\ \mathbf{be}\ n + 1\ \mathbf{in}\ n\text{: }\mathbf{val}[\mathbf{nat}]} \qquad n\text{: }\mathbf{val}[\mathbf{nat}]}{(\mathbf{let}\ n\ \mathbf{be}\ n + 1\ \mathbf{in}\ n) + n\text{: }\mathbf{val}[\mathbf{nat}]}\ (+)$$

Another use of the Local-Definition Rule then allows the cancellation of two occurrences of the assumption n: **val**[**nat**] and gives us the complete desired derivation of (4.1), with no uncancelled assumptions:

$$\cfrac{\cfrac{\cfrac{[n\colon \textbf{val}[\textbf{nat}]] \quad \overline{1\colon \textbf{val}[\textbf{nat}]}}{n+1\colon \textbf{val}[\textbf{nat}]} \qquad [n\colon \textbf{val}[\textbf{nat}]]}{2\colon \textbf{val}[\textbf{nat}] \qquad \cfrac{\textbf{let } n \textbf{ be } n+1 \textbf{ in } n\colon \textbf{val}[\textbf{nat}] \qquad\qquad\qquad [n\colon \textbf{val}[\textbf{nat}]]}{(\textbf{let } n \textbf{ be } n+1 \textbf{ in } n) + n\colon \textbf{val}[\textbf{nat}]}}}{\textbf{let } n \textbf{ be } 2 \textbf{ in } (\textbf{let } n \textbf{ be } n+1 \textbf{ in } n) + n\colon \textbf{val}[\textbf{nat}]} \quad \text{(let)}$$

We finally can turn to the semantics of the language. The sets of possible meanings for the phrase types are defined as follows:

$$\llbracket \textbf{val}[\tau] \rrbracket = \llbracket \tau \rrbracket$$
$$\llbracket \theta \to \theta' \rrbracket = \llbracket \theta \rrbracket \to \llbracket \theta' \rrbracket$$
$$\llbracket (\theta) \rrbracket = \llbracket \theta \rrbracket$$

where, as before $\llbracket \tau \rrbracket$ is the set of values for data type τ. On the right-hand side, $A \to B$ denotes the set of all (total) functions from A to B. Note that we must use an inductive definition because there is an infinite number of functional phrase types.

The reader may by now be wondering how *identifiers* are going to be treated. Consider a phrase P; the *type* of P can depend in general on the types of the identifiers used within it, and these are determined by a type assignment π such that $\pi \vdash P\colon \theta$. Similarly, the *meaning* of P can depend on the meanings of the identifiers used within it; these will be determined by a "phrase-meaning assignment" or *environment* u which is π-compatible in the sense that, for all $\iota \in \text{dom } \pi$, $u(\iota) \in \llbracket \pi(\iota) \rrbracket$. For any phrase-type assignment π, we can define the set of π-compatible environments, $\llbracket \pi \rrbracket$, as follows:

$$\llbracket \pi \rrbracket \;=\; \prod_{\iota \in \text{dom } \pi} \llbracket \pi(\iota) \rrbracket;$$

i.e., the set of all functions u with $\text{dom } u = \text{dom } \pi$ such that, for all $\iota \in \text{dom } \pi$, $u(\iota) \in \llbracket \pi(\iota) \rrbracket$.

Let $[\theta]_\pi$ be the set of all phrases P such that $\pi \vdash P\colon \theta$. We can now define valuations

$$\llbracket \cdot \rrbracket_{\pi\theta}\colon [\theta]_\pi \;\longrightarrow\; (\llbracket \pi \rrbracket \to \llbracket \theta \rrbracket)$$

mapping every phrase P such that $\pi \vdash P\colon \theta$ into a *function* from $\llbracket \pi \rrbracket$ to $\llbracket \theta \rrbracket$. The π and θ subscripts (or just the π) on phrase-valuation brackets will often be omitted.

For an identifier $\iota \in \text{dom } \pi$ with $\pi(\iota) = \theta$, the semantic equation is

$$\llbracket \iota \rrbracket_{\pi\theta}(u) = u(\iota),$$

for all $u \in \llbracket \pi \rrbracket$. To allow for the pre-defined identifiers, we assume a π_0-compatible initial environment $u_0 \in \llbracket \pi_0 \rrbracket$ that determines their meanings, and interpret *programs* relative to the appropriate restrictions of u_0.

For most value phrases V, $[\![V]\!]_{\pi \text{ } \mathbf{val}[\tau]}$ can be defined in the same way that the corresponding expression was defined in Section 3.1, but with environment arguments replacing state arguments throughout, as in

$$[\![B_0 \text{ and } B_1]\!]u = \begin{cases} true, & \text{if } [\![B_0]\!]u = true \text{ and } [\![B_1]\!]u = true \\ false, & \text{otherwise.} \end{cases}$$

The given environment is passed down to each sub-phrase, even if modified environments are created locally within them to handle identifier-binding constructions. Similarly, the conditional form can be interpreted as follows:

$$[\![\text{if } B \text{ then } X_0 \text{ else } X_1]\!]_\theta(u) = \begin{cases} [\![X_0]\!]_\theta(u), & \text{if } [\![B]\!]u = true \\ [\![X_1]\!]_\theta(u), & \text{if } [\![B]\!]u = false. \end{cases}$$

The semantic equation for function applications is as follows:

$$[\![P\,Q]\!]u = ([\![P]\!]u)([\![Q]\!]u);$$

the syntax and the interpretation of the phrase types ensure that $[\![P]\!]u$ is a mathematical function and that $[\![Q]\!]u$ is an element of its domain to which the function can be *applied*. We can reduce the number of parentheses needed by assuming that function application in the meta-language associates to the left:

$$[\![P\,Q]\!]u = [\![P]\!]u([\![Q]\!]u).$$

Finally, the semantic equation for the local-definition block is

$$[\![\text{let } \iota \text{ be } P \text{ in } Q]\!]u = [\![Q]\!](u \mid \iota \mapsto [\![P]\!]u),$$

where the notation $(u \mid \iota \mapsto m)$ is analogous to $(\pi \mid \iota \mapsto \theta)$; i.e., the body of the block, Q, is interpreted relative to a local environment that is like u, except that ι is bound to the meaning of P in the original environment. The difference between this and the valuation for assignment commands in the preceding chapter should be particularly noted:

$$[\![\iota := E]\!]s = (s \mid \iota \mapsto [\![E]\!]s).$$

In the valuation for assignment, the resulting state is passed on to other commands by sequencing or iteration of command meanings. In contrast, the new environment created by a definition is only used "locally" within the body of the block.

As an example, let u be any environment; then

$$
\begin{aligned}
& [\![\text{let } n \text{ be } 2 \text{ in } (\text{let } n \text{ be } n + 1 \text{ in } n) + n]\!]u \\
= \ & [\![(\text{let } n \text{ be } n + 1 \text{ in } n) + n]\!](u \mid n \mapsto 2) \\
= \ & [\![\text{let } n \text{ be } n + 1 \text{ in } n]\!](u \mid n \mapsto 2) + [\![n]\!](u \mid n \mapsto 2) \\
= \ & [\![n]\!](u \mid n \mapsto [\![n + 1]\!](u \mid n \mapsto 2)) + [\![n]\!](u \mid n \mapsto 2) \\
= \ & [\![n]\!](u \mid n \mapsto 3) + [\![n]\!](u \mid n \mapsto 2) \\
= \ & 3 + 2 \\
= \ & 5
\end{aligned}
$$

The local environment created by the inner **let** is not used for the evaluation of the occurrence of *n* that is outside the scope of that definition.

The following are some examples of equivalences that can be validated using the valuation for local-definition blocks:

$$\text{let } \iota \text{ be } \iota \text{ in } X \;\equiv\; X \;\equiv\; \text{let } \iota \text{ be } X \text{ in } \iota$$

$$\text{let } \iota \text{ be } X \text{ in } PQ$$
$$\equiv \quad (\text{let } \iota \text{ be } X \text{ in } P)\,(\text{let } \iota \text{ be } X \text{ in } Q)$$

$$\text{let } \iota \text{ be } P \text{ in } (\text{let } \iota \text{ be } Q \text{ in } R)$$
$$\equiv \quad \text{let } \iota \text{ be } (\text{let } \iota \text{ be } P \text{ in } Q) \text{ in } R$$

4.2   Function Definitions

The language fragment described in the preceding section allows a programmer to use pre-defined functions and also to re-name them using the local-definition block, but does not provide a way for a programmer to define "new" functions. We therefore introduce the following notation:

Function Definition:

$$
\begin{array}{cc}
[\iota_0\colon \theta_0] & [\iota\colon \theta_0 \rightarrow \theta] \\
\vdots & \vdots \\
P\colon \theta & Q\colon \theta' \\
\hline
\multicolumn{2}{c}{\text{let } \iota(\iota_0\colon \theta_0) = P \text{ in } Q\colon \theta'}
\end{array}
$$

This construction defines ι to be the local name (within Q) of a function defined by "formal parameter" ι_0 and "body" P. For example, the following block defines a function *Add2* that returns the result of adding 2 to its argument:

$$\text{let } Add2(n\colon \textbf{val}[\textbf{nat}]) = n + 2$$
$$\textbf{in } \cdots$$

The semantic equation for this construction is as follows:

$$[\![\text{let } \iota(\iota_0\colon \theta_0) = P \text{ in } Q]\!]u \;=\; [\![Q]\!](u \mid \iota \mapsto f)$$

where $f\colon [\![\theta_0]\!] \rightarrow [\![\theta]\!]$ is the function defined by

$$f(a) = [\![P]\!](u \mid \iota_0 \mapsto a)$$

for all $a \in [\![\theta_0]\!]$. Notice the environment used for P: the formal parameter ι_0 is bound to the value a (of some actual parameter), but other identifiers in the body are interpreted in the environment u for the *definition* of the function, rather than the environment for its *call*. For example, the function defined in

$$\textbf{let } Addm(n\colon \textbf{val}[\textbf{nat}]) = n + m$$
$$\textbf{in } \cdots$$

returns the result of adding m to its argument, where m is determined in the context where the function is *defined*, not where it happens to be *used*. Occurrences of the function name ι in P are *not* recursive uses of the function being defined; recursion will be discussed in the next chapter.

It is also convenient to introduce notation for defining "anonymous" functions:

Abstraction:

$$[\iota\colon \theta]$$
$$\vdots$$
$$\dfrac{P\colon \theta'}{\lambda\iota\colon \theta.\, P\colon \theta \rightarrow \theta'}$$

This kind of construct is termed a *lambda expression*; it appears in several programming languages, including LISP and ALGOL 68, and the similar notation $x \mapsto \ldots x \ldots$ is used in mathematics. The phrase $\lambda\iota\colon \theta.\, P$ denotes the function that maps arguments a of type θ into the meaning of P when ι denotes a. For example, $\lambda n\colon \textbf{val}[\textbf{nat}].\, n + m$ denotes the numerical function that returns the result of adding m to its argument, so that the value of

$$\big(\lambda n\colon \textbf{val}[\textbf{nat}].\, n + m\big)(3)$$

is that of $3 + m$. As usual, we assume that the syntactic scope of the lambda expression extends as far to the right as possible. The name of the syntax rule, Abstraction, derives from the fact that the notation defines a function by abstracting from a particular syntactic representation of it.

The semantic equation for the lambda expression is

$$[\![\lambda\iota\colon \theta.\, P]\!]_{\pi(\theta \rightarrow \theta')}(u) = f \in [\![\theta]\!] \rightarrow [\![\theta']\!]$$
$$\text{such that } f(a) = [\![P]\!]_{(\pi|\iota \rightarrow \theta)\theta'}(u \mid \iota \mapsto a) \text{ for all } a \in [\![\theta]\!].$$

As with the function definition block, the values of identifiers used in the body P (other than the formal parameter ι) are determined in the environment of the λ-expression, rather than in the environments in which the function happens to be used.

4.3 Defined Notation

Rules about user-coined names is an area in which we might expect to see the history of computer applications give ground to their logic. Another such area is in specifying functional relations. In fact these two areas are closely related since any use of a user-coined name implicitly involves a functional relation.

P. J. Landin (1966)

It is straightforward to use the semantic equations of the preceding section to prove that, in any appropriate phrase-type assignment, the function-definition block

$$\textbf{let } \iota(\iota_0\!:\theta_0) = P \textbf{ in } Q\!:\theta'$$

and the simple definition block

$$\textbf{let } \iota \textbf{ be } \lambda\iota_0\!:\theta_0.\, P \textbf{ in } Q$$

are semantically equivalent for any P and Q (of appropriate type); furthermore, for any P of type θ (in some type assignment), the simple definition block

$$\textbf{let } \iota \textbf{ be } P \textbf{ in } Q$$

and the function application

$$(\lambda\iota\!:\theta.\,Q)P$$

are semantically equivalent in that type assignment. We have essentially "reduced" our two forms of local-definition block to particular combinations of functional abstraction and application. We can subsequently treat the two local-definition forms as *defined notation*, rather than as basic features of our language, much as we treated **if** B **then** C as an abbreviation for **if** B **then** C **else skip**.

As another example of this technique, we can reduce functions with multiple parameters to single-parameter functions. For any sets A, B, and C, there is a one-to-one correspondence between the set of two-argument functions $A \times B \rightarrow C$ and the set of function-producing functions $A \rightarrow (B \rightarrow C)$: any $f\!:A \times B \rightarrow C$ corresponds to $g\!:A \rightarrow (B \rightarrow C)$ such that, for all $a \in A$, $g(a) = h_a \in B \rightarrow C$ such that $h_a(b) = f(a,b)$ for all $b \in B$; conversely, $g\!:A \rightarrow (B \rightarrow C)$ corresponds to $f\!:A \times B \rightarrow C$ such that for all $a \in A$ and $b \in B$, $f(a,b) = g(a)(b)$.

This correspondence allows us to regard a phrase type of the form

$$\theta_1 \times \theta_2 \times \cdots \times \theta_n \rightarrow \theta$$

as an alternative notation for

$$\theta_1 \rightarrow (\theta_2 \rightarrow (\cdots \rightarrow (\theta_n \rightarrow \theta)\cdots)),$$

which is essentially similar to the way "multi-dimensional arrays" are treated in the programming language PASCAL: they are really arrays of arrays. We then can make the following syntactic extensions:

Multiple Application:

$$\frac{P:\theta_1 \times \cdots \times \theta_n \longrightarrow \theta \qquad Q_i:\theta_i \quad \text{for } i = 1,2,\ldots,n}{P(Q_1,\ldots,Q_n):\theta}$$

Multiple Abstraction:

$$\frac{\begin{bmatrix} \iota_1:\theta_1 \\ \vdots \\ \iota_n:\theta_n \end{bmatrix} \\ \vdots \\ P:\theta}{\lambda(\iota_1:\theta_1,\ldots,\iota_n:\theta_n).\,P:\theta_1 \times \cdots \times \theta_n \longrightarrow \theta}$$

Multiple-Parameter Function Definition:

$$\frac{\begin{bmatrix} \iota_1:\theta_1 \\ \vdots \\ \iota_n:\theta_n \end{bmatrix} \quad [\iota:\theta_1 \times \cdots \times \theta_n \longrightarrow \theta] \\ \vdots \qquad\qquad\qquad \vdots \\ P:\theta \qquad\qquad\qquad Q:\theta'}{\textbf{let } \iota(\iota_1:\theta_1,\ldots,\iota_n:\theta_n) = P \textbf{ in } Q:\theta'}$$

The interpretations can be defined by the following equivalences:

$$P(Q_1,\ldots,Q_n) \quad \equiv \quad P(Q_1)\cdots(Q_n)$$

$$\lambda(\iota_1:\theta_1,\ldots,\iota_n:\theta_n).\,P \quad \equiv \quad \lambda\iota_1:\theta_1.\cdots.\lambda\iota_n:\theta_n.\,P$$

$$\textbf{let } \iota(\iota_1:\theta_1,\ldots,\iota_n:\theta_n) = P \textbf{ in } Q$$
$$\equiv \quad \bigl(\lambda\iota:\theta_1 \times \cdots \times \theta_n \longrightarrow \theta.\,Q\bigr)\bigl(\lambda(\iota_1:\theta_1,\ldots,\iota_n:\theta_n).\,P\bigr),$$

where we have omitted the obvious type subscripts on $\equiv$. Variants of the **let** forms with *multiple* definitions could be introduced in the same way.

Another example of defined notation is based on the notation for quantification in predicate logic:

Quantification:

$$\frac{Q:(\theta' \longrightarrow \theta'') \longrightarrow \theta \qquad \begin{matrix} [\iota:\theta'] \\ \vdots \\ P:\theta'' \end{matrix}}{\# Q \, \iota.\,P:\theta}$$

Phrase Q is the *quantifier*, ι is the bound identifier, and P is the body. The interpretation is defined by the following equivalence:

$$\# Q\,\iota.\,P \quad \equiv_\theta \quad Q(\lambda\iota\colon\theta'.\,P);$$

that is, for any appropriate environment u,

$$[\![\# Q\,\iota.\,P]\!]u \;=\; [\![Q]\!]u f,$$

where $f(a) = [\![P]\!](u \mid \iota \mapsto a)$ for all $a \in [\![\theta']\!]$. For example, a programmer can obtain the analog of

$$\sum_{i=a}^{b} \cdots i \cdots$$

by using a suitable higher-order function

$$sum\colon \mathbf{val}[\mathbf{nat}] \times \mathbf{val}[\mathbf{nat}] \rightarrow \big(\mathbf{val}[\mathbf{nat}] \rightarrow \mathbf{val}[\mathbf{nat}]\big) \rightarrow \mathbf{val}[\mathbf{nat}]$$

as follows:

$$\# sum(a,b)\,i.\cdots i\cdots.$$

This is by definition equivalent to

$$sum\big(a, b, \lambda i\colon \mathbf{val}[\mathbf{nat}].\cdots i\cdots\big),$$

but the advantages of the quantification notation are that the syntactic structure is clearer and the type of the bound identifier need not be stated explicitly (because it can be inferred from the type of the quantifier).

We will use the quantification notation to introduce in a uniform way a variety of language features involving identifier binding.

4.4   Elementary Properties

The language described in the preceding three sections of this chapter is termed an *explicitly-typed* language because it has the following two properties:

1. For any phrase X and phrase-type assignment π, $\pi \vdash X\colon\theta$ is derivable for at most *one* phrase type θ.

2. If it is defined at all, the type of any composite phrase X in a phrase-type assignment π is determined by the types of the immediate constituents of X in some determined phrase-type assignments (possibly, but not necessarily π).

For example, the type of $\lambda\iota\!:\!\theta.\,X$ in π is defined just if X has a type in $(\pi \mid \iota \mapsto \theta)$, and is then $\theta \longrightarrow \theta'$, where θ' is the *unique* type of X in that phrase-type assignment. If the syntax did not require that the type of ι be specified explicitly, a lambda expression could have many types; e.g., $\lambda x.\,x$ has type $\theta \longrightarrow \theta$ for *every* θ.

As another example, the type of **let** ι **be** P **in** Q in phrase-type assignment π is defined just if P has a type in π and Q has a type in $(\pi \mid \iota \mapsto \theta)$, where θ is *the* type of P in π, and is then *the* type of Q in $(\pi \mid \iota \mapsto \theta)$. The explicit-typing property makes it possible to *infer* the type of ι from the type of P, despite the fact that there is no *explicit* occurrence of the type of ι in the construction.

As a final example, consider the function-definition block

$$\textbf{let } \iota(\iota_0\!:\!\theta_0) = P \textbf{ in } Q\!:\!\theta'$$

The explicit occurrence of the argument type θ_0 is here essential to determine the phrase-type assignment used for P. On the other hand, the result type θ can be inferred from P.

We have seen that, given π, there is at most one θ such that $\pi \vdash X\!:\!\theta$ is derivable; but given some phrase type θ, it is not the case that there is at most one phrase-type assignment π such that $\pi \vdash X\!:\!\theta$. Let $\pi' \vdash \pi$ just if π' is an extension of π; i.e., $\pi' \vdash \pi$ if and only if $\operatorname{dom}\pi \subseteq \operatorname{dom}\pi'$ and, for all $\iota \in \operatorname{dom}\pi$, $\pi(\iota) = \pi'(\iota)$.

Proposition 4.1   *If $\pi' \vdash \pi$ and $\pi \vdash X\!:\!\theta$ is derivable then so is $\pi' \vdash X\!:\!\theta$.*

This can be proved by induction on the length of derivations of sequents in the formal system for syntax. If $\pi \vdash \iota\!:\!\pi(\iota)$ is derivable, then so is $\pi' \vdash \iota\!:\!\pi(\iota)$ because $\pi'(\iota) = \pi(\iota)$.

If $\pi \vdash \lambda\iota\!:\!\theta.\,P\!:\!\theta \longrightarrow \theta'$ is derivable, then this follows directly from the derivability of $(\pi \mid \iota \mapsto \theta) \vdash P\!:\!\theta'$; but $(\pi' \mid \iota \mapsto \theta)$ is an extension of $(\pi \mid \iota \mapsto \theta)$ and so, by induction, $(\pi' \mid \iota \mapsto \theta) \vdash P\!:\!\theta'$ is derivable and then it follows that $\pi' \vdash \lambda\iota\!:\!\theta.\,P\!:\!\theta \longrightarrow \theta'$ is derivable.

If $\pi \vdash \textbf{not } B\!:\!\textbf{val[bool]}$ is derivable, then this follows directly from derivability of $\pi \vdash B\!:\!\textbf{val[bool]}$; by induction, $\pi' \vdash B\!:\!\textbf{val[bool]}$ is derivable, so that $\pi' \vdash \textbf{not } B\!:\!\textbf{val[bool]}$ is also, and similarly for other composite phrases. $\square$

This syntactic "ambiguity" raises the possibility that the semantic interpretation of a phrase might be ambiguous because of dependence on "unnecessary" assumptions made in the derivation of its syntactic well-formedness. The following result shows that this is not the case.

Lemma 4.2 (Coherence)   *If $\pi \vdash X\!:\!\theta$ and $\pi' \vdash \pi$, then, for every $u' \in [\![\pi']\!]$, $[\![X]\!]_{\pi'\theta}(u') = [\![X]\!]_{\pi\theta}(u)$, where $u \in [\![\pi]\!]$ is the restriction of u' to $\operatorname{dom}\pi$.*

If we use the notation $[\![\pi' \vdash \pi]\!]$ to denote the function from $[\![\pi']\!]$ to $[\![\pi]\!]$ that restricts any $u' \in [\![\pi']\!]$ to dom π, the Coherence Lemma can be expressed as the commutativity of the following diagram:

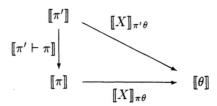

The Coherence Lemma can be proved by structural induction on the syntax of X. We discuss only the case that $X = \lambda\iota:\theta_0. P$. Suppose that

$$\pi \vdash \lambda\iota:\theta_0. P: \theta_0 \rightarrow \theta_1$$

is derivable and that π' is an extension of π; then $(\pi' \mid \iota \mapsto \theta_0)$ is an extension of $(\pi \mid \iota \mapsto \theta_0)$. Consider any $u' \in [\![\pi']\!]$ and let $u \in [\![\pi]\!]$ be its restriction to dom π; then, for any $a \in [\![\theta_0]\!]$, $(u \mid \iota \mapsto a)$ is the restriction of $(u' \mid \iota \mapsto a)$ to $\mathrm{dom}(\pi \mid \iota \mapsto \theta_0)$, and so

$$
\begin{aligned}
[\![\lambda\iota:\theta_0. P]\!]u'a &= [\![P]\!](u' \mid \iota \mapsto a) \\
&= [\![P]\!](u \mid \iota \mapsto a) \quad \text{(by induction)} \\
&= [\![\lambda\iota:\theta_0. P]\!]ua \quad \square
\end{aligned}
$$

The *minimal* dom π for which it is possible for a phrase X to be well-formed is the set $free(X)$ of all identifiers that occur "unbound" in X. This can be defined by induction on the structure of X as follows:

(i) $free(\iota) = \{\iota\}$;

(ii) $free(0) = \emptyset$, and similarly for the remaining basic phrases;

(iii) $free(\lambda\iota:\theta. P) = free(P) - \{\iota\}$;

(iv) $free(P\,Q) = free(P) \cup free(Q)$, and similarly for the remaining composite phrases that do not involve identifier binding.

The definitions of $free(\cdot)$ for the other phrase forms that involve identifier binding can be derived using the defining equivalences for those constructs, as in the following:

$$
\begin{aligned}
free(\textbf{let } \iota \textbf{ be } P \textbf{ in } Q) \\
&= free((\lambda\iota:\theta. Q)(P)) \\
&= (free(Q) - \{\iota\}) \cup free(P)
\end{aligned}
$$

For example,

$$
\begin{aligned}
free(\textbf{let } m \textbf{ be } m + n \textbf{ in } m + n) \\
&= (free(m + n) - \{m\}) \cup free(m + n) \\
&= \{n\} \cup \{m, n\} \\
&= \{m, n\}
\end{aligned}
$$

Notice that identifier m is both free and bound in this phrase.
    Similarly,

$$free(\textbf{let } \iota(\iota_0: \theta_0) = P \textbf{ in } Q: \theta')$$
$$= \quad free((\lambda\iota: \theta_0 \rightarrow \theta. Q)(\lambda\iota_0: \theta_0. P))$$
$$= \quad (free(Q) - \{\iota\}) \cup (free(P) - \{\iota_0\}).$$

The following proposition shows that $free(X)$ as defined above is neither
too large, nor too small:

Proposition 4.3

(a) If $\pi \vdash X: \theta$ then $free(X) \subseteq$ dom π.

(b) If $\pi \vdash X: \theta$ and π' is the restriction of π to $free(X)$ then $\pi' \vdash X: \theta$.

Each part can be proved by induction on the syntax of X. We discuss only
the case that $X = PQ$. Assume that $\pi \vdash PQ: \theta'$ because $\pi \vdash P: \theta \rightarrow \theta'$
and $\pi \vdash Q: \theta$:

(a) By induction, $free(P) \subseteq$ dom π and $free(Q) \subseteq$ dom π, and so

$$free(PQ) = free(P) \cup free(Q) \subseteq \text{dom } \pi,$$

as desired.

(b) Let π_1 be the restriction of π to $free(P)$ and π_2 be the restriction of
π to $free(Q)$; by induction, $\pi_1 \vdash P: \theta \rightarrow \theta'$ and $\pi_2 \vdash Q: \theta$. Let π'
be the restriction of π to $free(PQ)$; π' is an extension of both π_1 and
π_2, so that, by Proposition 4.1, $\pi' \vdash P: \theta \rightarrow \theta'$ and $\pi' \vdash Q: \theta$, and so
$\pi' \vdash PQ: \theta'$, as desired. □

Combining the Coherence Lemma with this proposition gives us the following useful fact.

Proposition 4.4   *For any phrase X, $[\![X]\!]u_1 = [\![X]\!]u_2$ whenever environments u_1 and u_2 agree on $free(X)$.*

Proof. By Proposition 4.3, X is well-formed in the phrase-type assignment
obtained by restricting to $free(X)$ and, by the Coherence Lemma, each side
is equal to $[\![X]\!]u$, where u is the restriction of u_1 and u_2 to $free(X)$. □

4.5   Programming Logic

In this section we describe a formal system for reasoning about semantic
equivalences in our applicative language.

4.5.1   Syntax and Semantics

We take the following formulas as the atomic specifications:

Equivalence:

$$\frac{X_0 : \theta \qquad X_1 : \theta}{X_0 \equiv_\theta X_1 : \mathbf{spec}}$$

We have been using equivalences in our meta-language; now, they are part of our formal object language as well. We adopt also all of the logical apparatus of Section 2.1: & (conjunction), $\Rightarrow$ (implication), and **absurd**; and we now add

Universal Quantification:

$$\frac{\begin{array}{c}[\iota : \theta]\\ \vdots \\ Z : \mathbf{spec}\end{array}}{\forall \iota : \theta.\, Z : \mathbf{spec}}$$

Intuitively, $\forall \iota : \theta.\, Z$ asserts that Z is *true* for ι denoting any element of $[\![\theta]\!]$. Note that the syntax rule is in natural-deduction format, and all the occurrences of ι in formula $\forall \iota : \theta.\, Z$ are bound; *free*$(\forall \iota : \theta.\, Z)$ can be defined by analogy with $\lambda \iota : \theta.\, X$, which has the same identifier-binding structure.

Semantically, we have $[\![\mathbf{spec}]\!] = \{true, false\}$, as before, but the interpretation of specification formulas must now use environments to allow determination of the meanings of the free identifiers: hence we define valuations

$$[\![\cdot]\!]_{\pi\,\mathbf{spec}} \colon [\mathbf{spec}]_\pi \longrightarrow \left([\![\pi]\!] \longrightarrow [\![\mathbf{spec}]\!]\right)$$

as follows:

$$[\![\forall \iota : \theta.\, Z]\!]u = \text{for all } m \in [\![\theta]\!],\, [\![Z]\!](u \mid \iota \mapsto m)$$

$$[\![\mathbf{absurd}]\!]u = false$$

$$[\![Z_0\ \&\ Z_1]\!]u = \begin{cases} true, & \text{if } [\![Z_0]\!]u = true \text{ and } [\![Z_1]\!]u = true \\ false, & \text{otherwise} \end{cases}$$

and similarly for the implication connective, and

$$[\![X_0 \equiv_\theta X_1]\!]u = \left([\![X_0]\!]u = [\![X_1]\!]u\right).$$

This completes the description of the syntax and semantics of the programming logic for our applicative language.

4.5.2 Substitution

Most formulations of the rule for substitution which were published, even by the ablest logicians, before 1940, were demonstrably incorrect.

H. B. Curry and R. Feys (1958)

In Section 3.6.2, we introduced the meta-linguistic notation $[P](\iota \mapsto E)$ to denote the result of substituting E for all occurrences of a variable-identifier ι in P and this concept played an important role in the programming logic for the simple imperative language. Substitution is also important in reasoning about programs in our applicative language, but we must first generalize the definition of substitution in several ways.

One generalization is that we must allow substitutions for *any* type of identifier, not just the variable-identifiers of Chapter 3. However, we must take into account identifier-binding constructions like the lambda expression; we do not want to substitute for *locally-bound* occurrences of identifiers. For example,

$$[\lambda n: \mathbf{val}[\mathbf{nat}].\, n + 1](n \mapsto a + 1)$$

should be equal to $\lambda n: \mathbf{val}[\mathbf{nat}].\, n + 1$; the occurrences of n in the lambda expression are to be regarded as occurrences of a different n than is being substituted for.

A further complication arises if an identifier is *both* free in a substituted phrase *and* locally-bound in the context of the substituted identifier; we do not want such a local binding to "capture" the free identifier of the substituted phrase. For example,

$$[\lambda n: \mathbf{val}[\mathbf{nat}].\, n + m](m \mapsto n + 2)$$

should *not* be $\lambda n: \mathbf{val}[\mathbf{nat}].\, n + (n + 2)$; the occurrence of n in the substituted phrase $n + 2$ is to be regarded as an occurrence of a different n than the formal parameter of the lambda expression. A solution to this problem is to take advantage of the fact that the choice of bound identifier is semantically irrelevant and change all bound occurrences of the local identifier to another identifier that does not appear free in the substituted phrase. For example, if we replace the bound identifier n by k, we obtain a semantically-equivalent phrase on which the substitution can be carried out without difficulty:

$$
\begin{aligned}
&[\lambda n: \mathbf{val}[\mathbf{nat}].\, n + m](m \mapsto n + 2)\\
\equiv\ &[\lambda k: \mathbf{val}[\mathbf{nat}].\, k + m](m \mapsto n + 2)\\
=\ &\lambda k: \mathbf{val}[\mathbf{nat}].\, k + (n + 2).
\end{aligned}
$$

Finally, it is technically convenient to treat simultaneous *multiple* substitution (of several identifiers) as the basic concept (with single-identifier substitution as a special case).

Substitutions will be specified by *phrase assignments*; i.e., functions from finite sets of identifiers to phrases, thought of as specifying simultaneous multiple substitutions of the phrases for the identifiers. If σ is a phrase assignment, let

$$free(\sigma) = \bigcup_{\iota \in \text{dom}\, \sigma} free(\sigma(\iota)).$$

For any phrase X and phrase assignment σ with dom $\sigma \supseteq free(X)$, we define $[X]\sigma$, the result of carrying out the substitutions specified by σ on X, by induction on the syntax of X as follows:

(i) $[\iota]\sigma = \sigma(\iota)$;

(ii) $[0]\sigma = 0$, and similarly for the remaining basic phrases;

(iii) $[\lambda\iota_0\colon\theta.\,P]\sigma = \lambda\iota_1\colon\theta.\,[P](\sigma \mid \iota_0 \mapsto \iota_1)$, where ι_1 can be any identifier not in $free(\sigma)$ (thereby precluding "capture" of free occurrences of ι_0 in the substituted phrases), and similarly for $[\forall\iota\colon\theta.\,Z]\sigma$;

(iv) $[P\,Q]\sigma = ([P]\sigma)\,([Q]\sigma)$, and similarly for the remaining composite phrases that do not involve identifier binding.

Strictly speaking, $[X]\sigma$ is not uniquely determined because of the choice allowed for identifier ι_1 in case (iii). If uniqueness is desired, it is necessary to select that identifier in some determinate way; for example, it is possible to order the set of identifiers (say, alphabetically) and then select the minimal identifier (according to this ordering) not free in σ.

The definition of substitution for the other phrase forms that involve identifier binding can be derived using the defining equivalences for those constructs, as in the following:

$$\begin{aligned}
&[\text{let } \iota_0 \text{ be } P \text{ in } Q]\sigma \\
&= \ [(\lambda\iota_0\colon\theta.\,Q)\,(P)]\sigma \\
&= \ (\lambda\iota_1\colon\theta.\,[Q](\sigma \mid \iota_0 \mapsto \iota_1))\,([P]\sigma) \\
&= \ \text{let } \iota_1 \text{ be } [P]\sigma \text{ in } [Q](\sigma \mid \iota_0 \mapsto \iota_1),
\end{aligned}$$

where ι_1 can be any identifier not in $free(\sigma)$. For example, for any phrase assignment σ,

$$\begin{aligned}
&[\text{let } m \text{ be } m + n \text{ in } m + n](\sigma \mid m \mapsto m \mid n \mapsto m + k) \\
&= \ \text{let } m' \text{ be } m + (m + k) \text{ in } m' + (m + k),
\end{aligned}$$

where m' is any identifier different from m and k.

In Chapter 3, we used substitutions only when substituting into a phrase would preserve its type. We still want substitutions to preserve types, but here the situation is more complicated because the type of a phrase can only be determined in a given type assignment to its free identifiers. For any phrase-type assignments π_0 and π_1, let $[\pi_0]_{\pi_1}$ denote the following set of *type-preserving* phrase assignments:

$$\prod_{\iota \in \text{dom } \pi_0} [\pi_0(\iota)]_{\pi_1};$$

that is, $\sigma \in [\pi_0]_{\pi_1}$ is required to be a function with the same domain as π_0 that maps each identifier $\iota \in \text{dom } \pi_0$ into a phrase $\sigma(\iota)$ such that, if $\pi_0(\iota) = \theta$, then $\pi_1 \vdash \sigma(\iota): \theta$.

For example, suppose that

$$\pi_0 = \{n: \mathbf{val}[\mathbf{nat}], b: \mathbf{val}[\mathbf{bool}]\}, \text{ and}$$

$$\pi_1 = \{m: \mathbf{val}[\mathbf{nat}]\},$$

and let σ be the phrase assignment such that

- $\text{dom } \sigma = \{n, b\}$,
- $\sigma(n) = (m + 1)$, and
- $\sigma(b) = (m > 0)$;

then $\sigma \in [\pi_0]_{\pi_1}$ because $(m+1) \in \left[\mathbf{val}[\mathbf{nat}]\right]_{\pi_1}$ and $(m > 0) \in \left[\mathbf{val}[\mathbf{bool}]\right]_{\pi_1}$.

The following proposition shows that our definition of substitution is syntactically sound in the sense that if π_0 is the phrase-type assignment for a phrase *before* a substitution, π_1 is the phrase-type assignment for the phrase *after* the substitution, and σ preserves types (with respect to π_0 and π_1), then any substitution specified by σ preserves the type of the phrase as a whole (with respect to π_0 and π_1).

Proposition 4.5   *If $X \in [\theta]_{\pi_0}$ and $\sigma \in [\pi_0]_{\pi_1}$, then $[X]\sigma \in [\theta]_{\pi_1}$.*

The phrase type θ here (and in the following lemma) may be **spec** as well as any of the ordinary phrase types.

The proposition can be proved by structural induction on the syntax of X. We discuss only the case that $X = \lambda \iota_0: \theta. P$. If $\lambda \iota_0: \theta. P \in [\theta \rightarrow \theta']_{\pi_0}$ then $P \in [\theta']_{(\pi_0 | \iota_0 \mapsto \theta)}$. We first verify that

$$(\sigma \mid \iota_0 \mapsto \iota_1) \in \left[(\pi_0 \mid \iota_0 \mapsto \theta)\right]_{(\pi_1 | \iota_1 \mapsto \theta)}$$

for any $\iota_1 \notin \text{free}(\sigma)$; we need to show that, for all $\iota \in (\text{dom } \pi_0 \cup \{\iota_0\})$,

$$(\pi_1 \mid \iota_1 \mapsto \theta) \vdash (\sigma \mid \iota_0 \mapsto \iota_1)(\iota) : (\pi_0 \mid \iota_0 \mapsto \theta)(\iota).$$

If $\iota = \iota_0$, $(\pi_1 \mid \iota_1 \mapsto \theta) \vdash \iota_1: \theta$; if $\iota \neq \iota_0$, $(\pi_1 \mid \iota_1 \mapsto \theta) \vdash \sigma(\iota): \pi_0(\iota)$ because $\sigma \in [\pi_0]_{\pi_1}$ and $\iota_1 \notin \text{free}(\sigma)$. By induction,

$$[P](\sigma \mid \iota_0 \mapsto \iota_1) \in [\theta']_{(\pi_1 | \iota_1 \mapsto \theta)},$$

and so

$$\lambda \iota_1: \theta. [P](\sigma \mid \iota_0 \mapsto \iota_1) \in [\theta \rightarrow \theta']_{\pi_1},$$

as desired. □

The next result shows that our definition of substitution is also *semantically* sound, in the sense that the meaning of a phrase obtained by doing the substitution specified by a phrase assignment σ is that of the *original* phrase in a certain environment definable from σ. For reasoning about program meanings in concrete applications, syntactic substitution is an essential technique; but for reasoning about properties of the language as a whole, the corresponding semantic definition is more convenient. The following lemma assures us that the definition of substitution is sound relative to the semantic interpretation.

Lemma 4.6 (Substitution)   *If $X \in [\theta]_{\pi_0}$, $\sigma \in [\pi_0]_{\pi_1}$, and $u_1 \in [\![\pi_1]\!]$, then*

$$[\![[X]\sigma]\!]_{\pi_1\theta}(u_1) \;\; = \;\; [\![X]\!]_{\pi_0\theta}(u_0),$$

where $u_0 \in [\![\pi_0]\!]$ is defined as follows: for all $\iota \in \operatorname{dom} \pi_0$,

$$u_0(\iota) = [\![\sigma(\iota)]\!]_{\pi_1\,\pi_0(\iota)}(u_1).$$

As a special case of the Substitution Lemma, let $\pi_0 = (\pi_1 \mid \iota \mapsto \theta')$, $P \in [\theta']_{\pi_1}$, and $\sigma \in [\pi_1]_{\pi_1}$ map every identifier in $\operatorname{dom} \pi_1$ to itself; then

$$[\![[X](\sigma \mid \iota \mapsto P)]\!]_{\pi_1\theta}(u_1) \;\; = \;\; [\![X]\!]_{\pi_0\theta}\bigl(u_1 \mid \iota \mapsto [\![P]\!]_{\pi_1\theta'}(u_1)\bigr),$$

which is comparable to (but much more general than) Proposition 3.3 in Section 3.6.3.

The Substitution Lemma can be proved by structural induction on X. We discuss only the lambda-expression case in detail. Omitting subscripts on valuation brackets, we must show that

$$[\![[\lambda\iota_0\!:\!\theta.\,P]\sigma]\!] u_1 a \;\; = \;\; [\![\lambda\iota_0\!:\!\theta.\,P]\!] u_0 a$$

for all $a \in [\![\theta]\!]$, where $u_0(\iota) = [\![\sigma(\iota)]\!] u_1$ for all $\iota \in \operatorname{dom} \pi_0$. The left-hand side equals

$$
\begin{aligned}
& [\![\lambda\iota_1\!:\!\theta.\,[P](\sigma \mid \iota_0 \mapsto \iota_1)]\!] u_1 a \qquad (\text{for } \iota_1 \notin \mathit{free}(\sigma)) \\
= \;& [\![[P](\sigma \mid \iota_0 \mapsto \iota_1)]\!](u_1 \mid \iota_1 \mapsto a) \\
= \;& [\![P]\!] u_0',
\end{aligned}
$$

where $u_0'(\iota) = [\![(\sigma \mid \iota_0 \mapsto \iota_1)(\iota)]\!](u_1 \mid \iota_1 \mapsto a)$ (by induction). The right-hand side equals $[\![P]\!](u_0 \mid \iota_0 \mapsto a)$, and so we need only show that

$$u_0'(\iota) \;\; = \;\; (u_0 \mid \iota_0 \mapsto a)(\iota)$$

for all $\iota \in \bigl(\operatorname{dom} \pi_0 \cup \{\iota_0\}\bigr)$. If $\iota = \iota_0$, both sides are equal to a; if $\iota \neq \iota_0$, both sides are equal to $[\![\sigma(\iota)]\!] u_1$, using Proposition 4.4 and the fact that $\iota_1 \notin \mathit{free}(\sigma(\iota))$. □

As a simple first application of this result, we can verify that, for any $P \in [\theta]_\pi$ and $Q \in [\theta']_{(\pi|\iota \mapsto \theta)}$,

$$\textbf{let } \iota \textbf{ be } P \textbf{ in } Q$$

is semantically equivalent in phrase-type assignment π to

$$[Q](\sigma \mid \iota \mapsto P),$$

where σ maps every identifier in dom π to itself. Consider any $u \in [\![\pi]\!]$; then

$$[\![\textbf{let } \iota \textbf{ be } P \textbf{ in } Q]\!]u$$

and

$$[\![[Q](\sigma \mid \iota \mapsto P)]\!]u$$

are both equal to

$$[\![Q]\!](u \mid \iota \mapsto [\![P]\!]u),$$

by the semantic equation for **let** and the Substitution Lemma, respectively.

We will regard

$$[Q](\iota \mapsto P)$$

as an abbreviation of $[Q](\sigma \mid \iota \mapsto P)$, where σ is a phrase assignment that maps every identifier free in Q to itself, and similarly for

$$[Q](\iota_1 \mapsto P_1 \mid \cdots \mid \iota_n \mapsto P_n).$$

4.5.3 Rules and Axioms

We are finally ready to present the formal system of axioms and rules for our programming logic. The formal system will involve sequents of the form

$$\pi, \Sigma \vdash Z,$$

where π is a phrase-type assignment, $\Sigma = \{\ldots, Z_i, \ldots\}$ is a finite set of formulas $Z_i \in [\textbf{spec}]_\pi$, and $Z \in [\textbf{spec}]_\pi$; that is, we now allow for assumptions of the form $\iota \colon \theta$. When dom $\pi = \emptyset$ we simplify $\pi, \Sigma \vdash Z$ to $\Sigma \vdash Z$, which is the form of sequent used previously. A sequent $\pi, \Sigma \vdash Z$ is *valid* just if, for all $u \in [\![\pi]\!]$, $[\![Z]\!]u = true$ whenever $[\![Z']\!]u = true$ for every $Z' \in \Sigma$.

Each of the inference rules in Table 2.3 of Section 2.1 preserves validity of sequents in this richer framework, as do the following new rules for the universal quantifier:

∀-*Introduction*:

$$\begin{array}{c} [\iota \colon \theta] \\ \vdots \\ Z \\ \hline \forall \iota \colon \theta.\, Z \end{array}$$

provided ι is not free in any of the (uncancelled) assumptions used to derive Z, and,

$\forall$-*Elimination*:

$$\frac{\forall \iota \colon \theta .\, Z \quad X \colon \theta}{[Z](\iota \mapsto X)}$$

The rule of $\forall$-Introduction should be interpreted in terms of sequents as follows: if

$$(\pi \mid \iota \mapsto \theta), \Sigma \vdash Z$$

is derivable, then so is

$$\pi, \Sigma \vdash \forall \iota \colon \theta .\, Z,$$

provided $\iota \notin free(\Sigma)$; i.e., $\iota \notin free(Z')$ for every $Z' \in \Sigma$. Similarly, the rule of $\forall$-Elimination is interpreted in terms of sequents as follows: if

$$\pi, \Sigma \vdash \forall \iota \colon \theta .\, Z$$

and

$$\pi \vdash X \colon \theta$$

are derivable, then so is

$$\pi, \Sigma \vdash [Z](\iota \mapsto X).$$

We will verify the soundness of the $\forall$-Introduction Rule. Assume that

$$(\pi \mid \iota \mapsto \theta), \Sigma \vdash Z$$

is valid, and consider $u \in [\![\pi]\!]$ such that $[\![Z']\!]u = true$ for all $Z' \in \Sigma$, and any $a \in [\![\theta]\!]$; then $[\![Z']\!]u' = true$ for all $Z' \in \Sigma$ where $u' = (u \mid \iota \mapsto a)$, by Proposition 4.4 because $\iota \notin free(Z')$. Hence, by assumption, $[\![Z]\!]u' = true$, as desired.

We can combine the rules of $\forall$-Introduction and $\forall$-Elimination to derive the following rule:

Free Substitution:

$$[\iota \colon \theta]$$

$$\vdots$$

$$\frac{Z \qquad X \colon \theta}{[Z](\iota \mapsto X)}$$

which allows substitution of any phrase (of appropriate type) for a free identifier of any provable specification, provided the identifier is not free in any uncancelled assumptions.

It can also be verified that if $\pi' \vdash \pi$ and $\Sigma' \vdash \Sigma$, and the sequent $\pi, \Sigma \vdash Z$ is derivable, then so is $\pi', \Sigma' \vdash Z$. Furthermore, we can add the following rule, which allows unnecessary typing assumptions to be dropped (the soundness of this rule depends on the fact that $[\![\theta]\!] \neq \emptyset$ for every θ): if π' is the *restriction* of π to $free(\Sigma) \cup free(Z)$ and $\pi, \Sigma \vdash Z$ is derivable, then so is $\pi', \Sigma \vdash Z$.

We now discuss the axioms. These will be presented as sequents of the form $\pi \vdash Z$, with $Z \in [\mathbf{spec}]_\pi$. We start with the general properties of equivalences.

    Reflexivity:

$$\pi \vdash X \equiv_\theta X,$$

when $X \in [\theta]_\pi$.

    Transitivity:

$$\pi \vdash X_0 \equiv_\theta X_1 \ \& \ X_1 \equiv_\theta X_2 \ \Rightarrow \ X_0 \equiv_\theta X_2,$$

when $X_0, X_1, X_2 \in [\theta]_\pi$.

    Symmetry:

$$\pi \vdash X_0 \equiv_\theta X_1 \ \Rightarrow \ X_1 \equiv_\theta X_0,$$

when $X_0, X_1 \in [\theta]_\pi$.

    Substitutivity:

$$\pi \vdash X_1 \equiv_{\theta_1} Q_1 \ \& \ \cdots \ \& \ X_n \equiv_{\theta_n} Q_n \ \& \ [Z](\iota_1 \mapsto X_1 \mid \cdots \mid \iota_n \mapsto X_n)$$
$$\Rightarrow \ [Z](\iota_1 \mapsto Q_1 \mid \cdots \mid \iota_n \mapsto Q_n),$$

when $X_i, Q_i \in [\theta_i]_\pi$, $Z \in [\mathbf{spec}]_{(\pi|\cdots|\iota_i \mapsto \theta_i|\cdots)}$.

Mathematical facts about the data types lead to domain-specific axioms; for example, we can have the following axiom:

$$\pi \vdash \forall n\colon \mathbf{val}[\mathbf{nat}]. \ \mathbf{succ}\, n \not\equiv_{\mathbf{val}[\mathbf{nat}]} 0,$$

where $X \not\equiv_\theta X'$ is an abbreviation for $X \equiv_\theta X' \Rightarrow \mathbf{absurd}$.

Reasoning about phrases of *functional* type can be based on the following axioms:

    Extensionality:

$$\pi \vdash \left(\forall \iota\colon \theta. \ F_0(\iota) \equiv_{\theta'} F_1(\iota)\right) \ \Longleftrightarrow \ F_0 \equiv_{\theta \longrightarrow \theta'} F_1,$$

when $F_0, F_1 \in [\theta \longrightarrow \theta']_\pi$ and $\iota \notin \mathrm{dom}\,\pi$.

    Alpha:

$$\pi \vdash \lambda \iota_0\colon \theta. \ P \ \equiv_{\theta \longrightarrow \theta'} \ \lambda \iota_1\colon \theta. \ [P](\iota_0 \mapsto \iota_1),$$

when $P \in [\theta']_{(\pi|\iota_0 \mapsto \theta)}$ and $\iota_1 \notin \mathrm{dom}\,\pi$.

    Beta:

$$(\pi \mid \iota \mapsto \theta) \vdash (\lambda \iota\colon \theta. \ Q)(\iota) \ \equiv_{\theta'} \ Q,$$

when $Q \in [\theta']_{(\pi|\iota \mapsto \theta)}$.

Eta:

$$\pi \vdash \lambda\iota\!:\!\theta.\, F(\iota) \equiv_{\theta \longrightarrow \theta'} F,$$

when $F \in [\theta \longrightarrow \theta']_\pi$ and $\iota \notin \operatorname{dom} \pi$.

The Extensionality Law states that the meanings of phrases of functional types are fully determined by their applicative behaviour. The Alpha Law justifies "systematic changes of identifier," as in the definition of substitution; and the Beta and Eta Laws assert that abstracting with respect to an identifier ι and applying to ι are inverse operations. The names of these axioms are those of the corresponding axioms in the (simply-typed) lambda calculus, which is the purely-equational form of this system.

The validity of all of these axioms can be verified using the semantic valuations; we discuss the Alpha Law. Consider any $u \in [\![\pi]\!]$ and $a \in [\![\theta]\!]$, and a phrase assignment σ that maps every element of $\operatorname{dom} \pi \cup \{\iota_1\}$ to itself; then

$$
\begin{aligned}
&[\![\lambda\iota_1\!:\!\theta.\,[P](\sigma \mid \iota_0 \mapsto \iota_1)]\!]ua \\
={} &[\![[P](\sigma \mid \iota_0 \mapsto \iota_1)]\!](u \mid \iota_1 \mapsto a) \\
={} &[\![P]\!](u \mid \iota_1 \mapsto a \mid \iota_0 \mapsto a) \quad \text{(by the Substitution Lemma)} \\
={} &[\![P]\!](u \mid \iota_0 \mapsto a) \quad \text{(by the Coherence Lemma, because } \iota_1 \notin \operatorname{dom} \pi) \\
={} &[\![\lambda\iota_0\!:\!\theta.\,P]\!]ua
\end{aligned}
$$

Further equivalences can be *derived* for defined notation; for example, the following derivation

$$
\cfrac{\cfrac{\cfrac{[\iota\!:\!\theta]}{(\lambda\iota\!:\!\theta.\,Q)(\iota) \equiv_{\theta'} Q}\text{(Beta)}}{\forall\iota\!:\!\theta.\,(\lambda\iota\!:\!\theta.\,Q)(\iota) \equiv_{\theta'} Q}\text{($\forall$-I)}}{[(\lambda\iota\!:\!\theta.\,Q)(\iota) \equiv_{\theta'} Q](\iota \mapsto P)}\text{($\forall$-E)}
$$

gives us the equivalence of **let** ι **be** P **in** Q and $[Q](\iota \mapsto P)$ that was verified semantically in Section 4.5.2.

Exercises

4.1   Can the syntax of the language discussed in this chapter be completely specified using BNF (Backus–Naur Formalism)?

4.2   What should $[\![\pi]\!]$ and $[\![X]\!]_{\pi\theta}$ be when $\operatorname{dom} \pi = \emptyset$ and $X \in [\theta]_\pi$?

4.3   Use the semantic interpretation (extended in the obvious way to handle value phrases of the form $N_0 + N_1$) to compute the value of each of the following expressions in any environment that maps m to the natural number 5.

(a) let n be $m + 1$ in
     let n be $n + 2$ in $m + n$

(b) let n be $m + 1$ in
     let m be 2 in $m + n$

(c) let $f(x: \mathbf{val}[\mathbf{nat}]) = x + m$ in
     let m be 2 in $f(5) + m$

4.4 Simplify each expression in the preceding exercise by using equivalences such as

$$\mathbf{let}\ \iota\ \mathbf{be}\ P\ \mathbf{in}\ Q\ \equiv\ [Q](\iota \mapsto P)$$

and obvious simplifications (such as $1 + 2 \equiv 3$). Try different simplification strategies and confirm that equivalent results are obtained.

4.5 Use the denotational semantics to verify the equivalences at the end of Section 4.1 and at the beginning of Section 4.3.

4.6 Is the following equivalence valid?

$$\mathbf{let}\ \iota\ \mathbf{be}\ P\ \mathbf{in}\ (\mathbf{let}\ \iota'\ \mathbf{be}\ Q\ \mathbf{in}\ R)$$
$$\equiv\quad \mathbf{let}\ \iota'\ \mathbf{be}\ (\mathbf{let}\ \iota\ \mathbf{be}\ P\ \mathbf{in}\ Q)\ \mathbf{in}\ (\mathbf{let}\ \iota\ \mathbf{be}\ P\ \mathbf{in}\ R)$$

If so, prove it using the semantic interpretation; if not, suggest sufficient syntactic conditions for the equivalence to be valid.

4.7 Let $B: \mathbf{val}[\mathbf{bool}]$, $F: \theta \to \theta'$ and $X_1, X_2: \theta$; is the following equivalence valid?

$$F(\mathbf{if}\ B\ \mathbf{then}\ X_1\ \mathbf{else}\ X_2)\ \equiv_{\theta'}\quad \mathbf{if}\ B\ \mathbf{then}\ F(X_1)\ \mathbf{else}\ F(X_2).$$

4.8 Complete the proofs of the Coherence Lemma (4.2) and Proposition 4.3.

4.9 Define how to do substitutions into the function-definition form of block.

4.10 Complete the proofs of Proposition 4.5 and the Substitution Lemma (4.6).

4.11 Define, for any phrase-type assignments π_0 and π_1, a substitution valuation function

$$[\![\cdot]\!]_{\pi_1 \pi_0} : [\pi_0]_{\pi_1} \to \left([\![\pi_1]\!] \to [\![\pi_0]\!]\right)$$

such that, for any $\sigma \in [\pi_0]_{\pi_1}$ and $X \in [\theta]_{\pi_0}$,

$$[\![[X]\sigma]\!]_{\pi_1 \theta} = [\![\sigma]\!]_{\pi_1 \pi_0} ; [\![X]\!]_{\pi_0 \theta}$$

Hint: use the Substitution Lemma.

4.12 Verify the equivalence of

$$\mathbf{let}\ \iota\ \mathbf{be}\ X\ \mathbf{in}\ P\,Q$$

and

$$(\mathbf{let}\ \iota\ \mathbf{be}\ X\ \mathbf{in}\ P)\,(\mathbf{let}\ \iota\ \mathbf{be}\ X\ \mathbf{in}\ Q),$$

both semantically and by using the formal system of Section 4.5.3.

4.13 Validate the remaining axioms of Section 4.5.3.

4.14 Consider the following description of the concept of "locality" in
ALGOL 60, from [N⁺63]:

> Any identifier occurring within the block may through a
> suitable declaration be specified to be local to the block in
> question. This means (a) that the entity represented by this
> identifier inside the block has no existence outside it, and
> (b) that any entity represented by this identifier outside the
> block is completely inaccessible inside the block.

Point out any inaccurate or misleading aspects of these statements.

4.15 The following explanation of the semantics of function application,
in ALGOL 60, called the "copy rule," is essentially as given in [N⁺63]:

> A function application serves to invoke the evaluation
> of a function body. The effect of this evaluation will be
> equivalent to the following operations on the program at
> the time of evaluation of the function application.
>
> The formal parameter is replaced, throughout the func-
> tion body, by the actual parameter after enclosing this lat-
> ter in parentheses. Possible conflicts between identifiers
> inserted through this process and other identifiers already
> present in the function body will be avoided by suitable sys-
> tematic changes of the formal or local identifiers involved.
>
> Finally, the function body, modified as above, is inserted
> in place of the function application and evaluated. If the
> function is called from a place outside the scope of any non-
> local quantity of the procedure body, the conflicts between
> the identifiers inserted through this process of body replace-
> ment and the identifiers whose declarations are valid at the
> place of the function application will be avoided through
> suitable systematic changes of the latter identifiers.

This explanation can be expressed more compactly for our language
as the equivalence of

$$\textbf{let } \iota(\iota_0\colon \theta_0) = P$$
$$\textbf{in } [Q]\big(\iota' \mapsto \iota(A)\big)$$

and

$$\textbf{let } \iota(\iota_0\colon \theta_0) = P$$
$$\textbf{in } [Q]\big(\iota' \mapsto [P](\iota_0 \mapsto A)\big)$$

where $\iota' \neq \iota$. Why is this equivalence not valid for our language?
Suggest a sufficient syntactic condition for validity of the equivalence.

Bibliographic Notes

The essential features of the language discussed in this chapter were first described in [Chu40]; modern presentations may be found in [Mit90] and [Bar91]. The treatment of multi-argument functions as function-producing functions is due to [Sch24], but the technique is often called "Currying," after [CF58]. The connections between Church's lambda calculi and programming languages, the applicative/imperative distinction, and the **let** notation are from [Lan64, Lan66]. The quantification notation is from [Ten87b]. Our treatment of substitution is based on the approach used in [EFT84, Ole87, Sto88b]. Completeness is treated in [Fri75].

Chapter 5

Recursion and Domain Theory

Fixed points of functional equations solve recursions. This explains our mathematical *concept of recursion. Note that there are no stacks, no pointers, no bookkeeping. None of those devices of implementation is relevant to the concept. That is why this is a mathematical semantics.*

D. S. Scott (1972)

Most programming languages allow *recursive* definitions, in which the name of the entity being defined can "recur" in its own definition. In this chapter we introduce recursive variants of the **let** forms of definition discussed in the preceding chapter. In order to interpret such definitions, we must discuss elementary aspects of the mathematical theory known as "domain theory," which provides the appropriate semantic constructions.

After presenting the domain-theoretic semantics of our applicative language (extended by recursion), we will go on to consider operational and axiomatic descriptions and their correctness, and discuss the question of full abstraction of the denotational semantics.

5.1 Recursive Definitions

Consider the following syntax rule:

Recursive Function Definition:

$$
\cfrac{\left[\begin{array}{c} \iota\colon \theta_0 \longrightarrow \theta \\ \iota_0\colon \theta_0 \end{array}\right] \qquad [\iota\colon \theta_0 \longrightarrow \theta]}{\begin{array}{cc} \vdots & \vdots \\ P\colon \theta & Q\colon \theta' \end{array}}
$$
$$
\textbf{letrec } \iota(\iota_0\colon \theta_0)\colon \theta = P \textbf{ in } Q\colon \theta'
$$

Note that free occurrences of ι in P are bound in the definition; that is, they are *recursive* uses of that function name (unless $\iota_0 = \iota$).

We can unify and simplify our treatment of recursion by also introducing the following construct:

Recursive Definition:

$$
\frac{\begin{array}{cc} [\iota:\theta] & [\iota:\theta] \\ \vdots & \vdots \\ P:\theta & Q:\theta' \end{array}}{\textbf{letrec } \iota{:}\theta \textbf{ be } P \textbf{ in } Q{:}\theta'}
$$

For example,

> **letrec** *double*: **val**[nat] $\rightarrow$ **val**[nat] **be**
> λn: **val**[nat]. **if** $n = 0$ **then** 0 **else** $2 + double(n - 1)$
> **in** $\cdots$

defines the function $double(n) = 2 \times n$. Note that the type of ι must be explicitly indicated here; it cannot be straightforwardly inferred from P (because ι will typically recur in P). We can now *define* (in the sense of Section 4.3) recursive function definitions by the following equivalence:

> **letrec** $\iota(\iota_0{:}\theta_0){:}\theta = P$ **in** Q
> $\equiv$ **letrec** $\iota{:}\theta_0 \rightarrow \theta$ **be** $\lambda\iota_0{:}\theta_0. P$ **in** Q.

In principle, the form of recursive definition block just introduced allows for recursive definitions of identifiers of *arbitrary* phrase types, rather than just functional types; but we will see that only trivial examples are practical for value types.

The key idea in the semantic interpretation of (simple) recursive definitions is that the meaning defined for ι by **letrec** $\iota{:}\theta$ **be** P **in** $\cdots$ is the appropriate solution of the following *equation*:

$$p = [\![P]\!](u \mid \iota \mapsto p).$$

Consider the definition of *double* above; if we substitute $2 \times (n - 1)$ for $double(n - 1)$ in the lambda expression we get

> λn: **val**[nat]. **if** $n = 0$ **then** 0 **else** $2 + (2 \times (n - 1))$
> $\equiv$ λn: **val**[nat]. **if** $n = 0$ **then** 0 **else** $2 + (2 \times n) - 2$
> $\equiv$ λn: **val**[nat]. $2 \times n$

and so the corresponding equation is indeed *satisfied* by the function defined by $double(n) = 2 \times n$.

It is also the case that $n = 0$ is the unique solution in N of the equation corresponding to the recursive definition

> **letrec** n: **val**[nat] **be** $n \times 0$ **in** $\cdots$;

however, it is less evident that this will be a satisfactory way of dealing
with recursive definitions such as

$$\textbf{letrec } n\text{: } \textbf{val}[\text{nat}] \textbf{ be } n + 1 \textbf{ in } \cdots,$$

the corresponding equation to which is not satisfied by *any* natural number,
or

$$\textbf{letrec } n\text{: } \textbf{val}[\text{nat}] \textbf{ be } n \textbf{ in } \cdots,$$

the corresponding equation to which is satisfied by *every* natural number!
Operationally, such recursive definitions lead to *non-terminating* computations; when we have allowed for this possibility in our semantic model, we
will have a way out of these difficulties.

In mathematics, an equation of the form

$$x \;\; = \;\; \cdots x \cdots$$

is termed a *fixed-point* equation (because a solution is preserved by substituting it into the right-hand side; i.e., it is a "fixed point" for the right-hand
side). Our intention is to solve such equations in the same way that we
solved an equation of the form

$$c \;\; = \;\; \cdots [\![B]\!] \cdots [\![C]\!] \cdots c \cdots$$

for the meaning of **while** B **do** C in Section 3.3; i.e., by taking the "limit"
of the sequence of approximations obtained by starting from a trivial initial
approximation and generating better-and-better approximations by substituting for the indeterminate of the equation on the right-hand side. What
are needed are generalizations of

- the meaning of **diverge**, which is the initial approximation appropriate
  to command meanings;
- the $\subseteq$ relation on partial-function graphs, which is the notion of approximation appropriate to command meanings; and
- the "limit" obtained by forming the *union* of the approximating partial
  functions.

The following two sections present enough of a theory of computation developed by Dana Scott called *domain theory* to allow us to deal with recursive
definitions in this way in Section 5.4.

5.2 Computational Domains

The first principle of Scott's theory of computation is that a necessary
condition for the computability of an infinitary object is that it be the *limit*
of a sequence of finitary approximations. For example, the meaning of a

while loop may be an infinitary mathematical object; but it is the union of finitary approximations to it, as in Section 3.3.

A partially-ordered set D is *ω-complete* if and only if, for every chain $d \in D^\omega$, the least upper bound $\bigsqcup_{i \in \omega} d_i$ exists in D. We define a *computational domain* (hereafter abbreviated to just *domain*) to be any partially-ordered set that is ω-complete. The intuition behind this definition is that the partial-order models approximation of computable entities; $d \sqsubseteq_D d'$ should be interpreted as saying that more computation might improve the partially-defined result d to the possibly better-defined result d'. The least upper bound of the components of a chain is the limit of that sequence of approximations, and the completeness requirement ensures that such a limit always exists. For example, we will see that the appropriate partial order on command meanings (partial functions on states) is graph inclusion, and the least upper bound of a chain of increasing command meanings is the partial function whose graph is their union.

If D is a domain, a chain $d \in D^\omega$ is termed *interesting* if it does not contain its own least upper bound; i.e., there is no $k \in \omega$ such that $d_{k+j} = d_k$ for all $j \in \omega$. The completeness requirement is vacuous for uninteresting chains because $\bigsqcup_{i \in \omega} d_i = d_k \in D$ for some $k \in \omega$. The limit of an interesting chain is termed a *limit point*.

The reader should be warned that the definition of a domain varies considerably in the literature. Some authors require every domain to have a least element or lubs of *all* subsets or all "directed" subsets, and for more advanced applications, domains must have additional properties.

Here are some general methods for constructing domains.

- Any set A can be discretely-ordered by the partial order $\sqsubseteq$ defined by $a \sqsubseteq a'$ just if $a = a'$; then $\ddot{A} = (A, \sqsubseteq)$ is a domain because the only chains have the form $a \sqsubseteq a \sqsubseteq a \sqsubseteq \cdots$, whose lub is a. $\ddot{A}$ does not have a least element unless A is a singleton set.

- If D and E are domains, then $D \times E$ (the *product* of D and E) is a domain such that $|D \times E| = |D| \times |E|$ and the partial order $\sqsubseteq_{D \times E}$ is defined component-wise; i.e., $(d, e) \sqsubseteq_{D \times E} (d', e')$ just if $d \sqsubseteq_D d'$ and $e \sqsubseteq_E e'$. The limits are as follows.

Proposition 5.1 *For any chain $p \in (D \times E)^\omega$,*

$$\bigsqcup_{i \in \omega} p_i = \left(\bigsqcup_{i \in \omega} d_i, \bigsqcup_{i \in \omega} e_i \right),$$

where $d \in |D|^\omega$ and $e \in |E|^\omega$ are defined by the requirement that $(d_i, e_i) = p_i$ for every $i \in \omega$.

Proof. Because $\sqsubseteq_{D \times E}$ is defined component-wise, d and e are chains and the limits $\bigsqcup_{i \in \omega} d_i$ and $\bigsqcup_{i \in \omega} e_i$ are well-defined. Let $d_\infty = \bigsqcup_{i \in \omega} d_i$ and $e_\infty = \bigsqcup_{i \in \omega} e_i$; then (d_∞, e_∞) is an upper bound of $\{p_i \mid i \in \omega\}$ because, for every $i \in \omega$, $d_i \sqsubseteq_D d_\infty$ and $e_i \sqsubseteq_E e_\infty$. Similarly, (d_∞, e_∞) is the *least upper bound* of $\{p_i \mid i \in \omega\}$ because, if (d', e') is any upper bound of the p_i, $d_i \sqsubseteq_D d'$ and $e_i \sqsubseteq_E e'$ for every $i \in \omega$, and so $d_\infty \sqsubseteq_D d'$ and $e_\infty \sqsubseteq_E e'$. $\square$

If D and E have least elements $\perp_D$ and $\perp_E$, respectively, $D \times E$ has a least element $\perp_{D \times E} = (\perp_D, \perp_E)$.

- If D and E are domains, then so is the poset $D + E$ (the *sum* of D and E) such that

$$|D + E| = |D| + |E| = \{(0, d) \mid d \in D\} \cup \{(1, e) \mid e \in E\}$$

and $\sqsubseteq_{D+E}$ is defined as follows: $(m, z) \sqsubseteq_{D+E} (n, z')$ just if $m = n$ and $z \sqsubseteq z'$ in either D or E (as determined by the "tags" m and n). Chains in $D + E$ consist of components that are all from $|D|$ or all from $|E|$, so that limits are inherited from D and E; however, $D + E$ does not have a least element (unless D or E is empty and the other has a least element).

- If D is a domain, then so is $D_\perp$ such that $|D_\perp|$ is $|D|$ with a new least element $\perp$ added; i.e., $D_\perp$ is the domain obtained by "lifting" D. Chains in $D_\perp$ are either trivial, or all in D, or have the general form $\perp \sqsubseteq d_0 \sqsubseteq d_1 \sqsubseteq \cdots$ where $d \in D^\omega$, and it is evident that lubs of all such chains exist in $D_\perp$.

If D is discretely ordered, $D_\perp$ is termed a *flat* domain. For example, if $T = \{true, false\}$, the Hasse diagram of $\ddot{T}_\perp$ is as follows:

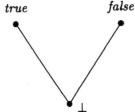

The least element represents "no information (yet)," which might be improved by more computation to either element of T. An example of a non-flat domain is $\ddot{T}_\perp \times \ddot{T}_\perp$:

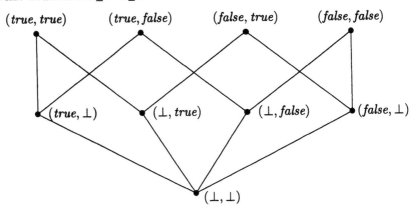

However, we have not as yet described a way of constructing domains with *interesting* chains; this will be possible with the following methods of construction.

- If A is a set and D is a domain, then $A \to D$ is the domain such that $|A \to D| = A \to |D|$ and $\sqsubseteq_{A \to D}$ is defined point-wise; i.e., $f \sqsubseteq_{A \to D} f'$ just if $f(a) \sqsubseteq_D f'(a)$ for every $a \in A$. It can be verified by a proof similar to that of Proposition 5.1 that, for $f \in (A \to D)^\omega$,

$$\left(\bigsqcup_{i \in \omega} f_i \right)(a) \;=\; \bigsqcup_{i \in \omega} f_i(a) \quad \text{for every } a \in A.$$

If D has a least element $\bot_D$, $A \to D$ has a least element; it is the constant function mapping all $a \in A$ to $\bot_D$.

    This construction is easily generalized to every product $\prod_{i \in I} D_i$ of domains.

- If A is a set and D is a domain, then $A \rightharpoonup D$ is the domain such that $|A \rightharpoonup D| = A \rightharpoonup |D|$ and $\sqsubseteq_{A \rightharpoonup D}$ is defined point-wise; i.e., $f \sqsubseteq_{A \rightharpoonup D} f'$ just if, for every $a \in A$, $f'(a)$ is defined whenever $f(a)$ is, and then $f(a) \sqsubseteq_D f'(a)$. It can be verified that, for $f \in (A \rightharpoonup D)^\omega$,

$$\left(\bigsqcup_{i \in \omega} f_i \right)(a) = \begin{cases} \text{undefined}, & \text{if } f_i(a) \text{ is undefined for all } i \in \omega \\ \bigsqcup_{j \in \omega} f_{i+j}(a), & \text{if } f_i(a) \text{ is defined for some } i \in \omega \end{cases}$$

for every $a \in A$. The least element of $A \rightharpoonup D$ is the empty partial function. When D is discretely-ordered, $f \sqsubseteq_{A \rightharpoonup D} f'$ if and only if graph $f \subseteq$ graph f', and

$$\text{graph}\left(\bigsqcup_{i \in \omega} f_i \right) \;=\; \bigcup_{i \in \omega} \text{graph } f_i$$

for any $f \in (A \rightharpoonup D)^\omega$. For example, the sequence of command meanings c_i defined in Section 3.3 can be regarded as a chain in $(S \rightharpoonup \ddot{S})^\omega$ and the least upper bound is c_∞, the meaning of the **while** loop.

In Section 5.3, constructions $D \to E$ and $D \rightharpoonup E$ will be generalized to allow D to be an arbitrary *domain*. Notice the difference between $A \to D_\bot$ and $A \rightharpoonup D$; an element of the first is a *total* function whose result for some argument in A might be $\bot$, the least element of $D_\bot$, and an element of the second is a *partial* function whose result for some argument in A might not be defined. Although these domains are isomorphic here, this will not be the case for the corresponding entities in the more general framework described in Chapter 9.

    We conclude this section with two useful results about limits in domains.

Lemma 5.2   *If D is a domain with partial ordering $\sqsubseteq$, and $a, b \in D^\omega$ are chains such that, for all $i \in \omega$ there exists $j \in \omega$ such that $a_i \sqsubseteq b_j$, then $\bigsqcup_{i \in \omega} a_i \sqsubseteq \bigsqcup_{j \in \omega} b_j$.*

Proof. For every $i \in \omega$ there is a $j \in \omega$ such that $a_i \sqsubseteq b_j \sqsubseteq \bigsqcup_{j \in \omega} b_j$ and so $\bigsqcup_{j \in \omega} b_j$ is an upper bound of the a_i; but then $\bigsqcup_{i \in \omega} a_i \sqsubseteq \bigsqcup_{j \in \omega} b_j$ because $\bigsqcup_{i \in \omega} a_i$ is the *least* upper bound of the a_i. $\square$

Let D be a domain with partial ordering $\sqsubseteq$; $d \in |D|^{\omega \times \omega}$ is termed a *double-chain* just if

$$d_{i0} \sqsubseteq d_{i1} \sqsubseteq d_{i2} \sqsubseteq \cdots \text{ for every } i \in \omega,$$

and

$$d_{0j} \sqsubseteq d_{1j} \sqsubseteq d_{2j} \sqsubseteq \cdots \text{ for every } j \in \omega.$$

Lemma 5.3   *If d is a double-chain in D, the following limits are well-defined and equivalent:*

$$\bigsqcup_{i \in \omega} \bigsqcup_{j \in \omega} d_{ij} \tag{5.1}$$

$$\bigsqcup_{j \in \omega} \bigsqcup_{i \in \omega} d_{ij} \tag{5.2}$$

$$\bigsqcup_{k \in \omega} d_{kk} \tag{5.3}$$

Proof. Let $d_{i\infty} = \bigsqcup_{j \in \omega} d_{ij}$ and $d_{\infty j} = \bigsqcup_{i \in \omega} d_{ij}$. To see that (5.1) is well-defined, we note that, for every $i \in \omega$, $d_{ij} \sqsubseteq d_{(i+1)j}$ for all $j \in \omega$, and so $d_{i\infty} \sqsubseteq d_{(i+1)\infty}$ by Lemma 5.2. Similarly, $d_{\infty j} \sqsubseteq d_{\infty(j+1)}$ for every $j \in \omega$, and so (5.2) is well-defined. Finally, for every $k \in \omega$, $d_{kk} \sqsubseteq d_{k(k+1)} \sqsubseteq d_{(k+1)(k+1)}$, and so (5.3) is well-defined.

To see that $d_{\infty j} \sqsubseteq$ (5.1) for every $j \in \omega$, we note that $d_{ij} \sqsubseteq d_{i\infty}$ for all $i \in \omega$ and so $\bigsqcup_{i \in \omega} d_{ij} \sqsubseteq \bigsqcup_{i \in \omega} d_{i\infty}$ by Lemma 5.2. But then (5.2), the least upper bound of the $d_{\infty j}$, is $\sqsubseteq$ (5.1). Similarly, it can be shown that (5.1) $\sqsubseteq$ (5.2), and so, by anti-symmetry of $\sqsubseteq$, (5.1) = (5.2).

To see that $d_{i\infty} \sqsubseteq$ (5.3) for every $i \in \omega$, we note that, for every $j \in \omega$, $d_{ij} \sqsubseteq d_{kk}$ for $k = \max(i,j)$, and so $\bigsqcup_{j \in \omega} d_{ij} \sqsubseteq \bigsqcup_{k \in \omega} d_{kk}$ by Lemma 5.2; therefore, (5.1) $\sqsubseteq$ (5.3). For the other direction, we note that, for every $k \in \omega$, $d_{kk} \sqsubseteq d_{k\infty} \sqsubseteq \bigsqcup_{i \in \omega} d_{i\infty}$, and so $\bigsqcup_{k \in \omega} d_{kk} \sqsubseteq$ (5.1) by Lemma 5.2. We conclude that (5.1) = (5.2) = (5.3). $\square$

5.3   Continuous Functions

The second principle of Scott's theory of computation is that computable functions on domains preserve domain structure. Let D and E be domains; a function $f \colon |D| \to |E|$ is termed

- *order-preserving* or *monotonic* if $f(d) \sqsubseteq_E f(d')$ when $d \sqsubseteq_D d'$; and
- *limit-preserving* or *ω-continuous* (hereafter, just *continuous*) if, for every chain $d \in D^\omega$,

$$f\left(\bigsqcup_{i \in \omega} d_i\right) = \bigsqcup_{i \in \omega} f(d_i).$$

It is easily verified using the chain $d_0 \sqsubseteq d_1 \sqsubseteq d_1 \sqsubseteq \cdots$ that continuity implies monotonicity. Hence Scott's thesis is that computable (total) functions are continuous. If D and E have least elements $\perp_D$ and $\perp_E$, respectively, $f: |D| \rightarrow |E|$ is termed *bottom-preserving* or *strict* if $f(\perp_D) = \perp_E$.

The following are some examples of continuous functions on domains.

- The identity function on any domain is continuous.

- If f and g are continuous functions with dom g = codom f then f ; g is continuous.

- If A and B are arbitrary sets and $f: A \rightarrow B$ is an arbitrary function, the *strict* extension of f to $A_\perp \rightarrow B_\perp$ is continuous, and similarly for extensions of elements of $\left(\prod_{i \in I} A_i\right) \rightarrow B$ that are strict ($\perp$-preserving) in all arguments.

- Any constant function is continuous, even if it is not strict.

- There are four continuous extensions of the disjunction operation $or: T \times T \rightarrow T$ to $T_\perp \times T_\perp \rightarrow T_\perp$, defined as follows: for all of them, $or(\perp, false)$ $= or(false, \perp) = or(\perp, \perp) = \perp$, but $or(\perp, true)$ and $or(true, \perp)$ can (independently) be either $\perp$ or *true*. If both are $\perp$, we have the "doubly-strict" *or*, which requires two non-$\perp$ argument values to produce a non-$\perp$ result; if one is *true* and the other is $\perp$ we have "sequential" *ors*, which can be implemented so that a possibly non-terminating evaluation of one argument is avoided if the other argument yields *true*; and if both are *true*, we have the "parallel" *or*, so-called because evaluation of the arguments must be concurrent or interleaved, in case either fails to terminate but the other produces *true*.

  The same kind of choice is available whenever the value of an operation is constant for some argument value; for example, $n \times m = 0$ if either n or m is 0, regardless of the value of the other argument, so that there are continuous sequential and parallel, as well as doubly-strict, multiplications on $N_\perp$.

- If D is any domain with least element $\perp$, the "sequential" $if: T_\perp \times D \times D \rightarrow D$ defined by

$$if(t, d_0, d_1) = \begin{cases} d_0, & \text{if } t = true \\ d_1, & \text{if } t = false \\ \perp_D, & \text{if } t = \perp_{T_\perp} \end{cases}$$

and, if D is a flat domain, the "parallel" $if_{\|}: T_\perp \times D \times D \rightarrow D$ defined by

$$if_{\|}(t, d_0, d_1) = \begin{cases} d_0, & \text{if } t = true \text{ or } d_0 = d_1 \\ d_1, & \text{if } t = false \text{ or } d_0 = d_1 \\ \perp_D, & \text{if } t = \perp_{T_\perp} \text{ and } d_0 \neq d_1 \end{cases}$$

are continuous.

- If I is a set, D is a domain, $d \in D$, and $u \in U = I \to D$, the operations

$$(\cdot \mid i \mapsto d): U \to U'$$

and

$$(u \mid i \mapsto \cdot): D \to U',$$

where $U' = (I \cup \{i\}) \to (D \cup \{d\})$, are continuous.

We now discuss two functions that are *not* continuous.

- Let D be any domain with a least element $\bot$ and consider the "defined-ness" predicate ∂ on D defined as follows:

$$\partial(d) = \begin{cases} true, & \text{if } d \neq \bot \\ false, & \text{if } d = \bot. \end{cases}$$

This predicate is not computable because an implementation cannot risk producing the result *false* in case the process computing d subsequently produces some information. If ∂ is regarded as mapping to the discretely-ordered domain $\ddot{T}$ or to the flat domain $\ddot{T}_\bot$ it is not monotonic, because $\partial(\bot) \not\sqsubseteq \partial(d)$ when $d \neq \bot$. However, if ∂ is regarded as mapping to the flat domain T' with $|T'| = \{true, false\}$ and *false* $\sqsubseteq$ *true*:

$$true$$

$$false$$

then ∂ *is* monotonic, and it is also intuitively computable because the ordering allows an implementation to "improve" a *false* result to *true*.

- Consider the predicate $total: (S \rightharpoonup \ddot{S}) \to T'$ on command meanings such that

$$total(c) = \begin{cases} true, & \text{if } c(s) \text{ is defined for all } s \in S \\ false, & \text{if } c(s) \text{ is undefined for some } s \in S \end{cases}$$

If S has an infinite number of elements, $total(c)$ is not computable because an implementation could not determine the totality of c from any finite amount of information about it. Predicate $total$ is monotonic, but it is not continuous. For example, suppose $S = N$ and consider $c \in (N \rightharpoonup \ddot{N})^\omega$ such that, for all $n \in N$,

$$c_i(n) = \begin{cases} 0, & \text{if } n < i \\ \text{undefined}, & \text{if } n \geq i; \end{cases}$$

then $total(c_i) = false$ for every $i \in \omega$, but $total\left(\bigsqcup_{i \in \omega} c_i\right) = true$ because $\left(\bigsqcup_{i \in \omega} c_i\right)(n) = 0$ for all $n \in N$.

Note that it is not being claimed that every continuous function *is* computable (in the sense of computability theory), but that a function that is non-continuous is *not* computable.

Similarly, a *partial* function $f: |D| \to |E|$ is termed

- *monotonic* if, when $f(d)$ is defined and $d \sqsubseteq_D d'$, then $f(d')$ is defined and $f(d) \sqsubseteq_E f(d')$; and

- *continuous* if it is monotonic and, for every chain $d \in D^\omega$, if $f(\bigsqcup_{i \in \omega} d_i)$ is defined then, for some $j \in \omega$, $f(d_j)$ is defined and

$$f\left(\bigsqcup_{i \in \omega} d_i\right) = \bigsqcup_{i \in \omega} f(d_{i+j}).$$

Notice that $f(d_i)$ might be undefined for $i < j$.

We can now define the $\to$ and $\rightharpoonup$ constructions for *domains* of arguments as follows.

- If D and E are domains, then $D \to E$ is the domain such that $|D \to E|$ is the set of all *continuous* functions from $|D|$ to $|E|$ and $\sqsubseteq_{D \to E}$ is defined point-wise; i.e., $f \sqsubseteq_{D \to E} f'$ just if $f(d) \sqsubseteq_E f'(d)$ for every $d \in |D|$. The limit of a chain is defined as in Section 5.2, but it must be verified that it is continuous.

Proposition 5.4   Let f be an ω-chain of continuous functions from D to E; then $\bigsqcup_{i \in \omega} f_i$ is continuous.

Proof. Consider $d \in D^\omega$; then

$$\left(\bigsqcup_{i \in \omega} f_i\right)\left(\bigsqcup_{j \in \omega} d_j\right)$$

$$= \bigsqcup_{i \in \omega} f_i\left(\bigsqcup_{j \in \omega} d_j\right) \quad \text{(limits in } D \to E)$$

$$= \bigsqcup_{i \in \omega} \bigsqcup_{j \in \omega} f_i(d_j) \quad \text{(by continuity of } f_i)$$

$$= \bigsqcup_{j \in \omega} \bigsqcup_{i \in \omega} f_i(d_j) \quad \text{(by Lemma 5.3)}$$

$$= \bigsqcup_{j \in \omega} \left(\bigsqcup_{i \in \omega} f_i\right)(d_j) \quad \text{(limits in } D \to E). \quad \square$$

- If D and E are domains, then $D \rightharpoonup E$ is the domain such that $|D \rightharpoonup E|$ is the set of all *continuous* partial functions from $|D|$ to $|E|$ and $\sqsubseteq_{D \rightharpoonup E}$ is defined point-wise; i.e., $f \sqsubseteq_{D \rightharpoonup E} f'$ just if $f'(d)$ is defined when $f(d)$ is and then $f(d) \sqsubseteq_E f'(d)$, for every $d \in D$. It can be verified that, for $f \in (D \rightharpoonup E)^\omega$, $\bigsqcup_{i \in \omega} f_i$ is as defined in Section 5.2 and is continuous.

Notice that if A is a set and D is a domain, $\ddot{A} \rightarrow D = A \rightarrow D$, and similarly for $\rightharpoonup$; i.e., for discretely-ordered domains of arguments, the constructions above coincide with those of the preceding section. Hereafter, we shall simply write A (rather than $\ddot{A}$) for the domain obtained by discretely-ordering set A whenever it is clear from the context that a domain is needed. This convention will apply at the lowest possible level; for example, if A and B are sets, $A \rightharpoonup B$ as a domain will be interpreted as being $\ddot{A} \rightharpoonup \ddot{B}$ (i.e., partial functions from A to B, ordered by graph inclusion), rather than the *discretely-ordered* domain of partial functions from A to B.

We conclude with a result that will be crucial to the treatment of recursion in the following section.

Theorem 5.5   *Let D be a domain with a least element $\perp$, and $f\colon D \rightarrow D$ be a continuous function; then $\bigsqcup_{i \in \omega} f^i(\perp)$ is the least fixed point of f.*

Proof.   It is easily proved by mathematical induction on i that $f^i(\perp) \sqsubseteq f^{i+1}(\perp)$ for every $i \in \omega$, so that the limit is well-defined. To see that it is a fixed point of f:

$$f\left(\bigsqcup_{i \in \omega} f^i(\perp)\right)$$

$$= \bigsqcup_{i \in \omega} f\left(f^i(\perp)\right) \qquad (f \text{ is continuous})$$

$$= \bigsqcup_{i \in \omega} f^{i+1}(\perp)$$

$$= \perp \sqcup \bigsqcup_{i \in \omega} f^{i+1}(\perp) \qquad (\perp \sqcup d = d)$$

$$= f^0(\perp) \sqcup \bigsqcup_{i \in \omega} f^{i+1}(\perp) \qquad (f^0(\perp) = \perp)$$

$$= \bigsqcup_{i \in \omega} f^i(\perp)$$

To see that $\bigsqcup_{i \in \omega} f^i(\perp)$ is the *least* fixed point, consider any fixed point d' of f; we first show by mathematical induction on i that, for every $i \in \omega$, $f^i(\perp) \sqsubseteq d'$: $f^0(\perp) = \perp \sqsubseteq d'$ and, if $f^i(\perp) \sqsubseteq d'$ then $f^{i+1}(\perp) \sqsubseteq f(d')$ (by monotonicity of f) and $f(d') = d'$ (by assumption). Hence, d' is an upper bound of $\{f^i(\perp) \mid i \in \omega\}$ and so $\bigsqcup_{i \in \omega} f^i(\perp) \sqsubseteq d'$.   □

5.4   Domain-Theoretic Semantics

In this section, we re-interpret the applicative language of Chapter 4 using *domains* and *continuous* functions, rather than *sets* and *arbitrary* functions, and then treat the recursive definitions introduced in this chapter using the least fixed points of Theorem 5.5.

We begin by re-interpreting the phrase types as domains. Although we could discretely-order the sets used previously, the resulting domains would not have least elements. If we want to allow use of recursively-defined functions in value phrases, the semantic model must allow for non-termination of their evaluation. Hence, we re-define $[\![\mathbf{val}[\tau]]\!]$ to be the flat domain $[\![\tau]\!]_{\perp}$, which has a least element. We can continue to write

$$[\![\theta \to \theta']\!] = [\![\theta]\!] \to [\![\theta']\!]$$

and

$$[\![\pi]\!] = \prod_{\iota \in \mathrm{dom}\, \pi} [\![\pi(\iota)]\!],$$

but these are now interpreted as definitions of *domains* with non-trivial orderings; for example, any $f \in [\![\theta \to \theta']\!]$ must now be a *continuous* function, preserving limits of chains in $[\![\theta]\!]$. Every $[\![\theta \to \theta']\!]$ and $[\![\pi]\!]$ now has a least element $\perp_{\theta \to \theta'}$ or $\perp_\pi$, given inductively by $\perp_{\theta \to \theta'}(a) = \perp_{\theta'}$ for all $a \in [\![\theta]\!]$, and $\perp_\pi(\iota) = \perp_{\pi(\iota)}$ for all $\iota \in \mathrm{dom}\, \pi$, respectively.

We now re-interpret the phrases of our applicative language by defining valuation functions

$$[\![\cdot]\!]_{\pi\theta} \colon [\![\theta]\!]_\pi \to ([\![\pi]\!] \to [\![\theta]\!])$$

so that all phrases P such that $\pi \vdash P \colon \theta$ are mapped into *continuous* functions from domain $[\![\pi]\!]$ to domain $[\![\theta]\!]$. In fact, it is much simpler to describe the small number of *changes* necessary than to present all the semantic equations again:

- Each of the primitive operations ($\mathbf{not}, <, =, \mathbf{succ}, \mathbf{and}, \dots$) must be interpreted by a monotonic extension on the flat domain of the corresponding function on the data types (such as the extension that is strict, that is to say, $\perp$-preserving, in all arguments).

- The conditional is interpreted as the "sequential" *if* of Section 5.3.

No other changes are needed; however, we must verify that the functions on domains are continuous.

Proposition 5.6   *For all* $P \in [\![\theta]\!]_\pi$, $[\![P]\!]_{\pi\theta}$ *is continuous and, when* $\theta = \theta' \to \theta''$, $[\![P]\!]_{\pi(\theta' \to \theta'')}(u)$ *is continuous for all* $u \in [\![\pi]\!]$.

Proof. By structural induction. If P is a constant, $[\![P]\!]$ is a constant function. (If we had constants of *functional* type, they would be required to denote continuous functions.)

For an application phrase $(P\,Q) \in [\theta]_\pi$, consider $u \in [\![\pi]\!]^\omega$;

$$[\![P\,Q]\!]\left(\bigsqcup_{i\in\omega} u_i\right)$$

$$= [\![P]\!]\left(\bigsqcup_{i\in\omega} u_i\right)\left([\![Q]\!]\left(\bigsqcup_{j\in\omega} u_j\right)\right)$$

$$= \left(\bigsqcup_{i\in\omega}[\![P]\!]u_i\right)\left(\bigsqcup_{j\in\omega}[\![Q]\!]u_j\right) \quad \text{(by the continuity of } [\![P]\!] \text{ and } [\![Q]\!])$$

$$= \bigsqcup_{i\in\omega}[\![P]\!]u_i\left(\bigsqcup_{j\in\omega}[\![Q]\!]u_j\right)$$

$$= \bigsqcup_{i\in\omega}\bigsqcup_{j\in\omega}[\![P]\!]u_i([\![Q]\!]u_j) \quad \text{(by the continuity of } [\![P]\!]u_i)$$

$$= \bigsqcup_{i\in\omega}[\![P]\!]u_i([\![Q]\!]u_i) \quad \text{(by Lemma 5.3)}$$

$$= \bigsqcup_{i\in\omega}[\![P\,Q]\!]u_i.$$

For an abstraction phrase $(\lambda\iota{:}\,\theta.\,P) \in [\theta \to \theta']_\pi$, consider $u \in [\![\pi]\!]^\omega$ and $a \in [\![\theta]\!]$;

$$[\![\lambda\iota{:}\,\theta.\,P]\!]\left(\bigsqcup_{i\in\omega} u_i\right)(a)$$

$$= [\![P]\!]\left(\bigsqcup_{i\in\omega} u_i \mid \iota \mapsto a\right)$$

$$= [\![P]\!]\left(\bigsqcup_{i\in\omega}(u_i \mid \iota \mapsto a)\right) \quad \text{(by the continuity of } (\,\cdot \mid \iota \mapsto a))$$

$$= \bigsqcup_{i\in\omega}[\![P]\!](u_i \mid \iota \mapsto a) \quad \text{(by the continuity of } [\![P]\!])$$

$$= \bigsqcup_{i\in\omega}[\![\lambda\iota{:}\,\theta.\,P]\!]u_i a$$

$$= \left(\bigsqcup_{i\in\omega}[\![\lambda\iota{:}\,\theta.\,P]\!]u_i\right)(a).$$

To show that $[\![\lambda\iota{:}\,\theta.\,P]\!]u$ is continuous for any $u \in [\![\pi]\!]$, consider $a \in [\![\theta]\!]^\omega$; then

$$[\![\lambda\iota{:}\,\theta.\,P]\!]u\left(\bigsqcup_{i\in\omega} a_i\right)$$

$$= [\![P]\!]\left(u \mid \iota \mapsto \bigsqcup_{i\in\omega} a_i\right)$$

$$= [\![P]\!]\Big(\bigsqcup_{i\in\omega}(u \mid \iota \mapsto a_i)\Big) \quad \text{(by the continuity of } (u \mid \iota \mapsto \cdot))$$

$$= \bigsqcup_{i\in\omega}[\![P]\!](u \mid \iota \mapsto a_i) \quad \text{(by the continuity of } [\![P]\!])$$

$$= \bigsqcup_{i\in\omega}[\![\lambda\iota\!:\!\theta.\,P]\!]ua_i.$$

The remaining cases are straightforward. □

The significance of this result goes beyond the particular programming language that we are considering: the result can in principle be "lifted" to the meta-language. We will not go through the exercise of formalizing the meta-language, but we can now take it for granted that any meta-linguistic expression that denotes a function and involves only continuous primitives and (typed) functional abstraction and application denotes a *continuous* function for all appropriate values of any free meta-variables occurring in the expression; for example, composition preserves continuity because $f \,;\, g = \lambda x.\,g(f(x))$.

Finally, we treat the recursive-definition form,

$$(\textbf{letrec } \iota\!:\!\theta \textbf{ be } P \textbf{ in } Q) \in [\theta']_\pi.$$

Consider any $u \in [\![\pi]\!]$ and define $f\!: [\![\theta]\!] \to [\![\theta]\!]$ as follows:

$$f(p) = [\![P]\!](u \mid \iota \mapsto p)$$

for every $p \in [\![\theta]\!]$; it is clear that f is continuous if $[\![P]\!]$ is, and so we define

$$[\![\textbf{letrec } \iota\!:\!\theta \textbf{ be } P \textbf{ in } Q]\!]u = [\![Q]\!]\Big(u \mid \iota \mapsto \bigsqcup_{i\in\omega} f^i(\bot_\theta)\Big).$$

From Theorem 5.5 we know that the limit is well-defined, and that the meaning defined for ι is the least solution of the equation

$$p = [\![P]\!](u \mid \iota \mapsto p).$$

For example, consider evaluating

$$\textbf{letrec } g\!: \textbf{val}[\textbf{nat}] \to \textbf{val}[\textbf{nat}] \textbf{ be}$$
$$\lambda n\!: \textbf{val}[\textbf{nat}].\,\textbf{if } n = 0 \textbf{ then } 0 \textbf{ else } 2 + g(n-1)$$
$$\textbf{in } \cdots;$$

in environment u; then

$$f(p) = [\![\lambda n\!: \textbf{val}[\textbf{nat}].\,\textbf{if } n = 0 \textbf{ then } 0 \textbf{ else } 2 + g(n-1)]\!](u \mid g \mapsto p),$$

for all $p \in [\![\textbf{val}[\textbf{nat}] \to \textbf{val}[\textbf{nat}]]\!]$, so that

$$f(p)(a) = \begin{cases} 0, & \text{if } a = 0 \\ 2 + p(a-1), & \text{if } a > 0 \\ \bot, & \text{if } a = \bot \end{cases}$$

for all $a \in [\![\textbf{val}[\textbf{nat}]]\!]$. The approximations to the least fixed point are the functions defined as follows:

$$p_0(a) \quad = \quad \bot$$

$$p_1(a) \quad = \quad \begin{cases} 0, & \text{if } a = 0 \\ 2 + p_0(a - 1), & \text{if } a > 0 \\ \bot, & \text{if } a = \bot \end{cases}$$

$$= \quad \begin{cases} 0, & \text{if } a = 0 \\ \bot, & \text{otherwise;} \end{cases}$$

$$p_2(a) \quad = \quad \begin{cases} 0, & \text{if } a = 0 \\ 2 + p_1(a - 1), & \text{if } a > 0 \\ \bot, & \text{if } a = \bot \end{cases}$$

$$= \quad \begin{cases} 0, & \text{if } a = 0 \\ 2, & \text{if } a = 1 \\ \bot, & \text{otherwise;} \end{cases}$$

$$p_3(a) \quad = \quad \begin{cases} 0, & \text{if } a = 0 \\ 2 + p_2(a - 1), & \text{if } a > 0 \\ \bot, & \text{if } a = \bot \end{cases}$$

$$= \quad \begin{cases} 0, & \text{if } a = 0 \\ 2, & \text{if } a = 1 \\ 4, & \text{if } a = 2 \\ \bot, & \text{otherwise;} \end{cases}$$

and so on; i.e., for any $i \in \omega$,

$$p_i(a) \quad = \quad \begin{cases} 2 \times a, & \text{if } a < i \\ \bot, & \text{otherwise,} \end{cases}$$

and so their least upper bound is the function p_∞ defined by

$$p_\infty(a) \quad = \quad \begin{cases} 2 \times a, & \text{if } a \neq \bot \\ \bot, & \text{if } a = \bot. \end{cases}$$

We must verify that $[\![\textbf{letrec } \iota\colon\theta \textbf{ be } P \textbf{ in } Q]\!]$ is continuous. We can simplify the problem by introducing a new constant

$$\textbf{rec}[\theta]\colon (\theta \longrightarrow \theta) \longrightarrow \theta$$

for every phrase type θ in our programming language, defining the **letrec** form by the following equivalence:

$$\textbf{letrec } \iota\colon\theta \textbf{ be } P \textbf{ in } Q \quad \equiv \quad \textbf{let } \iota \textbf{ be } \#\,\textbf{rec}[\theta]\,\iota.\,P \textbf{ in } Q$$
$$\equiv \quad \textbf{let } \iota \textbf{ be } \textbf{rec}[\theta](\lambda\iota\colon\theta.\,P) \textbf{ in } Q,$$

and defining the semantics of the constant $\textbf{rec}[\theta]$ by

$$[\![\textbf{rec}[\theta]]\!]\,uf = \bigsqcup_{i \in \omega} f^i(\bot_\theta)$$

for every environment u and $f \in [\![\theta]\!] \longrightarrow [\![\theta]\!]$. We now only need to show that $[\![\textbf{rec}[\theta]]\!]$ is continuous.

Proposition 5.7 *If $f \in D \to D$ is continuous and D has a least element $\bot$, the function $fix(f) = \bigsqcup_{i \in \omega} f^i(\bot)$ is continuous.*

Proof. Let $fix_i(f) = f^i(\bot)$ for every $i \in \omega$; then $fix(f) = \bigsqcup_{i \in \omega} f^i(\bot) = \bigsqcup_{i \in \omega} fix_i(f) = \left(\bigsqcup_{i \in \omega} fix_i\right)(f)$ by the definition of limits in domains of functions, so that $fix = \bigsqcup_{i \in \omega} fix_i$ and because the fix_i are easily shown to be continuous, so is the limit, by Proposition 5.4. □

Hence the interpretations of the constants **rec**$[\theta]$ are continuous functions, and so, by Proposition 5.6, the interpretation of the **letrec** definition is continuous.

Defining recursive definitions in terms of the constant **rec** also makes it easy to see that the Coherence and Substitution Lemmas remain valid if recursion is added to the applicative language. These results were proved by structural induction; the constant cases were always trivial, and the other cases are essentially unchanged. Because the Substitution Lemma remains valid, so does the equivalence

$$\textbf{let } \iota \textbf{ be } P \textbf{ in } Q \equiv [Q](\iota \mapsto P)$$

and this has an important consequence for implementations: a "call-by-name" or "lazy" implementation of parameter passing is called for. For example,

$$\textbf{let } n \textbf{ be } N \textbf{ in true},$$

which is by definition equivalent to

$$(\lambda n\!:\!\theta.\,\textbf{true})(N),$$

is semantically equivalent to $[\textbf{true}](n \mapsto N) = \textbf{true}$ for *every* $N\!:\!\theta$, even if an evaluation of N would fail to terminate. This can be seen semantically as well: for any appropriate environment u,

$$\begin{aligned}
&[\![\textbf{let } n \textbf{ be } N \textbf{ in true}]\!]u \\
&= [\![\textbf{true}]\!](u \mid n \mapsto [\![N]\!]u) \\
&= true
\end{aligned}$$

even if $[\![N]\!]u = \bot$. A straightforward (sequential) implementation must therefore defer evaluations of actual-parameter expressions like N until (if ever) the value of that expression is actually needed, unless it can be determined that the evaluation will terminate. In Section 6.3, we will discuss another approach to the semantics of function parameters which allows "call-by-value" or "eager" evaluation.

We can make explicit the parallel between our semantic valuation of **letrec** $\iota\!:\!\theta$ **be** P **in** Q and the interpretation of the **while** loop in Section 3.3 by using the Substitution Lemma. Let **undef**$[\theta]\!:\!\theta$ be a constant for every phrase type θ such that $[\![\textbf{undef}[\theta]]\!]u = \bot_\theta$ for every environment u. We can then define a sequence P_i for $i \in \omega$ of phrases of type θ as follows:

$$P_0 = \mathbf{undef}[\theta]$$

$$P_{i+1} = [P](\iota \mapsto P_i)$$

For any appropriate environment u, we can then define the corresponding sequence $p_i = [\![P_i]\!]u$ of elements of $[\![\theta]\!]$ as follows:

$$p_0 = [\![P_0]\!]u = \bot_\theta$$

$$
\begin{aligned}
p_{i+1} = \quad [\![P_{i+1}]\!]u \quad &= \quad [\![[P](\iota \mapsto P_i)]\!]u \\
&= \quad [\![P]\!](u \mid \iota \mapsto [\![P_i]\!]u) \quad \text{(by the Substitution Lemma)} \\
&= \quad [\![P]\!](u \mid \iota \mapsto p_i)
\end{aligned}
$$

It is clear that $p_i \sqsubseteq p_{i+1}$ for every $i \in \omega$ and hence the limit $p_\infty = \bigsqcup_{i \in \omega} p_i$ exists; then

$$[\![\mathbf{letrec}\ \iota{:}\,\theta\ \mathbf{be}\ P\ \mathbf{in}\ Q]\!]u = [\![Q]\!](u \mid \iota \mapsto p_\infty).$$

Clearly, if $f(p) = [\![P]\!](u \mid \iota \mapsto p)$, $p_i = f^i(\bot_\theta)$ for every $i \in \omega$, and $p_\infty = \bigsqcup_{i \in \omega} f^i(\bot_\theta)$.

We conclude this section with a result that will justify an important method of reasoning about meanings that are recursively-defined.

Theorem 5.8   *Let*

- *D be a domain having a least element $\bot$,*
- *φ be an ω-complete predicate on D; i.e., for any $d \in D^\omega$, $\varphi(d_i)$ for all $i \in \omega$ implies $\varphi(\bigsqcup_{i \in \omega} d_i)$, and*
- *$f\colon D \to D$ be a continuous function;*

if $\varphi(\bot)$ and, for all $d \in D$, $\varphi(d)$ implies $\varphi(f(d))$, then $\varphi(\mathit{fix}(f))$.

Proof. It can be shown by mathematical induction on i that $\varphi(f^i(\bot))$ for all $i \in \omega$; then the ω-completeness of φ allows us to conclude that $\varphi(\bigsqcup_{i \in \omega} f^i(\bot))$; i.e., $\varphi(\mathit{fix}(f))$. $\square$

This result justifies the following inductive method of reasoning known as *fixed-point* (or *computational*) induction: a predicate on a domain with a least element $\bot$ is proved

(i) for $\bot$ (the basis); and

(ii) for $f(d)$, on the assumption (the inductive hypothesis) that d has the property.

The conclusion is that $\mathit{fix}(f)$ has the property, provided that the property is "admissible for fixed-point induction," i.e., satisfies the ω-completeness requirement of the theorem. To see the necessity of the admissibility requirement, consider the predicate $\varphi(\cdot) = $ "$\cdot$ is strictly partial" on $N \to N$, and the chain $c \in (N \to N)^\omega$ defined by $c_i = f^i(\bot_{N \to N})$, where

$$
f(c)(n) = \begin{cases} 0, & \text{if } n = 0 \\ c(n-1), & \text{otherwise;} \end{cases}
$$

then the basis and inductive steps of fixed-point induction allow us to prove that $\varphi(c_i)$ for all $i \in \omega$, but *not* to conclude that $\varphi(fix(f))$, because φ is not ω-complete. In fact, $fix(f)(n) = 0$ for *all* $n \in N$.

Admissibility for fixed-point induction is a difficult issue in general. We will address it for a specific formal language of predicates in Section 5.6. A non-trivial use of fixed-point induction will be made in the proof of Proposition 5.9 in the following section.

5.5   Operational Semantics

In this section, we describe an operational semantics for our applicative language (with recursion), and verify its correctness using the denotational semantics. The operational semantics will be expressed as a family of binary relations $\triangleright_\theta$ on $[\theta]_{\pi_0}$ for every phrase type θ, where π_0 is the phrase-type assignment for pre-defined identifiers. For $P, P' \in [\theta]_{\pi_0}$, the relationship $P \triangleright_\theta P'$ should hold just when the change from P to P' is a single computational step.

The $\triangleright_\theta$ relations can be defined to be the smallest binary relations satisfying the axioms and rules of Table 5.1 and similar ones for the other operators of the language and for the pre-defined identifiers. Provided that the $\triangleright_\theta^*$ relations are functional for every θ, we can define valuations

$$\{\!|\cdot|\!\}_\tau \colon [\mathbf{val}[\tau]]_{\pi_0} \to [\![\mathbf{val}[\tau]]\!]$$

on programs as follows:

$$\{\!|P|\!\}_\tau = \begin{cases} [\![P']\!] u_0, & \text{if } P \triangleright_{\mathbf{val}[\tau]}^* P' \text{ and } P' \not\triangleright_{\mathbf{val}[\tau]} P'' \text{ for any } P'', \\ \bot, & \text{otherwise.} \end{cases}$$

The denotational valuation $[\![\cdot]\!]$ is used here only to map "canonical" (i.e., irreducible) programs (such as **true** and **false**) to their values.

We now want to prove that the operational and denotational valuations for programs are equivalent in the sense that $\{\!|P|\!\}_\tau = [\![P]\!]_{\pi_0 \mathbf{val}[\tau]}(u_0)$ for all programs $P \in [\mathbf{val}[\tau]]_{\pi_0}$. We can prove that $\{\!|P|\!\}_\tau \sqsubseteq [\![P]\!]_{\pi_0 \mathbf{val}[\tau]}(u_0)$ by showing that for each axiom in Table 5.1,

$$[\![P]\!] u_0 = [\![P']\!] u_0 \text{ when } P \triangleright_\theta P'$$

and that this property is preserved by each of the rules, and so if $P \triangleright_\theta^* P'$, then $\{\!|P|\!\}_\tau = [\![P']\!] u_0 = [\![P]\!] u_0$.

In the other direction, we show that $[\![P]\!]_{\pi_0 \mathbf{val}[\tau]}(u_0) \sqsubseteq \{\!|P|\!\}_\tau$ by proving a more general property by structural induction. We first define a family of binary relations $\|\theta\| \subseteq [\![\theta]\!] \times [\theta]_{\pi_0}$ by induction on the structure of θ as follows:

- $v \|\mathbf{val}[\tau]\| V$ if and only if $v \sqsubseteq \{\!|V|\!\}_\tau$;

$$\overline{(P) \; \triangleright_\theta \; P}$$

$$\overline{(\lambda \iota : \theta . \, P)Q \; \triangleright_{\theta'} \; [P](\iota \mapsto Q)}$$

$$\overline{\mathbf{rec}[\theta](F) \; \triangleright_\theta \; F(\mathbf{rec}[\theta](F))}$$

$$\frac{F \; \triangleright_{\theta \longrightarrow \theta'} \; F'}{F(A) \; \triangleright_{\theta'} \; F'(A)}$$

$$\overline{\mathbf{if\ true\ then}\ P_1\ \mathbf{else}\ P_2 \; \triangleright_\theta \; P_1}$$

$$\overline{\mathbf{if\ false\ then}\ P_1\ \mathbf{else}\ P_2 \; \triangleright_\theta \; P_2}$$

$$\frac{B \; \triangleright_{\mathbf{val[bool]}} \; B'}{\mathbf{if}\ B\ \mathbf{then}\ P_1\ \mathbf{else}\ P_2 \; \triangleright_\theta \; \mathbf{if}\ B'\ \mathbf{then}\ P_1\ \mathbf{else}\ P_2}$$

$$\overline{\mathbf{undef}[\theta] \; \triangleright_\theta \; \mathbf{undef}[\theta]}$$

$$\overline{\mathbf{not\ true} \; \triangleright_{\mathbf{val[bool]}} \; \mathbf{false}}$$

$$\overline{\mathbf{not\ false} \; \triangleright_{\mathbf{val[bool]}} \; \mathbf{true}}$$

$$\frac{B \; \triangleright_{\mathbf{val[bool]}} \; B'}{\mathbf{not}\ B \; \triangleright_{\mathbf{val[bool]}} \; \mathbf{not}\ B'}$$

Table 5.1 Operational semantics of the applicative language.

- $f \, \|\theta \longrightarrow \theta'\| \, F$ if and only if, for all $a \in [\![\theta]\!]$ and $A \in [\theta]_{\pi_0}$, $a \, \|\theta\| \, A$ implies $f(a) \, \|\theta'\| \, F(A)$.

Such families of relations, defined by induction on types so that related entities of functional type map related arguments to related results, are termed *logical relations*. Intuitively, $p \, \|\theta\| \, P$ holds when $p \in [\![\theta]\!]$ approximates (in the sense of $\sqsubseteq$) the "operational meaning" of P.

Proposition 5.9   *For all $u \in [\![\pi]\!]$, $\sigma \in [\pi]_{\pi_0}$ and $P \in [\theta]_\pi$, if*

$$u(\iota) \, \|\pi(\iota)\| \, \sigma(\iota)$$

for every $\iota \in \mathrm{dom}\,\pi$ then

$$[\![P]\!]_{\pi\theta}(u) \, \|\theta\| \, [P](\sigma).$$

Proof. The proof is by structural induction over P. We discuss only the case of $\mathbf{rec}[\theta]$ when $\theta = \mathbf{val}[\tau]$.

Consider any $f \in [\![\theta]\!] \to [\![\theta]\!]$ and $F \in [\theta \to \theta]_{\pi_0}$ such that $f \Vert \theta \to \theta \Vert F$, and let $m = \{\mathbf{rec}[\theta](F)\}_\tau$; then we show that $\mathit{fix}(f) \sqsubseteq m$ by fixed-point induction using $\varphi(d) = (d \sqsubseteq m)$, which is obviously admissible. The basis is clear. Assume $\varphi(d)$; i.e., $d \sqsubseteq m = \{\mathbf{rec}[\theta](F)\}_\tau$ (because $\theta = \mathbf{val}[\tau]$), and then $\varphi(f(d))$ follows from the assumption that $f \Vert \theta \to \theta \Vert F$ and the fact that $\mathbf{rec}[\theta](F) \triangleright_\theta F(\mathbf{rec}[\theta](F))$. $\square$

In particular, $[\![P]\!]_{\pi_0 \mathbf{val}[\tau]}(u_0) \sqsubseteq \{P\}_\tau$ for every program P, provided $u_0(\iota) \Vert \pi_0(\iota) \Vert \iota$ for every $\iota \in \mathrm{dom}\, \pi_0$ (i.e., the meanings of the pre-defined identifiers are correctly implemented), and so we can conclude that the operational and denotational valuations for programs are equivalent.

5.6 Programming Logic

In this section we describe a formal system for reasoning about programs in our language. It is in a class known as LCF ("Logic for Computable Functions"), for which there are several implementations that are widely used for reasoning about programs in applicative languages. The most important axiom is a formalization of the method of fixed-point induction discussed after Theorem 5.8 in Section 5.4.

5.6.1 Syntax and Semantics

The language of specifications will be identical to that of Section 4.5, except that we take *approximation* formulas as the atomic specifications:

Approximation:

$$\frac{X_0 : \theta \qquad X_1 : \theta}{X_0 \sqsubseteq_\theta X_1 : \mathbf{spec}}$$

with

$$[\![X_0 \sqsubseteq_\theta X_1]\!]u = ([\![X_0]\!]u \sqsubseteq [\![X_1]\!]u),$$

and then *define* $X_0 \equiv_\theta X_1$ to be an abbreviation for $X_0 \sqsubseteq_\theta X_1 \,\&\, X_1 \sqsubseteq_\theta X_0$.

5.6.2 Rules and Axioms

The syntax and interpretation of sequents, and the inference rules are exactly as in Section 4.5. The axioms are as follows: the Substitutivity, Alpha, Beta, and Eta Laws of Section 4.5 and the following:

Reflexivity:

$$\pi \vdash X \sqsubseteq_\theta X,$$

when $X \in [\theta]_\pi$.

Transitivity:

$$\pi \vdash X_0 \sqsubseteq_\theta X_1 \ \& \ X_1 \sqsubseteq_\theta X_2 \ \Rightarrow \ X_0 \sqsubseteq_\theta X_2,$$

when $X_0, X_1, X_2 \in [\theta]_\pi$.

Monotonicity:

$$\pi \vdash X_0 \sqsubseteq_\theta X_1 \Rightarrow F(X_0) \sqsubseteq_{\theta'} F(X_1),$$

when $X_0, X_1 \in [\theta]_\pi$ and $F \in [\theta \to \theta']_\pi$.

Extensionality:

$$\pi \vdash \big(\forall \iota : \theta.\, F_0(\iota) \sqsubseteq_{\theta'} F_1(\iota)\big) \ \Longleftrightarrow \ F_0 \sqsubseteq_{\theta \to \theta'} F_1,$$

when $F_0, F_1 \in [\theta \to \theta']_\pi$ and $\iota \notin \mathrm{dom}\,\pi$.

Undefined:

$$\pi \vdash \mathbf{undef}[\theta] \sqsubseteq_\theta X,$$

when $X \in [\theta]_\pi$.

Fixed Point:

$$\pi \vdash \mathbf{rec}[\theta](F) \equiv_\theta F(\mathbf{rec}[\theta](F)),$$

when $F \in [\theta \to \theta]_\pi$.

Fixed-Point Induction:

$$\pi \vdash [Z](\iota \mapsto \mathbf{undef}[\theta]) \ \& \ \Big(\forall \iota : \theta.\, Z \Rightarrow [Z]\big(\iota \mapsto F(\iota)\big)\Big)$$
$$\Rightarrow [Z]\big(\iota \mapsto \mathbf{rec}[\theta](F)\big),$$

when $Z \in [\mathbf{spec}]_{(\pi | \iota \mapsto \theta)}$ and $F \in [\theta \to \theta]_\pi$, provided that $\iota \notin \mathrm{dom}\,\pi$ and, to ensure its admissibility for fixed-point induction, Z satisfies the following requirement: $\iota \notin \mathit{free}_-(Z)$, where, for any $Z \in [\mathbf{spec}]_\pi$, $\mathit{free}_-(Z)$ and $\mathit{free}_+(Z)$ are subsets of $\mathit{free}(Z)$ simultaneously defined by induction on Z as follows:

$$\mathit{free}_-(X_0 \sqsubseteq_{\theta'} X_1) = \emptyset$$
$$\mathit{free}_-(\mathbf{absurd}) = \emptyset$$
$$\mathit{free}_-(Z_0 \ \& \ Z_1) = \mathit{free}_-(Z_0) \cup \mathit{free}_-(Z_1)$$
$$\mathit{free}_-(Z_0 \Rightarrow Z_1) = \mathit{free}_+(Z_0) \cup \mathit{free}_-(Z_1)$$
$$\mathit{free}_-(\forall \iota' : \theta'.\, Z') = \mathit{free}_-(Z') - \{\iota'\}$$

$$\mathit{free}_+(X_0 \sqsubseteq_{\theta'} X_1) = \mathit{free}(X_1)$$
$$\mathit{free}_+(\mathbf{absurd}) = \emptyset$$
$$\mathit{free}_+(Z_0 \ \& \ Z_1) = \mathit{free}_+(Z_0) \cup \mathit{free}_+(Z_1)$$
$$\mathit{free}_+(Z_0 \Rightarrow Z_1) = \mathit{free}(Z_0) \cup \mathit{free}_+(Z_1)$$
$$\mathit{free}_+(\forall \iota' : \theta'.\, Z') = \mathit{free}_+(Z') - \{\iota'\}$$

The negative sign in *free_* refers to its use as a side condition in the Induction axiom, and the positive sign in *free_+* refers to its use on the "negative" (left) argument of the implication in the definition of $free_-(Z_0 \Rightarrow Z_1)$. These definitions make the sets *free_* and *free_+* as small as possible, while maintaining the following semantic properties.

Proposition 5.10 *Let* $Z \in [\mathbf{spec}]_{(\pi|\iota\mapsto\theta)}$;

(a) *if* $\iota \notin free_-(Z)$ *then, for all* $u \in \llbracket\pi\rrbracket$ *and interesting chains* $d \in \llbracket\theta\rrbracket^\omega$, *if* $\llbracket Z\rrbracket(u \mid \iota \mapsto d_i)$ *for all* $i \in \omega$ *then* $\llbracket Z\rrbracket(u \mid \iota \mapsto \bigsqcup_{i\in\omega} d_i)$; *and*

(b) *if* $\iota \notin free_+(Z)$ *then, for all* $u \in \llbracket\pi\rrbracket$ *and limit points* $d_\infty \in \llbracket\theta\rrbracket$, *if* $\llbracket Z\rrbracket(u \mid \iota \mapsto d_\infty)$ *then, for all* $d \sqsubseteq d_\infty$, $\llbracket Z\rrbracket(u \mid \iota \mapsto d)$.

Proof. This can be proved by a simultaneous structural induction over Z. We will discuss several cases in detail.

If $\iota \notin free_-(X_0 \sqsubseteq_{\theta'} X_1)$, consider any $u \in \llbracket\pi\rrbracket$ and interesting chain $d \in \llbracket\theta\rrbracket^\omega$, and assume that $\llbracket X_0\rrbracket(u \mid \iota \mapsto d_i) \sqsubseteq \llbracket X_1\rrbracket(u \mid \iota \mapsto d_i)$ for all $i \in \omega$; then $\llbracket X_0\rrbracket(u \mid \iota \mapsto \bigsqcup_{i\in\omega} d_i) \sqsubseteq \llbracket X_1\rrbracket(u \mid \iota \mapsto \bigsqcup_{i\in\omega} d_i)$ by the continuity of $\llbracket X_0\rrbracket$ and $\llbracket X_1\rrbracket$, and Lemma 5.2.

If $\iota \notin free_-(Z_0 \Rightarrow Z_1)$, consider any $u \in \llbracket\pi\rrbracket$ and interesting chain $d \in \llbracket\theta\rrbracket^\omega$, and assume that $\llbracket Z_0\rrbracket(u \mid \iota \mapsto d_i)$ implies $\llbracket Z_1\rrbracket(u \mid \iota \mapsto d_i)$ for all $i \in \omega$, and that $\llbracket Z_0\rrbracket(u \mid \iota \mapsto \bigsqcup_{i\in\omega} d_i)$; then $\llbracket Z_0\rrbracket(u \mid \iota \mapsto d_i)$ for all $i \in \omega$, by the induction hypothesis and the fact that $i \notin free_+(Z_0)$, and so $\llbracket Z_1\rrbracket(u \mid \iota \mapsto d_i)$ for all $i \in \omega$, and hence $\llbracket S_1\rrbracket(u \mid \iota \mapsto \bigsqcup_{i\in\omega} d_i)$ by the induction hypothesis and the fact that $\iota \notin free_-(Z_1)$.

If $\iota \notin free_-(\forall\iota':\theta'.Z')$, consider any $u \in \llbracket\pi\rrbracket$ and interesting chain $d \in \llbracket\theta\rrbracket^\omega$, and assume that, for all $d' \in \llbracket\theta'\rrbracket$, $\llbracket Z'\rrbracket(u \mid \iota \mapsto d_i \mid \iota' \mapsto d')$ for all $i \in \omega$. If $\iota = \iota'$,

$$\llbracket Z'\rrbracket(u \mid \iota \mapsto d_i \mid \iota' \mapsto d') \quad = \quad \llbracket Z'\rrbracket\Big(u \mid \iota \mapsto \bigsqcup_{i\in\omega} d_i \mid \iota' \mapsto d'\Big)$$

for all $d' \in \llbracket\theta'\rrbracket$. If $\iota \neq \iota'$, consider $d' \in \llbracket\theta'\rrbracket$; then, for all $i \in \omega$, $\llbracket Z'\rrbracket(u \mid \iota' \mapsto d' \mid \iota \mapsto d_i)$, and so $\llbracket Z'\rrbracket(u \mid \iota' \mapsto d' \mid \iota \mapsto \bigsqcup_{i\in\omega} d_i)$ by the induction hypothesis and the fact that $\iota \notin free_-(Z')$, and hence $\llbracket Z'\rrbracket(u \mid \iota \mapsto \bigsqcup_{i\in\omega} d_i \mid \iota' \mapsto d')$.

If $\iota \notin free_+(X_0 \sqsubseteq_{\theta'} X_1)$, consider any $u \in \llbracket\pi\rrbracket$, limit point $d_\infty \in \llbracket\theta\rrbracket$, and $d \sqsubseteq d_\infty$, and assume that $\llbracket X_0\rrbracket(u \mid \iota \mapsto d_\infty) \sqsubseteq \llbracket X_1\rrbracket(u \mid \iota \mapsto d_\infty)$; then

$$\begin{aligned}
&\llbracket X_0\rrbracket(u \mid \iota \mapsto d) \\
&\sqsubseteq \llbracket X_0\rrbracket(u \mid \iota \mapsto d_\infty) \qquad \text{(by the continuity of } \llbracket X_0\rrbracket) \\
&\sqsubseteq \llbracket X_1\rrbracket(u \mid \iota \mapsto d_\infty) \qquad \text{(by assumption)} \\
&= \llbracket X_1\rrbracket(u \mid \iota \mapsto d) \qquad \text{(because } \iota \notin free(X_1))
\end{aligned}$$

If $\iota \notin free_+(Z_0 \Rightarrow Z_1)$, consider any $u \in \llbracket\pi\rrbracket$, limit point $d_\infty \in \llbracket\theta\rrbracket$, and $d \sqsubseteq d_\infty$, and assume that $\llbracket Z_0\rrbracket(u \mid \iota \mapsto d_\infty)$ implies $\llbracket Z_1\rrbracket(u \mid \iota \mapsto d_\infty)$, and that $\llbracket Z_0\rrbracket(u \mid \iota \mapsto d)$; then $\llbracket Z_0\rrbracket(u \mid \iota \mapsto d_\infty)$ because $i \notin free(Z_0)$,

$$\frac{\dfrac{[x\!:\theta]\quad[x\sqsubseteq_\theta A]}{F(x)\sqsubseteq_\theta F(A)}\;(\text{Monot.})\quad [F(A)\sqsubseteq_\theta A]}{F(x)\sqsubseteq_\theta A}\;(\text{Trans.})$$

$$\dfrac{F(x)\sqsubseteq_\theta A}{x\sqsubseteq_\theta A\Rightarrow F(x)\sqsubseteq_\theta A}\;(\Rightarrow\text{-I})$$

$$\dfrac{}{\mathbf{undef}[\theta]\sqsubseteq_\theta A}\;(\text{Undef.})\qquad \dfrac{\forall x\!:\theta.\,x\sqsubseteq_\theta A\Rightarrow F(x)\sqsubseteq_\theta A}{}\;(\forall\text{-I})$$

$$\dfrac{}{\mathbf{rec}[\theta](F)\sqsubseteq_\theta A}\;(\text{Induct.})$$

$$\dfrac{}{F(A)\sqsubseteq_\theta A\Rightarrow \mathbf{rec}[\theta](F)\sqsubseteq_\theta A}\;(\Rightarrow\text{-I})$$

Table 5.2 A derivation of Park's Theorem in LCF.

and so $[\![Z_1]\!](u\mid\iota\mapsto d_\infty)$ by assumption, and hence $[\![Z_1]\!](u\mid\iota\mapsto d)$ by the induction hypothesis and the fact that $\iota\notin free_+(Z_1)$. Note that $\iota\notin free_-(Z_0)$ would not be sufficient here.   □

Validity of the fixed-point induction axiom follows from the Substitution Lemma, Theorem 5.8 and the above proposition, which shows that the syntactic condition $\iota\notin free_-(Z)$ is sufficient to ensure admissibility for fixed-point induction of Z with respect to ι. Validity of the other axioms is obvious.

Table 5.2 is an example of a derivation in this system. This is a formal proof (with a few steps omitted) of what is known as Park's Theorem [Par69]: $F(A)\sqsubseteq_\theta A\Rightarrow\mathbf{rec}[\theta](F)\sqsubseteq_\theta A$, when $F\in[\theta\to\theta]_\pi$ and $A\in[\theta]_\pi$.

5.7   Full Abstraction

We conclude our study of the semantics of the purely-applicative language by stating (without proof) some important results about full abstraction. It may be recalled from Section 1.2.2 that a semantic interpretation is said to be fully abstract if and only if phrase meanings are not distinguished unless there is a program context in which the phrases can be used that allows the distinction to be observed at the program level.

It can be proved using domain-theoretic techniques beyond the scope of this book that the semantic interpretation of our language is in fact fully abstract, provided "parallel conditionals" are added for types of the form **val**[τ]; i.e., **parif** conditionals that are like the conventional **if** conditionals except that

$$\mathbf{parif}\ \mathbf{undef}[\mathbf{bool}]\ \mathbf{then}\ V\ \mathbf{else}\ V\ \equiv_{\mathbf{val}[\tau]}\ V$$

for all $V\!:\mathbf{val}[\tau]$.

To see the necessity for these conditionals, let θ_0 be an abbreviation for **val[bool]** $\times$ **val[bool]** $\longrightarrow$ **val[bool]** and consider the following phrases F_i of type $\theta_0 \longrightarrow$ **val[nat]**:

$$F_i = \lambda f{:}\theta_0. \text{ if } f(\textbf{true}, \textbf{undef[val[bool]]}) \text{ then}$$
$$\text{if } f(\textbf{undef[val[bool]]}, \textbf{true}) \text{ then}$$
$$\text{if } f(\textbf{false}, \textbf{false}) \text{ then } \textbf{undef[val[nat]]} \text{ else } i$$
$$\text{else } \textbf{undef[val[nat]]}$$
$$\text{else } \textbf{undef[val[nat]]}$$

It is easy to see that $F_i(f) = i$ if f denotes the "parallel *or*" operation and $F_i(f) = \bot$ for all other f, and so

$$F_0 \quad \not\equiv_{\theta_0 \longrightarrow \textbf{val[nat]}} \quad F_1;$$

but, in fact,

$$F_0(A) \quad \equiv_{\textbf{val[nat]}} \quad F_1(A)$$

for all $A \in [\theta_0]_{\pi_0}$, because the parallel *or* (the only element of $[\![\theta_0]\!]$ that can be used as an argument to distinguish the outcomes of applying F_0 and F_1) is *not* expressible in our language. This can be proved using the obvious sequentiality properties of the operational semantics, or by showing by structural induction on the denotational semantics that every expressible function has a "stability" property that parallel *or* lacks. By adding parallel conditionals to the language, the parallel *or* (and other meanings necessary to make such distinctions) become definable.

Another approach to achieving full abstraction is to define "smaller" domains. For example, in this case we might want only "sequentially-implementable" functions that would not include operations like the parallel *or*; however, despite considerable effort, the problem of characterizing sequentially-implementable higher-order functions rigorously has not been solved.

Exercises

5.1 Why is $\omega = (N, \leq)$ not a domain? Let N' be the set $N \cup \{\infty\}$; define a partial ordering $\sqsubseteq$ on N' that extends $\leq$ on N such that $(N', \sqsubseteq)$ is a domain. What function from this domain to $\{\textit{true}\}_\bot$ is monotonic but not continuous?

5.2 Let D and E be domains; prove that if $f{:}|D| \longrightarrow |E|$ is continuous, it is also monotonic.

5.3 A *partial* function is continuous if and only if it is monotonic and it preserves least upper bounds of ω-chains. Show that the first

requirement is necessary by defining a partial function that preserves
least upper bounds of chains but is non-monotonic.

5.4   Prove directly from the definition of continuity that constant and
identity functions are continuous.

5.5   Prove that if $f: A \rightarrow B$ is everywhere-defined, it is continuous as a
partial function if and only if it is continuous as a total function.

5.6   Prove directly from the definition of continuity that, if f and g are
continuous functions, so is $f;g$. Do the same if f and g are continuous
partial functions.

5.7   Prove directly from the definition of continuity that if A and B are
domains, a function $f: A \times B \rightarrow C$ of two arguments is continuous if and only if it is continuous in each argument separately; i.e.,
$f_a(b) = f(a, b)$ is continuous for every $a \in A$, and $f_b(a) = f(a, b)$ is
continuous for every $b \in B$.

5.8   Let S be a set, D be a domain, and $f \in (S \rightarrow D)^\omega$; prove that
$\bigsqcup_{i \in \omega} f_i$ is the function $g \in S \rightarrow D$ defined by $g(s) = \bigsqcup_{i \in \omega} f_i(s)$ for
all $s \in S$, and similarly if $f: (S \rightarrow D)^\omega$.

5.9   Show that the functions fix_i used in the proof of Proposition 5.7 are
continuous.

5.10 What are the iterative approximations and the fixed-point meanings
of the defined identifiers in each of the following definitions?

   (a) **letrec** n: **val**[nat] **be** n **in** $\cdots$;
   (b) **letrec** n: **val**[nat] **be** 0 **in** $\cdots$;
   (c) **letrec** n: **val**[nat] **be** $n + 1$ **in** $\cdots$;
   (d) **letrec** n: **val**[nat] **be** $n \times 0$ **in** $\cdots$, for both the strict multipli-
        cation ($\perp \times 0 = \perp$) and the "parallel" multiplication ($\perp \times 0 = 0$);
   (e) **letrec** g: **val**[nat] $\rightarrow$ **val**[nat] **be**
        λn: **val**[nat]. **if** $n = 0$ **then** 0 **else** $g(n + 1)$
        in $\cdots$;
   (f) **letrec** g: **val**[nat] $\rightarrow$ **val**[nat] **be**
        λn: **val**[nat]. **if** $n = 0$ **then** 0 **else** $g(n - 1)$
        in $\cdots$.

5.11 Prove the cases $P = \lambda \iota: \theta. Q$ and $F(A)$ of Proposition 5.9. Hint: any
functional type in our language can be written in the form

$$\theta_1 \rightarrow (\theta_2 \rightarrow (\cdots \rightarrow (\theta_n \rightarrow \mathbf{val}[\tau]) \cdots)).$$

5.12 Where would the proof of Proposition 5.9 break down if $v \|\mathbf{val}[\tau]\| V$
were defined to be $v = \{V\}_\tau$? (This would permit the equivalence
of the denotational and operational valuations to be shown with a
single induction.)

5.13 Let B: **val**[**bool**], $F: \theta \rightarrow \theta'$ and $X_1, X_2: \theta$; is the following equivalence valid?

$$F(\textbf{if } B \textbf{ then } X_1 \textbf{ else } X_2) \ \equiv_{\theta'} \ \textbf{if } B \textbf{ then } F(X_1) \textbf{ else } F(X_2).$$

5.14 Programming languages often allow "mutually-recursive" (simultaneous) definitions of *several* identifiers, as in

$$\textbf{letrec } \iota_1: \theta_1 \textbf{ be } P_1, \iota_2: \theta_2 \textbf{ be } P_2, \dots, \iota_n: \theta_n \textbf{ be } P_n \textbf{ in } Q$$

Any free occurrences of identifiers $\iota_1, \iota_2, \dots, \iota_n$ in phrases Q or $P_1, P_2, \dots, P_n$ are bound by the recursive definition.

(a) Give a syntax rule for this construction.

(b) Give a semantic interpretation of mutually-recursive definitions; for simplicity, you may assume that $n = 2$.

(c) Mutually-recursive definitions can also be treated as defined notation. The idea is to use the following equivalence as a transformation until only *simple* recursive definitions remain:

$$\begin{aligned}
&\textbf{letrec } \iota_1: \theta_1 \textbf{ be } P_1, \iota_2: \theta_2 \textbf{ be } P_2, \dots, \iota_n: \theta_n \textbf{ be } P_n \textbf{ in } Q \\
\equiv \ &\textbf{letrec } \iota_1: \theta_1 \textbf{ be} \\
&\quad (\textbf{letrec } \iota_2: \theta_2 \textbf{ be } P_2, \dots, \iota_n: \theta_n \textbf{ be } P_n \textbf{ in } P_1) \\
&\textbf{in} \\
&\quad (\textbf{letrec } \iota_2: \theta_2 \textbf{ be } P_2, \dots, \iota_n: \theta_n \textbf{ be } P_n \textbf{ in } Q)
\end{aligned}$$

The equivalence shows how to "factor out" a simple recursive definition of ι_1 by using *separate* recursive definitions of the remaining identifiers $\iota_2, \dots, \iota_n$ for P_1 and Q. Prove that this gives the same interpretation as you gave directly in part (b); you may again assume $n = 2$.

Bibliographic Notes

The applicative language with recursion treated here is essentially what is termed PCF in [Plo77]. The treatment of recursion in terms of fixed points of continuous functions in domain-like structures was first outlined in a privately-circulated memo [Sco69]; [Mil73] is a detailed exposition of this work. Two of the best presentations of elementary domain theory are [Wad78] and [Plo78], which originated as sets of lecture notes, but have been widely circulated. Other expositions may be found in many places, such as [LS84, Sch86, RR91].

Logical relations are discussed in [Plo80, Sta85, Mit90]. Various versions of the formal system called LCF have been described in [Sco69, Mil72, MMN75, GMW79, Pau87, Sta90]. Our treatment of admissibility for fixed-point induction is based on the approach used (for a different language of predicates) in [Rey82]. The results on full abstraction are from [Plo77]; other work on full abstraction may be found in [Mil77, BCL85, Mul87, Sto88a]. The reduction of simultaneous recursion to iterated simple recursion in Exercise 5.14 was first presented in [Bek69].

PART III

An Algol-Like Language

Chapter 6

An Algol-Like Language I

Algol is obtained from the simple imperative language by imposing a proce-
dure mechanism based on a fully typed call-by-name lambda calculus.

J. C. Reynolds (1981)

In the preceding chapters, we have analyzed two programming languages:

- a simple *imperative* language with state-dependent expressions and state-changing commands; and

- a purely *applicative* language with state-independent expressions and functions, and recursion.

For each language we presented denotational, operational, and axiomatic semantics, and used the denotational description to verify the correctness of the operational and axiomatic ones. The reader may be wondering whether the methods described so far are also applicable to the "procedural" languages used in practice, which have both applicative and imperative aspects.

In this chapter, we will see that this is definitely the case. The (syntax and semantics of the) two mini-languages will essentially be *combined* to form the "core" of a procedural language. Remarkably, the combined language retains nearly all of the logical properties of the "pure" languages and can reasonably be described as being *both* imperative *and* applicative.

In the following chapters, we will add important new facilities such as jumps, local-variable declarations, data structures, and modules to this core. The real-life language that our language most closely resembles in semantic structure is ALGOL 60 [N$^+$63], and so we term it an *Algol-like* language. An alternative approach to combining imperative and applicative concepts will be discussed briefly for comparison purposes in Section 6.3, which can be skipped without loss of continuity.

6.1   Syntax

We begin by combining the type rules for the simple imperative and applicative languages as follows:

$$\theta ::= \mathbf{val}[\tau] \mid \mathbf{exp}[\tau] \mid \mathbf{comm} \mid \theta \rightarrow \theta' \mid (\theta)$$

where, as before, τ ranges over data types. This combination gives us more than the *union* of the phrase types of those languages: we now have new *procedural* phrase types of the forms $\theta \rightarrow \mathbf{exp}[\tau]$ and $\theta \rightarrow \mathbf{comm}$. Meanings of these types are like the "functions" and procedures, respectively, of a language like PASCAL.

In the imperative language of Chapter 3, *all* identifiers were variable-identifiers, whereas in the applicative language of the preceding two chapters, identifiers denoted values and functions but *not* variables. To allow here for variable-identifiers (and other kinds of variable-denoting phrases), we add new primitive phrase types of the form $\mathbf{var}[\tau]$ for every data type τ:

$$\theta ::= \cdots \mid \mathbf{var}[\tau]$$

A variable-identifier for values of type τ is now just an identifier having phrase type $\mathbf{var}[\tau]$.

This now also gives us procedural types of the forms $\mathbf{var}[\tau] \rightarrow \theta$ and $\theta \rightarrow \mathbf{var}[\tau]$. The former are just procedures with variable parameters. Procedures with **var** result types have been termed "selectors"; for example, conventional *arrays* ("subscriptable variables") are essentially procedures with an **exp** argument type and a **var** result type.

As the initial syntax of our language, we take *all* of the rules of the preceding three chapters (including the "defined" notations of Sections 4.3, 5.1 and 5.4), with a few small changes as follows.

The rules for variable-identifier expressions and assignment commands in Section 3.2 are no longer appropriate because we now have identifiers that do not denote variables. Also, we will want to have variable phrases that are not identifiers; for example, if ι_1 and ι_2 are variable-identifiers for values of type τ, $E\colon \mathbf{exp}[\tau]$, and $B\colon \mathbf{exp}[\mathbf{bool}]$, then one would expect the assignment command

$$(\mathbf{if}\ B\ \mathbf{then}\ \iota_1\ \mathbf{else}\ \iota_2) := E,$$

which uses a "conditional variable," to be equivalent to the following conditional command:

$$\mathbf{if}\ B\ \mathbf{then}\ (\iota_1 := E)\ \mathbf{else}\ (\iota_2 := E).$$

This illustrates that the left-hand sides of assignments can be more complex than simple identifiers. (In fact, few programming languages allow conditional variables, but the same kind of syntactic and semantic complexity

is exhibited by many other features, such as subscripted array variables.)
The following syntax rules will therefore replace those of Section 3.2:

De-referencing:

$$\frac{V:\mathbf{var}[\tau]}{V:\mathbf{exp}[\tau]}$$

Assignment:

$$\frac{V:\mathbf{var}[\tau] \quad E:\mathbf{exp}[\tau]}{V := E:\mathbf{comm}}$$

De-referencing is an example of a *coercion*: a phrase of one type ($\mathbf{var}[\tau]$) can
be used as a phrase of another type ($\mathbf{exp}[\tau]$) without requiring an explicit
conversion operator.

Coercions are convenient for programmers, but introduce several theoretical problems. One is that the language no longer has the property that,
for any phrase-type assignment π, a phrase P has at most one type in π;
for example, if $\pi(\iota) = \mathbf{var}[\tau]$, then $\pi \vdash \iota : \mathbf{var}[\tau]$ *and* $\pi \vdash \iota : \mathbf{exp}[\tau]$. But, we
will show in Section 7.1 that, in any phrase-type assignment, every phrase
that has a type has a "most-general" type, which coerces into every other
type that the phrase can have.

Another potential problem with coercions is that there can be ambiguity
when they are combined with generic constructions. In fact, if $B: \mathbf{exp}[\mathbf{bool}]$
and $V_0, V_1 : \mathbf{var}[\tau]$, the conditional variable

$$\mathbf{if}\ B\ \mathbf{then}\ V_0\ \mathbf{else}\ V_1$$

is a phrase of type $\mathbf{exp}[\tau]$ in *two* ways: either as a de-referenced conditional
variable, or as a conditional expression whose two "arms" are expressions
obtained by de-referencing variables. The two derivations are as follows:

$$\frac{\dfrac{B:\mathbf{exp}[\mathbf{bool}] \quad V_0:\mathbf{var}[\tau] \quad V_1:\mathbf{var}[\tau]}{\mathbf{if}\ B\ \mathbf{then}\ V_0\ \mathbf{else}\ V_1:\mathbf{var}[\tau]}}{\mathbf{if}\ B\ \mathbf{then}\ V_0\ \mathbf{else}\ V_1:\mathbf{exp}[\tau]}$$

and

$$\frac{B:\mathbf{exp}[\mathbf{bool}] \quad \dfrac{V_0:\mathbf{var}[\tau]}{V_0:\mathbf{exp}[\tau]} \quad \dfrac{V_1:\mathbf{var}[\tau]}{V_1:\mathbf{exp}[\tau]}}{\mathbf{if}\ B\ \mathbf{then}\ V_0\ \mathbf{else}\ V_1:\mathbf{exp}[\tau]}$$

But it will turn out that there is no *semantic* ambiguity here, and so all
is well. The question will be considered for the language as a whole in
Section 7.1.

It is also convenient to introduce the following coercion to allow *any*
phrase of type $\mathbf{val}[\tau]$ to be used in contexts where phrases of type $\mathbf{exp}[\tau]$
are expected, such as the right-hand sides of assignments:

Constant Expression:

$$\frac{K:\mathbf{val}[\tau]}{K:\mathbf{exp}[\tau]}$$

Finally, we consider the conditional form

if B **then** X_0 **else** X_1

with $B:\mathbf{exp}[\mathbf{bool}]$ and $X_0, X_1: \theta$, which was originally defined for θ ranging over $\mathbf{exp}[\tau]$ and **comm** only. Ideally we would want θ to range now over *all* phrase types. For example, the following equivalence shows how to deal with procedural types (when the result type is one for which a conditional can be defined):

(**if** B **then** X_1 **else** $X_2)(A)$ $\equiv_{\theta'}$ **if** B **then** $X_1(A)$ **else** $X_2(A)$,

where $X_1, X_2: \theta'' \rightarrow \theta'$ and $A: \theta''$. However, it does not seem to be feasible to have such a conditional form for phrases of type θ when θ is a "purely-applicative" phrase type such as $\mathbf{val}[\tau]$ or $\theta' \rightarrow \mathbf{val}[\tau]$, because the Boolean condition is state-dependent in general. Hence, in the following syntax rule

Expression Conditional:

$$\frac{B:\mathbf{exp}[\mathbf{bool}] \quad X_0:\theta \quad X_1:\theta}{\mathbf{if}\ B\ \mathbf{then}\ X_0\ \mathbf{else}\ X_1:\theta}$$

we must require that θ *not* be a *value-like* phrase type, where the value-like phrase types are as follows: $\mathbf{val}[\tau]$ for any data type τ, and any functional phrase type of the form $\theta'' \rightarrow \theta'$ when θ' is value-like. The following syntax rule is applicable with *any* phrase type θ:

Value Conditional:

$$\frac{K:\mathbf{val}[\mathbf{bool}] \quad X_0:\theta \quad X_1:\theta}{\mathbf{if}\ K\ \mathbf{then}\ X_0\ \mathbf{else}\ X_1:\theta}$$

but the Boolean condition K here must be state-independent. We take *programs* to be elements of $[\mathbf{comm}]_{\pi_0}$; i.e., phrases that are well-formed as commands in the initial phrase-type assignment for pre-defined identifiers. This completes the syntactic description of the initial fragment of our Algol-like language.

Our language allows programming in both the imperative style of the language of Chapter 3 and the applicative style of the language of Chapters 4 and 5, and furthermore allows these styles to be used *together*. For example, the following defines a factorial-computing procedure recursively:

> **letrec** $fact(n: \mathbf{exp}[\mathbf{nat}], f: \mathbf{var}[\mathbf{nat}]): \mathbf{comm} =$
>   **if** $n = 0$ **then** $f := 1$ **else** $fact(n - 1, f)\,;\, f := n \times f$
> **in** $\cdots$

The following is semantically equivalent to this (except for the use of a non-local counter variable k), but uses iteration rather than recursion:

$$\textbf{let } fact(n\colon \textbf{exp}[\textbf{nat}], f\colon \textbf{var}[\textbf{nat}]) =$$
$$k := 0 \; ; f := 1;$$
$$\textbf{while } k \neq n \textbf{ do}$$
$$k := k + 1 \; ; f := k \times f$$
$$\textbf{in } \quad \cdots$$

A facility for declaring *local* variables will be introduced in Section 7.2.

Here is an example involving a parameter of type **comm**:

$$\textbf{let } repeat(b\colon \textbf{exp}[\textbf{bool}], c\colon \textbf{comm}) =$$
$$c \; ; \textbf{while not } b \textbf{ do } c$$
$$\textbf{in } \quad \cdots$$

Notice that, if this is to work as expected, the actual parameter corresponding to expression parameter b must be evaluated after *each* execution of the command parameter, c; in other words, parameters should be passed "by name."

Finally, we present an example with a procedural parameter:

$$\textbf{letrec } iterate(a\colon \textbf{exp}[\textbf{nat}], b\colon \textbf{exp}[\textbf{nat}], p\colon \textbf{exp}[\textbf{nat}] \rightarrow \textbf{comm}) =$$
$$\textbf{if } a \leq b \textbf{ then } p(a) \; ; iterate(\textbf{succ } a, b, p)$$
$$\textbf{in } \quad \cdots$$

The intended effect of $iterate(a, b, p)$ is to apply p successively to $a, a + 1, \ldots, b$. For example,

$$iterate(a, b, \lambda i : \textbf{exp}[\textbf{nat}]. \, s := s + i \times i)$$

or, alternatively,

$$\# \, iterate(a, b) \, i.$$
$$s := s + i \times i$$

have the overall effect of adding $\sum_{i=a}^{b} i^2$ to a variable s of type **var**[**nat**].

6.2 Semantics

The semantic interpretation of the combined language can be obtained by combining the semantics of the simple imperative and applicative languages. The following domain definitions are essentially taken from the preceding chapters:

$$[\![\textbf{val}[\tau]]\!] = [\![\tau]\!]_\bot$$
$$[\![\textbf{exp}[\tau]]\!] = S \rightarrow [\![\textbf{val}[\tau]]\!]$$

$$[\mathbf{comm}] = S \rightharpoonup S$$
$$[\theta \rightarrow \theta'] = [\theta] \rightarrow [\theta']$$
$$[(\theta)] = [\theta]$$
$$[\pi] = \prod_{\iota \in \mathrm{dom}\,\pi} [\pi(\iota)],$$

where, as before, S is the set of states (to be defined below), and, for every data type τ, $[\tau]$ is the set of τ-values. The only notable change is that evaluation of a phrase of type $\mathbf{exp}[\tau]$ at some state can now yield $\bot$ (signifying non-termination) as well as an element of $[\tau]$; in Chapter 3 we could use $[\mathbf{exp}[\tau]] = S \rightarrow [\tau]$ because expression evaluations there always terminated.

Notice that all functional and procedural types $\theta \rightarrow \theta'$ are treated uniformly. As an example of the interpretation of a procedural type, consider

$$[\mathbf{exp}[\mathbf{nat}] \rightarrow \mathbf{comm}] = (S \rightarrow N_\bot) \rightarrow (S \rightharpoonup S);$$

i.e., the domain of continuous functions from meanings of expressions for natural numbers to command meanings.

We must also define $[\mathbf{var}[\tau]]$. To allow for conditional variables and recursive definitions of variables and variable-returning procedures, and analogously to

$$[\mathbf{exp}[\tau]] = S \rightarrow [\tau]_\bot,$$

we define

$$[\mathbf{var}[\tau]] = S \rightarrow [\tau]_\bot,$$

where

$$[\tau] = \{\iota \in \mathrm{dom}\,\pi_0 \mid \pi_0(\iota) = \mathbf{var}[\tau]\}$$

is the set of pre-defined τ-valued variable identifiers; that is, a phrase of type $\mathbf{var}[\tau]$ denotes a function that, given any state, yields $\bot$ (signifying non-termination) or a pre-defined variable-identifier for values of type τ. As before, a state is any function s whose domain is the set of all identifiers ι such that $\pi_0(\iota) = \mathbf{var}[\tau]$ for some data type τ, and $s(\iota) \in [\tau]$ for all $\iota \in [\tau]$; S is the set of all such states.

We can now define the semantic valuation functions

$$[\cdot]_{\pi\theta}: [\theta]_\pi \rightarrow ([\pi] \rightarrow [\theta]),$$

where, as before, $[\theta]_\pi$ is the set of all phrases X such that $\pi \vdash X:\theta$. For the applicative aspects of the language, the semantic equations in Chapters 4 and 5 can be used without any changes whatsoever, even when imperative phrases such as variables or commands are involved. The most important of these equations are as follows:

$$[\iota]u = u(\iota)$$

$$\llbracket P\,Q \rrbracket u = \llbracket P \rrbracket u(\llbracket Q \rrbracket u)$$

$$\llbracket \lambda\iota\colon\theta.\,P \rrbracket ua = \llbracket P \rrbracket(u \mid \iota \mapsto a), \text{ for all } a \in \llbracket \theta \rrbracket$$

$$\llbracket \mathbf{undef}[\theta] \rrbracket u = \bot_\theta$$

$$\llbracket \mathbf{rec}[\theta] \rrbracket uf = \textstyle\bigsqcup_{i\in\omega} f^i(\bot_\theta), \text{ for all } f \in \llbracket \theta \rrbracket \to \llbracket \theta \rrbracket$$

$$\llbracket \mathbf{if}\ K\ \mathbf{then}\ X_0\ \mathbf{else}\ X_1 \rrbracket_\theta(u) = \begin{cases} \llbracket X_0 \rrbracket_\theta(u), & \text{if } \llbracket K \rrbracket u = \textit{true} \\ \llbracket X_1 \rrbracket_\theta(u), & \text{if } \llbracket K \rrbracket u = \textit{false} \\ \bot_\theta, & \text{if } \llbracket K \rrbracket u = \bot \end{cases}$$

where $K\colon\mathbf{val}[\mathbf{bool}]$. Notice that if the actual parameter (Q) in a procedure application $P\,Q$ is an expression, variable, or command, it is not evaluated (or executed) by the call (the state argument is not supplied); i.e., "lazy evaluation" or call-by-name parameter passing is specified.

For the imperative aspects, the semantic equations of Sections 3.1 and 3.3 need to be changed only by adding environment arguments to valuations throughout to account for identifier binding, and allowing for $\bot$ as a possible result of sub-expression evaluation, as in the following:

$$\llbracket \mathbf{not}\ B \rrbracket us = \begin{cases} \textit{false}, & \text{if } \llbracket B \rrbracket us = \textit{true} \\ \textit{true}, & \text{if } \llbracket B \rrbracket us = \textit{false} \\ \bot, & \text{if } \llbracket B \rrbracket us = \bot \end{cases}$$

$$\llbracket \mathbf{skip} \rrbracket u = \mathrm{id}_S$$

$$\llbracket C_0\ ;\ C_1 \rrbracket u = \llbracket C_0 \rrbracket u\ ;\ \llbracket C_1 \rrbracket u$$

$$\llbracket \mathbf{diverge} \rrbracket u = \bot_{\mathbf{comm}}$$

$$\llbracket \mathbf{while}\ B\ \mathbf{do}\ C \rrbracket u = \textstyle\bigsqcup_{i\in\omega} f^i(\bot_{\mathbf{comm}}),$$

$$\text{where } f(c)(s) = \begin{cases} (\llbracket C \rrbracket u\ ;\ c)(s), & \text{if } \llbracket B \rrbracket us = \textit{true} \\ s, & \text{if } \llbracket B \rrbracket us = \textit{false} \\ \text{undefined}, & \text{if } \llbracket B \rrbracket us = \bot \end{cases}$$

To interpret the expression-conditional forms we must resort to an induction on types as follows: for $B\colon\mathbf{exp}[\mathbf{bool}]$ and $X_0, X_1\colon\theta$ (θ not value-like),

$$\llbracket \mathbf{if}\ B\ \mathbf{then}\ X_0\ \mathbf{else}\ X_1 \rrbracket_\theta(u) = \textit{cond}_\theta(\llbracket B \rrbracket u, \llbracket X_0 \rrbracket_\theta(u), \llbracket X_1 \rrbracket_\theta(u))$$

where the auxiliary functions $\textit{cond}_\theta\colon \llbracket \mathbf{exp}[\mathbf{bool}] \rrbracket \times \llbracket \theta \rrbracket \times \llbracket \theta \rrbracket \to \llbracket \theta \rrbracket$ are defined by induction on the structure of θ as follows:

$$\textit{cond}_{\mathbf{exp}[\tau]}(b, e_0, e_1)(s) = \begin{cases} e_0(s), & \text{if } b(s) = \textit{true} \\ e_1(s), & \text{if } b(s) = \textit{false} \\ \bot, & \text{if } b(s) = \bot \end{cases}$$

$$\textit{cond}_{\mathbf{var}[\tau]}(b, v_0, v_1)(s) = \begin{cases} v_0(s), & \text{if } b(s) = \textit{true} \\ v_1(s), & \text{if } b(s) = \textit{false} \\ \bot, & \text{if } b(s) = \bot \end{cases}$$

$$\textit{cond}_{\mathbf{comm}}(b, c_0, c_1)(s) = \begin{cases} c_0(s), & \text{if } b(s) = \textit{true} \\ c_1(s), & \text{if } b(s) = \textit{false} \\ \text{undefined}, & \text{if } b(s) = \bot \end{cases}$$

$cond_{\theta \longrightarrow \theta'}(b, p_0, p_1)(a) = cond_{\theta'}(b, p_0(a), p_1(a))$, for all $a \in [\![\theta]\!]$,

where $cond_{\theta'}$ must exist because θ' is not value–like.

The semantic equations for constant expressions, assignment commands, and de-referencing are as follows:

$$[\![K]\!]_{\mathbf{exp}[\tau]}(u)(s) = [\![K]\!]_{\mathbf{val}[\tau]}(u)$$

$$[\![V := E]\!]us$$
$$= \begin{cases} (s \mid \iota \mapsto n), & \text{if } [\![V]\!]_{\mathbf{var}[\tau]}(u)(s) = \iota \in [\tau] \text{ and } [\![E]\!]us = n \in [\![\tau]\!] \\ \text{undefined}, & \text{if } [\![V]\!]_{\mathbf{var}[\tau]}(u)(s) = \bot \text{ or } [\![E]\!]us = \bot \end{cases}$$

$$[\![V]\!]_{\mathbf{exp}[\tau]}(u)(s) = \begin{cases} s(\iota), & \text{if } [\![V]\!]_{\mathbf{var}[\tau]}(u)(s) = \iota \in [\tau] \\ \bot, & \text{if } [\![V]\!]_{\mathbf{var}[\tau]}(u)(s) = \bot \end{cases}$$

for any $s \in S$. We can now verify that both derivations of

$$\textbf{if } B \textbf{ then } V_0 \textbf{ else } V_1 : \mathbf{exp}[\tau]$$

from $B: \mathbf{exp}[\mathbf{bool}]$, $V_0: \mathbf{var}[\tau]$, and $V_1: \mathbf{var}[\tau]$ yield the same interpretation. For the derivation

$$\frac{B: \mathbf{exp}[\mathbf{bool}] \quad V_0: \mathbf{var}[\tau] \quad V_1: \mathbf{var}[\tau]}{\dfrac{\textbf{if } B \textbf{ then } V_0 \textbf{ else } V_1 : \mathbf{var}[\tau]}{\textbf{if } B \textbf{ then } V_0 \textbf{ else } V_1 : \mathbf{exp}[\tau]}}$$

we get

$$[\![\textbf{if } B \textbf{ then } V_0 \textbf{ else } V_1]\!]_{\mathbf{exp}[\tau]}(u)(s)$$
$$= \begin{cases} s(\iota), & \text{if } [\![\textbf{if } B \textbf{ then } V_0 \textbf{ else } V_1]\!]_{\mathbf{var}[\tau]}(u)(s) = \iota \in [\tau] \\ \bot, & \text{otherwise} \end{cases}$$
$$= \begin{cases} s(\iota_0), & \text{if } [\![B]\!]us = true \text{ and } [\![V_0]\!]_{\mathbf{var}[\tau]}(u)(s) = \iota_0 \in [\tau] \\ s(\iota_1), & \text{if } [\![B]\!]us = false \text{ and } [\![V_1]\!]_{\mathbf{var}[\tau]}(u)(s) = \iota_1 \in [\tau] \\ \bot, & \text{otherwise,} \end{cases}$$

and for the derivation

$$\frac{B: \mathbf{exp}[\mathbf{bool}] \quad \dfrac{V_0: \mathbf{var}[\tau]}{V_0: \mathbf{exp}[\tau]} \quad \dfrac{V_1: \mathbf{var}[\tau]}{V_1: \mathbf{exp}[\tau]}}{\textbf{if } B \textbf{ then } V_0 \textbf{ else } V_1 : \mathbf{exp}[\tau]}$$

we get

$$[\![\textbf{if } B \textbf{ then } V_0 \textbf{ else } V_1]\!]_{\mathbf{exp}[\tau]}(u)(s)$$
$$= \begin{cases} [\![V_0]\!]_{\mathbf{exp}[\tau]}(u)(s), & \text{if } [\![B]\!]us = true \\ [\![V_1]\!]_{\mathbf{exp}[\tau]}(u)(s), & \text{if } [\![B]\!]us = false \\ \bot, & \text{otherwise} \end{cases}$$
$$= \begin{cases} s(\iota_0), & \text{if } [\![B]\!]us = true \text{ and } [\![V_0]\!]_{\mathbf{var}[\tau]}(u)(s) = \iota_0 \in [\tau] \\ s(\iota_1), & \text{if } [\![B]\!]us = false \text{ and } [\![V_1]\!]_{\mathbf{var}[\tau]}(u)(s) = \iota_1 \in [\tau] \\ \bot, & \text{otherwise.} \end{cases}$$

A complete treatment of coercions and the question of ambiguity will be given in Section 7.1.

We define the meanings of variable-identifiers in the "initial" environment u_0 as follows: for all $\iota \in [\tau]$ and $s \in S$, $u_0(\iota)(s) = \iota$. This gives us essentially the same semantics as before for variable-identifiers.

This completes the semantic interpretation of the Algol-like language obtained by combining the facilities of the simple imperative and applicative languages of the preceding chapters. It is noteworthy that the language retains virtually all of the logical properties of the "pure" languages, as shown by the following facts:

- All of the command equivalences of Sections 3.1, 3.2 and 3.3 continue to be valid.

- The Coherence and Substitution Lemmas and the other propositions of Section 4.4 continue to hold.

- All of the axioms of Sections 4.5 and 5.6 (including Substitutivity and the Beta and Eta Laws) are valid, even for imperative phrases such as variables or commands.

- We will see in Section 6.4 that, with only one exception, all of the Hoare-logic axioms of Section 3.6.2 remain valid with only minor modifications.

We also have some additional equational axioms relating conditionals and variables or procedures. When $B \in \left[\mathbf{exp}[\mathbf{bool}]\right]_\pi$, $V_0, V_1 \in \left[\mathbf{var}[\tau]\right]_\pi$, and $E \in \left[\mathbf{exp}[\tau]\right]_\pi$,

$$\pi \vdash (\textbf{if } B \textbf{ then } V_0 \textbf{ else } V_1) := E \equiv_{\textbf{comm}} \textbf{if } B \textbf{ then } V_0 := E \textbf{ else } V_1 := E$$

When $B \in \left[\mathbf{exp}[\mathbf{bool}]\right]_\pi$, $X_1, X_2 \in [\theta \rightarrow \theta']_\pi$ and $A \in [\theta]_\pi$,

$$\pi \vdash (\textbf{if } B \textbf{ then } X_1 \textbf{ else } X_2)(A) \equiv_{\theta'} \textbf{if } B \textbf{ then } X_1(A) \textbf{ else } X_2(A),$$

and, when $X_1, X_2 \in [\theta']_{(\pi|_{\iota \mapsto \theta})}$, $B \in \left[\mathbf{exp}[\mathbf{bool}]\right]_\pi$, and $\iota \notin \operatorname{dom} \pi$,

$$\pi \vdash \lambda\iota : \theta. \, \textbf{if } B \textbf{ then } X_1 \textbf{ else } X_2 \equiv_{\theta \rightarrow \theta'} \textbf{if } B \textbf{ then } \lambda\iota : \theta. \, X_1 \textbf{ else } \lambda\iota : \theta. \, X_2,$$

and similarly if $B : \mathbf{val}[\mathbf{bool}]$.

6.3 Call by Value

Two of the most important design principles underlying the language described in the preceding sections of this chapter are as follows:

- As in the applicative language, parameter passing is "by name," so that an actual parameter is evaluated (or executed) whenever its value or effect is actually needed by the calling procedure (if ever), rather than at the call.

- As in the simple imperative language, commands and expressions are distinguished in that commands can change the computational state but do not have values, and expressions can have values but cannot change the state.

Although virtually all practical programming languages combine applicative and imperative aspects, few of them adhere to these design principles.

To justify our apparently eccentric choice of example language and for comparison, we briefly discuss in this section a language that illustrates the combination of applicative and imperative features according to different language-design principles, as follows.

- "Eager" evaluation (call by value), in which an actual parameter is always evaluated *exactly once* before evaluation of the calling procedure, is usually more efficient than "lazy" evaluation (call by name).

- If expression "evaluation" can *change* (as well as access) the state, the type structure can be simplified by treating commands and expressions uniformly.

The syntactic-type structure for the language we consider in this section is as follows:

$$\tau ::= \textbf{unit} \mid \textbf{bool} \mid \textbf{nat} \qquad\qquad \text{data types}$$
$$\theta ::= \textbf{exp}[\tau] \mid \textbf{var}[\tau] \mid \theta \rightarrow \theta' \mid (\theta) \quad \text{phrase types}$$

Expressions of type **unit** always have a "dummy" value *nil*; they are normally "evaluated" solely for their effect on the state. For example, assignments here are expressions of type **unit**:

Assignment:

$$\frac{V : \textbf{var}[\tau] \quad E : \textbf{exp}[\tau]}{V := E : \textbf{exp}[\textbf{unit}]}$$

The semi-colon operator is generalized to allow sequential evaluation of arbitrary expressions:

Sequencing:

$$\frac{E_0 : \textbf{exp}[\tau_0] \quad E_1 : \textbf{exp}[\tau_1]}{E_0 \,;\, E_1 : \textbf{exp}[\tau_1]}$$

The value is that of E_1 after evaluation of E_0 for its effect on the computational state; the value of E_0 is simply discarded.

We now describe the semantics of the language. As before, we use environments for the applicative aspects and states for the imperative aspects. We interpret the data types as follows:

$$[\![\textbf{unit}]\!] = \{nil\}$$
$$[\![\textbf{bool}]\!] = \{true, false\}$$

$$\llbracket\mathbf{nat}\rrbracket = \{0, 1, 2, \ldots\}$$

For phrase types, the call-by-value regime forces us to distinguish between the *denotable* and the *expressible* entities of each phrase type. The former are the values denoted by identifiers of that phrase type (after evaluation); the latter are the meanings expressed by phrases of that type (before evaluation). We continue to use $\llbracket\theta\rrbracket$ for the domain of *denotable* values of phrase type θ, and define the operation

$$\mathcal{E}(D) = S \rightarrow D \times S$$

on domains D, so that $\mathcal{E}\llbracket\theta\rrbracket$ is the domain of *expressible* meanings of phrase type θ; as usual, S is an appropriate set of states. This definition allows evaluation at some state either to fail to terminate or to terminate with a value and a possibly updated state.

The domain of denotable values for any phrase type θ and the domain of environments appropriate to any phrase-type assignment π are defined as follows:

$$\llbracket\mathbf{exp}[\tau]\rrbracket = \llbracket\tau\rrbracket$$
$$\llbracket\mathbf{var}[\tau]\rrbracket = [\tau]$$
$$\llbracket\theta \rightarrow \theta'\rrbracket = \llbracket\theta\rrbracket \rightarrow \mathcal{E}\llbracket\theta'\rrbracket$$
$$\llbracket(\theta)\rrbracket = \llbracket\theta\rrbracket$$
$$\llbracket\pi\rrbracket = \prod_{\iota\in\mathrm{dom}\,\pi} \llbracket\pi(\iota)\rrbracket,$$

where $[\tau]$ is, as before, the set of pre-defined τ-valued variable-identifiers. Notice that an identifier of type $\theta \rightarrow \theta'$ denotes a function mapping each *denotable* value of type θ to an *expressible* meaning of type θ'.

The valuation functions map phrases into continuous functions from appropriate environments to *expressible* meanings of appropriate type, as follows: for every phrase-type assignment π and phrase type θ,

$$\llbracket\cdot\rrbracket_{\pi\theta}\colon [\theta]_\pi \rightarrow \left(\llbracket\pi\rrbracket \rightarrow \mathcal{E}\llbracket\theta\rrbracket\right).$$

Here are some typical semantic equations; as before, u and s range over environments and states, respectively:

$$\llbracket 0 \rrbracket us = (0, s)$$
$$\llbracket\mathbf{skip}\rrbracket us = (nil, s)$$
$$\llbracket\mathbf{diverge}\rrbracket us = \text{undefined}$$
$$\llbracket\iota\rrbracket us = \left(u(\iota), s\right)$$
$$\llbracket\lambda\iota\colon\theta.\,P\rrbracket us = (f, s), \text{ where } f(a) = \llbracket P\rrbracket(u \mid \iota \mapsto a) \text{ for all } a \in \llbracket\theta\rrbracket$$
$$\llbracket P\,Q\rrbracket us = \begin{cases} f(a)(s''), & \text{if } \llbracket P\rrbracket us = (f, s') \text{ and } \llbracket Q\rrbracket us' = (a, s'') \\ \text{undefined}, & \text{otherwise} \end{cases}$$

$\llbracket V := E \rrbracket us$

$$= \begin{cases} \bigl(nil, (s'' \mid \iota \mapsto v)\bigr), & \text{if } \llbracket V \rrbracket us = (\iota, s') \text{ and } \llbracket E \rrbracket us' = (v, s'') \\ \text{undefined}, & \text{otherwise} \end{cases}$$

$$\llbracket E_0 \,;\, E_1 \rrbracket us = \begin{cases} \llbracket E_1 \rrbracket us', & \text{if } \llbracket E_0 \rrbracket us = (v, s') \\ \text{undefined}, & \text{otherwise} \end{cases}$$

$\llbracket \textbf{if } B \textbf{ then } X_0 \textbf{ else } X_1 \rrbracket us$

$$= \begin{cases} \llbracket X_0 \rrbracket us', & \text{if } \llbracket B \rrbracket us = (true, s') \\ \llbracket X_1 \rrbracket us', & \text{if } \llbracket B \rrbracket us = (false, s') \\ \text{undefined}, & \text{otherwise} \end{cases}$$

Evaluation of identifiers, abstractions, and constants such as **skip** and 0 yield values and the *same* state; other expressions, such as the assignment, can yield *new* states. In general, *any* sub-expression evaluation might, as a *side effect*, change the computational state or fail to terminate, as well as yield a value, and these possibilities must be "propagated." Notice that the actual parameter in the procedure-application form is evaluated before the procedure is applied to the resulting argument value. This captures the call-by-value regime; for example, $\llbracket P(\textbf{diverge}) \rrbracket us$ is always undefined.

This completes the semantic description of the call-by-value language. Although it is only slightly more complicated than that for the Algol-like language of the preceding sections, its *logical* properties are very different. The key difference is that, because of the distinction between denotable values and expressible meanings, the Substitution Lemma fails. This means that none of the logical rules or axioms (such as ∀-elimination) whose validity depends on this lemma can be used without restrictions. Another important difference is that expression evaluation can have side effects on the computational state, and this means that conventional "algebraic" reasoning cannot be used with expressions. Furthermore, it does not seem possible to reason about assignments using substitution of an expression for a variable in an assertion because we cannot deal with side effects in an assertion.

These difficulties are the subjects of current research. It remains to be seen whether the *operational* advantage of call by value can be obtained without significant *logical* cost.

In summary, many programming languages (LISP, ALGOL 68, SCHEME, ML, ...) use variants of lambda notation for functions or procedures; but only ALGOL 60, which does not even have lambda expressions, and its very close relations (such as the language described in the preceding sections) combine applicative and imperative features in a way that preserves the *logical principles*, and not merely the *notation*, of the lambda calculus.

6.4 Programming Logic

In this section, we consider how Hoare's logic for the simple imperative language (Section 3.6) can be adapted to the Algol-like language of this chapter, which has both commands and procedures.

6.4.1 Syntax and Semantics

We first consider how assertions (phrase type **assert**) can be treated. In Section 3.6, assertions and Boolean expressions were regarded as identical. But this would be difficult now, because evaluation of a Boolean expression may fail to terminate. Instead, we continue to use

$$[\![\textbf{assert}]\!] = S \rightarrow [\![\textbf{bool}]\!],$$

so that an assertion yields a truth value in every state, whereas

$$[\![\textbf{exp}[\textbf{bool}]]\!] = S \rightarrow [\![\textbf{bool}]\!]_{\perp}.$$

For example, instead of the doubly-strict interpretation used for the *Boolean expression* $N < N'$, we define the *assertion* $N < N'$ as follows:

$$[\![N < N']\!]_{\textbf{assert}}(u)(s)$$
$$= \begin{cases} true, & \text{if } [\![N]\!]us \neq \perp, [\![N']\!]us \neq \perp, [\![N]\!]us < [\![N']\!]us; \\ false, & \text{otherwise}, \end{cases}$$

and similarly for the other primitive assertions. This approach "localizes" the problems created by non-termination as much as possible; in particular, the assertional operators **not**, **and**, $\supset$, and so on can be treated exactly as before.

We will treat equality assertions in the same way, so that $[\![E = E']\!]_{\textbf{assert}}(u)(s) = true$ just if both operands have the same value which is *not* $\perp$. For some applications, an equality assertion $E \equiv E'$ over the *whole* domain, including $\perp$, is needed. This can be added to the syntax as follows:

Reflexive Equality:

$$\frac{E : \textbf{exp}[\tau] \quad E' : \textbf{exp}[\tau]}{E \equiv E' : \textbf{assert}}$$

and interpreted as follows:

$$[\![E \equiv E']\!]_{\textbf{assert}}(u)(s) = ([\![E]\!]us = [\![E']\!]us)$$

for all $s \in S$. Note that the assertion $E = E$ is *true* exactly when the evaluation of E terminates, but $E \equiv E$ is *true* in *every* state.

By introducing suitable constants **forall**$[\tau]$ and **exists**$[\tau]$ of phrase type (**val**$[\tau] \rightarrow$ **assert**) $\rightarrow$ **assert** for every data type τ, we can obtain universal and existential quantification in the assertion language as follows:

$$\# \, \mathbf{forall}[\tau] \, \iota. \, P$$

$$\# \, \mathbf{exists}[\tau] \, \iota. \, P$$

An appropriate interpretation of these quantifier constants is as follows: for all environments u, $f \in [\![\mathbf{val}[\tau]]\!] \to [\![\mathbf{assert}]\!]$, and states s,

$$[\![\mathbf{forall}[\tau]]\!] u f s = (\text{for all } v \in [\![\mathbf{val}[\tau]]\!], f(v)(s) = \mathit{true})$$

$$[\![\mathbf{exists}[\tau]]\!] u f s = (\text{for some } v \in [\![\mathbf{val}[\tau]]\!], f(v)(s) = \mathit{true})$$

This gives us, for example,

$$
\begin{aligned}
[\![\# \, \mathbf{forall}[\tau] \, \iota. \, P]\!] u s \; &= \; [\![\mathbf{forall}[\tau](\lambda\iota\colon \mathbf{val}[\tau]. \, P)]\!] u s \\
&= \; [\![\mathbf{forall}[\tau]]\!] u ([\![\lambda\iota\colon \mathbf{val}[\tau]. \, P]\!] u) s \\
&= \; (\text{for all } v \in [\![\mathbf{val}[\tau]]\!], [\![P]\!] (u \mid \iota \mapsto v) s = \mathit{true})
\end{aligned}
$$

and similarly for $\mathbf{exists}[\tau]$.

Specification formulas can be treated as in Sections 4.5 and 5.6, but using Hoare triples as the atomic formulas; the semantic equation for Hoare triples in this context is as follows:

$$
\begin{aligned}
&[\![\{P\}C\{Q\}]\!] u \\
&= \text{for all } s_0, s_1 \in S, \text{ if } [\![P]\!] u s_0 \text{ and } [\![C]\!] u s_0 = s_1 \text{ then } [\![Q]\!] u s_1
\end{aligned}
$$

An environment argument has been added to each valuation to handle free identifiers.

6.4.2   Axioms and Derived Rules

The simplest forms of assignment lend themselves to very simple explications. But this simplicity is deceptive; the examples are themselves special cases of a more general form and the first explications which come to mind will not generalise satisfactorily.

C. Strachey (1967)

We now discuss axioms for reasoning about Hoare-triple specifications for our combined language. A minor problem with two of the axioms of Section 3.6.2 is that they are no longer syntactically well-formed because we now distinguish between assertions and Boolean expressions; hence, we must revise the axioms for the conditional and iterative forms of command as follows:

$$\{P \text{ and } (B = \mathbf{true})\} C_0 \{Q\} \; \& $$

$$\{P \text{ and } (B = \mathbf{false})\} C_1 \{Q\} \; \Rightarrow$$

$$\{P\} \mathbf{if} \, B \, \mathbf{then} \, C_0 \, \mathbf{else} \, C_1 \{Q\}$$

$$\{P \text{ and } (B = \mathbf{true})\}C\{P\} \Rightarrow$$

$$\{P\}\mathbf{while}\ B\ \mathbf{do}\ C\{P \text{ and } (B = \mathbf{false})\}$$

With one exception, all of the other axioms presented in Section 3.6.2 remain valid without any changes. Unfortunately, the exception is the most fundamental axiom in Hoare-logic reasoning, the assignment axiom:

$$\{[P](\iota \mapsto E)\}\iota := E\{P\}.$$

There are essentially two difficulties:

1. It is no longer true that assigning to one variable identifier cannot affect any other variable identifier. For example, suppose $b: \mathbf{var}[\mathbf{bool}]$ and consider

$$\mathbf{let}\ c\ \mathbf{be}\ b\ \mathbf{in}$$
$$b := \mathbf{not}\ b\ ;\ \cdots$$

then, the value of c is affected by the assignment to b because c is an *alias* for the same variable in the scope of the definition. The assignment axiom of Section 3.6.2 would allow us to derive

$$\{[c = \mathbf{not}\ b](b \mapsto \mathbf{not}\ b)\}b := \mathbf{not}\ b\{c = \mathbf{not}\ b\}$$

which is

$$\{c = \mathbf{not}\ \mathbf{not}\ b\}b := \mathbf{not}\ b\{c = \mathbf{not}\ b\}$$

and this is clearly invalid if b and c denote the *same* variable.

A more subtle kind of aliasing can arise from the use of non-local variables or procedures in procedure bodies. For example, suppose $m: \mathbf{var}[\mathbf{nat}]$ and consider

$$\mathbf{let}\ addm(x: \mathbf{exp}[\mathbf{nat}]) = x + m$$
$$\mathbf{in}\ \cdots$$

Any assignment to m interferes with assertions that involve $addm$; for example, the following instance of Hoare's assignment axiom

$$\{a = addm(b)\}m := \mathbf{succ}\ m\{a = addm(b)\}$$

is clearly invalid.

2. It is no longer true in general that, immediately after assigning to a variable, the value of that variable is the value just assigned! For example, suppose that $b0, b1: \mathbf{var}[\mathbf{bool}]$ and consider the assignment $B := \mathbf{true}$ when B is the conditional variable

$$\mathbf{if}\ b1\ \mathbf{then}\ b0\ \mathbf{else}\ b1$$

If $b1$ is *false* initially, the assignment is equivalent to $b1 := \mathbf{true}$, and so the value of the conditional variable after the assignment is the value of $b0$, which might happen to be *false*.

A variable phrase $V \in [\mathbf{var}[\tau]]_\pi$ is termed *good* just if, for all $E \in [\mathbf{exp}[\tau]]_\pi$, $u \in [\![\pi]\!]$, and $s \in S$, if $[\![V := E]\!]us = s'$, then

$$[\![V]\!]_{\pi\,\mathbf{exp}[\tau]}(u)(s') = [\![E]\!]us;$$

that is, immediately after assigning to a good variable, the value of the variable is the value just assigned. The difficulty with conditional variable phrases is that they may not be good variables, even when their two sub-variables are good variables. The same kind of difficulty arises whenever variable phrases can have expressions as components; in a language with subscripted array variables, for example, $a[a[i]]$ is not a good variable because, when $a[i] = i$, an assignment to $a[a[i]]$ may change the value of the outer subscript.

There are basically two approaches to these problems. One is to design a language in which aliasing and bad variables can easily be precluded or detected *syntactically*; the other is to introduce new atomic specification formulas that allow relevant assumptions about variables and assertions to be stated and reasoned about in the programming logic. The first approach is beyond the scope of this text, but we will consider the second approach in Section 9.6 and give there a generally-valid axiom for assignments in our language.

We conclude by briefly discussing inference rules that can be *derived* for some of the command forms that were *defined* in terms of lambda abstraction and application. It is an important benefit of the use of defined notation that these natural but complex rules can be derived fairly straightforwardly from fundamental axioms.

We first consider the local-definition block

$$\mathbf{let}\ \iota\ \mathbf{be}\ X\ \mathbf{in}\ C,$$

where $X\colon \theta$ and $C\colon \mathbf{comm}$. The following natural-deduction rule allows one to derive a Hoare-triple specification for the block by proving a property Z of X and assuming that ι has that property in reasoning about C:

$$[Z]$$
$$\vdots$$
$$\frac{[Z](\iota \mapsto X) \qquad \{P\}C\{Q\}}{\{P\}\mathbf{let}\ \iota\ \mathbf{be}\ X\ \mathbf{in}\ C\{Q\}}$$

provided ι is not free in P, Q, or any uncancelled assumptions. This rule may be derived from the equivalence

$$\mathbf{let}\ \iota\ \mathbf{be}\ X\ \mathbf{in}\ C \quad \equiv_{\mathbf{comm}} \quad [C](\iota \mapsto X)$$

using the rules for $\forall$ and $\Rightarrow$.

Similarly, the following rule may be derived for reasoning about command blocks in which an expression procedure is defined.

$$[Z]$$
$$\vdots$$
$$\frac{\{P\}C\{Q\}}{\{P\}\textbf{let } \iota(\iota_1\!:\!\theta_1,\ldots,\iota_n\!:\!\theta_n) = E \textbf{ in } C\{Q\}}$$

where Z is

$$\forall \iota_1\!:\!\theta_1.\cdots.\forall \iota_n\!:\!\theta_n.\,\{\iota(\iota_1,\ldots,\iota_n) \equiv E\}\,,$$

ι, ι_1, ..., ι_n are all distinct, and ι is not free in P, Q, E, or uncancelled assumptions. Note the use of $\equiv$, the reflexive assertional equality, in Z to ensure that the assertion is true for *all* states, even if evaluation of the body E should fail to terminate.

We also give a rule for reasoning about command blocks in which a *command* procedure is defined; this is more complex because the property that must be assumed about calls of the procedure is itself a Hoare-triple specification subject to assumptions.

$$[Z'] \qquad\qquad [Z]$$
$$\vdots \qquad\qquad\quad \vdots$$
$$\frac{\{P'\}C'\{Q'\} \qquad \{P\}C\{Q\}}{\{P\}\textbf{let } \iota(\iota_1\!:\!\theta_1,\ldots,\iota_n\!:\!\theta_n) = C' \textbf{ in } C\{Q\}}$$

where Z is

$$\forall \iota_1\!:\!\theta_1.\cdots.\forall \iota_n\!:\!\theta_n.\forall \iota_1'\!:\!\theta_1'.\cdots.\forall \iota_m'\!:\!\theta_m'.$$
$$Z' \Rightarrow \{P'\}\iota(\iota_1,\ldots,\iota_n)\{Q'\},$$

ι, ι_1, ..., ι_n, ι_1', ..., ι_m' are all distinct, ι is not free in P, Q, P', Q', C', Z', or uncancelled assumptions, ι_1, ..., ι_n are not free in uncancelled assumptions, and ι_1', ..., ι_m' are not free in C' or uncancelled assumptions (but can occur freely in Z', P', or Q'). The formula Z' specifies *assumptions* about the formal parameters and other free identifiers of P' and Q'.

As an example of how this rule would be used, consider a command block of the following form:

$$\textbf{let } repeat(b\!:\textbf{exp[bool]}, c\!:\textbf{comm}) =$$
$$c\,;\textbf{while not } b \textbf{ do } c$$
$$\textbf{in } \quad \cdots$$

The minimum we would need to know about b and c to be able to reason about

$$c\,;\textbf{while not } b \textbf{ do } c$$

is that some assertion i is an invariant for **while not** b **do** c, and that an assertion p is a sufficient pre-condition for c to achieve i; hence, we take Z' to be

$$\{p\}c\{i\} \ \& \ \{i \textbf{ and } (b = \textbf{false})\}c\{i\}$$

and, from this assumption, one can use the axioms for ; and **while** to prove the specification

$$\{p\}c \; ; \; \textbf{while not } b \textbf{ do } c\{i \textbf{ and } (b = \textbf{true})\}.$$

Hence, Z is as follows:

$$\forall b: \textbf{exp[bool]}. \; \forall c: \textbf{comm}. \; \forall p: \textbf{assert}. \; \forall i: \textbf{assert}.$$
$$\{p\}c\{i\} \; \& \; \{i \textbf{ and } (b = \textbf{false})\}c\{i\} \Rightarrow$$
$$\{p\}repeat(b, c)\{i \textbf{ and } (b = \textbf{true})\},$$

and this can be used to reason about uses of *repeat* in C just as if a **repeat** command form had been provided in the language.

We present a rule for only one of the *recursive* forms of these definition constructs; it is identical to the rule above for the command block defining a non-recursive command procedure, except that the procedure name ι is allowed to occur freely in C' and specification Z is added as a further assumption which can be used in reasoning about C':

$$
\begin{array}{cc}
[Z' \; \& \; Z] & [Z] \\
\vdots & \vdots \\
\{P'\}C'\{Q'\} & \{P\}C\{Q\} \\
\hline
\multicolumn{2}{c}{\{P\}\textbf{letrec } \iota(\iota_1: \theta_1, \ldots, \iota_n: \theta_n): \textbf{comm} = C' \textbf{ in } C\{Q\}}
\end{array}
$$

Strictly speaking, this rule cannot be derived from axioms or rules we have already discussed, because it is necessary to use fixed-point induction and we have not addressed the issue of admissibility for Hoare triples. But it is easy to prove that formulas of the form

$$\forall \iota_1: \theta_1. \cdots . \forall \iota_n: \theta_n. \forall \iota_1': \theta_1'. \cdots . \forall \iota_m': \theta_m'.$$
$$Z' \Rightarrow \{P'\}\iota(\iota_1, \ldots, \iota_n)\{Q'\}$$

are admissible for fixed-point induction with respect to ι, and, with this, the rule above can be validated using the axiom for fixed-point induction.

Exercises

6.1 Is it possible to define a procedure of type **comm** $\longrightarrow$ **val[bool]** in our language?

6.2 Verify that syntactically-ambiguous use of the de-referencing coercion and the generic parenthesization construct does not lead to *semantic* ambiguities.

6.3 Validate the command equivalences at the end of Section 6.2.

6.4 Which of the equivalences of Exercises 3, 6, and 9 in Chapter 3 are valid for the Algol-like language of this chapter?

6.5 Validate the equivalences at the end of Section 6.2.

6.6 In Section 6.2, the domains of *all* procedural and functional types are uniformly defined by

$$[\![\theta \to \theta']\!] = [\![\theta]\!] \to [\![\theta']\!].$$

This interpretation is unrealistic for some procedural types; for example, consider

$$[\![\mathbf{exp}[\tau] \to \mathbf{exp}[\tau']]\!] = (S \to [\![\tau]\!]_\perp) \to (S \to [\![\tau']\!]_\perp).$$

This domain allows the meaning of the actual parameter (of type $\mathbf{exp}[\tau]$) of a call and the call itself (of type $\mathbf{exp}[\tau']$) to be evaluated at *different* states. But in fact, the actual parameter (if it is evaluated at all) can only be evaluated at the *same* state as is used for the call. This suggests that the following domain is more realistic:

$$[\![\mathbf{exp}[\tau] \to \mathbf{exp}[\tau']]\!] = S \to ([\![\tau]\!]_\perp \to [\![\tau']\!]_\perp).$$

Give semantic valuations for abstraction and application of such procedures using this domain and verify the appropriate properties. Generalize this approach to other "expression-like" types.

6.7 (a) Let N and N' be numerical expressions; prove that the assertions $(N < N') = \mathbf{true}$ and $N < N'$ are equivalent.

(b) Let B and B' be Boolean expressions; for which interpretation of the Boolean-expression **or** are assertions

$$(B \mathbf{\ or\ } B') = \mathbf{true}$$

and

$$(B = \mathbf{true}) \mathbf{\ or\ } (B' = \mathbf{true})$$

equivalent?

(c) Investigate other assertions of the forms $B = \mathbf{true}$ or $B = \mathbf{false}$.

6.8 Prove that, if conditional variables were removed, all of the variables expressible in our Algol-like language would be "good" variables.

6.9 An example in Section 6.4.2 gives a specification Z of a procedure *repeat*; use this specification as an additional assumption to prove that the procedure body in

> **letrec** *repeat*(*b*: **exp**[**bool**], *c*: **comm**): **comm** =
>   *c* ; **if not** *B* **then** *repeat*(*b*, *c*)
> **in** $\cdots$

satisfies its specification.

6.10 The following axiom for assignment commands was proposed in [Flo67]:

$$\{P\}\; \iota := E \; \{\# \, \mathbf{exists}[\tau]\iota_0 . \iota = [E](\iota \mapsto \iota_0) \; \mathbf{and} \; [P](\iota \mapsto \iota_0)\}$$

where $\iota \in [\tau]$ and ι_0 is any identifier both distinct from ι and not free in E or P.

(a) Verify the validity of this axiom for the simple imperative language of Chapter 3.

(b) Is this axiom valid for the Algol-like language discussed in this chapter?

6.11 Discuss the syntax and semantics of

(a) recursion, and
(b) multi-parameter functions

in the call-by-value language of Section 6.3.

6.12 Define operational semantics for the languages described in this chapter and verify their correctness.

Bibliographic Notes

The key reference for this chapter and the following one is [Rey81b]; see also [Rey78, Rey81a, Rey82, Ten89]. The semantics and logic of call-by-value languages are discussed in [Lan66, Plo75, Ros86, Fel87, FF89, Mog88, Mog89, Rie90]. The treatment of Boolean expressions and assertions is from [Ten87a]. A syntactic approach to the problems of aliasing and interference in Algol-like languages is discussed in [Rey78, Ten83, Rey89, O'H90].

Chapter 7

An Algol-Like Language II

ALGOL 60 is a language so far ahead of its time that it was not only an improvement on its predecessors but also on nearly all its successors.

C. A. R. Hoare (1974)

In this chapter, we continue the design of the Algol-like language whose "core" was discussed in Chapter 6. We begin with a detailed consideration of coercions, addressing the questions raised about syntactic and semantic ambiguity. We then go on to consider local-variable declarations, data structures, "write-only variables," jumps, and block expressions. Many of these discussions will illustrate the usefulness of rigorous semantic analysis in language design.

7.1 Coercions

Many language designers in recent years have tried to avoid implicit conversions as much as possible because of the many difficulties and surprises encountered by programmers using languages such as PL/I and ALGOL 68, which had very complex systems of coercions. But coercions are too convenient to abandon completely: every imperative high-level programming language has at least de-referencing and a coercion from integer to real-valued expressions. The aim of this section is to describe a relatively simple approach to coercions for our Algol-like language and verify that it has appropriate theoretical properties.

We can avoid one kind of syntactic complexity by deciding that the applicability of any coercion from one type to another should not be dependent on syntactic context. Then coercibility can be specified by means of a binary relation on phrase-type expressions, which we denote by ⊢. The

135

relationship $\theta \vdash \theta'$ may be regarded as an abbreviation for the syntax rule

$$\frac{X:\theta}{X:\theta'}$$

i.e., for any type assignment π and phrase X, $\pi \vdash X:\theta$ implies $\pi \vdash X:\theta'$, so that, in any context where phrases of type θ' are expected, any phrase of type θ can be used as well. Sometimes θ is termed a "sub-type" of θ'; however, a "sub-type" need not be interpreted as a subset. For example, consider the following coercions, which we have already discussed:

$$\mathbf{var}[\tau] \vdash \mathbf{exp}[\tau]$$

$$\mathbf{val}[\tau] \vdash \mathbf{exp}[\tau]$$

for every data type τ. The domains of variable and value meanings are not subsets of the domain of expression meanings.

It is natural to require reflexivity ($\theta \vdash \theta$) and transitivity ($\theta_1 \vdash \theta_2$ and $\theta_2 \vdash \theta_3$ imply $\theta_1 \vdash \theta_3$), so that $\vdash$ is in general a pre-order. We write $\theta \simeq \theta'$ if $\theta \vdash \theta'$ and $\theta' \vdash \theta$; it is easily proved that $\simeq$ is an equivalence relation. Requiring that $\vdash$ be anti-symmetric ($\theta \simeq \theta'$ only if $\theta = \theta'$) would ensure that $\vdash$ is always a partial order, but this is undesirable when it becomes necessary to choose arbitrarily a canonical representative of a $\simeq$-equivalence class.

Semantically, we need to define a *conversion* function

$$[\![\theta \vdash \theta']\!]: [\![\theta]\!] \longrightarrow [\![\theta']\!]$$

whenever $\theta \vdash \theta'$, so that, for any phrase X such that $\pi \vdash X:\theta$,

$$[\![X]\!]_{\pi\theta'} = [\![X]\!]_{\pi\theta} \,;\, [\![\theta \vdash \theta']\!]$$

whenever $\theta \vdash \theta'$. For computational phrase types, we will require that these conversions be strict ($\bot$-preserving) and continuous. For example, the conversion for de-referencing may be defined as follows:

$$[\![\mathbf{var}(\tau) \vdash \mathbf{exp}[\tau]]\!]vs = \begin{cases} s(v(s)), & \text{if } v(s) \in [\tau] \\ \bot, & \text{if } v(s) = \bot. \end{cases}$$

To preclude ambiguity, we require that $[\![\theta \vdash \theta]\!]$ be the identity function on $[\![\theta]\!]$, and that, when $\theta_1 \vdash \theta_2$ and $\theta_2 \vdash \theta_3$, $[\![\theta_1 \vdash \theta_3]\!]$ be equal to the composite conversion $[\![\theta_1 \vdash \theta_2]\!] \,;\, [\![\theta_2 \vdash \theta_3]\!]$.

We will also want to define a non-trivial pre-order (also denoted $\vdash$) on *data-type* names. For example, we can introduce new data-type symbols **int** and **real** with $[\![\mathbf{int}]\!]$ and $[\![\mathbf{real}]\!]$ as the sets of integer and real numbers, respectively, and then specify that $\mathbf{nat} \vdash \mathbf{int} \vdash \mathbf{real}$, with the corresponding conversions, $[\![\mathbf{nat} \vdash \mathbf{int}]\!]$ and $[\![\mathbf{int} \vdash \mathbf{real}]\!]$, being the obvious injections. A Hasse diagram of the resulting data-type pre-order is then

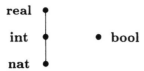

We will then want every such data-type coercion $\tau \vdash \tau'$ to induce the following coercions on *phrase* types:

$$\mathbf{val}[\tau] \vdash \mathbf{val}[\tau']$$

$$\mathbf{exp}[\tau] \vdash \mathbf{exp}[\tau']$$

For example, an integer-valued expression should be usable wherever an expression producing reals is, because any integer value it produces can be converted to a real number. In general:

$$[\![\mathbf{val}[\tau] \vdash \mathbf{val}[\tau']]\!] = [\![\tau \vdash \tau']\!]_\perp$$
$$[\![\mathbf{exp}[\tau] \vdash \mathbf{exp}[\tau']]\!]e = e \,;\, [\![\tau \vdash \tau']\!]_\perp,$$

for all $e \in [\![\mathbf{exp}[\tau]]\!]$, where $[\![\tau \vdash \tau']\!]_\perp$ is the strict extension of

$$[\![\tau \vdash \tau']\!]\colon [\![\tau]\!] \to [\![\tau']\!]$$

to $[\![\tau]\!]_\perp \to [\![\tau']\!]_\perp$.

We can also introduce coercions on *functional* and *procedural* types; these are determined by the coercibility of their argument and result types as follows:

$$\theta_0 \to \theta_1 \vdash \theta_0' \to \theta_1' \text{ whenever } \theta_0' \vdash \theta_0 \text{ and } \theta_1 \vdash \theta_1'.$$

Notice that the $\to$ operator is monotone in its second operand but *anti-monotone* in its first operand. For example, a procedure expecting a **real**-valued phrase should be usable wherever it is possible to use a procedure with the same result type but expecting an **int**-valued phrase as an actual parameter, because an integer argument can be converted to a real value for the procedure. The conversion in general is defined by

$$[\![\theta_0 \to \theta_1 \vdash \theta_0' \to \theta_1']\!]f = [\![\theta_0' \vdash \theta_0]\!] \,;\, f \,;\, [\![\theta_1 \vdash \theta_1']\!],$$

where f is a function from $[\![\theta_0]\!]$ to $[\![\theta_1]\!]$.

Finally, it is convenient to introduce new phrase types **1** and **0** such that

$$\theta \vdash \mathbf{1} \text{ and } \mathbf{0} \vdash \theta$$

for *every* phrase type θ. As a result, **1** is a *greatest* type and **0** is a *least* type in the pre-order of phrase types.

We allow *every* phrase to have type **1** by adding the syntax rule

$$\overline{X \colon \mathbf{1}}$$

so that any phrase X has (at least) type **1** in *every* phrase-type assignment. But only phrases that are intuitively type-incorrect in a phrase-type assignment will have **1** as their *least* type in that phrase-type assignment. Phrase type **1** can be interpreted as denoting a singleton domain $\{\bot\}$; then $[\![\theta \vdash \mathbf{1}]\!]$ would be the unique function from $[\![\theta]\!]$ to $[\![\mathbf{1}]\!]$, and

$$cond_1(e, m_0, m_1) = \bot.$$

A complete program whose least type is **1** should be considered as erroneous, and need not be executed because it has a trivial meaning. But, in order that errors can be localized, we would expect a compiler to generate a message for any phrase whose least type is **1** when none of its sub-phrases have least type **1**; however, this should be only a *warning* message, because, in general, a phrase need not have least type **1** when a proper component does. For example,

let x be P in skip

has type **comm**, even when the least type of P is **1**.

The least type **0** and the coercion $\mathbf{0} \vdash \theta$ are interpreted as follows:

$$[\![\mathbf{0}]\!] = \{\bot\}$$
$$[\![\mathbf{0} \vdash \theta]\!]z = \bot_\theta$$

Type **0** is not particularly useful, but we can replace the family of constants **undef**$[\theta]$ by the following single constant:

Undefined:

$\overline{\textbf{undef}: \mathbf{0}}$

because its value $(\bot)$ converts to the least element of any phrase type.

This completes the description of the coercion system for our language. Our aim now is to demonstrate that the design is satisfactory by proving that the syntax and semantics have appropriate properties.

The first step is to demonstrate that there is a syntactic valuation $\langle \cdot \rangle$ on phrases such that, for any phrase X and phrase-type assignment π with $free(X) \subseteq \mathrm{dom}\,\pi$, $\langle X \rangle \pi$ is a *least* type of X in π. This ensures that the language with coercions has most of the desirable attributes of explicitly-typed languages.

Some of the equations defining $\langle \cdot \rangle$ are as follows:

$$\langle 0 \rangle \pi = \mathbf{val}[\mathbf{nat}]$$
$$\langle \iota \rangle \pi = \pi(\iota)$$
$$\langle \lambda \iota {:} \theta.\, P \rangle \pi = \theta \rightarrow (\langle P \rangle(\pi \mid \iota \mapsto \theta))$$
$$\langle P\,Q \rangle \pi = \begin{cases} \theta', & \text{if } \langle P \rangle \pi = \theta \rightarrow \theta' \text{ and } \langle Q \rangle \pi \vdash \theta, \\ \mathbf{1}, & \text{otherwise}; \end{cases}$$
$$\langle \mathbf{let}\ \iota\ \mathbf{be}\ P\ \mathbf{in}\ Q \rangle \pi = \langle Q \rangle(\pi \mid \iota \mapsto \langle P \rangle \pi)$$
$$\langle V := E \rangle \pi = \begin{cases} \mathbf{comm}, & \text{if } \langle V \rangle \pi = \mathbf{var}[\tau] \text{ and } \langle E \rangle \pi \vdash \mathbf{exp}[\tau], \\ \mathbf{1}, & \text{otherwise}; \end{cases}$$

$$\langle \mathbf{not}\, B\rangle\pi = \begin{cases} \mathbf{val[bool]}, & \text{if } \langle B\rangle\pi \vdash \mathbf{val[bool]}, \\ \mathbf{exp[bool]}, & \text{if } \langle B\rangle\pi \vdash \mathbf{val[bool]} \text{ fails to hold} \\ & \text{but } \langle B\rangle\pi \vdash \mathbf{exp[bool]}, \\ \mathbf{1}, & \text{otherwise}; \end{cases}$$

Most of the remaining equations would be similar, but *conditional* phrases require a detailed treatment.

Suppose $\langle B\rangle\pi \vdash \mathbf{val[bool]}$; then the least type of **if** B **then** X_0 **else** X_1 in π should be a *least upper bound* of $\langle X_0\rangle\pi$ and $\langle X_1\rangle\pi$, and similarly if $\langle B\rangle\pi \vdash \mathbf{val[bool]}$ fails to hold but $\langle B\rangle\pi \vdash \mathbf{exp[bool]}$, except that if the least upper bound is a value-like type ($\mathbf{val}[\tau]$ or of the form $\theta \to \theta'$ for θ' value-like), it must be "raised" to the corresponding expression-like type (respectively, $\mathbf{exp}[\tau]$ or $\theta \to \theta''$, where θ'' is the expression-like type corresponding to θ'). If $\langle B\rangle\pi \vdash \mathbf{exp[bool]}$ fails to hold, then the least type of **if** B **then** X_0 **else** X_1 in π is **1**.

This means that, for any pair of types θ and θ', there must be a *least upper bound* $\theta \sqcup \theta'$ in the phrase-type pre-order. For example, the least upper bound of $\mathbf{val[int]}$ and $\mathbf{var[real]}$ is $\mathbf{exp[real]}$. For the non-procedural types, the existence of a least upper bound $\theta \sqcup \theta'$ for any pair of types θ and θ' is easily checked. For procedural types with a non-trivial common upper bound,

$$(\theta_0 \to \theta_0') \sqcup (\theta_1 \to \theta_1') = (\theta_0 \sqcap \theta_1) \to (\theta_0' \sqcup \theta_1')$$

and so we *also* need the existence of a greatest lower bound $\theta \sqcap \theta'$ for any pair of types θ and θ' that have a common lower bound; but this is also true for our system of types, and in particular,

$$(\theta_0 \to \theta_0') \sqcap (\theta_1 \to \theta_1') = (\theta_0 \sqcup \theta_1) \to (\theta_0' \sqcap \theta_1').$$

We now verify that valuation $\langle \cdot \rangle$ has the desired properties; i.e., that any phrase has its least type as one of its types, and that the least type of a phrase does coerce into any type that the phrase has.

Proposition 7.1 *For any phrase X and phrase-type assignment π with* $\mathrm{dom}\, \pi \supseteq \mathit{free}(X)$,

(a) $\pi \vdash X : \langle X\rangle\pi$;

(b) *if* $\pi \vdash X : \theta$ *then* $\langle X\rangle\pi \vdash \theta$.

Each part can be proved by structural induction; we present two cases.

1. Case $X = P\,Q$. Assume $\langle P\,Q\rangle\pi = \theta' \not\simeq \mathbf{1}$; then, for some θ, $\langle P\rangle\pi = \theta \to \theta'$ and $\langle Q\rangle\pi \vdash \theta$. But then, by induction, $\pi \vdash P : \theta \to \theta'$ and $\pi \vdash Q : \theta$, and so $\pi \vdash P\,Q : \theta'$. For the second part, assume that $\pi \vdash P\,Q : \theta'$ because $\pi \vdash P : \theta \to \theta'$ and $\pi \vdash Q : \theta$; we need to prove that $\langle P\,Q\rangle\pi \vdash \theta'$. By induction, $\langle P\rangle\pi \vdash \theta \to \theta'$ and so $\langle P\rangle\pi = \hat\theta \to \hat\theta'$ such that $\theta \vdash \hat\theta$ and $\hat\theta' \vdash \theta'$. By induction, $\langle Q\rangle\pi \vdash \theta \vdash \hat\theta$, and so, from the definition of $\langle \cdot \rangle$, $\langle P\,Q\rangle\pi = \hat\theta' \vdash \theta'$.

2. Case $X = \lambda\iota\!:\!\theta.\,P$. Assume $\langle\lambda\iota\!:\!\theta.\,P\rangle\pi = \theta \to \theta'$ with $\langle P\rangle(\pi \mid \iota \mapsto \theta) = \theta'$; then, by induction, $(\pi \mid \iota \mapsto \theta) \vdash P\!:\!\theta'$, and so $\pi \vdash \lambda\iota\!:\!\theta.\,P\!:\!\theta \to \theta'$. For the second part, assume $(\pi \mid \iota \mapsto \theta) \vdash P\!:\!\theta'$ and so $\pi \vdash \lambda\iota\!:\!\theta.\,P\!:\!\theta \to \theta'$; then, by induction, $\langle P\rangle(\pi \mid \iota \mapsto \theta) \vdash \theta'$ and so

$$\langle\lambda\iota\!:\!\theta.\,P\rangle\pi = \theta \to \langle P\rangle(\pi \mid \iota \mapsto \theta) \vdash \theta \to \theta'. \quad \square$$

It is evident that, for any $\iota \in (\mathrm{dom}\,\pi' \cap \mathrm{dom}\,\pi)$, if $\pi'(\iota) \vdash \pi(\iota)$ then $\langle\iota\rangle\pi' \vdash \langle\iota\rangle\pi$; remarkably, a property of this kind can be proved for *all* phrases in our language. In order to state the general result compactly, we re-define $\pi' \vdash \pi$ as follows:

$$\pi' \vdash \pi \text{ iff } \mathrm{dom}\,\pi \subseteq \mathrm{dom}\,\pi' \text{ and, for all } \iota \in \mathrm{dom}\,\pi, \pi'(\iota) \vdash \pi(\iota)$$

It is easily verified that $\pi' \vdash X\!:\!\theta$ whenever $\pi' \vdash \pi$ and $\pi \vdash X\!:\!\theta$. Notice that, when the pre-order on phrase types is discrete ($\theta' \vdash \theta$ only if $\theta' = \theta$), the definition of $\pi' \vdash \pi$ reduces to the definition given in Section 4.1, and that $\vdash$, viewed as a binary relation on phrase-type assignments, is a pre-order.

Proposition 7.2 (Monotonicity of $\langle\cdot\rangle$)   *For any phrase X and phrase-type assignments π' and π with $\mathrm{dom}\,\pi \supseteq \mathrm{free}(X)$, if $\pi' \vdash \pi$ then $\langle X\rangle\pi' \vdash \langle X\rangle\pi$.*

The proof is by structural induction; we present two cases:

1. Case $X = PQ$. Assume $\langle PQ\rangle\pi = \theta_1$ with $\langle P\rangle\pi = \theta_0 \to \theta_1$ and $\langle Q\rangle\pi \vdash \theta_0$. By induction, $\langle P\rangle\pi' = \theta_0' \to \theta_1'$ with $\theta_0' \to \theta_1' \vdash \theta_0 \to \theta_1$, and

$$\langle Q\rangle\pi' \vdash \langle Q\rangle\pi \vdash \theta_0 \vdash \theta_0'$$

and so $\langle PQ\rangle\pi' = \theta_1' \vdash \theta_1$.

2. Case $X = \lambda\iota\!:\!\theta.\,P$. Assume $\langle\lambda\iota\!:\!\theta.\,P\rangle\pi = \theta \to \langle P\rangle(\pi \mid \iota \mapsto \theta)$; $\pi' \vdash \pi$ implies $(\pi' \mid \iota \mapsto \theta) \vdash (\pi \mid \iota \mapsto \theta)$ so that, by induction,

$$\langle P\rangle(\pi' \mid \iota \mapsto \theta) \vdash \langle P\rangle(\pi \mid \iota \mapsto \theta)$$

and so

$$\langle\lambda\iota\!:\!\theta.\,P\rangle\pi' = \theta \to \langle P\rangle(\pi' \mid \iota \mapsto \theta) \vdash \theta \to \langle P\rangle(\pi \mid \iota \mapsto \theta). \quad \square$$

Our final task is to ensure that no combination of coercions and generic constructions is semantically ambiguous. We do this by proving the following strengthening of the Coherence Lemma (4.2):

Proposition 7.3   *If π' and π are phrase-type assignments such that $\pi' \vdash \pi$, then, for any phrase X with $\mathrm{dom}\,\pi \supseteq \mathrm{free}(X)$,*

$$[\![X]\!]_{\pi'\theta'} \; ; [\![\theta' \vdash \theta]\!] = [\![\pi' \vdash \pi]\!] \; ; [\![X]\!]_{\pi\theta},$$

where $\theta' = \langle X \rangle \pi'$, $\theta = \langle X \rangle \pi$, and $[\![\pi' \vdash \pi]\!]: [\![\pi']\!] \to [\![\pi]\!]$ is defined component-wise; i.e.,

$$[\![\pi' \vdash \pi]\!] u' \iota = [\![\pi'(\iota) \vdash \pi(\iota)]\!] (u'(\iota))$$

for every $u' \in [\![\pi']\!]$ and $\iota \in \text{dom}\,\pi$.

The proposition states that the following diagram commutes:

where θ' and θ are the least types of X in π' and π, respectively, so that $\theta' \vdash \theta$, by Proposition 7.2.

For example, suppose $\pi' \vdash \pi$ with $\pi'(b) = \pi(b) = \text{exp[bool]}$, $\pi'(v_1) = \pi'(v_2) = \text{var}[\tau]$, and $\pi(v_1) = \pi(v_2) = \text{exp}[\tau]$, so that

$$\theta' = \langle \text{if } b \text{ then } v_1 \text{ else } v_2 \rangle \pi' = \text{var}[\tau]$$

and

$$\theta = \langle \text{if } b \text{ then } v_1 \text{ else } v_2 \rangle \pi = \text{exp}[\tau];$$

then the proposition ensures that both derivations of

$$\pi' \vdash \text{if } b \text{ then } v_1 \text{ else } v_2 \colon \text{exp}[\tau]$$

yield the same semantics, and similarly for other combinations of coercions and generic constructions.

The proposition can be proved by structural induction; the two basic cases are as follows:

1. Case $X = P\,Q$. Let $\langle P\,Q \rangle \pi' = \theta'_1$ with $\langle P \rangle \pi' = \theta'_0 \to \theta'_1$ and $\langle Q \rangle \pi' \vdash \theta'_0$, and $\langle P\,Q \rangle \pi = \theta_1$ with $\langle P \rangle \pi = \theta_0 \to \theta_1$ and $\langle Q \rangle \pi \vdash \theta_0$, and consider any $u' \in [\![\pi']\!]$; then

$$[\![P\,Q]\!]_{\pi \theta_1} ([\![\pi' \vdash \pi]\!] u')$$
$$= [\![P]\!]_{\pi(\theta_0 \to \theta_1)} ([\![\pi' \vdash \pi]\!] u') \Big([\![Q]\!]_{\pi \theta_0} ([\![\pi' \vdash \pi]\!] u') \Big)$$
$$= [\![\theta'_0 \to \theta'_1 \vdash \theta_0 \to \theta_1]\!] ([\![P]\!]_{\pi'(\theta'_0 \to \theta'_1)} (u')) \Big([\![Q]\!]_{\pi \theta_0} ([\![\pi' \vdash \pi]\!] u') \Big)$$
(by induction on P)
$$= [\![\theta'_1 \vdash \theta_1]\!] ([\![P]\!]_{\pi'(\theta'_0 \to \theta'_1)} (u')(q))$$

where

$$q = [\![\theta_0 \vdash \theta_0']\!]\Big([\![Q]\!]_{\pi\theta_0}([\![\pi' \vdash \pi]\!]u')\Big)$$

$$= [\![\langle Q \rangle \pi \vdash \theta_0']\!]\Big([\![Q]\!]_{\pi(\langle Q \rangle \pi)}([\![\pi' \vdash \pi]\!]u')\Big)$$

$$= [\![\langle Q \rangle \pi' \vdash \theta_0']\!]([\![Q]\!]_{\pi'(\langle Q \rangle \pi')}(u'))$$

(by induction on Q)

$$= [\![Q]\!]_{\pi'\theta_0'}.$$

2. Case $X = \lambda\iota\!:\!\theta.\,P$. Let $\langle \lambda\iota\!:\!\theta.\,P \rangle \pi' = \theta \to \theta_1'$ with $\theta_1' = \langle P \rangle (\pi' \mid \iota \mapsto \theta)$, and $\langle \lambda\iota\!:\!\theta.\,P \rangle \pi = \theta \to \theta_1$ with $\theta_1 = \langle P \rangle (\pi \mid \iota \mapsto \theta)$, and consider any $u' \in [\![\pi']\!]$ and $a \in [\![\theta]\!]$; then

$$[\![\lambda\iota\!:\!\theta.\,P]\!]_{\pi(\theta \to \theta_1)}([\![\pi' \vdash \pi]\!]u')(a)$$

$$= [\![P]\!]_{(\pi\mid\iota\mapsto\theta)\theta_1}([\![\pi' \vdash \pi]\!]u' \mid \iota \mapsto a)$$

$$= [\![P]\!]_{(\pi\mid\iota\mapsto\theta)\theta_1}\Big([\![(\pi' \mid \iota \mapsto \theta) \vdash (\pi \mid \iota \mapsto \theta)]\!](u' \mid \iota \mapsto a)\Big)$$

$$= [\![\theta_1' \vdash \theta_1]\!]([\![P]\!]_{(\pi\mid\iota\mapsto\theta)\theta_1'}(u' \mid \iota \mapsto a)) \qquad \text{(by induction)}$$

$$= [\![\theta \to \theta_1' \vdash \theta \to \theta_1]\!]([\![\lambda\iota\!:\!\theta.\,P]\!]_{\pi'(\theta \to \theta_1')}(u'))(a). \quad \square$$

The case $X = (E_0 = E_1)$ is noteworthy when both operands are of type **nat** because it is indeterminate whether the equality operation on natural, integer, or real numbers is used, and similarly if both operands are of type **int**; but there is no semantic ambiguity because the corresponding numerical conversions are *injective* (one-to-one) functions.

Similarly, we could add a generic addition operation to the language as follows:

Addition:

$$\frac{E_1\!:\mathbf{val}[\tau] \quad E_2\!:\mathbf{val}[\tau]}{E_1 + E_2\!:\mathbf{val}[\tau]}$$

where **nat** $\vdash \tau \vdash$ **real**; to prevent ambiguity, the following diagram must commute whenever **nat** $\vdash \tau' \vdash \tau \vdash$ **real**:

$$
\begin{array}{ccc}
[\![\tau']\!] \times [\![\tau']\!] & \xrightarrow{\;[\![+]\!]_{\tau'}\;} & [\![\tau']\!] \\
\downarrow \qquad \downarrow & & \downarrow \\
[\![\tau]\!] \times [\![\tau]\!] & \xrightarrow{\;[\![+]\!]_{\tau}\;} & [\![\tau]\!]
\end{array}
$$

where the horizontal arrows are the meanings of the addition operator for data types τ' and τ, and each of the vertical arrows is the conversion $[\![\tau' \vdash \tau]\!]$. This condition is satisfied by the usual definitions of addition on natural numbers, integers, and reals (disregarding overflow and round-off errors).

We can also allow the operator + to be used on numerical *expressions* because we have the following kind of commutativity:

$$
\begin{array}{ccc}
[\![\mathbf{val}[\tau]]\!] \times [\![\mathbf{val}[\tau]]\!] & \xrightarrow{\;[\![+]\!]_{\mathbf{val}[\tau]}\;} & [\![\mathbf{val}[\tau]]\!] \\
\downarrow \qquad\quad \downarrow & & \downarrow \\
[\![\mathbf{exp}[\tau]]\!] \times [\![\mathbf{exp}[\tau]]\!] & \xrightarrow{\;[\![+]\!]_{\mathbf{exp}[\tau]}\;} & [\![\mathbf{exp}[\tau]]\!]
\end{array}
$$

where the vertical arrows are conversions, and similarly for all of the other operators that might be used on both expressions and value phrases, such as =, **not**, **and**, <, **succ**, etc.

In summary, our language demonstrates that coercions are not *necessarily* undesirable, provided that the appropriate syntactic and semantic properties are rigorously verified to ensure non-ambiguity.

7.2   Local Variables

Instead of providing all of the variables once and for all in the initial environment, programming languages since ALGOL 60 have allowed for *dynamically-created* variables; i.e., provided a way for a programmer to specify the creation of "new" variables during program execution, and, sometimes, a way to dispose of such variables. In fact, ALGOL 60 provided only a very structured form of dynamic storage, the *locally-declared* variable, whose lifetime is determined by the scope of the identifier that denotes it. This allows for more efficient use of memory and more control of interference between program parts than fully-static storage, but is much simpler to use and implement than fully-dynamic storage.

To provide this kind of facility in our example language, we introduce a family of quantifier constants

$$\mathbf{new}[\tau]\colon (\mathbf{var}[\tau] \to \mathbf{comm}) \to \mathbf{comm}$$

so that

$$\# \, \mathbf{new}[\tau] \, \iota . \, C$$

is a variable-declaration block with command C as its body. A new variable is created for each execution of such a block, and that variable can be de-allocated by the implementation when that execution is finished. For example, the simple **for** loop described in Section 3.1 can now be defined by the following equivalence:

$$\mathbf{for} \; N \; \mathbf{do} \; C \; \equiv \; \# \, \mathbf{new}[\mathbf{nat}] \, \iota . \, \iota := N \, ; \, \mathbf{while} \; \iota \neq 0 \; \mathbf{do} \; \iota := \iota - 1 \, ; C$$

where ι is not free in N or C; more complex loop forms can be similarly treated.

In the rest of this section, we briefly describe the technique that has traditionally been used in denotational semantics to treat dynamic storage. The essential idea is that components of the state are indexed, not by identifiers, but by special values, termed *locations*, which can be thought of as abstract storage addresses. Allocation and de-allocation of variables can then be treated by recording in the state itself whether or not each component is currently "in use." If locations themselves are storable values, it is possible to describe the semantics of features such as the "pointer" types in PASCAL that permit creation and use of dynamically-linked structures.

This suggests the following definition of the set of states:

$$S = L \longrightarrow (V + \{unused\}),$$

where L is a suitable set of locations (e.g., the set of natural numbers), V is the set of storable values, and $+$ denotes disjoint union of sets. For simplicity, in this section we shall assume that there is a single set V containing all of the storable values, and that $unused \notin V$, so that "tags" are unnecessary in forming elements of the disjoint union. The following functions would then allow storage components to be allocated and de-allocated, and the values of the components to be accessed and updated:

$$new\colon S \longrightarrow L_{\perp}$$
$$lose\colon L \longrightarrow [\![\mathbf{comm}]\!]$$
$$contents\colon L \longrightarrow (S \longrightarrow V_{\perp})$$
$$update\colon L \longrightarrow (V \longrightarrow [\![\mathbf{comm}]\!])$$

The first of these can be any "choice" function such that, for any $s \in S$, $s(new(s)) = unused$ if there exists some $l \in L$ such that $s(l) = unused$, and $new(s) = \perp$ otherwise. The remaining functions are defined as follows:

$$lose(l)(s) = (s \mid l \mapsto unused)$$
$$contents(l)(s) = \begin{cases} v, & \text{if } s(l) = v \in V; \\ \perp, & \text{if } s(l) = unused. \end{cases}$$
$$update(l)(v)(s) = (s \mid l \mapsto v)$$

This approach to the semantics of dynamic storage corresponds to the way implementations deal with fully-dynamic storage, but not to the conventional implementation of local-variable declarations. The unsatisfactory nature of the semantic interpretation can be seen by trying to show the equivalence of

$$\# \, \mathbf{new}[\mathbf{nat}] \, n.\, n := 0;$$
$$c;$$
$$\mathbf{if} \, n = 0 \, \mathbf{then} \, \mathbf{diverge}$$

and **diverge**, where c is a non-local identifier of type **comm**. Intuitively, the meaning of c cannot access the "new" local variable n, and so the value of n must still be 0 after execution of c (unless the execution of c itself fails to terminate), and so any execution of the block must fail to terminate; but, semantically, c can range over *arbitrary* command meanings, including those that can update the location denoted by n, and so the equivalence fails.

A more sophisticated approach to the semantics of local-variable declarations will be described in Section 9.4.

7.3   Product Types and Arrays

In this section, we add to our language a simple form of "structured" type similar to the "classes" of SIMULA, the "records" of ALGOL W, PASCAL and ML, and the "modules" of languages such as MODULA 2, and consider how *arrays* can be treated.

The first step is to introduce a new kind of phrase-type expression, as follows:

$$\theta ::= \cdots \mid \iota_1 \mapsto \theta_1 \,\&\, \cdots \,\&\, \iota_n \mapsto \theta_n \quad (\iota_i \text{ distinct})$$

The new types are termed *product* types; notice that they are *phrase* types, rather than *data* types. Each of the *field types* θ_i can be any of the (phrase) types, and each of the *field names* ι_i can be any identifier (different from the other field names of that product type). Semantically,

$$[\![\iota_1 \mapsto \theta_1 \,\&\, \cdots \,\&\, \iota_n \mapsto \theta_n]\!] = \prod_{i=1}^{n} [\![\theta_i]\!]$$

that is, a product type denotes the set of all n-tuples of meanings of appropriate type, ordered component-wise.

We now consider what coercions are to be allowed on products. We want product types to be monotonic with respect to their component types:

$$\iota_1 \mapsto \theta_1 \,\&\, \cdots \,\&\, \iota_n \mapsto \theta_n \vdash \iota_1 \mapsto \theta'_1 \,\&\, \cdots \,\&\, \iota_n \mapsto \theta'_n$$

if, for all $1 \le i \le n$, $\theta_i \vdash \theta'_i$. But we also want to allow components that are unnecessary in some context to be "dropped"; the general coercion on product types should then be as follows:

$$\iota_1 \mapsto \theta_1 \,\&\, \cdots \,\&\, \iota_n \mapsto \theta_n \vdash \iota'_1 \mapsto \theta'_1 \,\&\, \cdots \,\&\, \iota'_m \mapsto \theta'_m$$

if $\{\iota'_1, \ldots, \iota'_m\} \subseteq \{\iota_1, \ldots, \iota_n\}$ and $\theta_i \vdash \theta'_j$ whenever $\iota'_j = \iota_i$. Notice that, as a binary relation on phrase-type expressions, $\vdash$ is now a pre-order that is *not* a partial order: product types that differ only by a permutation of

---

let *counter*(*user*: (*inc* $\mapsto$ **comm** & *val* $\mapsto$ **exp**[**nat**]) $\rightarrow$ **comm**) =
  # new[**nat**] *n*. *n* := 0;
    user(*inc* $\mapsto$ *n* := *n* + 1, *val* $\mapsto$ *n*)
  in

$\vdots$

(**#** *counter c*.
  $\cdots$ *c.inc* ; $\cdots$ *c.val* $\cdots$)

$\vdots$

Table 7.1 A class of counter objects.

fields are $\simeq$-equivalent but not equal. The conversion corresponding to the coercion is defined as follows:

$$\llbracket \iota_1 \mapsto \theta_1 \& \cdots \& \iota_n \mapsto \theta_n \vdash \iota_1' \mapsto \theta_1' \& \cdots \& \iota_m' \mapsto \theta_m' \rrbracket(p)(j)$$
$$= \quad \llbracket \theta_i \vdash \theta_j' \rrbracket(p(i))$$

when $\iota_j' = \iota_i$.

To allow meanings of product types to be expressed and used, we add the following syntax rules:

Product Introduction:

$$\frac{X_i\colon \theta_i \quad \text{for every } i = 1, \ldots . n}{\iota_1 \mapsto X_1, \ldots, \iota_n \mapsto X_n\colon \iota_1 \mapsto \theta_1 \& \cdots \& \iota_n \mapsto \theta_n} \quad (\iota_i \text{ distinct})$$

Field Selection:

$$\frac{P\colon \iota \mapsto \theta}{P.\iota\colon \theta}$$

The rule for Field Selection can be particularly simple because only the field being selected need be mentioned explicitly; the other fields are simply dropped by the coercion on product types. The occurrences of ι as a field name in $\ldots, \iota \mapsto X, \ldots$ and $P.\iota$ are not conventional identifier occurrences; for example, they are not subject to substitutions.

We present an example of how these facilities could be used for doing "object-oriented" programming. The program fragment in Table 7.1 illustrates how to define a class of "counter" objects, whose capabilities are limited to incrementation and evaluation, and create an instance of the class. The procedural parameter *user* may be thought of as a typical "customer" for an instance of the counter class. Note that the representation of a counter (i.e., variable n) is a "private" variable, not directly accessible to users. In more complex examples, private *procedures* might also be necessary.

Semantically, we define

$$[\![\iota_1 \mapsto X_1, \ldots, \iota_n \mapsto X_n]\!](u)(i) = [\![X_i]\!]u,$$

for $1 \leq i \leq n$,

$$[\![P.\iota]\!]_{\pi\theta}(u) = [\![P]\!]_{\pi(\iota \mapsto \theta)}(u)(1)$$

and

$$cond_{\iota_1 \mapsto \theta_1 \& \cdots \& \iota_n \mapsto \theta_n}(b, p_1, p_2)(i) = cond_{\theta_i}(b, p_1(i), p_2(i))$$

for $1 \leq i \leq n$, provided $cond_{\theta_i}$ is definable for each of the θ_i.

The following equivalences can now be validated:

- for any $X_i \colon \theta_i$ $(1 \leq i \leq n)$,

$$(\iota_1 \mapsto X_1, \ldots, \iota_n \mapsto X_n).\iota_i \quad \equiv_{\theta_i} \quad X_i;$$

- for $\theta = \iota_1 \mapsto \theta_1 \& \cdots \& \iota_n \mapsto \theta_n$ and any $P \colon \theta$,

$$(\iota_1 \mapsto P.\iota_1, \ldots, \iota_n \mapsto P.\iota_n) \quad \equiv_\theta \quad P;$$

- for any $B \colon \mathbf{exp[bool]}$ and $P_1, P_2 \colon \iota \mapsto \theta$,

$$(\textbf{if } B \textbf{ then } P_1 \textbf{ else } P_2).\iota \quad \equiv_\theta \quad \textbf{if } B \textbf{ then } P_1.\iota \textbf{ else } P_2.\iota,$$

and similarly if $B \colon \mathbf{val[bool]}$.

Arrays differ from products in two ways: components of arrays can be selected by using a *computed* "index" (rather than an explicit field name), and, to allow a practical implementation and type-checking, all of the components of an array must have the same type. Programming languages typically provide arrays in two specialized and unrelated forms: as conventional arrays of variables and in "case" constructions, which involve indexing into what are essentially arrays of commands or expressions. Furthermore, the only substantive difference between conventional arrays and procedures with **var** result types is representation. We can unify and generalize all of these possibilities by simply regarding arrays as procedures, rather than introducing specialized types into the language.

For example, a programmer can, in principle, define a procedure *NewRealVarArray* as in Table 7.2; then,

$$\# \, NewRealVarArray(n)A. \; \cdots A(i) \cdots$$

declares A to be an "array" of n new real-valued variables. The allowable "subscripts" are expressions whose values are natural numbers less than n.

The implementation of *NewRealVarArray* works as follows. Each call of *allocate* (except the last) declares one real variable, passing on a procedure that allows access to this new variable and also to previously-allocated ones. The last call of *allocate* (when i reaches *size*) applies the *user* procedure to the array of variables, represented by the procedure. This technique is

---

```
let NewRealVarArray
    (size: exp[nat],
     user: (exp[nat] → var[real]) → comm) =
    letrec allocate(i: exp[nat], a: exp[nat] → var[real]): comm =
    if i = size then user(a) else
        # new[real] x.
        let newa(j: exp[nat]) = if i = j then x else a(j)
        in allocate(succ i, newa)
    in allocate(0, undef[exp[nat] → var[real]])
in   · · ·
```

Table 7.2 An array declarator.

possible even in languages such as PASCAL that are supposed not to have
dynamic arrays. In practice, equivalent but more efficient implementations
of *NewRealVarArray* and similar quantifiers should be provided as the values of constants or pre-defined identifiers.

7.4   Acceptors

The treatment of variables in our Algol-like language, though typical of
most existing languages, is somewhat asymmetric in that, for every data
type τ, phrases of type **var**$[\tau]$ can be used as both the left- *and* right-hand
sides of assignments, but phrases of type **exp**$[\tau]$ can be used as right-hand
sides *only*. A more symmetric treatment of variables can be achieved by
introducing "write-only variables," phrases that can be used as left-hand
sides of assignments, but not as right-hand sides. For example, if it is
intended that the formal parameter of a procedure is to be used *only* as a
"result" parameter, this should be made explicit in the argument type of
the procedure. Such write-only variables will be termed *acceptors*.

We therefore add new phrase types as follows:

$$\theta ::= \cdots \mid \mathbf{acc}[\tau],$$

replace the syntax rule for assignments by the following rule:

Assignment:

$$\frac{A: \mathbf{acc}[\tau] \quad E: \mathbf{exp}[\tau]}{A := E: \mathbf{comm}}$$

and add a new coercion

$$\mathbf{var}[\tau] \vdash \mathbf{acc}[\tau]$$

for every data type τ to allow conventional variables to be used as left-hand sides of assignments.

Semantically, it is now convenient to regard a variable abstractly as an "object" consisting of two components that correspond to the two ways it can be used: on the right-hand side of assignments as an expression, and on the left-hand side of assignments as an acceptor which accepts an expression meaning and then behaves like a command. Sometimes, the acceptor and expression components of a variable meaning are termed its *l-value* and *r-value*, respectively, referring to the left and right-hand sides of the assignment command. The appropriate domain definitions are as follows:

$$[\![\mathbf{acc}[\tau]]\!] = [\![\mathbf{exp}[\tau]]\!] \to [\![\mathbf{comm}]\!]$$
$$[\![\mathbf{var}[\tau]]\!] = [\![\mathbf{acc}[\tau]]\!] \times [\![\mathbf{exp}[\tau]]\!]$$

The semantic equation for assignment commands is then

$$[\![A := E]\!]u = [\![A]\!]u([\![E]\!]u)$$

and the coercions for variables are interpreted as follows:

$$[\![\mathbf{var}[\tau] \vdash \mathbf{exp}[\tau]]\!](a, e) = e$$
$$[\![\mathbf{var}[\tau] \vdash \mathbf{acc}[\tau]]\!](a, e) = a$$

The variables in the initial environment u_0 for programs can be defined to access and update the "components" of states as follows. For all $\iota \in [\tau]$ for some τ,

$$u_0(\iota) = (a_\iota, e_\iota)$$
$$\text{where } a_\iota(e)(s) = \begin{cases} \text{undefined}, & \text{if } e(s) = \bot \\ (s \mid \iota \mapsto e(s)), & \text{otherwise} \end{cases}$$
$$\text{and } e_\iota(s) = s(\iota).$$

Finally, to allow for conditional acceptors and variables, we define

$$cond_{\mathbf{acc}[\tau]}(b, a_0, a_1)(e) = cond_{\mathbf{comm}}(b, a_0(e), a_1(e))$$

for all $e \in [\![\mathbf{exp}[\tau]]\!]$, and

$$cond_{\mathbf{var}[\tau]}(b, (a_0, e_0), (a_1, e_1)) = (a, e)$$
$$\text{where } a = cond_{\mathbf{acc}[\tau]}(b, a_0, a_1)$$
$$\text{and } e = cond_{\mathbf{exp}[\tau]}(b, e_0, e_1)$$

Note that it is consistent to regard $\mathbf{acc}[\tau]$ as an *abbreviation* of the procedural type $\mathbf{exp}[\tau] \to \mathbf{comm}$, rather than as an additional primitive type. This suggests that any data-type coercion $\tau \vdash \tau'$ should also induce the following coercion on acceptor phrase types:

$$\mathbf{acc}[\tau'] \vdash \mathbf{acc}[\tau],$$

because $\mathbf{exp}[\tau] \vdash \mathbf{exp}[\tau']$. For example, an acceptor for real numbers should be coercible to an acceptor for integers; if the latter is applied to an integer-producing expression, the integer can be converted to a real number.

The addition of acceptor phrases as described above has, however, a subtle defect: if τ_1 and τ_2 are comparable but inequivalent data types, the phrase types $\mathbf{var}[\tau_1]$ and $\mathbf{var}[\tau_2]$ have upper bounds but do not have a *least* upper bound, and this means that the conditional phrase

$$\mathbf{if}\ B\ \mathbf{then}\ X_1\ \mathbf{else}\ X_2$$

is not well-formed if $X_1 \colon \mathbf{var}[\tau_1]$ and $X_2 \colon \mathbf{var}[\tau_2]$. For example, if $\tau_1 = \mathbf{real}$ and $\tau_2 = \mathbf{int}$, both $\mathbf{acc}[\mathbf{int}]$ and $\mathbf{exp}[\mathbf{real}]$ are common upper bounds of $\mathbf{var}[\mathbf{real}]$ and $\mathbf{var}[\mathbf{int}]$, but there is no *least* upper bound:

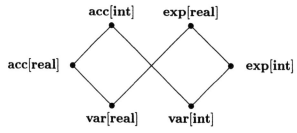

The problem is that the conditional phrase is essentially a variable that can be used as an integer acceptor and as a real expression; however, our type system does not allow for such variables of "mixed type."

The solution to this problem is to introduce new types of the form $\mathbf{acc}[\tau]\ \&\ \mathbf{exp}[\tau']$, which would coerce *both* to $\mathbf{acc}[\tau]$ *and* to $\mathbf{exp}[\tau']$, and would also be greater than any other lower bound. For example, the unlabelled point in the middle of the following Hasse diagram is the new type $\mathbf{acc}[\mathbf{int}]\ \&\ \mathbf{exp}[\mathbf{real}]$, and is now a *least* upper bound for $\mathbf{var}[\mathbf{real}]$ and $\mathbf{var}[\mathbf{int}]$:

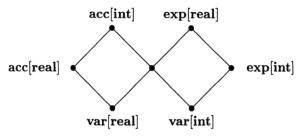

This allows $\mathbf{if}\ B\ \mathbf{then}\ X_1\ \mathbf{else}\ X_2$ when $X_1 \colon \mathbf{var}[\mathbf{real}]$ and $X_2 \colon \mathbf{var}[\mathbf{int}]$. It is actually possible to define a binary operation $\&$ applicable to *any* types, but we will only need types of the form $\mathbf{acc}[\tau]\ \&\ \mathbf{exp}[\tau']$ here.

Semantically, we want $[\![\mathbf{acc}[\tau]\ \&\ \mathbf{exp}[\tau']]\!] = [\![\mathbf{acc}[\tau]]\!] \times [\![\mathbf{exp}[\tau']]\!]$; the coercions from $\mathbf{acc}[\tau]\ \&\ \mathbf{exp}[\tau']$ to $\mathbf{acc}[\tau]$ and $\mathbf{exp}[\tau']$ are the projection functions on $[\![\mathbf{acc}[\tau]]\!] \times [\![\mathbf{exp}[\tau']]\!]$. We can now *define* $\mathbf{var}[\tau]$ to be an abbreviation for $\mathbf{acc}[\tau]\&\mathbf{exp}[\tau]$ (rather than a primitive type); the coercions on the type $\mathbf{acc}[\tau]$ & $\mathbf{exp}[\tau]$ are the coercions desired for $\mathbf{var}[\tau]$.

7.5 Jumps

Those of us who have worked with continuations for some time have soon learned to think of them as natural and in fact often simpler than the earlier methods.

C. Strachey and C. P. Wadsworth (1974)

In this section, we introduce "jumps" into our Algol-like language and discuss the technique of *continuations*, which makes it possible to define compositional semantics of such features.

7.5.1 Completions

The reader may recall that it was convenient in Section 3.4 to assume a program-completion function $k_0 \colon S \rightharpoonup O$ that mapped final states of program execution to program outputs. To allow other ways of "completing" program execution, we introduce a new phrase type of *completions*:

$$\theta ::= \cdots \mid \mathbf{compl}$$

with

$$[\![\mathbf{compl}]\!] = S \rightharpoonup O$$

As examples of completions, we introduce the following new syntax:

Immediate Termination:

$$\overline{\mathbf{stop}\colon \mathbf{compl}}$$

Abortion:

$$\overline{\mathbf{abort}\colon \mathbf{compl}}$$

The intention is that a programmer can use **stop** or **abort** to immediately terminate program execution; **stop** does the usual program finalisation (such as output), whereas **abort** produces an error message.

To specify the semantics of these, we partition the domain of outputs as follows:

$$O = A + \{error\}$$

where *error* represents the error message produced by **abort**, and A is a suitable domain of "answers" (i.e., outputs that are *not* error messages). If we assume $error \notin A$, tags are unnecessary in forming elements of the disjoint union, and then we can define

$$\llbracket \mathbf{skip} \rrbracket uks = k(s)$$

$$\llbracket C_0 \,;\, C_1 \rrbracket uks = \llbracket C_0 \rrbracket u(\llbracket C_1 \rrbracket uk)(s)$$

$$\llbracket \mathbf{diverge} \rrbracket uks = \text{undefined}$$

$$cond_{\mathbf{compl}}(b, k_0, k_1)(s) = \begin{cases} k_0(s), & \text{if } b(s) = \textit{true} \\ k_1(s), & \text{if } b(s) = \textit{false} \\ \text{undefined}, & \text{if } b(s) = \bot \end{cases}$$

$$cond_{\mathbf{comm}}(b, c_0, c_1)(k) = cond_{\mathbf{compl}}(b, c_0(k), c_1(k))$$

Table 7.3 Continuation semantics.

$$\llbracket \mathbf{stop} \rrbracket us = k_0(s)$$

$$\llbracket \mathbf{abort} \rrbracket us = \textit{error}$$

for any environment u and state s, where $k_0 \colon S \rightharpoonup O$ is the standard program-completion function.

However, we have not yet provided a way that such completions can actually be used by a programmer. In many languages, this is done by introducing a command form **goto** K, where K is a completion, but it is simpler to introduce the coercion **compl** ⊢ **comm**, so that a completion can be used wherever a command is expected; the command resulting from the conversion ignores the "normal" continuation of the computation, simply initiating execution of the completion.

To describe the semantics of jumps, we cannot continue to use

$$\llbracket \mathbf{comm} \rrbracket = S \rightharpoonup S,$$

because a command containing a completion might produce a final program output and not an (intermediate) state. Hence, we *re-define* $\llbracket \mathbf{comm} \rrbracket$ to be $\llbracket \mathbf{compl} \rrbracket \rightarrow \llbracket \mathbf{compl} \rrbracket$. Expanding this out, we get

$$\llbracket \mathbf{comm} \rrbracket = (S \rightharpoonup O) \rightarrow S \rightharpoonup O$$

so that, if $c \in \llbracket \mathbf{comm} \rrbracket$, $c(k)(s)$ is a *program output*. The second argument, $s \in S$, is the state *before* execution of the command. The first argument, $k \in (S \rightharpoonup O)$, is termed the *continuation* for the command execution; the continuation specifies how the state *after* execution of the command (if the execution terminates without a jump) is to be mapped into the output for the whole program.

We must now re-define the semantics of all of the forms of command. This new "continuation semantics" for commands is given in Table 7.3; k ranges over $\llbracket \mathbf{compl} \rrbracket$. Intuitively, the equation for command sequencing states that, to execute $C_0 \,;\, C_1$ with continuation k, execute C_0 with a continuation that executes C_1 with continuation k. Note that the first two equations can be simplified to

$$[\![\mathbf{skip}]\!]u = \mathrm{id}_{(S \longrightarrow O)}$$
$$[\![C_0\,;C_1]\!]u = [\![C_0]\!]u \cdot [\![C_1]\!]u$$

It can be verified by a structural induction that, for any command C that does not involve completions, $[\![C]\!]uk$ is equal to $[\![C]\!]u\,;k$, where, in the latter, $[\![\cdot]\!]$ is the "direct" (i.e., non-continuation) semantic valuation for commands used previously. The coercion from completions to commands is then interpreted as follows:

$$[\![\mathbf{compl} \vdash \mathbf{comm}]\!]kk' = k$$

so that

$$[\![K]\!]_{\mathbf{comm}}(u)(k')(s) \;=\; [\![K]\!]_{\mathbf{compl}}(u)(s).$$

The program output will be produced by executing the completion and the "normal" command continuation k' is simply ignored.

Complete programs are now interpreted as follows:

$$[\![C]\!]_{\mathbf{prog}} = g_0\,;[\![C]\!]_{\mathbf{comm}}(u_0)(k_0)$$

where g_0, k_0, and u_0 are the appropriate initialization, completion, and initial environment, respectively, for all programs. The "initial" continuation, k_0, will be applied to the *final* state of program execution, unless there is a "jump" (such as an **abort**) or execution does not terminate.

At present, the only completions explicitly available for use by a programmer are the ones denoted by **stop** and **abort**, which terminate program execution. We can provide for more localized jumps by introducing procedural constants

$$\mathbf{label}, \mathbf{escape} \colon (\mathbf{compl} \rightarrow \mathbf{comm}) \rightarrow \mathbf{comm}$$

and defining them so that the quantified commands

$$\#\,\mathbf{label}\,\iota.\,C$$

and

$$\#\,\mathbf{escape}\,\iota.\,C$$

are executed by executing C in the environment such that execution of ι results in an immediate jump to the *beginning* or *end*, respectively, of C; for the former, execution continues with C itself, and for the latter, execution continues with the rest of the program. Notice that the bound identifier ι can be used in an actual parameter to a non-local procedure, and so it is possible to "jump" out of the body of a procedure to the (beginning or end of) the calling context.

As an example, the following code does a linear search for $x: \mathbf{exp}[\tau]$ in an "array" $f: \mathbf{exp}[\mathbf{nat}] \rightarrow \mathbf{exp}[\tau]$ over the range of "subscripts" from a to b, both of type $\mathbf{exp}[\mathbf{nat}]$:

$$
\begin{aligned}
&\#\ \mathbf{new}[\mathbf{bool}]\ present. \\
&(\#\ \mathbf{escape}\ xFound. \\
&\quad (\#\ iterate(a, b)\ i. \\
&\qquad \mathbf{if}\ f(i) = x\ \mathbf{then} \\
&\qquad\qquad present := \mathbf{true}\ ;\ xFound); \\
&\quad present := \mathbf{false}) \\
&\{present = (x \in f(a..b))\}
\end{aligned}
$$

Quantifier $iterate$ is as defined at the end of Section 6.1. The completion $xFound$ is used to terminate the search as soon as a component equal to x is found.

The semantic equations for the new quantifier constants are as follows:

$$[\mathbf{label}]upk = \bigsqcup\nolimits_{i \in \omega} f^i(\bot), \quad \text{where } f(k') = p(k')(k)$$

$$[\mathbf{escape}]upk = p(k)(k)$$

where p ranges over $[\mathbf{compl}] \rightarrow [\mathbf{comm}]$. From these we derive

$$
\begin{aligned}
[\#\,\mathbf{label}\ \iota.\, C]uk\ &=\ [\mathbf{label}(\lambda\iota : \mathbf{compl}.\, C)]uk \\
&=\ [\mathbf{label}]u([\lambda\iota : \mathbf{compl}.\, C]u)k \\
&=\ \bigsqcup_{i \in \omega} f^i(\bot), \quad \text{where } f(k') = [C](u \mid \iota \mapsto k')(k),
\end{aligned}
$$

and

$$
\begin{aligned}
[\#\,\mathbf{escape}\ \iota.\, C]uk\ &=\ [\mathbf{escape}(\lambda\iota : \mathbf{compl}.\, C)]uk \\
&=\ [\mathbf{escape}]u([\lambda\iota : \mathbf{compl}.\, C]u)(k) \\
&=\ [C](u \mid \iota \mapsto k)(k).
\end{aligned}
$$

Also, we can generalize the sequencing operator to completions, as follows:

Sequencing:

$$\frac{C : \mathbf{comm} \quad K : \mathbf{compl}}{C\ ;\ K : \mathbf{compl}}$$

with interpretation

$$[C\ ;\ K]_{\mathbf{compl}}(u)(s) = [C]u([K]u)s$$

It can be verified that, although $C\ ;\ K$ and $\mathbf{if}\ B\ \mathbf{then}\ K_0\ \mathbf{else}\ K_1$ (for completions K, K_0 and K_1) can be syntactically analyzed as *commands* in two ways, the semantic interpretations are not ambiguous.

7.5.2 Programming Logic

We now consider the effect on our programming logic of introducing jumps into the programming language. First, we must re-interpret the Hoare-triple formula in this context. This is most conveniently done by introducing a new atomic formula, as follows:

Hoare Double:

$$\frac{P: \textbf{assert} \quad K: \textbf{compl}}{\{P\}K: \textbf{spec}}$$

The "Hoare-double" formula, $\{P\}K$, asserts that P is a sufficient precondition on initial states to ensure that terminating executions of K lead to acceptable program output (where, for example, an error message is *not* acceptable). We can then *define* the conventional Hoare triple for commands C by the following equivalence:

$$\{P\}C\{Q\} \quad \equiv_{\textbf{spec}} \quad \forall \iota: \textbf{compl.} \ \{Q\}\iota \Rightarrow \{P\}(C \ ; \iota)$$

for ι not free in P, Q or C. In this context, $\{P\}C\{Q\}$ asserts that P is sufficient to ensure that terminating executions of C lead to acceptable program output when supplied with a continuation for which Q is sufficient to ensure acceptable output on termination.

To define the semantics of the Hoare-double formula, let ϕ be the characteristic function of the A-subset of O; i.e., $\phi(o) = true$ just if $o \in A$. In effect, ϕ is the (implicit) post-condition for *all* completions. We now interpret Hoare-double specifications as follows:

$$[\![\{P\}K]\!]u = \text{for all } s \in S \text{ and } o \in O, [\![P]\!]us \text{ and } [\![K]\!]us = o \text{ imply } \phi(o),$$

which is analogous to the interpretation of Hoare triples in "direct" (i.e., non-continuation) semantics.

The continuation-semantic interpretation of the Hoare triple is now derivable as follows:

$$[\![\{P\}C\{Q\}]\!]u$$
$$= \quad [\![\forall \iota: \textbf{compl.} \ \{Q\}\iota \Rightarrow \{P\}(C;\iota)]\!]u \quad (\iota \text{ not free in } P, Q, \text{ or } C)$$
$$= \quad \text{for all } k \in [\![\textbf{compl}]\!],$$

$$\quad\quad \text{if} \quad \text{for all } s \in S \text{ and } o \in O,$$
$$\quad\quad\quad\quad [\![Q]\!]us \text{ and } k(s) = o \text{ imply } \phi(o)$$
$$\quad\quad \text{then for all } s \in S \text{ and } o \in O,$$
$$\quad\quad\quad\quad [\![P]\!]us \text{ and } [\![C]\!]uks = o \text{ imply } \phi(o).$$

Surprisingly, the re-interpretation of the Hoare-triple formula does not necessitate substantial modification of the formal system. All of the axioms previously discussed remain valid in the present context, except for the following:

$$\{P\}C\{Q_1\} \& \cdots \& \{P\}C\{Q_n\}$$
$$\Rightarrow \{P\}C\{Q_1 \text{ and } \cdots \text{ and } Q_n\}$$

For example, suppose $C = $ **abort** and $n = 0$; the specification

$$\{P\}\textbf{abort}\{\textbf{true}\}$$

is *not* valid (for arbitrary P) because the output will be *error*. The failure of this axiom seems to be the only objective evidence for the widely expressed opinion that reasoning about programs is more difficult if jumps are used. Another example of a formula that was valid in direct semantics, but is invalid in the present context is the equivalence

$$C \text{ ; } \textbf{diverge} \equiv_{\textbf{comm}} \textbf{diverge}$$

The Hoare-like axioms relevant to **stop**, **abort**, labels and escapes are as follows:

$$\{P\}\textbf{stop}\{\textbf{false}\}$$

$$\{\textbf{false}\}\textbf{abort}\{\textbf{false}\}$$

$$\big(\forall \iota\!: \textbf{compl. } \{P\}\iota\{\textbf{false}\} \;\Rightarrow\; \{P\}C\{Q\}\big) \;\Rightarrow\; \{P\}\,\#\,\textbf{label } \iota.\,C\{Q\}$$

$$\big(\forall \iota\!: \textbf{compl. } \{Q\}\iota\{\textbf{false}\} \;\Rightarrow\; \{P\}C\{Q\}\big) \;\Rightarrow\; \{P\}\,\#\,\textbf{escape } \iota.\,C\{Q\}$$

where, in the latter two axioms, ι should not be free in P or Q; see [Rey81a] for an example of a verification using an axiom similar to these. We can also state command equivalences such as

$$\#\,\textbf{label } \iota.\,\iota \;\equiv\; \textbf{diverge}$$

$$\#\,\textbf{escape } \iota.\,\iota \;\equiv\; \textbf{skip}$$

$$K \text{ ; } C \;\equiv\; K$$

where C is a command and K is a completion.

7.6   Block Expressions

Most programming languages allow command-like phrases to be components of expression-like ones. For example, consider adding a family of quantifier constants

$$\textbf{result}[\tau]\!: \big((\textbf{exp}[\tau] \to \textbf{compl}) \to \textbf{compl}\big) \to \textbf{exp}[\tau]$$

such that the value of $\#\,\textbf{result}[\tau]\iota.\,K$ is the value of the expression to which the procedure ι is applied during the execution of $K\colon\textbf{compl}$. This kind of facility is sometimes termed a *block expression*, but in many programming languages is allowed only in expression-procedure definitions.

Block expressions introduce the possibility of side effects to *non-local* variables during execution of an *expression*. We do not want to allow such side effects because of their drastic effects on the programming logic. But then the semantical problem is to restrict execution of the body of a block expression so that it cannot change the values of non-local variables, even if non-local commands or procedures are invoked.

Another problem with block expressions in the presence of jumps is that a non-local completion might be invoked, so that "evaluation" of an expression might even fail to produce a value. If this were to be allowed, it would be necessary to re-define the domain of expression meanings as follows:

$$\llbracket\textbf{exp}[\tau]\rrbracket = G \rightarrow \llbracket\textbf{compl}\rrbracket$$

where $G = \llbracket\tau\rrbracket \rightarrow \llbracket\textbf{compl}\rrbracket$ is the domain of *expression continuations*. An expression meaning is then a function transforming an expression continuation into a command continuation; for example,

$$\llbracket N_0 + N_1 \rrbracket ug = \llbracket N_0 \rrbracket ug_1$$
$$\text{where } g_1(n_0) = \llbracket N_1 \rrbracket ug_2$$
$$\text{where } g_2(n_1) = g(n_0 + n_1)$$

where $n_0, n_1 \in \llbracket\textbf{nat}\rrbracket$, and $g, g_1, g_2 \in G$, and

$$\llbracket\textbf{result}[\tau]\rrbracket upg = p(q)$$

for all $p \in \llbracket(\textbf{exp}[\tau] \rightarrow \textbf{compl}) \rightarrow \textbf{compl}\rrbracket$ and q is the element of $\llbracket\textbf{exp}[\tau] \rightarrow \textbf{compl}\rrbracket$ such that $q(e) = e(g)$ for all $e \in \llbracket\textbf{exp}[\tau]\rrbracket$, so that

$$\llbracket\#\,\textbf{result}[\tau]\,\iota.\,K\rrbracket ug = \llbracket K\rrbracket(u \mid \iota \mapsto q),$$

for q defined similarly.

Notice, however, that the interpretation of $N_0 + N_1$ specifies the order of evaluation of the sub-expressions, and even equivalences such as

$$N_0 + N_1 \equiv N_1 + N_0$$

would fail in this framework, even if there are no side effects, since the two sub-expressions might jump to different places. In order to preserve the familiar "algebraic" properties of expressions, we must instead try to give an interpretation that precludes non-local jumps (other than error stops) as well as side effects. This will be discussed in Section 9.7.

Exercises

7.1 Prove the following syntactic analogue of the Substitution Lemma; for all phrases X, phrase assignments σ, and phrase-type assignments π_1 with dom $\sigma \supseteq free(X)$ and dom $\pi_1 \supseteq free(\sigma(\iota))$ for all $\iota \in$ dom σ,

$$\langle [X]\sigma \rangle \pi_1 = \langle X \rangle \pi_0,$$

where π_0 is defined as follows: for all $\iota \in$ dom σ, $\pi_0(\iota) = \langle \sigma(\iota) \rangle \pi_1$.

7.2 Prove that, for any phrase X and phrase-type assignment π with dom $\pi \supseteq \big(free(X) \cup \{\iota\}\big)$,

$$\langle X \rangle \pi \vdash \big\langle (\lambda \iota\colon \theta.\, X)(\iota) \big\rangle \pi.$$

How can this be strengthened when $\pi(\iota) = \theta$?

7.3 Define detailed semantics of **new**$[\tau]$, the assignment command, and the de-referencing coercion using the model of dynamic storage discussed in Section 7.2.

7.4 Extend the definition of $\langle \cdot \rangle \pi$ and the proofs of Propositions 7.1, 7.2, and 7.3 to allow for the syntactic facilities introduced in Section 7.3, and similarly for those in Section 7.4.

7.5 What goes wrong if the Product-Introduction Rule of Section 7.3 is replaced by the following simpler and more flexible rules:

Tag Introduction:

$$\frac{Z\colon \theta}{\iota \mapsto Z\colon \iota \mapsto \theta}$$

Merging:

$$\frac{P\colon \iota_1 \mapsto \theta_1 \;\&\; \cdots \;\&\; \iota_n \mapsto \theta_n \qquad P'\colon \iota_1' \mapsto \theta_1' \;\&\; \cdots \;\&\; \iota_m' \mapsto \theta_m'}{P, P'\colon \iota_1 \mapsto \theta_1 \;\&\; \cdots \;\&\; \iota_n \mapsto \theta_n \;\&\; \iota_1' \mapsto \theta_1' \;\&\; \cdots \;\&\; \iota_m' \mapsto \theta_m'}$$

where $\iota_1, \ldots, \iota_n, \iota_1', \ldots, \iota_m'$ are all distinct?

7.6 Suppose that we add the following new construct to our language:

Case Selection:

$$\frac{N\colon \mathbf{exp[nat]} \qquad F\colon \mathbf{exp[nat]} \to \theta}{\mathbf{case}\ N\ \mathbf{of}\ F\colon \theta}$$

and interpret it by the following equivalence:

$$\mathbf{case}\ N\ \mathbf{of}\ F \;\equiv_\theta\; F(N);$$

that is, the **case** construction is an alternative notation for a procedure call. For this approach to **case** selection to be useful, it is necessary to add new notation for defining procedures by explicit enumeration of argument-to-result associations. Design such notation, including a specification of the syntax and semantics.

7.7   Validate the conventional control-structure axioms of Hoare's logic using the continuation semantics of Section 7.5.2. Do the same for the new axioms (relevant to **abort**, labels, and escapes) introduced in that section.

7.8   Devise an operational semantics for the language of Section 7.5 (with jumps) and verify its correctness relative to the continuation form of denotational semantics.

Bibliographic Notes

The treatment of coercions in Section 7.1 is based on [Rey80b, Rey81b, Rey85, Ole82, Ole87]. The treatment of dynamic storage in Section 7.2 is based on [SS71, Sco72a, Str72]. Many authors have expressed the view that a more abstract approach to local variables would be desirable: [Sco72a, Don77, Rey81b, Ole82, HMT83, Ole85, Bro85, MS88]. The use of procedural parameters and product types to construct "objects" with hidden representations is a well-known technique; see, for example, the Appendix of [Rey78].

Acceptors are proposed in [Rey80b, Rey81b]. Phrase types of the form $\mathbf{acc}[\tau] \& \mathbf{exp}[\tau']$ (Section 7.4) are special cases of *conjunctive* types as introduced in [CD78] in the context of type assignment for untyped languages, and applied to explicitly-typed languages in [Rey87, Rey88]. Further discussion of data-structuring facilities in Algol-like languages may be found in [Ten89].

The use of continuations to treat the semantics of jumps was introduced in [SW74]. The "Hoare-double" form of specification formula is from [TT91]; for related treatments, see [CH72, dB80b, Rey81a].

PART IV

Advanced Techniques

Chapter 8

An Introduction to Category Theory

In designing a programming language, the central problem is to organize a variety of concepts in a way which exhibits uniformity and generality. Substantial leverage can be gained in attacking this problem if these concepts can be defined concisely within a framework which has already proven its ability to impose uniformity and generality upon a wide variety of mathematics.

J. C. Reynolds (1980)

The theory of categories was developed when mathematicians noticed that some simple abstract concepts were applicable in many branches of mathematics. The main advantage of abstraction in mathematics is efficiency: a general theorem can be proved once, instead of several times in many specific contexts; often the proof of the general theorem is simpler and clearer than its special cases. Another advantage is flexibility: often, a definition formulated in categorical terms can be used in many frameworks, much as programmers can change the representation of an abstract data type without affecting code that depends only on the abstract properties.

Category theory should be particularly relevant to a relatively young subject such as Computer Science for which the fundamental concepts are not yet known. When fundamental concepts can be formulated in categorical terms, there is some assurance that the definitions are not "slightly wrong" or presented in a way that is biased by the context. This is especially true in the area of *semantics*, where the primary goal of the field is to provide "good" definitions.

In this chapter, we discuss several category-theoretical concepts that seem to be especially relevant to semantics of programming languages: categories, isomorphisms, terminal and initial objects, products, sums, and exponentials of objects and morphisms, functors, natural transformations, and functor categories.

8.1   Categories

A category consists of a collection of *objects* and a collection of *morphisms* (also called "arrows" or "maps") such that,

- for each morphism f, there is a *domain* object, dom f, and a *co-domain* object, codom f (so that we can write $f\colon x \longrightarrow y$ to indicate that $x =$ dom f and $y =$ codom f); and

- for each object x, there is an *identity* morphism, $\mathrm{id}_x\colon x \longrightarrow x$.

Furthermore, there is a (partial) binary operation ; of *composition* on morphisms such that, whenever dom g = codom f, a composite morphism $f\,; g\colon$ dom $f \longrightarrow$ codom g exists and the following properties hold.

- *Associativity:* for all morphisms $f\colon x \longrightarrow y$, $g\colon y \longrightarrow z$, and $h\colon z \longrightarrow w$,

$$(f\,; g)\,; h \;=\; f\,; (g : h).$$

- *Identity:* for every morphism $f\colon x \longrightarrow y$,

$$\mathrm{id}_x\,; f \;=\; f \quad \text{and} \quad f\,; \mathrm{id}_y \;=\; f.$$

We shall use bold-face letters such as **C** as names of categories. The other notation will already be familiar to the reader because we have used it for *functions* on *sets*. In fact, our first example of a category will be the category **S** of sets and functions, which is defined as follows.

- The objects are sets; i.e., every set is an object.

- The morphisms with domain A and co-domain B are functions from A to B.

- The composition operation is function composition, which is easily proved to be associative.

- The identity morphism on an object is the identity function on that set, which is easily proved to be the identity for function composition.

Similarly, we can define the category **D** of domains (that is, ω-complete partially-ordered sets) and continuous functions:

- The objects are domains.

- The morphisms from D to E are triples $(f, \sqsubseteq_D, \sqsubseteq_E)$, where f is a continuous function from D to E, and $\sqsubseteq_D$ and $\sqsubseteq_E$ are the partial orderings for domains D and E. The partial orderings are included to allow the domain and co-domain objects of a morphism to be uniquely determined, in the same way that a *function* uniquely determines its domain and co-domain sets as well as its graph. In practice, this subtlety is usually ignored and the function itself is treated as the morphism.

- The composition of $(f, \sqsubseteq_D, \sqsubseteq_E)$ and $(g, \sqsubseteq_E, \sqsubseteq_F)$ is the morphism $(f \,;\, g, \sqsubseteq_D, \sqsubseteq_F)$; we know that function composition preserves continuity.

- The identity morphism on a domain D is $(\mathrm{id}_D, \sqsubseteq_D, \sqsubseteq_D)$; we know that the identity function on any domain is continuous.

S and **D** are termed *large* categories because the collection of all objects is not itself a set. (There is no set of *all* sets.) If the collections of all objects and all morphisms for a category are sets, the category is termed *small*. An example of a (very) small category is as follows. There is just a single object and a single morphism, the identity on that object. It isn't at all important what the object or the morphism is. In particular, the object need not be a set, and we cannot in general talk about the (set-theoretical) members of objects in arbitrary categories.

We now give a whole class of such examples. Suppose $\sqsubseteq$ is a pre-ordering (i.e., a reflexive and transitive relation) on a set A; then we can define a category as follows:

- The objects are the elements of A.

- The morphisms are the pairs (a, a') for all $a, a' \in A$ such that $a \sqsubseteq a'$; the domain of (a, a') is a and the co-domain is a'.

- The composite morphism (a, a'') exists whenever (a, a') and (a', a'') do because of the transitivity of $\sqsubseteq$.

- The identity morphism (a, a) exists for every object $a \in A$ because of the reflexivity of $\sqsubseteq$.

Conversely, for any category with at most one morphism between any pair of objects, we can define a pre-ordered set, and these constructions are mutually inverse.

As another example, for any *monoid* we can define an associated category, where a monoid is a triple $(M, \cdot, 1)$ such that M is a non-empty set, $\cdot$ is an associative binary operation on M, and $1 \in M$ is the identity for $\cdot$. The category has a single object and the morphisms are the elements of M. The composite $m_0 \,;\, m_1$ is defined to be $m_0 \cdot m_1$, and the identity morphism on the object is the identity of the $\cdot$ operation. Conversely, for any category with a single object, we can define a monoid, and these constructions are mutually inverse.

We can also define categories in terms of existing categories. We give three examples. If **C** is a category, the *opposite* category $\mathbf{C}^{\mathrm{op}}$ is defined as follows:

- The $\mathbf{C}^{\mathrm{op}}$-objects are the **C**-objects.

- The $\mathbf{C}^{\mathrm{op}}$-morphisms are the **C**-morphisms, but with the domain and co-domain exchanged; i.e., if $f : x \longrightarrow y$ in **C**, then $f : y \longrightarrow x$ in $\mathbf{C}^{\mathrm{op}}$.

- The composite morphism $f \,;\, g$ in $\mathbf{C}^{\mathrm{op}}$ is equal to $g \,;\, f$ in **C**.

- id_x in $\mathbf{C}^{op}$ is id_x in $\mathbf{C}$.

If $\mathbf{C}_0$ and $\mathbf{C}_1$ are categories, their *product* is the category $\mathbf{C}_0 \times \mathbf{C}_1$ defined as follows:

- The objects are the pairs (c_0, c_1) such that c_0 is a $\mathbf{C}_0$-object and c_1 is a $\mathbf{C}_1$-object.
- The morphisms are the pairs (f_0, f_1) such that f_0 is a $\mathbf{C}_0$-morphism and f_1 is a $\mathbf{C}_1$-morphism, and then $\mathrm{dom}(f_0, f_1) = (\mathrm{dom}\, f_0, \mathrm{dom}\, f_1)$ and $\mathrm{codom}(f_0, f_1) = (\mathrm{codom}\, f_0, \mathrm{codom}\, f_1)$.
- The composite $(f, g) \,;\, (f', g')$ is $(f \,;\, f', g \,;\, g')$.
- The identity $id_{(c_0, c_1)}$ is (id_{c_0}, id_{c_1}).

If $\mathbf{C}$ is a category, the corresponding *arrow category*, $\mathbf{C}^{\rightarrow}$, is defined as follows:

- The objects of $\mathbf{C}^{\rightarrow}$ are the morphisms of $\mathbf{C}$.
- A $\mathbf{C}^{\rightarrow}$-morphism from $f : c \rightarrow d$ to $f' : c' \rightarrow d'$ is a pair (g, h) of $\mathbf{C}$-morphisms $g : c \rightarrow c'$ and $h : d \rightarrow d'$ such that the following diagram commutes:

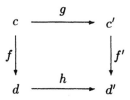

- The composite $(g_0, h_0) \,;\, (g_1, h_1)$ is $(g_0 \,;\, g_1, h_0 \,;\, h_1)$; we can verify that, in the following diagram,

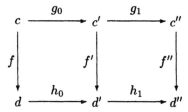

the outer rectangle commutes whenever both of the inner squares do:

$$
\begin{aligned}
f \,;\, (h_0 \,;\, h_1) &= (f \,;\, h_0) \,;\, h_1 && \text{(by associativity)} \\
&= (g_0 \,;\, f') \,;\, h_1 && \text{(by commutativity)} \\
&= g_0 \,;\, (f' \,;\, h_1) && \text{(by associativity)} \\
&= g_0 \,;\, (g_1 \,;\, f'') && \text{(by commutativity)} \\
&= (g_0 \,;\, g_1) \,;\, f'' && \text{(by associativity).}
\end{aligned}
$$

- For any $\mathbf{C}$-morphism $f : c \rightarrow d$, the $\mathbf{C}^{\rightarrow}$-identity $id_f : f \rightarrow f$ is (id_c, id_d):

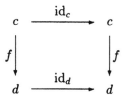

8.2 Special Objects and Morphisms

Categorical definitions characterize objects and morphisms in terms of their interactions with other objects and morphisms, rather than by reference to their "internal" structure. Here is an example. An object c_1 in a category **C** is termed a *terminal* object if, for every **C**-object c, there is exactly one **C**-morphism from c to c_1.

The following are some instances of this concept:

- Any singleton set is terminal in **S** or **D**. For any non-empty set A, there is exactly one (constant) function from A to a singleton set. There is also only one function from the empty set to any set; its graph is the empty set.

- The category associated with a pre-ordered set has a terminal object if and only if the pre-ordered set has a greatest element.

- The category associated with a monoid does not have a terminal object, unless the monoid has just one element.

- If **C** has a terminal object c_1 and **C**' has a termimal object c_1', then (c_1, c_1') is a terminal object in **C** × **C**'. The unique morphism from (c, c') is (f, f'), where f and f' are the unique morphisms from c to c_1 in **C** and from c' to c_1' in **C**', respectively.

- If **C** has a terminal object c_1, then id_{c_1} is a terminal object in **C**$^{\rightarrow}$. The unique morphism from $f: c \rightarrow d$ is (g, h), where $g: c \rightarrow c_1$ and $h: d \rightarrow c_1$ are the unique morphisms from c and d to c_1 in **C**.

Note that a category may have more than one terminal object. If there is more than one terminal object, they are "essentially equivalent" in the following sense: two **C**-objects c and c' are termed *isomorphic* (written $c \cong c'$) just if there exist morphisms $f: c \rightarrow c'$ and $f': c' \rightarrow c$ such that $f ; f' = \mathrm{id}_c$ and $f' ; f = \mathrm{id}_{c'}$. These morphisms are termed *isomorphisms*.

To see that terminal objects in *any* category are isomorphic (if they exist at all), suppose c_1 and c_1' are both terminal in a category **C**. There is a morphism $f: c_1 \rightarrow c_1'$, by terminality of c_1', and a morphism $f': c_1' \rightarrow c_1$, by terminality of c_1. But then $f ; f'$ and id_{c_1} are both morphisms from c_1 to

c_1 and must be equal by uniqueness, and similarly f' ; f and $\text{id}_{c_1'}$ must be equal morphisms from c_1' to c_1', and so f and f' are mutual inverses with respect to composition:

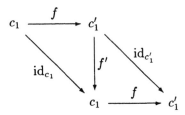

In **S**, sets are isomorphic if and only if they have the same cardinality (i.e., they can be put into one-to-one correspondence). In the category associated with a pre-ordered set, objects a and a' are isomorphic if and only if $a \sqsubseteq a'$ and $a' \sqsubseteq a$.

Many categorical concepts have *duals*, obtained by "reversing the arrows" in the definition. For example, an object c_0 in a category **C** is an *initial* object if, for every **C**-object c, there is exactly one **C**-morphism from c_0 to c. Equivalently, an object is initial in **C** if and only if it is terminal in $\mathbf{C}^{op}$. For example, the empty set is initial in **S** or **D**, because there is exactly one function (with an empty graph) from the empty set to any set, and the category associated with a pre-ordered set has an initial object if and only if it has a least element.

One of the most important categorical concepts is that of *products* of objects and morphisms. A (categorical) product of objects c_0 and c_1 is an object $c_0 \times c_1$ together with *projection* morphisms $\pi_0 \colon c_0 \times c_1 \to c_0$ and $\pi_1 \colon c_0 \times c_1 \to c_1$ such that, for any object x and morphisms $f_0 \colon x \to c_0$ and $f_1 \colon x \to c_1$, there is exactly one morphism $h \colon x \to c_0 \times c_1$ such that the following diagram commutes:

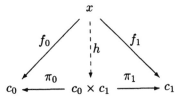

i.e., $f_i = h \, ; \pi_i$. Dashed arrows are used in diagrams to indicate morphisms that make the diagram commute and whose existence is being asserted. This definition characterizes the triple

$$(c_0 \times c_1, \ \pi_0 \colon c_0 \times c_1 \to c_0, \ \pi_1 \colon c_0 \times c_1 \to c_1)$$

as being *most general* (up to isomorphism) of all triples of the form

$$(x, \ f_0 \colon x \to c_0, \ f_1 \colon x \to c_1).$$

In the category $\mathbf{S}$, the Cartesian product $A \times B$ together with the usual projection functions from $A \times B$ to A and to B is a (categorical) product. For any set S and any functions $f: S \to A$ and $g: S \to B$, the function $h: S \to A \times B$ is defined by $h(s) = \big(f(s), g(s)\big)$, and it is clear that this is the only function that has the necessary commutativity properties.

Similarly, the domain product $D \times E$ of domains D and E together with the projection functions from $D \times E$ to D and to E is a categorical product in $\mathbf{D}$. If a and a' are objects in the category associated with a pre-ordered set, a greatest lower bound of a and a' (if it exists) is a categorical product of a and a'.

As with terminal objects, products need not be unique. For example, in $\mathbf{S}$ the Cartesian product $B \times A$ is also a categorical product of A and B, provided that the projections are as follows: $\pi_0(b, a) = a$ and $\pi_1(b, a) = b$. It can be verified that, if p and p' are both product objects in an arbitrary category, p and p' are isomorphic.

We can also define products of *morphisms*. Suppose that $f_0: c_0 \to c_0'$ and $f_1: c_1 \to c_1'$ are morphisms, and that a product $c_0 \times c_1$ (with projections π_i), and a product $c_0' \times c_1'$ (with projections π_i') both exist. We can then define

$$f_0 \times f_1 : (c_0 \times c_1) \to (c_0' \times c_1')$$

to be the unique morphism for which the following diagram commutes:

$$
\begin{array}{ccccc}
c_0 & \xleftarrow{\ \pi_0\ } & c_0 \times c_1 & \xrightarrow{\ \pi_1\ } & c_1 \\
\downarrow{\scriptstyle f_0} & & \vdots\,{\scriptstyle f_0 \times f_1} & & \downarrow{\scriptstyle f_1} \\
c_0' & \xleftarrow{\ \pi_0'\ } & c_0' \times c_1' & \xrightarrow{\ \pi_1'\ } & c_1'
\end{array}
$$

In category $\mathbf{S}$, for example, $f_0 \times f_1$ is the function such that

$$(f_0 \times f_1)(x, y) = \big(f_0(x), f_1(y)\big)$$

for all $x \in c_0$ and $y \in c_1$.

The dual to the concept of product is termed the *sum* or "co-product." An object $c_0 + c_1$ together with *injection* morphisms $\iota_0: c_0 \to c_0 + c_1$ and $\iota_1: c_1 \to c_0 + c_1$ is a categorical sum of c_0 and c_1 if, for any object x and morphisms $f_0: c_0 \to x$ and $f_1: c_1 \to x$, there is exactly one morphism $h: c_0 + c_1 \to x$ such that the following diagram commutes:

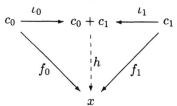

A sum

$$(c_0 + c_1, \ \iota_0 \colon c_0 \rightarrow c_0 + c_1, \ \iota_1 \colon c_1 \rightarrow c_0 + c_1)$$

is thus a most general (up to isomorphism) triple of the form

$$(x, \ f_0 \colon c_0 \rightarrow x, \ f_1 \colon c_1 \rightarrow x).$$

In category $\mathbf{S}$, the disjoint union

$$A_0 + A_1 \ = \ \{(0, a_0) \mid a_0 \in A_0\} \cup \{(1, a_1) \mid a_1 \in A_1\}$$

together with the injection functions $\iota_i(z) = (i, z)$ from A_i into $A_0 + A_1$ is a categorical sum of A_0 and A_1. For any functions $f_0 \colon A_0 \rightarrow S$ and $f_1 \colon A_1 \rightarrow S$, the function $h \colon A_0 + A_1 \rightarrow S$ is defined by $h(i, z) = f_i(z)$, and similarly in $\mathbf{D}$. In the category associated with a pre-ordered set, a least upper bound of a and a' (if it exists) is a categorical sum of a and a'.

Sums of *morphisms* can be defined as well. The reader is invited to infer the definition from the following diagram:

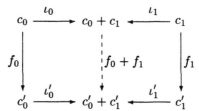

In $\mathbf{S}$, for example, $f_0 + f_1$ is the function defined by

$$(f_0 + f_1)(i, z) = (i, f_i(z)).$$

There is also a categorical notion of exponentiation. Suppose that, for all objects c_0 and c_1 in category $\mathbf{C}$, there is a product $c_0 \times c_1$ of c_0 and c_1. An object $c \Rightarrow d$, together with an *evaluation* morphism $\eta \colon (c \Rightarrow d) \times c \rightarrow d$, is called an *exponentiation* of objects c and d if and only if, for any object x and morphism $f \colon x \times c \rightarrow d$, there is exactly one morphism $h \colon x \rightarrow (c \Rightarrow d)$ such that the following diagram commutes:

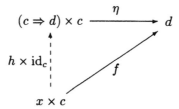

In category $\mathbf{S}$, the set of all functions $A \rightarrow B$, together with the function $apply \colon (A \rightarrow B) \times A \rightarrow B$ defined by $apply(g, a) = g(a)$, is an exponential of sets A and B. Notice that in "$apply \colon (A \rightarrow B) \times A \rightarrow B$" the $\rightarrow$ symbol is used in two distinct ways: to denote the exponential object $A \rightarrow B$, and to specify that the domain and co-domain for *apply* are $(A \rightarrow B) \times A$

and B, respectively. For any set S and any function $f: S \times A \to B$, the function $h: S \to (A \to B)$ is defined by $h(s)(a) = f(s, a)$, for all $s \in S$ and $a \in A$; i.e., h is the "Curried" form of f. Object exponentiation in $\mathbf{D}$ is defined similarly, and we have shown that application is in fact a continuous function.

We can also define exponentiation of *morphisms*. For any morphisms $f: c \to c'$ and $g: d \to d'$,

$$f \Rightarrow g: (c' \Rightarrow d) \to (c \Rightarrow d')$$

can be defined as the unique morphism such that the following diagram commutes:

where $\eta_{cd'}$ and $\eta_{c'd}$ are the evaluation morphisms for the exponential objects $c \Rightarrow d'$ and $c' \Rightarrow d$, respectively. In $\mathbf{S}$, for example, $f \Rightarrow g$ is the function defined by $(f \Rightarrow g)(h) = f \; ; h \; ; g$ for all $h: c' \to d$.

A category in which a terminal object and products and exponentials of all pairs of objects can be specified is termed *Cartesian closed*; for example, $\mathbf{S}$ and $\mathbf{D}$ are Cartesian-closed categories. It can be shown that every Cartesian-closed category provides an interpretation of functional abstraction and application that validates the laws of the typed lambda calculus.

8.3   Functors and Natural Transformations

"Category" has been defined in order to define "functor," and "functor" has been defined in order to define "natural transformation."

S. Mac Lane (1971)

In algebra, the concept of *homomorphism*, or "structure-preserving map" is very fundamental. For example, a monoid homomorphism from monoid $(M, \cdot, 1)$ to monoid $(M', \cdot, 1')$ is a function $f: M \to M'$ such that $f(1) = 1'$ and $f(m_0 \cdot m_1) = f(m_0) \cdot f(m_1)$.

The comparable concept in category theory is that of *functors*, mappings of categories that preserve categorical structure. We say that F is a (covariant) functor from category $\mathbf{C}$ to category $\mathbf{C}'$ (written $F: \mathbf{C} \to \mathbf{C}'$) just if, for every $\mathbf{C}$-object c there is a $\mathbf{C}'$-object $F(c)$, and, for every $\mathbf{C}$-morphism $f: c \to d$ there is a $\mathbf{C}'$-morphism $F(f): F(c) \to F(d)$ such that

- for every **C**-object c, $F(\mathrm{id}_c) = \mathrm{id}_{F(c)}$; and
- for all **C**-morphisms $f: c \to d$ and $g: d \to e$, $F(f \,;\, g) = F(f) \,;\, F(g)$:

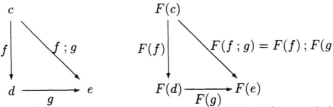

where the left part of the diagram is in **C** and the right part is in **C'**.

It is a conventional abuse of notation to use the same symbol to denote a functor, its object part (mapping objects to objects), and its morphism part (mapping morphisms to morphisms).

Here is an example of a functor. Let Θ be the category associated with the pre-ordered set of phrase types for the Algol-like language of Chapters 6 and 7. Then $[\![\cdot]\!]$ is a functor from Θ to the category $\mathbf{D}_\perp$ of domains with least elements and strict continuous functions, because we have imposed the requirements that $[\![\theta \vdash \theta]\!]$ be the identity function on $[\![\theta]\!]$ and that $[\![\theta_0 \vdash \theta_2]\!] = [\![\theta_0 \vdash \theta_1]\!] \,;\, [\![\theta_1 \vdash \theta_2]\!]$ whenever $\theta_0 \vdash \theta_1 \vdash \theta_2$.

Here are some other examples of functors:

- There is a *forgetful* functor $F: \mathbf{D} \to \mathbf{S}$ that "forgets" domain structure; for any domain D, $F(D)$ is the set underlying D and, for any continuous function f, $F(f)$ is f, regarded as a function on the underlying sets.

- There is an *embedding* functor $E: \mathbf{S} \to \mathbf{D}$ such that, for any set A, $E(A)$ is the domain obtained by discretely ordering A and, for any function f, $E(f)$ is f, regarded as a continuous function.

- For any **C'**-object c', there is a *constant* functor $F: \mathbf{C} \to \mathbf{C'}$ such that $F(c) = c'$ for all **C**-objects c, and $F(f) = \mathrm{id}_{c'}$ for every **C**-morphism f.

- For any category **C**, there is an *identity* functor $\mathrm{id}_{\mathbf{C}}: \mathbf{C} \to \mathbf{C}$ such that $\mathrm{id}_{\mathbf{C}}(c) = c$ for every **C**-object c and $\mathrm{id}_{\mathbf{C}}(f) = f$ for every **C**-morphism f.

- If **C** and **C'** are the categories associated with pre-ordered sets, a functor from **C** to **C'** corresponds to a monotonic function from one pre-ordered set to the other.

- If **C** and **C'** are the categories associated with monoids, a functor from **C** to **C'** corresponds to a monoid homomorphism from one monoid to the other.

- If $F: \mathbf{C} \to \mathbf{C'}$ and $G: \mathbf{C'} \to \mathbf{C''}$ are functors, then there is a composite functor $F;G: \mathbf{C} \to \mathbf{C''}$ such that $(F;G)(c) = G\big(F(c)\big)$ for every **C**-object c, and $(F \,;\, G)(f) = G\big(F(f)\big)$ for every **C**-morphism f.

• Let $\mathbf{C}$ be a category and c_0 be a $\mathbf{C}$-object, and suppose that there is a product object $c_0 \times c$ for every $\mathbf{C}$-object c; then $(c_0 \times \cdot): \mathbf{C} \to \mathbf{C}$ is the functor such that, for every $\mathbf{C}$-object c, $c_0 \times c$ is the specified product of c_0 and c, and, for every $\mathbf{C}$-morphism $f: c \to c'$, $c_0 \times f$ is the product of morphisms id_{c_0} and f.

A *contravariant functor* from $\mathbf{C}$ to $\mathbf{C}'$ is a *covariant* functor from $\mathbf{C}^{\mathrm{op}}$ to $\mathbf{C}'$, so that the direction of the arrows is reversed: $F(f): F(d) \to F(c)$ for every $\mathbf{C}$-morphism $f: c \to d$, and $F(f \mathbin{;} g) = F(g) \mathbin{;} F(f)$.

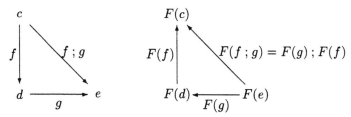

We now define the very important concept of *natural transformations*. Suppose F and G are both functors from category $\mathbf{C}$ to category $\mathbf{C}'$; then a natural transformation η from F to G (written $\eta: F \xrightarrow{\cdot} G$) is a family of $\mathbf{C}'$-morphisms

$$\{\eta_c: F(c) \to G(c) \mid c \text{ is a } \mathbf{C}\text{-object}\}$$

satisfying the following commutativity condition: for every $\mathbf{C}$-morphism $f: c_0 \to c_1$, the following diagram commutes:

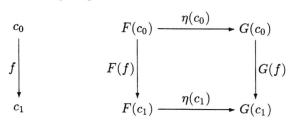

Intuitively, $\eta: F \xrightarrow{\cdot} G$ is a family of $\mathbf{C}'$-morphisms that are *uniform* with respect to the F and G images of $\mathbf{C}$-morphisms.

For example, suppose that a is a $\mathbf{C}$-object and that there exist exponential objects $a \Rightarrow c$ and product objects $c \times a$ for every $\mathbf{C}$-object c. For any $\mathbf{C}$-morphism $f: c_0 \to c_1$, consider the following diagram:

$$
\begin{array}{ccc}
c_0 & (a \Rightarrow c_0) \times a \xrightarrow{\eta(c_0)} c_0 \\
\\
f \Big\downarrow \quad (\mathrm{id}_a \Rightarrow f) \times \mathrm{id}_a \Big\downarrow & \quad \Big\downarrow f \\
\\
c_1 & (a \Rightarrow c_1) \times a \xrightarrow{\eta(c_1)} c_1
\end{array}
$$

where $\eta(c_i)$ is the evaluation morphism associated with the exponential object $a \Rightarrow c_i$; from the definition of morphism exponentiation, we know that the diagram commutes. But this means that η is a natural transformation from the functor $F\colon \mathbf{C} \to \mathbf{C}$ defined by

- $F(c) = (a \Rightarrow c) \times a$, and
- $F(f) = (\mathrm{id}_a \Rightarrow f) \times \mathrm{id}_a$,

to the identity functor $\mathrm{id}_{\mathbf{C}}\colon \mathbf{C} \to \mathbf{C}$.

As a second example, let $\mathbf{\Pi}$ be the category associated with the set of phrase-type assignments pre-ordered by the $\vdash$ relation defined in Section 7.1 and consider the following diagram:

$$
\begin{array}{ccc}
\pi_0 & [\![\pi_0]\!] \xrightarrow{\ [\![X]\!]_{\pi_0\theta_0}\ } [\![\theta_0]\!] \\[1em]
\Big\downarrow{\scriptstyle \pi_0 \vdash \pi_1} & \Big\downarrow{\scriptstyle [\![\pi_0 \vdash \pi_1]\!]} \qquad\qquad \Big\downarrow{\scriptstyle [\![\theta_0 \vdash \theta_1]\!]} \\[1em]
\pi_1 & [\![\pi_1]\!] \xrightarrow{\ [\![X]\!]_{\pi_1\theta_1}\ } [\![\theta_1]\!]
\end{array}
$$

where $\theta_i = \langle X \rangle \pi_i$; Proposition 7.3 tells us that the diagram commutes. But this means that we can define a natural tranformation $\eta\colon F \to G$ by

$$\eta(\pi) = [\![X]\!]_{\pi(\langle X \rangle \pi)},$$

where the functors $F, G\colon \mathbf{\Pi} \to \mathbf{D}_\perp$ are defined by

- $F(\pi) = [\![\pi]\!]$, and
- $F(\pi_0 \vdash \pi_1) = [\![\pi_0 \vdash \pi_1]\!]$,

and

- $G(\pi) = [\![\langle X \rangle \pi]\!]$, and
- $G(\pi_0 \vdash \pi_1) = [\![\langle X \rangle \pi_0 \vdash \langle X \rangle \pi_1]\!]$.

Our final topic is that of *functor categories*, categories whose objects are functors and whose morphisms are natural transformations. For any functor $F\colon \mathbf{C} \to \mathbf{C}'$, there is a natural transformation $\mathrm{id}_F\colon F \to F$ defined by $\mathrm{id}_F(c) = \mathrm{id}_{F(c)}$ for every $\mathbf{C}$-object c:

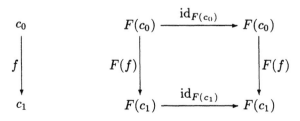

Furthermore, if F, G and H are all functors from $\mathbf{C}$ to $\mathbf{C}'$ and $\eta\colon F \to G$ and $\tau\colon G \to H$ are natural transformations, there is a composite natural transformation $\eta\,;\tau\colon F \to H$ defined by $(\eta\,;\tau)(c) = \eta(c)\,;\tau(c)$ for every $\mathbf{C}$-object c:

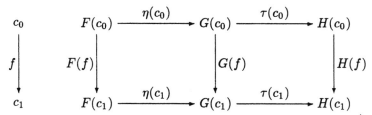

It is also evident that $\mathrm{id}_F\,;\eta = \eta = \eta\,;\mathrm{id}_G$, and that composition of natural transformations is associative. These facts allow us to define a category $\mathbf{C} \Rightarrow \mathbf{C}'$ whose objects are all the functors from $\mathbf{C}$ to $\mathbf{C}'$ and whose objects are all the natural transformations of those functors.

For example, let $\mathbf{C}$ be an arbitrary category and $\mathbf{2}$ be the category associated with the partially-ordered set whose Hasse diagram is as follows:

The functor category $\mathbf{2} \Rightarrow \mathbf{C}$ is isomorphic to the arrow category $\mathbf{C}^{\to}$, in the sense that we can define the following invertible functors between them:

- For every functor $F\colon \mathbf{2} \to \mathbf{C}$, there is exactly one $\mathbf{C}$-morphism $f\colon c \to d$ with $c = F(0)$, $d = F(1)$ and $f = F(0,1)$, and conversely.
- For every natural transformation $\eta\colon F \to G$ for $F, G\colon \mathbf{2} \to \mathbf{C}$, there is exactly one pair (f_0, f_1) of $\mathbf{C}$-morphisms with $f_0 = \eta(0)$ and $f_1 = \eta(1)$ such that the following diagram commutes:

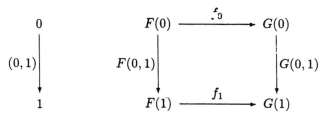

and conversely.

In the following chapter, we will be interpreting programming languages in functor categories of the forms $\mathbf{W} \Rightarrow \mathbf{S}$ and $\mathbf{W} \Rightarrow \mathbf{D}$ for appropriate categories $\mathbf{W}$ of "possible worlds."

Exercises

8.1 Show that, in every category **C**, the identity morphism id_c on any object c is the only morphism that can satisfy the Identity laws.

8.2 Define a category of sets and *partial* functions.

8.3 Define a category $\mathbf{D}_\perp$ of domains with least elements and strict ($\perp$-preserving) continuous functions.

8.4 Define a sum $\mathbf{C}_0 + \mathbf{C}_1$ of arbitrary categories $\mathbf{C}_0$ and $\mathbf{C}_1$.

8.5 Verify that $(\mathbf{C}^{\mathrm{op}})^{\mathrm{op}} = \mathbf{C}$.

8.6 Show that the binary relation R on the objects of a category defined by cRc' if and only if $c \cong c'$ is an equivalence relation.

8.7 What object in the category $\mathbf{D}_\perp$ of Exercise 3 is both an initial and a terminal object?

8.8 Consider a category of *propositions*, where $(p,q)\colon p \longrightarrow q$ is a morphism if and only if $p \vdash q$ (q is derivable from p) in some formal system. What would terminal objects, and products and exponentials of objects be in such a category?

8.9 Show that any functor preserves isomorphisms; i.e., if $c \cong d$ in **C** and $F\colon \mathbf{C} \longrightarrow \mathbf{C}'$ is a functor, then $F(c) \cong F(d)$ in $\mathbf{C}'$.

8.10 Generalize the concepts of products and sums of *pairs* of objects or morphisms to products and sums of I-indexed *families* of objects or morphisms, for sets I. What is obtained if $I = \emptyset$?

8.11 Prove that a natural transformation $\eta\colon F \xrightarrow{\cdot} G$ is an isomorphism in $\mathbf{C} \Rightarrow \mathbf{C}'$ whenever $\eta(c)\colon F(c) \longrightarrow G(c)$ is an isomorphism in **C** for every **C**-object c.

8.12 Prove that if $\mathbf{C}'$ has terminal (initial) objects, so does $\mathbf{C} \Rightarrow \mathbf{C}'$, for any **C**.

8.13 Suppose **C** is a Cartesian-closed category and that c_0 is a **C**-object. Verify the functorial properties of the functor $c_0 \Rightarrow \cdot \colon \mathbf{C} \longrightarrow \mathbf{C}$ defined by

- $(c_0 \Rightarrow \cdot)(c) = c_0 \Rightarrow c$ for every **C**-object c, and
- $(c_0 \Rightarrow \cdot)(f) = \mathrm{id}_{c_0} \Rightarrow f$ for every **C**-morphism f.

Do the same for the similarly-defined *contravariant* functor $\cdot \Rightarrow c_0$.

Bibliographic Notes

Good presentations of category theory include [ML71, AM75, HS79, Gol79, RB88, Pie91, BW90, AL91].

Chapter 9

Possible Worlds

If this is the best of possible worlds, what then are the others?

Voltaire, *Candide* (1759)

In this chapter we discuss a semantic technique that will allow us to solve three difficult problems that arose in earlier chapters:

- a good semantics for local-variable declarations;

- a semantics for a "non-interference" formula that allows Hoare-like reasoning about assignment commands in a language with procedures; and

- a semantics that allows commands to be used in expressions without causing side effects or non-local jumps.

The method is known as *possible-world semantics*, and is well-known to logicians, who have used it to interpret modal and intuitionistic logics.

Possible-world semantics is appropriate when it is necessary to import non-locally defined meanings into a context where some local conditions are applicable to the semantic domains and valuations. For example, a local-variable declaration is most appropriately thought of as temporarily "expanding" the set of states from some non-local set S to a new local set $S \times V$, where V is the set of values possible for the new variable. In a conventional interpretation, non-local procedures and command meanings are defined for the non-local set S of states, and are not usable with the expanded local set of states $S \times V$. Possible-world interpretations will allow us to deal coherently with such changes of context.

9.1 Functor-Category Semantics

Suppose that $X \in [\theta]_\pi$ and that w ranges over a set of objects, termed *possible worlds*, that determine certain "local" aspects of the interpretation;

177

that is, the sets or domains of environments and meanings and the valuation functions are now all "parameterized" by possible worlds w:

$$[\![\pi]\!]w \xrightarrow{\;[\![X]\!]_{\pi\theta}(w)\;} [\![\theta]\!]w$$

But the domains and valuation functions for different possible worlds should not be arbitrarily different from one another. To arrive at an appropriate uniformity condition, suppose that x is another possible world and that $f\colon w \longrightarrow x$ is one way of "changing" from w to x. It is reasonable to require that, for any possible world w, there is a "null" change-of-possible-world $\mathrm{id}_w\colon w \longrightarrow w$ and that, if $f\colon w \longrightarrow x$ and $g\colon x \longrightarrow y$ are changes-of-possible-world, there is a composite change $f\,;\,g\colon w \longrightarrow y$ such that composition is associative and id_w is the identity. In short, possible worlds and changes-of-possible-world must form a *category* **W**.

Now, a **W**-morphism $f\colon w \longrightarrow x$ induces a change-of-meaning

$$[\![\theta]\!]f\colon [\![\theta]\!]w \longrightarrow [\![\theta]\!]x$$

for every phrase type θ. Similarly,

$$[\![\pi]\!]f\colon [\![\pi]\!]w \longrightarrow [\![\pi]\!]x$$

should do the same kind of thing component-wise to π-compatible environments. It is reasonable to require that these induced mappings should preserve identities and composites. In short, $[\![\pi]\!]$ and $[\![\theta]\!]$ must be *functors* from **W**, a category of possible worlds, to a suitable category of semantic domains:

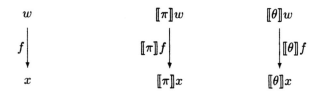

Finally, the appropriate uniformity condition on the valuations is that, for every $X \in [\theta]_\pi$, $[\![X]\!]_{\pi\theta}$ should be a *natural transformation* from $[\![\pi]\!]$ to $[\![\theta]\!]$; that is, the following diagram should commute for every **W**-morphism $f\colon w \longrightarrow x$:

$$
\begin{array}{ccccc}
w & & [\![\pi]\!]w & \xrightarrow{\;[\![X]\!]_{\pi\theta}(w)\;} & [\![\theta]\!]w \\[2pt]
{\scriptstyle f}\Big\downarrow & & {\scriptstyle [\![\pi]\!]f}\Big\downarrow & & \Big\downarrow{\scriptstyle [\![\theta]\!]f} \\[2pt]
x & & [\![\pi]\!]x & \xrightarrow{\;[\![X]\!]_{\pi\theta}(x)\;} & [\![\theta]\!]x
\end{array}
$$

Note that this picture reduces to the conventional one when **W** is the trivial (one-object and one-morphism) category.

The basic idea of the possible-world approach then is to move from the usual categories **S**, of sets and functions, or **D**, of domains and continuous functions, to more general *functor categories* **W** $\Rightarrow$ **S** and **W** $\Rightarrow$ **D** whose objects are the functors from a suitable (small) category **W** of possible worlds to **S** or to **D**, and whose morphisms are the natural transformations of these functors.

9.2   Semantic-Domain Functors

In this section, we first define constructions on functors that are generalizations of the set and domain constructions used previously, and then show how to define semantic-domain functors $[\![\tau]\!]$, $[\![\theta]\!]$, and $[\![\pi]\!]$ for every data type τ, phrase type θ, and phrase-type assignment π.

If **W** is *any* category (of possible worlds), we can define the following constructions of functors from **W** to **D** from functors D and E from **W** to **D**; w, x, and y are **W**-objects, and $f: w \to x$ and $g: x \to y$ are **W**-morphisms.

- $D \times E$:

$$
(D \times E)(w) = D(w) \times E(w),
$$

  and

$$
(D \times E)(f)(a, b) = \big(D(f)(a), E(f)(b)\big);
$$

- $D_\perp$:

$$
D_\perp(w) = \big(D(w)\big)_\perp,
$$

  and

$$
D_\perp(f)(a) = \begin{cases} \perp, & \text{if } a = \perp \\ D(f)(a), & \text{otherwise;} \end{cases}
$$

- $D \to E$:

$(D \to E)(w)$

$$= \left\{ m \in \prod_{f:w \to x} (D(x) \to E(x)) \ \middle| \ \begin{array}{c} \text{for all } f\colon w \to x \text{ and } g\colon x \to y, \\ m(f) : E(g) = D(g) ; m(f ; g) \end{array} \right\},$$

ordered pointwise (i.e., $m_1 \sqsubseteq m_2$ iff $m_1(f) \sqsubseteq m_2(f)$ for every $f\colon w \to x$), where

$$\prod_{f:w \to x} \cdots x \cdots$$

here and in subsequent definitions is an abuse of notation for

$$\prod_{f \in \mathbf{W}(w,\cdot)} \cdots \operatorname{codom} f \cdots,$$

where $\mathbf{W}(w, \cdot)$ is the set of all $\mathbf{W}$-morphisms with domain w, and

$$(D \to E)(f)(m)(g) = m(f ; g);$$

To motivate the $\to$ construction, consider that a procedure defined in possible world w might be called in any possible world x accessible from w using an $\mathbf{W}$-morphism $f\colon w \to x$, and it is the domain structure determined by x which should be in effect when the procedure body is executed. This suggests that we cannot just define $(D \to E)(w)$ to be $D(w) \to E(w)$; the meaning of a procedure defined in possible world w must be a *family* of functions, indexed by $\mathbf{W}$-morphisms $f\colon w \to x$. But such families of functions must be appropriately *uniform*; the uniformity condition is commutativity of all diagrams

$$
\begin{array}{ccc}
 & m(f\colon w \to x) & \\
D(x) & \xrightarrow{\hspace{3cm}} & E(x) \\
{\scriptstyle D(g\colon x \to y)} \Big\downarrow & & \Big\downarrow {\scriptstyle E(g\colon x \to y)} \\
D(y) & \xrightarrow[\ m(f ; g\colon w \to y)\ ]{} & E(y)
\end{array}
$$

For $D \rightharpoonup E$, the construction is similar, but the uniformity condition only requires commutativity when the result of the partial mapping along the top of the diagram is defined:

$(D \rightharpoonup E)(w)$

$$= \left\{ m \in \prod_{f:w \to x} (D(x) \rightharpoonup E(x)) \ \middle| \ \begin{array}{c} \text{for all } f\colon w \to x \text{ and } g\colon x \to y, \\ m(f) ; E(g) \subseteq D(g) ; m(f ; g) \end{array} \right\},$$

ordered pointwise, where the $\subseteq$ relation on partial functions is graph inclusion, and

$$(D \longrightarrow E)(f)(m)(g) = m(f\,;g).$$

Intuitively, a function defined at some argument in one world should also be defined and have a corresponding result for a corresponding argument at all derived worlds.

Finally, if I is a finite set and, for every $i \in I$, D_i is a functor from $\mathbf{W}$ to $\mathbf{D}$, then we define $\prod_{i \in I} D_i$ by

$$\left(\prod_{i \in I} D_i\right)(w) = \prod_{i \in I} D_i(w),$$

and

$$\left(\prod_{i \in I} D_i\right)(f)(d)(j) = D_j(f)(d_j).$$

For functors to $\mathbf{S}$, rather than $\mathbf{D}$, the constructions are defined in the same way, but are based on the corresponding construction in $\mathbf{S}$, and the component sets are not partially-ordered. It is easily verified that these are all functors, and that the constructions reduce to the conventional ones when $\mathbf{W}$ is trivial. It can be shown that, for *any* $\mathbf{W}$, functor categories $\mathbf{W} \Rightarrow \mathbf{S}$ and $\mathbf{W} \Rightarrow \mathbf{D}$ are Cartesian-closed, and that the $\times$ and $\longrightarrow$ defined above construct product and exponential objects, respectively, in these categories.

We will also use these constructions on *contravariant* functors. The product and lifting operations construct contravariant functors when applied to contravariant functors. For the exponentiation operations, the uniformity conditions are obtained by reversing the appropriate arrows and, for $\longrightarrow$, reversing the partial ordering if the "argument" functor is contravariant; for example, for D and E contravariant,

$(D \longrightarrow E)(w)$

$$= \left\{ m \in \prod_{f:w \longrightarrow x} (D(x) \longrightarrow E(x)) \;\middle|\; \begin{array}{l} \text{for all } f\colon w \longrightarrow x \text{ and } g\colon x \longrightarrow y, \\ m(f\,;g)\,;E(g) \subseteq D(g)\,;m(f) \end{array} \right\},$$

so that commutativity of

$$
\begin{array}{ccc}
 & m(f\colon w \longrightarrow x) & \\
D(x) & \xrightarrow{\hspace{2.5cm}} & E(x) \\
{\scriptstyle D(g\colon x \longrightarrow y)}\Big\uparrow & & \Big\uparrow{\scriptstyle E(g\colon x \longrightarrow y)} \\
D(y) & \xrightarrow[\;m(f\,;g\colon w \longrightarrow y)\;]{} & E(y)
\end{array}
$$

$$\llbracket \mathbf{val}[\tau] \rrbracket = \llbracket \tau \rrbracket_\bot$$

$$\llbracket \mathbf{exp}[\tau] \rrbracket = S \to \llbracket \mathbf{val}[\tau] \rrbracket$$

$$\llbracket \mathbf{assert} \rrbracket = S \to \llbracket \mathbf{bool} \rrbracket$$

$$\llbracket \mathbf{comm} \rrbracket = S \rightharpoonup S$$

$$\llbracket \mathbf{acc}[\tau] \rrbracket = \llbracket \mathbf{exp}[\tau] \rrbracket \to \llbracket \mathbf{comm} \rrbracket$$

$$\llbracket \mathbf{var}[\tau] \rrbracket = \llbracket \mathbf{acc}[\tau] \rrbracket \times \llbracket \mathbf{exp}[\tau] \rrbracket$$

$$\llbracket \theta \to \theta' \rrbracket = \llbracket \theta \rrbracket \to \llbracket \theta' \rrbracket$$

$$\llbracket \iota_1 \mapsto \theta_1 \,\&\, \cdots \,\&\, \iota_n \mapsto \theta_n \rrbracket = \prod_{1 \le i \le n} \llbracket \theta_i \rrbracket$$

$$\llbracket \pi \rrbracket = \prod_{\iota \in \mathrm{dom}\,\pi} \llbracket \pi(\iota) \rrbracket$$

Table 9.1 Semantic-domain functors.

is required whenever the partial function at the *bottom* gives a defined result. The morphism parts are defined as for covariant functors, so that $D \to E$ and $D \rightharpoonup E$ are always covariant, even when D or E is contravariant.

We now show how, for any category $\mathbf{W}$ of possible worlds, we can define functors $\llbracket \tau \rrbracket$, $\llbracket \theta \rrbracket$, and $\llbracket \pi \rrbracket$ for every data type τ, phrase type θ, and phrase-type assignment π. We can actually use exactly the same definitions as before, but with the names of primitive sets and domains re-interpreted as being primitive functors, and the set and domain constructions re-interpreted as the functor constructions defined above.

For every data type τ, $\llbracket \tau \rrbracket$ is a constant functor (covariant or contravariant, as appropriate) such that, for every $\mathbf{W}$-object w, $\llbracket \tau \rrbracket w$ is the set of values of type τ. Then, if S is a (possibly contravariant) functor such that $S(w)$ is the set of computational states appropriate to possible world w, the definitions of Table 9.1, which in earlier chapters were definitions of *sets* or *domains*, may now be re-interpreted as definitions of direct-semantic *functors* from $\mathbf{W}$ to $\mathbf{S}$, or to $\mathbf{D}$, as appropriate. Note that expression, assertion, acceptor, and command meanings are, like procedures, *families* of functions, indexed by changes of possible worlds.

Similarly, if O is re-defined to be a suitable output functor, the following functor definitions are appropriate for continuation semantics:

$$\llbracket \mathbf{compl} \rrbracket = S \rightharpoonup O$$

$$\llbracket \mathbf{comm} \rrbracket = \llbracket \mathbf{compl} \rrbracket \to \llbracket \mathbf{compl} \rrbracket$$

The functor $\llbracket \mathbf{spec} \rrbracket$ for specifications will be discussed in Section 9.5.

$$[\![\textbf{if } K \textbf{ then } X_0 \textbf{ else } X_1]\!]wu = \begin{cases} [\![X_0]\!]wu, & \text{if } [\![K]\!]wu = \textit{true} \\ [\![X_1]\!]wu, & \text{if } [\![K]\!]wu = \textit{false} \\ \bot, & \text{if } [\![K]\!]wu = \bot \end{cases}$$

$$[\![\textbf{if } B \textbf{ then } X_0 \textbf{ else } X_1]\!]_\theta(w)(u)$$
$$= cond_\theta(w)\big([\![B]\!]wu, [\![X_0]\!]_\theta(w)(u), [\![X_1]\!]_\theta(w)(u)\big)$$

$$[\![\textbf{true}]\!]wu = \textit{true}$$

$$[\![\textbf{not } B]\!]wufs = \begin{cases} \textit{false}, & \text{if } [\![B]\!]wufs = \textit{true} \\ \textit{true}, & \text{if } [\![B]\!]wufs = \textit{false} \\ \bot, & \text{if } [\![B]\!]wufs = \bot \end{cases}$$

$$[\![\textbf{skip}]\!]wuf = \text{id}_{S(x)}$$

$$[\![C_0 \,;\, C_1]\!]wuf = [\![C_0]\!]wuf \,;\, [\![C_1]\!]wuf$$

$$[\![A := E]\!]wu = [\![A]\!]wu(\text{id}_w)([\![E]\!]wu)$$

$$[\![\iota]\!]wu = u(\iota)$$

$$[\![\lambda\iota{:}\,\theta.\, P]\!]wufa = [\![P]\!]x\big([\![\pi]\!]fu \mid \iota \mapsto a\big), \text{ for } a \in [\![\theta]\!]x$$

$$[\![PQ]\!]wu = [\![P]\!]wu(\text{id}_w)([\![Q]\!]wu)$$

$$[\![\textbf{forall}[\tau]]\!]wufpgs = \text{for all } v \in [\![\textbf{val}[\tau]]\!]x, p(\text{id}_x)(v)(g)(s),$$
$$\text{for } p \in [\![\textbf{val}[\tau] \rightarrow \textbf{assert}]\!]x, g{:}\, x \rightarrow y, s \in S(y)$$

$$[\![\textbf{rec}[\theta]]\!]wufpg = \bigsqcup_{i \in \omega} (p(g))^i(\bot_\theta), \text{ for } p \in [\![\theta \rightarrow \theta]\!]x, g{:}\, x \rightarrow y$$

Table 9.2 Semantic equations.

9.3 Semantic Valuations

It remains to define a *natural transformation*

$$[\![X]\!]_{\pi\theta}{:}\, [\![\pi]\!] \dashrightarrow [\![\theta]\!]$$

for every phrase $X \in [\theta]_\pi$. In this section we discuss the valuations for several of the constructs discussed earlier. These do not depend on the category **W** of possible worlds. The semantic equations for direct semantics are given in Table 9.2; w and x are **W**-objects, $u \in [\![\pi]\!]w$, $f{:}\, w \rightarrow x$ is an **W**-morphism, $s \in S(x)$, $K \in [\![\textbf{val}[\textbf{bool}]]\!]_\pi$, $B \in [\![\textbf{exp}[\textbf{bool}]]\!]_\pi$, and natural transformations

$$cond_\theta{:}\, [\![\textbf{exp}[\textbf{bool}]]\!] \times [\![\theta]\!] \times [\![\theta]\!] \dashrightarrow [\![\theta]\!]$$

may be defined by induction on θ as follows:

$$cond_{\textbf{exp}[\tau]}(w)(b, e_0, e_1)(f)(s) = \begin{cases} e_0(f)(s), & \text{if } b(f)(s) = \textit{true} \\ e_1(f)(s), & \text{if } b(f)(s) = \textit{false} \\ \bot, & \text{if } b(f)(s) = \bot \end{cases}$$

$$cond_{\mathbf{assert}}(w)(b, p_0, p_1)(f)(s) = \begin{cases} p_0(f)(s), & \text{if } b(f)(s) = \textit{true} \\ p_1(f)(s), & \text{if } b(f)(s) = \textit{false} \\ \textit{false}, & \text{if } b(f)(s) = \perp \end{cases}$$

$$cond_{\mathbf{comm}}(w)(b, c_0, c_1)(f)(s) = \begin{cases} c_0(f)(s), & \text{if } b(f)(s) = \textit{true} \\ c_1(f)(s), & \text{if } b(f)(s) = \textit{false} \\ \textit{undefined}, & \text{if } b(f)(s) = \perp \end{cases}$$

$cond_{\mathbf{acc}[\tau]}(w)(b, a_0, a_1)(f)(e)$
$$= cond_{\mathbf{comm}}(x)\Big([\![\mathbf{exp[bool]}]\!]fb, a_0(f)(e). \, a_1(f)(e)\Big)$$

$cond_{\mathbf{var}[\tau]}(w)\big(b, (a_0, e_0), (a_1, e_1)\big) = (a, e)$
where $a = cond_{\mathbf{acc}[\tau]}(w)(b, a_0, a_1)$
and $e = cond_{\mathbf{exp}[\tau]}(w)(b, e_0, e_1)$

$cond_{\theta \to \theta'}(w)(b, p_0, p_1)(f)(a)$
$$= cond_{\theta'}(x)\Big([\![\mathbf{exp[bool]}]\!]fb, p_0(f)(a), p_1(f)(a)\Big), \text{ for } a \in [\![\theta]\!]x.$$

It can be verified by a simultaneous structural induction that all of these valuations define natural transformations, and that all of the uniformity conditions are satisfied. For example, to show that $[\![PQ]\!]$ is natural, where $P \in [\theta \to \theta']_\pi$ and $Q \in [\theta]_\pi$, consider any **W**-morphism $f \colon w \to x$; we must show that the following diagram commutes:

$$
\begin{array}{ccc}
[\![\pi]\!]w & \xrightarrow{\;[\![PQ]\!]_{\pi\theta'}(w)\;} & [\![\theta']\!]w \\[4pt]
{\scriptstyle [\![\pi]\!]f}\Big\downarrow & & \Big\downarrow{\scriptstyle [\![\theta']\!]f} \\[4pt]
[\![\pi]\!]x & \xrightarrow{\;[\![PQ]\!]_{\pi\theta'}(x)\;} & [\![\theta']\!]x
\end{array}
$$

Consider any $u \in [\![\pi]\!]$; then

$[\![PQ]\!]x([\![\pi]\!]fu)$
$$= [\![P]\!]x([\![\pi]\!]fu)(\mathrm{id}_x)\Big([\![Q]\!]x([\![\pi]\!]fu)\Big)$$
$$= [\theta \to \theta']f([\![P]\!]wu)(\mathrm{id}_x)\Big([\![\theta]\!]f([\![Q]\!]wu)\Big)$$
(by induction)
$$= [\![P]\!]wuf\Big([\![\theta]\!]f([\![Q]\!]wu)\Big)$$
(by the definition of $[\theta \to \theta']f$)
$$= [\![\theta']\!]f([\![P]\!]wu(\mathrm{id}_w))([\![Q]\!]wu)$$
(by the definition of $[\theta \to \theta']w$)
$$= [\![\theta']\!]f([\![PQ]\!]wu),$$

where the second-last step is justified by the commutativity of

$$
\begin{array}{ccc}
[\![\theta]\!]w & \xrightarrow{\;[\![P]\!]wu(\mathrm{id}_w)\;} & [\![\theta']\!]w \\[2pt]
{\scriptstyle[\![\theta]\!]f}\Big\downarrow & & \Big\downarrow{\scriptstyle[\![\theta']\!]f} \\[2pt]
[\![\theta]\!]x & \xrightarrow[\;[\![P]\!]wuf\;]{} & [\![\theta']\!]x
\end{array}
$$

To show that $[\![\lambda\iota\colon\theta.\,P]\!]wu$ is a uniform family of functions, where $P \in [\![\theta']\!]_{(\pi|\iota\mapsto\theta)}$ and $u \in [\![\pi]\!]w$, consider any **W**-morphisms $f\colon w \to x$ and $g\colon x \to y$; we must verify the commutativity of the following diagram:

$$
\begin{array}{ccc}
[\![\theta]\!]x & \xrightarrow{\;[\![\lambda\iota\colon\theta.\,P]\!]wuf\;} & [\![\theta']\!]x \\[2pt]
{\scriptstyle[\![\theta]\!]g}\Big\downarrow & & \Big\downarrow{\scriptstyle[\![\theta']\!]g} \\[2pt]
[\![\theta]\!]y & \xrightarrow[\;[\![\lambda\iota\colon\theta.\,P]\!]wu(f\,;g)\;]{} & [\![\theta']\!]y
\end{array}
$$

Consider any $a \in [\![\theta]\!]x$; then

$$
\begin{aligned}
& [\![\lambda\iota\colon\theta.\,P]\!]wu(f\,;g)\big([\![\theta]\!]ga\big) \\
={}& [\![P]\!]y\big([\![\pi]\!](f\,;g)u \mid \iota \mapsto [\![\theta]\!]ga\big) \\
={}& [\![\theta']\!]g\Big([\![P]\!]x\big([\![\pi]\!]fu \mid \iota \mapsto a\big)\Big) \\
={}& [\![\theta']\!]g\big([\![\lambda\iota\colon\theta.\,P]\!]wufa\big),
\end{aligned}
$$

where the second-last step is justified by the commutativity of the following diagram:

$$
\begin{array}{ccc}
[\![\pi']\!]x & \xrightarrow{\;[\![P]\!]x\;} & [\![\theta']\!]x \\[2pt]
{\scriptstyle[\![\pi']\!]g}\Big\downarrow & & \Big\downarrow{\scriptstyle[\![\theta']\!]g} \\[2pt]
[\![\pi']\!]y & \xrightarrow[\;[\![P]\!]y\;]{} & [\![\theta']\!]y
\end{array}
$$

where $\pi' = (\pi \mid \iota \mapsto \theta)$, because $[\![P]\!]$ is a natural transformation.

It can also be verified that the Coherence and Substitution Lemmas hold. Continuation-semantic valuations for the commands and completions would be similar.

9.4   Semantics of Local Variables

In this section, we begin to exploit the additional flexibility available to us in the possible-world framework by treating local-variable declarations. Intuitively, the effect of a local-variable declaration is to expand the set of states to allow for use of the new variable during an execution of the block body. Thus, if S is the set of states for an execution of a block $\#\,\mathbf{new}[\tau]\iota.\,C$, the meaning of the block should be, as usual, a partial function on S, but this will be defined in terms of the meaning of C when the set of allowed states is $S \times V_\tau$, where V_τ is the set of values of type τ. Notice, however, that the storage structure relevant to a procedure is that of the *call*, rather than the *definition*, of the procedure, and similarly if a command meaning is defined in one context and used in another.

We can formalize these intuitions by using a possible-world semantics in which the possible worlds are sets of states, and the changes of possible world are "expansions" from any set S to $S \times V_\tau$. We define a category $\mathbf{W}$ of possible worlds as follows. The objects are sets, $W, X, \ldots$, interpreted as sets of states representable by the run-time stack; the morphisms from W to X are pairs f, Q where f is a function from X to W and Q is an equivalence relation on X such that the following is a product diagram in $\mathbf{S}$:

$$W \xleftarrow{\;\;f\;\;} X \xrightarrow{\;\;q\;\;} X/Q$$

where q maps every element of X to its Q-equivalence class. Intuitively, f extracts the small stack embedded in a larger one, and Q relates large stacks with identical "expansion components." This is just the category-theoretic way of saying that larger stacks are formed from smaller ones by adding independent components for local variables. It can be verified that $X \cong W \times X/Q$ and that f is bijective (a one-to-one correspondence) on Q-equivalence classes.

The identity morphism id_W on an object W has as its two components: the identity function on W, and the universally-true binary relation on W. The composition (in diagrammatic order) $(f, Q)\,;\,(g, R)\colon W \longrightarrow Z$ of morphisms $f, Q\colon W \longrightarrow X$ and $g, R\colon X \longrightarrow Y$ has as its two components: the functional composition of f and g, and the equivalence relation on Y that relates $s_0, s_1 \in Y$ just if they are R-related and Q relates $g(s_0)$ and $g(s_1)$. To see that these components have the required product property, let $h, S = (f, Q)\,;\,(g, R)$ and note that

$$
\begin{aligned}
Y &\cong X \times Y/R \\
  &\cong (W \times X/Q) \times Y/R \\
  &\cong W \times (X/Q \times Y/R)
\end{aligned}
$$

$$\cong\ W \times Y/S,$$

by the isomorphism between Y/S and $X/Q \times Y/R$ established by the function mapping $[y]_S$ to $([g(y)]_Q, [y]_R)$, whose inverse is the function mapping $([x]_Q, [y]_R)$ to $\{y' \in [y]_R \mid g(y')Qx\}$.

An important kind of morphism in this category is "expansion by a set." If V is a set, then the morphism $\times V\colon W \to W \times V$ has as its components: the projection function from $W \times V$ to W, and the equivalence relation that relates (s_0, v_0) and (s_1, v_1) just if $v_0 = v_1$. Strictly speaking, the notation $\times V$ is inadequate because the domain and co-domain objects for the expansion morphism are not uniquely-determined; but these will always be evident from context.

The state-set functor S for this category of possible worlds is defined by $S(W) = W$, discretely-ordered, and $S(f, Q) = f$. Notice that S is *contravariant*.

We now consider local-variable declarations. First, we define a functor $expand_\tau\colon \mathbf{W} \to \mathbf{W}$ for each data type τ as follows:

$$expand_\tau(W) = W \times [\![\tau]\!]W$$

and

$$expand_\tau(f, Q\colon W \to X) = f_\tau, Q_\tau$$
$$\text{where } f_\tau(x, v) = \big(f(x), v\big)$$
$$\text{and } (x_0, v_0)Q_\tau(x_1, v_1) \text{ if and only if } x_0 Q x_1.$$

For any $\mathbf{W}$-morphism $f, Q\colon W \to X$, the following diagram commutes:

We can now define the acceptor and expression components

$$a_\tau(W) \in [\![\mathbf{acc}[\tau]]\!]\big(expand_\tau(W)\big)$$

and

$$e_\tau(W) \in [\![\mathbf{exp}[\tau]]\!]\big(expand_\tau(W)\big)$$

of a "new" local variable of data type τ in an expanded possible world $expand_\tau(W)$; we assume direct semantics. If $f, Q\colon expand_\tau(W) \to X$ and

$g, R\colon X \to Y$ are **W**-morphisms, and $e \in [\![\mathbf{exp}[\tau]]\!]X$,

$$a_\tau(W)(f, Q)(e)(g, R)(y_0 \in Y)$$
$$= \begin{cases} \text{undefined,} & \text{if } e(g, R)(y_0) = \bot \\ y_1, & \text{if } e(g, R)(y_0) = v_1 \in [\![\tau]\!]X \end{cases}$$

where

(i) $y_0 R y_1$ and $g(y_0)Qg(y_1)$; and

(ii) $f\big(g(y_1)\big) = (w, v_1)$, where $(w, v_0) = f\big(g(y_0)\big)$;

and

$$e_\tau(W)(f, Q)(x_0 \in X) = v, \text{ where } (w, v) = f(x_0).$$

In the definition of a_τ, a state y_1 satisfying the two conditions must exist and be unique by the "product" property of **W**-morphism (f, Q) ; (g, R). Intuitively, the effect of assigning to the acceptor is to replace the old value v_0 in the appropriate component of the stack by a new value v_1, without changing more local components (ensured by condition (i)) or more global components (i.e., the w in condition (ii)).

The variable-declaration quantifiers

$$\mathbf{new}[\tau]\colon (\mathbf{var}[\tau] \to \mathbf{comm}) \to \mathbf{comm}$$

for every data type τ may now be defined as follows. Let w, x and y be **W**-objects, $f\colon w \to x$ and $g\colon x \to y$ be **W**-morphisms, u be any environment, $p \in [\![\mathbf{var}[\tau] \to \mathbf{comm}]\!]x$, and $s \in S(y)$; then

$$[\![\mathbf{new}[\tau]]\!]wufpgs$$
$$= \begin{cases} s', & \text{if } p\big(\times [\![\tau]\!]x\big)\big(a_\tau(x), e_\tau(x)\big)\big(expand_\tau(g)\big)(s, v_\tau) \\ & \quad = (s', v'); \\ \text{undefined,} & \text{otherwise,} \end{cases}$$

where, as in Section 3.4, v_τ is an initial value for all variables of type τ. Then, using the syntactic equivalence for quantification and the valuations for abstraction and application, the derived direct-semantic interpretation of a block command declaring a local τ-variable is as follows:

$$[\![\#\,\mathbf{new}[\tau]\,\iota.\,C]\!]_{\pi\,\mathbf{comm}}wufs$$
$$= \begin{cases} s', & \text{if } [\![C]\!]w'u'f'(s, v_\tau) = (s', v'); \\ \text{undefined,} & \text{otherwise,} \end{cases}$$
$$\text{where } w' = expand_\tau(w)$$
$$\text{and } u' = \Big([\![\pi]\!]\big(\times [\![\tau]\!]w\big)(u) \mid \iota \mapsto \big(a_\tau(w), e_\tau(w)\big)\Big)$$
$$\text{and } f' = expand_\tau(f).$$

9.5   Specifications

As there are an infinity of possible worlds, there are also an infinity of laws, some proper to one, others to another, and each possible individual of any world contains in its notion the laws of its world.

G. W. Leibnitz (1686)

We now consider how to define the semantic-domain functor $[\![\mathbf{spec}]\!]$ and interpret the logical operators in the possible-world context. It might seem reasonable to make $[\![\mathbf{spec}]\!]$ a constant functor with $[\![\mathbf{spec}]\!]w = \{true, false\}$ for all w. This does not work, however, because the truth value of a formula can change as the result of a change of possible world, and this would violate the uniformity requirement for natural transformations.

A fairly general solution (i.e., one suitable for *any* category of possible worlds) with acceptable *logical* properties is to define $[\![\mathbf{spec}]\!]w$ to be the set of all families of $\mathbf{W}$-morphisms with domain w satisfying the constraint that, if $f: w \longrightarrow x$ is in such a family, then so is $f \,; g$ for *every* $g: x \longrightarrow y$; such a composition-closed family of morphisms is termed a *sieve on w*. Note that on any $\mathbf{W}$-object w there are always at least two sieves: the empty set of morphisms, and the family of all $\mathbf{W}$-morphisms with domain w. Intuitively, if the meaning of a formula in possible world w is a sieve on w and $f: w \longrightarrow x$ is an element of that sieve, then f is a change of possible world sufficient to make the formula true (and all *further* changes must maintain the truth of the formula). In effect, instead of recording the truth value of a formula at w alone, an element of $[\![\mathbf{spec}]\!]w$ records its truth value for every way of changing from possible world w (including, of course, the identity change).

An elegant way of formulating this construction is to let $[\![\mathbf{spec}]\!]$ be $1 \longrightarrow 1$, where $1: \mathbf{W} \longrightarrow \mathbf{S}$ is the (covariant) constant functor defined by $1(w) = \{*\}$ (or any other singleton set) for every w. The identity function on $\{*\}$ may be identified with *true*, and the undefined function on $\{*\}$ with *false*. Each element of $[\![\mathbf{spec}]\!]w$ is a family m of partial functions on $\{*\}$ indexed by the $\mathbf{W}$-morphisms from w and subject to the condition that, if $m(f)(*)$ is defined, then so is $m(f \,; g)(*)$; in effect, m is just the "characteristic function" of a sieve on w.

The valuations for the purely-logical forms of specification in this framework are given in Table 9.3. Note the "implicit" quantifications over changes of possible world in the valuations for implication and quantification. These are required in general to ensure the following "monotonicity" property, which is required by the naturality condition on valuations: for any specification S, $[\![S]\!]wuf$ implies $[\![S]\!]wu(f; g)$ for every appropriate g. It can be verified that all of the inference rules in Sections 2.1 and 4.5.3 preserve validity of sequents if these valuations are used.

This semantics is a category-theoretic formulation of an interpretation due to S. Kripke for *intuitionistic* logic, which is a formalization of *construc-*

$[\![\mathbf{absurd}]\!]wuf = false$

$[\![S_1 \ \& \ S_2]\!]wuf = [\![S_1]\!]wuf \ \text{ and } \ [\![S_2]\!]wuf$

$[\![S_1 \Rightarrow S_2]\!]wuf = \text{for all } g\colon x \longrightarrow y, \text{ if } [\![S_1]\!]wu(f \ ; g) \text{ then } [\![S_2]\!]wu(f \ ; g)$

$[\![\forall \iota\colon \theta. \ S]\!]wuf = \quad \text{for all } g\colon x \longrightarrow y \text{ and } m \in [\![\theta]\!]y,$

$\qquad\qquad\qquad [\![S]\!]y\big([\![\pi]\!](f \ ; g)(u) \mid \iota \mapsto m\big)(\mathrm{id}_y)$

Table 9.3 Semantics of specifications.

tive reasoning principles. As a pure logic, intuitionistic logic is weaker than classical logic; but the axioms of an intuitionistic *theory* can be stronger than would be possible in a corresponding classical theory. This additional generality will prove to be essential in our applications, and this explains why in Section 2.1 we did *not* adopt the following logical rule, which is a formalization of the non-constructive method of proof by contradiction:

Reductio ad Absurdum:

$$[\neg Z]$$

$$\vdots$$

$$\frac{\mathbf{absurd}}{Z}$$

where $\neg Z$ is an abbreviation for $Z \Rightarrow \mathbf{absurd}$. .

We conclude this section by presenting the valuations for the atomic formulas that we have used in our programming logics. For equivalence and approximation,

$[\![Z_1 \equiv_\theta Z_2]\!]wuf$
$= \text{for all } g\colon x \longrightarrow y, \ [\![\theta]\!](f \ ; g)([\![Z_1]\!]wu) = [\![\theta]\!](f \ ; g)([\![Z_2]\!]wu)$

$[\![Z_1 \sqsubseteq_\theta Z_2]\!]wuf$
$= \text{for all } g\colon x \longrightarrow y, \ [\![\theta]\!](f \ ; g)([\![Z_1]\!]wu) \sqsubseteq [\![\theta]\!](f \ ; g)([\![Z_2]\!]wu)$

For Hoare triples (using direct semantics):

$[\![\{P\}C\{Q\}]\!]wuf \quad = \quad \text{for all } s_0, s_1 \in S(x),$

$\qquad\qquad\qquad\qquad [\![P]\!]wufs_0 \text{ and } [\![C]\!]wufs_0 = s_1 \text{ imply } [\![Q]\!]wufs_1$

and for Hoare doubles (using continuation semantics):

$[\![\{P\}K]\!]wuf \quad = \quad \text{for all } s \in S(x) \text{ and } o \in O(x),$

$\qquad\qquad\qquad\qquad [\![P]\!]wufs \text{ and } [\![K]\!]wufs = o \text{ imply } \phi(o)$

All of the axioms for our Algol-like language are valid with these interpretations. For example, we will show the validity of the Eta Law. Suppose that $F \in [\theta \longrightarrow \theta']_\pi$ with $\iota \notin \mathrm{dom}\,\pi$ and consider any $u \in [\![\pi]\!]$; we must show that $[\![\lambda\iota\!:\!\theta.\,F(\iota)\ \equiv_{\theta\longrightarrow\theta'}\ F]\!]wu(\mathrm{id}_w)$. Consider any **W**-morphism $f\!:\!w\to x$; we now must show that

$$[\![\theta\to\theta']\!](f)([\![\lambda\iota\!:\!\theta.\,F(\iota)]\!]wu)\ =\ [\![\theta\to\theta']\!](f)([\![F]\!]wu).$$

Consider any **W**-morphism $g\!:\!x\to y$ and $a\in[\![\theta]\!]y$; then

$$
\begin{aligned}
&[\![\theta\to\theta']\!](f)([\![\lambda\iota\!:\!\theta.\,F(\iota)]\!]wu)(g)(a)\\
=\ &[\![\lambda\iota\!:\!\theta.\,F(\iota)]\!]wu(f\,;g)(a)\\
=\ &[\![F(\iota)]\!]yu',\quad\text{where } u' = ([\![\pi]\!](f\,;g)u\mid\iota\mapsto a)\\
=\ &[\![F]\!]yu'(\mathrm{id}_y)([\![\iota]\!]yu')\\
=\ &[\![F]\!]y([\![\pi]\!](f\,;g)u)(\mathrm{id}_y)(a)\quad\text{(because } \iota\notin\mathrm{dom}\,\pi)\\
=\ &[\![\theta\to\theta']\!](f\,;g)([\![F]\!]wu)(\mathrm{id}_y)(a)\quad\text{(by the naturality of } [\![F]\!])\\
=\ &[\![\theta\to\theta']\!](f)([\![F]\!]wu)(g)(a)\quad\text{(by the definition of } [\![\theta\to\theta']\!]j).
\end{aligned}
$$

9.6   Non-Interference Specifications

Intuitionistic logic is, when measured along certain dimensions, weaker than its classical counterpart. This very weakness, however, holds tremendous potential value: intuitionistic logic allows axioms which are classically false but mathematically efficient to be consistent with powerful theories.

C. McCarty (1984)

It was pointed out in Section 6.4 that Hoare-like reasoning about assignment commands in the presence of procedures is quite problematical because of the possibilities of interference through non-local variables, aliasing, and bad variables. In this section, we describe one approach to dealing with these issues. The basic idea is to introduce new atomic specification formulas as follows:

Good Variable:

$$\frac{V\!:\mathbf{var}[\tau]}{\mathbf{gv}_\tau(V)\!:\mathbf{spec}}$$

Non-Interference:

$$\frac{C\!:\theta\quad E\!:\theta'}{C\mathbin{\#}E\!:\mathbf{spec}}$$

Informally, $\mathbf{gv}_\tau(V)$ asserts that V is a good variable, and $C\mathbin{\#}E$ asserts that every way of using C preserves any value produced by using E. For example, if C is a command and E is an assertion, then every execution of C preserves the truth or falsity of E; if C is an acceptor, then no assignment to C can interfere with E; and if C is a procedure, then no call of C can interfere with E other than by using an argument that interferes with E.

Then, an axiom scheme for assignment commands in the presence of procedures is

$$\pi \vdash \mathbf{gv}_\tau(V) \,\&\, V \,\#\, Q \Rightarrow \{Q(E)\}V := E\{Q(V)\},$$

when $V \in \left[\mathbf{var}[\tau]\right]_\pi$, $E \in \left[\mathbf{exp}[\tau]\right]_\pi$, and $Q \in \left[\mathbf{exp}[\tau] \rightarrow \mathbf{assert}\right]_\pi$. The consequent of the axiom is essentially similar to Hoare's axiom discussed in Section 3.6, but, in the more general context, the antecedents guard against possible bad variables, interference through non-locals, or aliasing.

Of course, the formal system must provide ways to discharge good-variable and non-interference assumptions. The following axiom allows a non-interference specification to be "decomposed" into a conjunction of non-interference formulas for its free identifiers:

Non-Interference Decomposition:

$$\pi \vdash \iota \,\#\, \iota' \text{ for every } \iota \in \mathit{free}(X) \text{ and } \iota' \in \mathit{free}(X')$$
$$\Rightarrow X \,\#\, X'$$

Intuitively, this axiom captures the fact that there are no *anonymous* "channels of interference" in our language.

The following axiom allows good-variable and non-interference assumptions about locally-declared variables to be discharged:

Local-Variable Declaration:

$$\pi \vdash \big(\forall \iota{:}\,\mathbf{var}[\tau].\,\mathbf{gv}_\tau(\iota) \,\&\, \cdots \,\&\, \iota \,\#\, E_i \,\&\, \cdots \,\&\, C_j \,\#\, \iota \,\&\, \cdots$$
$$\Rightarrow \{P\}C\{Q\}\big)$$
$$\Rightarrow \{P\} \,\#\, \mathbf{new}[\tau]\,\iota.\,C\{Q\},$$

when $\iota \notin \mathrm{dom}\,\pi$, $P, Q \in [\mathbf{assert}]_\pi$, $C \in [\mathbf{comm}]_{(\pi|\iota \mapsto \mathbf{var}[\tau])}$, and the E_i and C_j are arbitrary phrases in π. Essentially, this states that the identifiers declared by local-variable declarations denote variables that

- are good variables;
- do not interfere with non-local entities; and
- are not interfered with by non-local entities.

Before discussing further axioms for non-interference formulas, consider the following "weak" interpretation of $C \,\#\, P$ when C is a command and P is an assertion (in conventional direct semantics):

$$[\![C \,\#\, P]\!]u$$
$$= \text{ for all } s_0, s_1 \in S, \text{ if } [\![C]\!]us_0 = s_1 \text{ then } [\![P]\!]us_1 = [\![P]\!]us_0;$$

that is, every *complete* execution of C leaves the value of assertion P unchanged. This would be satisfactory for some applications, but a stronger and more useful interpretation of $C \,\#\, P$ is possible: intuitively, the value of P is to remain constant *throughout* the (terminating) executions of C. To see the motivation for this, consider the following axiom:

Constancy:

$$\pi \vdash C \# R \ \& \ (\{R\} \Rightarrow \{P\}C\{Q\}) \ \Rightarrow \ \{P \text{ and } R\}C\{Q \text{ and } R\}$$

when $C \in [\mathbf{comm}]_\pi$ and $P, Q, R \in [\mathbf{assert}]_\pi$. This asserts that, if no execution of C interferes with assertion R and R holds before an execution of C, then R will continue to hold throughout the execution, and so it is possible to treat R as a static assertion in partial-correctness reasoning about C.

For example, suppose that C is a binary-search algorithm and R asserts that the array being searched is sorted; it is obvious by inspection that $C \# R$, and so the axiom justifies "factoring" R out of the pre and post-conditions for the algorithm and *also* assuming R whenever necessary in the verification of C. With the weaker interpretation of non-interference, only the following weaker form of Constancy would be valid:

$$C \# R \ \& \ \{P\}C\{Q\} \ \Rightarrow \ \{P \text{ and } R\}C\{Q \text{ and } R\},$$

and R could not be used as a "local" mathematical fact in reasoning about C.

Similarly, the following axiom requires the stronger interpretation of non-interference:

Non-Interference Composition:

$$\pi \vdash C \# E \ \& \ (X \# E \Rightarrow \{P\}C\{Q\}) \ \Rightarrow \ \{P\}C\{Q\}$$

when $C \in [\mathbf{comm}]_\pi$ and $P, Q \in [\mathbf{assert}]_\pi$. It asserts that, if C does not interfere with E, then it is possible to assume that no phrase interferes with E in partial-correctness reasoning about C.

A small example will demonstrate the use of some of the axioms for good-variable and non-interference specifications. We can use *Constancy* and *Non-Interference Decomposition* to derive

$$c \# n \ \Rightarrow \ \{n = 0\}c\{n = 0\}$$

for $c : \mathbf{comm}$ and $n : \mathbf{var}[\mathbf{nat}]$, and then conventional Hoare-logic axioms to derive

$$c \# n \ \& \ \mathbf{gv}(n) \ \Rightarrow \ \{\mathbf{true}\}n := 0 \, ; c \, ; \mathbf{if} \, n = 0 \, \mathbf{then} \, \mathbf{diverge}\{\mathbf{false}\}$$

Finally, the *Local-Variable Declaration* axiom can be used to show that the following block B

> $\# \, \mathbf{new}[\mathbf{nat}] \, n. \, n := 0;$
> $c;$
> $\mathbf{if} \, n = 0 \, \mathbf{then} \, \mathbf{diverge}$

discussed at the end of Section 7.2 satisfies the specification $\{\mathbf{true}\}B\{\mathbf{false}\}$, and so is equivalent to **diverge**, as expected.

We now turn to a detailed consideration of the interpretation of non-interference formulas. At first sight, the strong interpretation $C \# P$ seems to require treating the semantics of commands in an "operational" way; i.e., dealing explicitly with "intermediate" states of command executions. But the desired strong interpretation of $C \# P$ can be specified in a more elegant and satisfactory way by using possible-world semantics. The category of possible worlds $\mathbf{W}$ is re-defined so that the objects and morphisms are sets of (allowed) states and pairs f, Q, as before, but we now weaken the condition on f and Q so that f is required only to be *injective* on Q-equivalence classes; i.e., $f, Q: W \to X$ is an $\mathbf{W}$-morphism if and only if

- f is a function from X to W;

- Q is an equivalence relation on X; and

- for all $x, x' \in X$, xQx' and $f(x) = f(x')$ imply $x = x'$.

The identity morphisms and composites are as before.

We can show that, for $h, S = (f, Q) ; (g, R): W \to Y$, h is injective on S-equivalence classes as follows. Consider $y, y' \in Y$ such that ySy' and $h(y) = h(y')$; then yRy' and $g(y)Qg(y')$ by the definition of S, and $f\bigl(g(y)\bigr) = f\bigl(g(y')\bigr)$ by the definition of h. By the injectivity of f on Q-equivalence classes, $g(y) = g(y')$, and then, by the injectivity of g on R-equivalence classes, $y = y'$.

In this richer category, there is, as previously, an expansion morphism, $\times V: W \to W \times V$, for any data type V, and also

- a *state-set restriction* morphism, $\lceil W': W \to W'$, for any $W' \subseteq W$, where the components are: the insertion function from W' to W, and the universally-true binary relation on W'; and

- a *state-change restriction* morphism, $\lceil Q: W \to W$, for any equivalence relation Q on W, where the components are: the identity function on W, and Q.

Intuitively, $\lceil W'$ changes worlds so that command executions must stay within W' (or fail to terminate), and $\lceil Q$ imposes the constraint that a command execution can change the state from s to s' only if sQs'. State-change restrictions are enforced by defining $[\![\mathbf{comm}]\!]$ to be the following *sub*-functor of $S \to S$:

$[\![\mathbf{comm}]\!]w$

$$= \left\{ c \in (S \to S)(w) \;\middle|\; \begin{array}{c} \text{for all } f: w \to x \text{ and } s \in S(x), \\ S(\lceil X') ; c(f, Q) = c\bigl((f, Q)\bigr) ; \lceil X') ; S(\lceil X'), \\ \text{where } X' = \{s' \in S(x) \mid s'Qs\} \end{array} \right\},$$

where S is, as before, the state-set functor. The condition ensures that, for every $\mathbf{W}$-morphism $f, Q: w \to x$, execution of $c(f, Q)$ stays within a Q-equivalence class. For the morphism part,

$$[\![\mathbf{comm}]\!](f, Q)(c)(g, R) = c\bigl((f, Q) ; (g, R)\bigr)$$

and it can be verified that this defines a functor from $\mathbf{W}$ to $\mathbf{D}$.

With $[\![\tau]\!]$ as before, the remaining definitions of Table 9.1 define the other semantic-domain functors appropriate to our new category of possible worlds. The semantic equations of Section 9.3 may also be adopted without modification. For variable declarations, the only change from Section 9.4 is that, in the definition of $a_\tau(W)$, an updated state $y_1 \in Y$ satisfying the two conditions need not exist, and then

$$a_\tau(W)(f, Q: W \longrightarrow X)(e)(g, R: X \longrightarrow Y)(y_0 \in Y)$$

must be undefined; but if such a state exists, the injectivity requirement on morphisms ensures that it is unique.

We now interpret $C \mathbin{\#} P$ for $C: \theta$ and $P: \mathbf{assert}$ using a state-change restriction morphism as follows: for $f: w \longrightarrow x$ in $\mathbf{W}$,

$$[\![C \mathbin{\#} P]\!]wuf \;=\; \Big([\![\theta]\!]f\big([\![C]\!]wu\big) = [\![\theta]\!]\big(f; \lceil R\rceil\big)\big([\![C]\!]wu\big)\Big)$$

where, for $s, s' \in S(x)$, sRs' if and only if $[\![P]\!]wufs = [\![P]\!]wufs'$. Intuitively, the equation asserts that C does not interfere with P just if restricting C so that the value of P is invariant does not make the execution less defined. A use of C that, at some point, attempts to change the value of P will be non-terminating if this state-change is not "allowed" by equivalence relation R, and this difference between the restricted and the unrestricted use of C indicates potential interference. A natural generalization of this interpretation also allows treating $C \mathbin{\#} E$ when E is *any* (possibly higher-order) expression-like phrase; we refer the reader to [O'H90, OT91] for details.

We can now use this interpretation of $C \mathbin{\#} E$ to give the following definition of good-variable specifications:

$$\mathbf{gv}_\tau(V) \;\equiv\; \forall \iota_0: \mathbf{exp}[\tau].\, \forall \iota_1: \mathbf{exp}[\tau] \longrightarrow \mathbf{assert}.$$
$$V \mathbin{\#} \iota_1 \Rightarrow \{\iota_1(\iota_0)\}V := \iota_0\{\iota_1(V)\}$$

for any ι_0 and ι_1 not free in V. Intuitively, this states that a good variable is one for which Hoare's assignment axiom is always valid (provided that the variable does not interfere inappropriately with the assertion).

Using these interpretations, it is possible to validate all of the axioms we have discussed; see [O'H90, OT91]. A key point for the validation of Non-Interference Composition and Constancy is that the implicit quantification in the possible-world valuation for intuitionistic implication allows restriction to a subset of states for which an assertion or an expression has a constant value, and, in fact, it can be shown that only trivial models would be possible if the non-constructive *Reductio ad Absurdum* were added to the logical rules.

9.7   Semantics of Block Expressions

To interpret block expressions (Section 7.6), it again seems necessary to use
the possible-world approach, because we need to impose local constraints
that preclude side effects to non-local variables and non-local jumps.

We first enrich the category of possible worlds to allow for "local" answer
domains. Consider the category whose objects are domains, interpreted as
domains of local answers, and whose morphisms are injective continuous
functions, interpreted as mapping non-local answers into their local repre-
sentatives. Then we take $\mathbf{W}$, our category of possible worlds, to be the
product of the state-set category used before and this answer-domain category; that is, the objects of $\mathbf{W}$ are pairs W, D, where W is the local set of
states and D is the domain of local answers, and the morphisms from W, D
to X, E have the form $(f, Q), i$ where f is a function from X to W, Q is an
equivalence relation on X, i is an injection from D to E, and f is injective
on Q-equivalence classes.

In this category, we can define, for every object W, D, a *state-set restriction* morphism

$$\lceil W' \colon W, D \to W', D$$

for any subset W' of W, a *state-change restriction* morphism

$$\lceil Q \colon W, D \to W, D$$

for any equivalence relation Q on W, and a *state-set expansion* morphism

$$\times V \colon W, D \to (W \times V), D$$

for any set V, essentially as before, but ignoring the answer-related components. Furthermore, we can now define an *answer-domain adjunction*
morphism

$$+D' \colon W, D \to W, (D + D')$$

for any domain D' which is to be "added" to the local-answer component;
$+D'$ is like the identity morphism except that the second component is the
canonical injection from D into the domain sum $D + D'$.

We now re-define S to be the (contravariant) functor such that $S(W, D) =
W$ and $S((f, Q), i) = f$, and O to be the (covariant) functor such that
$O(W, D) = A + E + D$ and $O((f, Q), i) = \mathrm{id}_A + \mathrm{id}_E + i$, where A is the domain
of *program answers* and E is the domain of "erroneous outputs." Then, as
before, we have $[\![\mathbf{compl}]\!] = S \to O$, so that the uniformity condition on
any $k \in (S \to O)(w)$ requires commutativity of

$$
\begin{array}{ccc}
S(x) & \xrightarrow{\ k(f)\ } & O(x) \\[4pt]
{\scriptstyle S(g)}\Big\uparrow & & \Big\downarrow{\scriptstyle O(g)} \\[4pt]
S(y) & \xrightarrow{\ k(f\,;\,g)\ } & O(y)
\end{array}
$$

for all changes of possible world $f\colon w \to x$ and $g\colon x \to y$ whenever $k(f\,;\,g)$ gives a defined result.

In this context, ϕ, the "post-condition" for outputs, must be the natural transformation from O to $[\![\mathbf{bool}]\!]$ whose components act as before on global outputs (elements of A or E), and map all local answers to *true*. Then,

$$[\![\{P\}K]\!]wuf \;=\; \text{for all } s \in S(x) \text{ and } o \in O(x),$$
$$[\![P]\!]wufs \text{ and } [\![K]\!]wufs = o \text{ imply } \phi_x(o)$$

Finally, to treat the block-expression quantifier **result**$[\tau]$, we define a functor $adjoin_\tau\colon \mathbf{W} \to \mathbf{W}$ as follows:

$$adjoin_\tau(W, D) = W, (D + V)$$
$$adjoin_\tau\big((f, Q), i\colon W, D \to W', D'\big) = (f, Q), i'$$

where $i' = i + \mathrm{id}_V$, for $V = [\![\tau]\!](W, D)$. For any change of possible worlds $f\colon w \to x$, the following diagram commutes:

$$
\begin{array}{ccc}
w & \xrightarrow{\ +[\![\tau]\!]w\ } & adjoin_\tau(w) \\[4pt]
{\scriptstyle f}\Big\downarrow & & \Big\downarrow{\scriptstyle adjoin_\tau(f)} \\[4pt]
x & \xrightarrow{\ +[\![\tau]\!]x\ } & adjoin_\tau(x)
\end{array}
$$

Then, if w, x and y are **W**-objects, $f\colon w \to x$ and $g\colon x \to y$ are **W**-morphisms, u is any environment, $p \in [\![(\mathbf{exp}[\tau] \to \mathbf{compl}) \to \mathbf{compl}]\!]x$, and $s \in S(y)$,

$$[\![\mathbf{result}[\tau]]\!]wufpgs$$
$$= \begin{cases} v, & \text{if } p\big(+[\![\tau]\!]x\big)(q)\Big(adjoin_\tau\big(g\,;\,\lceil\{s\}\rceil\big)\Big)(s) = v \in [\![\tau]\!]x \\ \bot, & \text{otherwise,} \end{cases}$$

where $q \in [\![\mathbf{exp}[\tau] \to \mathbf{compl}]\!]x'$ for $x' = adjoin_\tau(x)$ is defined as follows: for $h\colon x' \to y$, $e \in [\![\mathbf{exp}[\tau]]\!]y$, $i\colon y \to w$, and $s' \in S(w)$,

$$q(h)(e)(i)(s') = \begin{cases} \text{undefined,} & \text{if } e(i)(s') = \bot; \\ O(h\,;\,i)\big(e(i)(s') \text{ in } O(x')\big), & \text{otherwise.} \end{cases}$$

This yields the following interpretation for the block expression:

$$\llbracket \# \, \textbf{result}[\tau] \, \iota. \, K \rrbracket wufs = \begin{cases} v, & \text{if } \llbracket K \rrbracket w'u'f's = v \in \llbracket \tau \rrbracket x \text{ in } O(x'); \\ \bot, & \text{otherwise,} \end{cases}$$

where $w' = adjoin_\tau(w)$ and $x' = adjoin_\tau(x)$

and $u' = \left(\llbracket \pi \rrbracket (+ \llbracket \tau \rrbracket w)(u) \mid \iota \mapsto q \right)$

and $f' = adjoin_\tau(f; \lceil \{s\} \rceil),$

and $q \in \llbracket \textbf{exp}[\tau] \longrightarrow \textbf{compl} \rrbracket w'$ is defined in the same way as the q above. The restriction to $\{s\}$ precludes side effects, and the ability to discriminate between "local" and "non-local" answers allows us to produce $\bot$ if there is a non-local jump.

It must be admitted, however, that the treatment of side effects given above is not entirely satisfactory. There are side effects that can be regarded as "benevolent" in the sense that, when viewed from a sufficiently abstract point of view, they do *not* change the state. A typical example is "path compression" while accessing the root of a tree when using the rooted-tree representation of a set partition; the change in the representation does not change the abstract partition being represented. Such benevolent side effects should be allowed, but it is not clear how this can be done without opening the door to non-benevolent ones as well.

It is also not clear how to reason about block expressions. The fundamental difficulty is that assertions about the value of a block expression must allow for the possibility that the body may fail to terminate (or attempt a side effect or non-local jump); but, in our intuitionistic partial-correctness framework, there is no way to express that completions or commands terminate. This is surprising, because $\{\textbf{true}\}C\{\textbf{false}\}$ asserts that C never terminates. But $\neg\{\textbf{true}\}C\{\textbf{false}\}$ (i.e., $\{\textbf{true}\}C\{\textbf{false}\} \Rightarrow \textbf{absurd}$) asserts that, in every possible world, C sometimes terminates; this is false for *every* C because there are possible worlds with *empty* state-sets.

Exercises

9.1   Verify that for any category **W** and functors $D, E \colon \textbf{W} \longrightarrow \textbf{D}$, $D \times E$, $D_\bot$, $D \longrightarrow E$, and $D \longrightarrow E$, as defined in Section 9.2, are functors from **W** to **D**, that they reduce to the conventional domain constructions if **W** is the trivial (single-object and single-morphism) category, and similarly if D and E are functors from **W** to **S**.

9.2   Verify that all of the semantic equations in this chapter define natural transformations, and that all uniformity conditions on families of functions are satisfied.

9.3 State and prove generalizations of the Coherence and Substitution Lemmas for the semantics of Section 9.3.

9.4 Verify that validity is preserved by all of the inference rules of Sections 2.1 and 4.5.3 using the valuations of Section 9.3.

9.5 Verify the validity of all of the axioms of Sections 4.5 and 5.6 using the valuations of Sections 9.3 and 9.5.

Bibliographic Notes

Kripke's semantics of intuitionistic logic is given in [Kri65]; see also [vD83, Dum77, Gol79]. Application of the functor-category approach to semantics of programming languages was initiated by [Rey81b, Ole82, Ole85] and extended to programming logics in [Ten86, Ten91]. The use of non-interference and good-variable formulas to allow Hoare-like reasoning about programs in Algol-like languages with procedures is from [Rey81a, Rey82]. The interpretation of non-interference formulas presented here is a simplified version of the interpretation given in [O'H90, OT91] which evolved from [Ten91]. The treatment of block expressions is from [TT91].

Chapter 10

Recursively-Defined Domains

We cannot feel happy with any domains defined by a self-referential equation until we have proved their existence.

C. Strachey (1972)

Recursive definitions of domain elements were discussed in Chapter 5. For some applications it is necessary or convenient to define entire sets or domains recursively. For example, it is natural to define the set of all finite sequences of elements of $T = \{true, false\}$ by the equation

$$D = \{nil\} + T \times D.$$

This says that a sequence of truth values is either *nil*, the zero-component sequence, or a non-nil sequence having a first component that is a truth value and a remainder that is a sequence of truth values. In this chapter, we discuss the solution of such equations.

We begin by discussing some simple examples in an *ad hoc* fashion in order to convey the essential ideas underlying the solution method, and then turn to a general treatment using category-theoretic techniques. Some applications are discussed in the final section.

10.1   Examples

To solve the equation

$$D = \{nil\} + T \times D,$$

we proceed by analogy with the method used to solve equations of the form

$$c = \cdots c \cdots$$

in Section 3.3; i.e., start with an initial object c_0, define better-and-better approximations by the inductive rule $c_{i+1} = \cdots c_i \cdots$, and obtain the desired "least" solution as the limit (union) of all of the c_i. Here, we let $D_0 = \emptyset$ (the empty set) and define

$$D_{i+1} = \{nil\} + T \times D_i$$

for every $i \in \omega$. This gives us

- $D_0 \;\; = \;\; \emptyset$
- $D_1 \;\; = \;\; \{nil\} + T \times \emptyset \;\; = \;\; \{nil\} + \emptyset \;\; = \;\; \{(0, nil)\}$
- $D_2 \;\; = \;\; \{nil\} + T \times D_1$
  $= \;\; \{(0, nil)\} \cup \{(1, (true, (0, nil))), (1, (false, (0, nil)))\}$
- $D_3 \;\; = \;\; \{nil\} + T \times D_2$
  $= \;\; \{(0, nil)\} \cup \{(1, (true, (0, nil))), (1, (false, (0, nil)))\}$
  $\cup \; \{ \; (1, (true, (1, (true, (0, nil))))),$
  $\qquad (1, (true, (1, (false, (0, nil))))),$
  $\qquad (1, (false, (1, (true, (0, nil))))),$
  $\qquad (1, (false, (1, (false, (0, nil))))) \; \},$

and so on. If we regard element $(0, nil)$ as representing the empty sequence, and an element of the form $(1, (t, s))$ as representing the non-empty sequence with first component t and remainder s, we see that, for each $i \in \omega$, D_i is the set of truth-value sequences having length less than i.

Each D_i can be embedded in D_{i+j} for all $j \in \omega$. In fact, $D_i \subseteq D_{i+j}$, and so we can define the set

$$D_\infty \;\; = \;\; \bigcup_{i \in \omega} D_i$$

which is a set of (representations of) all finite sequences of truth values, and this set does satisfy the equation

$$D \;\; = \;\; \{nil\} + T \times D$$

when it is substituted for D. Of course, there is no reason to distinguish between isomorphic domains and so the set $T^* = \sum_{i \in \omega} T^i$, which is isomorphic to D_∞, can also be regarded as a solution to the equation. In general, we will interpret an equation $D = \cdots D \cdots$ as if it were $D \cong \cdots D \cdots$.

There are also solutions to the equation that are *not* isomorphic to D_∞; for example, the set $T^* \cup T^\omega$ of all finite *and* denumerably-infinite truth-value sequences satisfies the isomorphism

$$D \;\; \cong \;\; \{nil\} + T \times D.$$

The special significance of D_∞ is that it is, up to isomorphism, the *least* such solution of the equation in a certain sense that will be defined later.

Consider now the equation

$$D \;\; = \;\; (T \times D)_\perp.$$

We again start with $D_0 = \emptyset$ and, for every $i \in \omega$, define

$$D_{i+1} = (T \times D_i)_\perp.$$

This gives us

- $D_0 = \emptyset$
- $D_1 = (T \times D_0)_\perp = \{\perp\}$
- $D_2 = (T \times D_1)_\perp =$

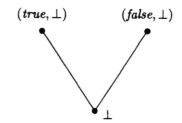

- $D_3 = (T \times D_2)_\perp =$

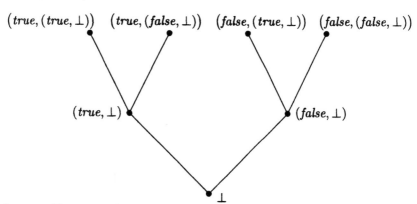

and so on. If we regard $\perp$ as representing the empty sequence and (t, s) as representing the non-empty sequence with first component t and remainder s, we see that each D_i is the domain of truth-value sequences having length less than i, ordered by the *prefix* ordering; i.e., $s \sqsubseteq s'$ if and only if s is a prefix (initial subsequence) of s'.

For every i, D_i is, in a sense to be defined precisely later, a *sub-domain* of D_{i+j} for all $j \in \omega$. In fact, if we identify the least elements, D_i is a sub-poset of each of the D_{i+j}, and so we can define the union $\bigcup_{i \in \omega} D_i$ and partially-order it by the prefix relation, which extends the ordering in each of the D_i. This poset satisfies the equation

$$D = (T \times D)_\perp;$$

however, it is not a satisfactory solution. The problem is that $\bigcup_{i \in \omega} D_i$ is not a domain! Consider any ω-sequence of truth values

$$t_0, t_1, t_2, \ldots, t_j, \ldots;$$

the ω-chain of its finite prefixes

$$\bot \sqsubseteq (t_0, \bot) \sqsubseteq (t_0, (t_1, \bot)) \sqsubseteq (t_0, (t_1, (t_2, \bot))) \sqsubseteq \cdots$$

must have as its least upper bound a representation of the *infinite* sequence of truth values; but every element of the union represents a *finite* sequence, and so the union is not ω-chain complete.

The union must be completed by adding a "top layer" of limit points which are essentially denumerably-infinite sequences of truth values. Each such limit point is approximated by all of its finite prefixes, as in the following Hasse-diagram fragment:

$$\bullet \ (t_0, (t_1, (t_2, \ldots, (t_j, \ldots) \ldots)))$$

$$\vdots$$

$$\bullet \ (t_0, (t_1, (t_2, \bot)))$$
$$\bullet \ (t_0, (t_1, \bot))$$
$$\bullet \ (t_0, \bot)$$
$$\bullet \ \bot$$

As a final example, consider the equation

$$D = B + (D \to D).$$

If $D \to D$ is the set of all functions on set D, this equation does not have non-trivial solutions. To see this, notice that d, the number of elements of D, must satisfy the equation $d = b + d^d$, where b is the cardinality of B, and the only possibility is $d = 1$ when $b = 0$. To obtain a domain of values appropriate to this application, one must allow for possible *non-termination* of execution by either using partial functions, as in

$$D = B + (D \rightharpoonup D),$$

or "lifting," as in

$$D = \big(B + (D \to D)\big)_{\bot}.$$

By ensuring that D is a domain with a non-trivial ordering, the cardinality of the function spaces is reduced because the functions are required to be *continuous*, and we will see that the equations have non-trivial solutions.

In the following two sections, we discuss recursive definitions of domains in more detail. The general method we describe is closely analogous to the way recursive definitions were solved within domains in Chapter 5. We will define analogs for **D**, the category of domains, of the concepts of partial ordering, least element, least upper bound, continuity, and least fixed point *in* domains.

10.2   Embeddings of Domains

And embed D_n into D_{n+1}? Yes, but with care. I consider this the most original step in my construction: once I had this straight all else was forced.

D. S. Scott (1972)

In this section, we first define how one domain might be embeddable as a "sub-domain" of another. This is the analog of the $\sqsubseteq$ relations in domains, but the situation is slightly more complex here because a domain can be a sub-domain of another in more than one way. We then show the existence of "least upper bounds" of ω-sequences of domain embeddings.

If D and E are domains, a continuous function $f: D \to E$ is an *embedding* (of domains) just if there is a continuous partial function $g: E \rightharpoonup D$ (termed a *projection*) such that

- $f \,;\, g = \mathrm{id}_D$, and
- $g \,;\, f \sqsubseteq \mathrm{id}_E$.

The first requirement ensures that f is an injection of D into E, and the second requirement ensures that the projection function maps each E-element into its "best-defined" analog in D (if there is one).

Proposition 10.1   *If $f: D \to E$ is an embedding with $g, g': E \rightharpoonup D$ as corresponding projections, then $g = g'$.*

Proof. We can show that $g' \sqsubseteq g$ as follows:

$$g' = g' \,;\, \mathrm{id}_D = g' \,;\, f \,;\, g \sqsubseteq \mathrm{id}_E \,;\, g = g$$

The proof in the other direction is similar. $\square$

This shows that an embedding uniquely determines a corresponding projection. We will use the notation f^P for the projection corresponding to an embedding f, and write $f: D \lhd E$ to express that f is an embedding of D into E.

We now show that there is a *category*, which we call $\mathbf{D}^E$, with the same objects as $\mathbf{D}$ and domain embeddings as the morphisms.

Proposition 10.2

(a) $\mathrm{id}_D: D \lhd D$, with $\mathrm{id}_D^P = \mathrm{id}_D$.

(b) *If $f: D \lhd E$ and $g: E \lhd F$, then $f \,;\, g: D \lhd F$ with $(f \,;\, g)^P = g^P \,;\, f^P$.*

Proof. The first part is trivial. For the second part, $f \,;\, g \,;\, g^P \,;\, f^P = f \,;\, f^P = \mathrm{id}_D$ and $g^P \,;\, f^P \,;\, f \,;\, g \sqsubseteq g^P \,;\, g \sqsubseteq \mathrm{id}_E$. $\square$

The category $\mathbf{D}^E$ has an initial object: it is the empty set, $\emptyset$. The unique embedding from $\emptyset$ to any domain D is the empty function, the corresponding projection being the everywhere-undefined partial function from D to $\emptyset$. This is the analog of the least element $\bot$ in a domain.

We also want to show that $\mathbf{D}^E$ is "ω-complete." Let Δ be an ω-sequence of domains and embeddings, as follows:

$$D_0 \overset{f_0}{\vartriangleleft} D_1 \overset{f_1}{\vartriangleleft} D_2 \overset{f_2}{\vartriangleleft} \cdots \overset{f_{i-1}}{\vartriangleleft} D_i \overset{f_i}{\vartriangleleft} D_{i+1} \overset{f_{i+1}}{\vartriangleleft} \cdots,$$

which we abbreviate by

$$\Delta = \{f_i : D_i \vartriangleleft D_{i+1} \mid i \in \omega\}.$$

We can define a domain that will turn out to be a "least upper bound" for Δ as follows. Let D_∞ be the domain whose elements are all of the *partial* ω-sequences

$$s \in \omega \longrightarrow \bigcup_{i\in\omega} D_i$$

such that

1. s_j is defined for some $j \in \omega$;
2. for all $j \in \omega$, if s_j is defined then $s_j \in D_j$;
3. for all $j \in \omega$, if either s_j or $f_j^P(s_{j+1})$ is defined, then both are defined and then $s_j = f_j^P(s_{j+1})$,

with the pointwise ordering; that is, $s \sqsubseteq s'$ in D_∞ if and only if, for every $j \in \omega$, if s_j is defined, then so is s'_j and then $s_j \sqsubseteq s'_j$ in D_j. The least upper bound of an ω-chain $s \in (D_\infty)^\omega$ is given by

$$\left(\bigsqcup_{i\in\omega} s_{i\cdot}\right)(j) = \bigsqcup_{i\in\omega} s_i(j)$$

for every $j \in \omega$.

For every $i \in \omega$, we can define embeddings $\eta_i : D_i \vartriangleleft D_\infty$ as follows:

$$\eta_i(d)(j) = \begin{cases} (f_i \, ; f_{i+1} \, ; \cdots ; f_{j-1})(d), & \text{if } i \le j \\ (f_{i-1}^P \, ; f_{i-2}^P \, ; \cdots ; f_j^P)(d), & \text{if } i > j, \end{cases}$$

for every $d \in D_i$ and $j \in \omega$, where the corresponding projection function $\eta_i^P : D_\infty \longrightarrow D_i$ is as follows:

$$\eta_i^P(s) = s_i$$

for every $s \in D_\infty$. It can easily be verified that the family

$$\{\eta_i : D_i \vartriangleleft D_\infty \mid i \in \omega\}$$

of embeddings has the following commutativity property for every $i \in \omega$:

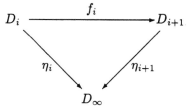

Any such commuting family of embeddings is termed a *cone from* Δ; we write $\eta\colon \Delta \longrightarrow D_\infty$, and call D_∞ the *vertex* of the cone. Any such cone is analogous to an upper bound of an ω-chain in a domain. In fact, the following theorem shows that η as defined above is the *co-limiting* (or universal, or most-general) cone from Δ, up to isomorphism of the vertex; this is the analog of verifying the existence of a *least* upper bound of an ω-chain in a domain.

Theorem 10.3   Let $\Delta = \{f_i\colon D_i \lhd D_{i+1} \mid i \in \omega\}$ be an ω-sequence of domains and embeddings, and $\eta\colon \Delta \longrightarrow D_\infty$ be the cone from Δ defined as above; then, if $\psi\colon \Delta \longrightarrow D$ is any cone from Δ, there is a unique embedding $h\colon D_\infty \lhd D$ such that the following diagram commutes for every $i \in \omega$:

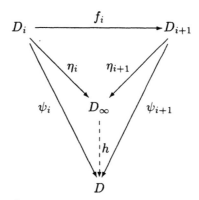

Proof. We first show that

$$\bigsqcup_{i\in\omega} \eta_i^P \; ; \eta_i = \mathrm{id}_{D_\times}.$$

For every $i \in \omega$, $\eta_i^P \; ; \eta_i \sqsubseteq \mathrm{id}_{D_\times}$ because η_i is an embedding; furthermore,

$$\begin{aligned}
\eta_i^P \; ; \eta_i &= (f_i \; ; \eta_{i+1})^P \; ; (f_i \; ; \eta_{i+1}) \\
&= \eta_{i+1}^P \; ; f_i^P \; ; f_i \; ; \eta_{i+1} \\
&\sqsubseteq \eta_{i+1}^P \; ; \eta_{i+1}
\end{aligned}$$

because $f_i^P \; ; f_i \sqsubseteq \mathrm{id}_{D_i}$ and composition is monotonic, and so the least upper bound is defined and $\bigsqcup_{i\in\omega} \eta_i^P \; ; \eta_i \sqsubseteq \mathrm{id}_{D_\times}$. In the other direction, consider any $s \in D_\infty$ and $i \in \omega$; then

$$\begin{aligned}
s_i &= \eta_i(s_i)(i) \\
&= (\eta_i^P \; ; \eta_i)(s)(i)
\end{aligned}$$

by the definitions of η_i and η_i^P, respectively, and so $\mathrm{id}_{D_\times} \sqsubseteq \bigsqcup_{i\in\omega} \eta_i^P \; ; \eta_i$. Now, consider

$$h = \bigsqcup_{i\in\omega} \eta_i^P \; ; \psi_i.$$

This is well-defined because $\eta_i^P \, ; \psi_i \sqsubseteq \eta_{i+1}^P \, ; \psi_{i+1}$. We show that $h \colon D_\infty \lhd D$ with corresponding projection

$$h^P \;=\; \bigsqcup_{i \in \omega} \psi_i^P \, ; \eta_i$$

as follows:

$$
\begin{aligned}
h \, ; h^P \;&=\; \left(\bigsqcup_{i \in \omega} \eta_i^P \, ; \psi_i \right) ; \left(\bigsqcup_{i \in \omega} \psi_i^P \, ; \eta_i \right) \\
&=\; \bigsqcup_{i \in \omega} \eta_i^P \, ; \psi_i : \psi_i^P \, ; \eta_i \\
&=\; \bigsqcup_{i \in \omega} \eta_i^P \, ; \eta_i \\
&=\; \mathrm{id}_{D_\infty} \,,
\end{aligned}
$$

and

$$
\begin{aligned}
h^P \, ; h \;&=\; \left(\bigsqcup_{i \in \omega} \psi_i^P \, ; \eta_i \right) ; \left(\bigsqcup_{i \in \omega} \eta_i^P \, ; \psi_i \right) \\
&=\; \bigsqcup_{i \in \omega} \psi_i^P \, ; \eta_i \, ; \eta_i^P \, ; \psi_i \\
&=\; \bigsqcup_{i \in \omega} \psi_i^P \, ; \psi_i \\
&\sqsubseteq\; \mathrm{id}_D .
\end{aligned}
$$

To show commutativity for every $i \in \omega$:

$$
\begin{aligned}
\eta_i \, ; h \;&=\; \eta_i \, ; \bigsqcup_{j \in \omega} \eta_j^P \, ; \psi_j \\
&=\; \bigsqcup_{j \in \omega} \eta_i \, ; \eta_j^P \, ; \psi_j \\
&=\; \bigsqcup_{j \geq i} (f_{i-1}^P \, ; \cdots \, ; f_j^P \, ; \eta_j) \, ; \eta_j^P \, ; \psi_j \\
&=\; \bigsqcup_{j \geq i} f_{i-1}^P \, ; \cdots \, ; f_j^P \, ; \psi_j \\
&=\; \bigsqcup_{j \geq i} \psi_i \\
&=\; \psi_i .
\end{aligned}
$$

Finally, suppose $h' \colon D_\infty \lhd D$ is any embedding for which the diagram above commutes; then

$$h' \;=\; \left(\bigsqcup_{i \in \omega} \eta_i^P \, ; \eta_i \right) ; h'$$

$$= \bigsqcup_{i\in\omega} \eta_i^P \; ; \eta_i \; ; h'$$

$$= \bigsqcup_{i\in\omega} \eta_i^P \; ; \psi_i$$

$$= h,$$

and so we have shown uniqueness. □

Corollary 10.4   *If both $\eta\colon \Delta \to D$ and $\psi\colon \Delta \to D'$ are co-limiting cones from Δ, then D and D' are isomorphic.*

Proof. Consider the following diagram:

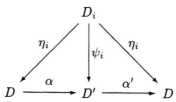

By the theorem, embeddings $\alpha\colon D \lhd D'$ and $\alpha'\colon D' \lhd D$ exist such that the left and right parts of the diagram commute, and this means that both $\alpha;\alpha'$ and id_D are embeddings of D into D such that

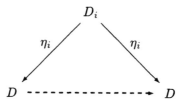

commutes. But, according to the theorem, such an embedding is unique, and so we have that $\alpha\,;\alpha' = \mathrm{id}_D$, and similarly for $\alpha'\,;\alpha = \mathrm{id}_{D'}$. □

Corollary 10.5   *If $\eta\colon \Delta \to D$ is a cone from Δ such that*

$$\bigsqcup_{i\in\omega} \eta_i^P \; ; \eta_i = \mathrm{id}_D,$$

then η is co-limiting.

Proof. $\bigsqcup_{i\in\omega} \eta_i^P \; ; \eta_i = \mathrm{id}_{D_\times}$ is the only property of $\eta\colon \Delta \to D_\infty$ used in the proof of the theorem. □

10.3   Least Fixed Points of Functors

In this section, we continue developing the analogy with the treatment of recursive definitions in domains by studying when domain equations

$D = \cdots D \cdots$ determine *functors* on $\mathbf{D}^E$ that are, in an appropriate sense, *continuous*, and showing that such functors have least fixed points.

A functor $F: \mathbf{D}^E \to \mathbf{D}^E$ is said to *preserve co-limiting cones* if and only if, for any ω-sequence

$$\Delta = \{f_i: D_i \lhd D_{i+1} \mid i \in \omega\}$$

of domains and embeddings, if $\eta: \Delta \to D$ is a co-limiting cone from Δ, then

$$F(\eta) = \{F(\eta_i): F(D_i) \lhd F(D) \mid i \in \omega\}$$

is a co-limiting cone from

$$F(\Delta) = \{F(f_i): F(D_i) \lhd F(D_{i+1}) \mid i \in \omega\}.$$

For any functor $F: \mathbf{D}^E \to \mathbf{D}^E$, we can define the following ω-sequence of domains and embeddings:

$$\emptyset \overset{!}{\lhd} F(\emptyset) \overset{F(!)}{\lhd} F^2(\emptyset) \overset{F^2(!)}{\lhd} \cdots \overset{F^{i-1}(!)}{\lhd} F^i(\emptyset) \overset{F^i(!)}{\lhd} F^{i+1}(\emptyset) \overset{F^{i+1}(!)}{\lhd} \cdots,$$

where ! is the unique embedding of $\emptyset$ into $F(\emptyset)$. The following theorem shows that, if F preserves co-limiting cones, the vertex of a co-limiting cone from this sequence is a least fixed point of F.

Theorem 10.6 *If functor $F: \mathbf{D}^E \to \mathbf{D}^E$ preserves co-limiting cones, and $\eta: \Delta_F \to D$ is a co-limiting cone from*

$$\Delta_F = \{F^i(!): F^i(\emptyset) \lhd F^{i+1}(\emptyset) \mid i \in \omega\},$$

then there exists an embedding $\alpha: F(D) \lhd D$ which is an isomorphism; furthermore, for any embedding of the form $\alpha': F(D') \lhd D'$, there is a unique embedding $h: D \lhd D'$ that makes the following diagram commute:

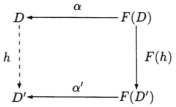

Proof. By assumption, $\eta: \Delta_F \to D$ is a co-limiting cone from Δ_F, and so

$$\{\eta_{i+1}: F^{i+1}(\emptyset) \lhd D \mid i \in \omega\}$$

is a co-limiting cone from

$$\Delta_{\bar{F}} = \{F^{i+1}(!): F^{i+1}(\emptyset) \lhd F^{i+2}(\emptyset) \mid i \in \omega\},$$

because $\Delta_{\bar{F}}$ is just Δ_F without the first component. But F preserves co-limiting cones, and so

$$\{F(\eta_i): F^{i+1}(\emptyset) \lhd F(D) \mid i \in \omega\}$$

is also a co-limiting cone from $\Delta_{\bar{F}} = F(\Delta)$. By Corollary 10.4, there is an isomorphism $\alpha: F(D) \lhd D$ such that the following diagram commutes for every $i \in \omega$:

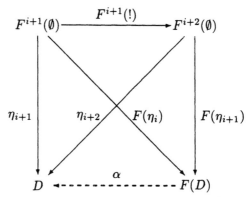

Now, consider any embedding $\alpha': F(D') \lhd D'$; we can define embeddings $\psi_i: F^i(\emptyset) \lhd D'$ as follows:

- ψ_0 is the unique embedding from $\emptyset$ into D', and,
- for every $i \in \omega$, $\psi_{i+1} = F(\psi_i)\,;\alpha'$.

We can show that $\{\psi_i: F^i(\emptyset) \lhd D' \mid i \in \omega\}$ is a cone from Δ_F by proving by induction on i that the following diagram commutes for every $i \in \omega$:

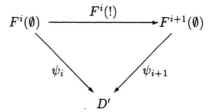

For $i = 0$, $\psi_0 = F^0(!)\,;\psi_1$ because $F^0(\emptyset)$ is the initial object in $\mathbf{D}^E$. Assume commutativity for $i = n$; then

$$
\begin{aligned}
F^{n+1}(!)\,;\psi_{n+2} &= F^{n+1}(!)\,;F(\psi_{n+1})\,;\alpha' &&\text{(definition of } \psi_{n+2}) \\
&= F(F^n(!)\,;\psi_{n+1})\,;\alpha' &&\text{(} F \text{ is a functor)} \\
&= F(\psi_n)\,;\alpha' &&\text{(by induction)} \\
&= \psi_{n+1} &&\text{(definition of } \psi_{n+1})
\end{aligned}
$$

By Theorem 10.3, there exists a unique embedding $h: D \lhd D'$ such that $\psi_i = \eta_i\,;h$ for all $i \in \omega$.

To show the commutativity of

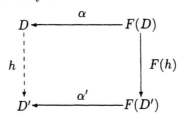

we note that

$$
\begin{aligned}
F(\eta_i)\,;\alpha\,;h &= \eta_{i+1}\,;h \quad \text{(definition of } \alpha) \\
&= \psi_{i+1}, \quad \text{(definition of } h)
\end{aligned}
$$

and also

$$
\begin{aligned}
F(\eta_i)\,;F(h)\,;\alpha' &= F(\eta_i\,;h)\,;\alpha' \quad (F \text{ is a functor}) \\
&= F(\psi_i)\,;\alpha' \quad \text{(definition of } h) \\
&= \psi_{i+1} \quad \text{(definition of } \psi_{i+1})
\end{aligned}
$$

and so $\alpha\,;h = F(h)\,;\alpha'$ because there is only *one* embedding that commutes as above from the vertex $F(D)$ of co-limiting cone $F(\eta)\colon F(\Delta) \to F(D)$ to the vertex D' of cone $\psi\colon F(\Delta) \to D'$.

Finally, to show uniqueness, assume $h'\colon F(D') \lhd D'$ is an embedding such that $\alpha\,;h' = F(h')\,;\alpha'$. We can prove by induction that $\psi_i = \eta_i\,;h'$ for every $i \in \omega$. For $i = 0$, $\emptyset$ is the initial object; for $i = n+1$,

$$
\begin{aligned}
\eta_{n+1}\,;h' &= F(\eta_n)\,;\alpha\,;h' . \quad \text{(definition of } \alpha) \\
&= F(\eta_n)\,;F(h')\,;\alpha' \quad \text{(assumption)} \\
&= F(\eta_n\,;h')\,;\alpha' \quad (F \text{ is a functor}) \\
&= F(\psi_n)\,;\alpha' \quad \text{(induction)} \\
&= \psi_{n+1} \quad \text{(definition of } \psi_{n+1})
\end{aligned}
$$

But there is only *one* embedding that commutes in this way from the vertex D of the co-limiting cone $\eta\colon \Delta \to D$ to the vertex D' of the cone $\psi\colon \Delta \to D'$, and so $h' = h$. $\square$

To use this result to solve domain equations, we must define how domain equations determine colimit-preserving functors F on $\mathbf{D}^E$. We first specify how some of our domain constructions are functors on $\mathbf{D}^E$ by defining corresponding operations on embeddings.

For the "lifting" construction $(\cdot)_\bot$, let $f_\bot\colon D_\bot \lhd E_\bot$ for any embedding $f\colon D \lhd E$ be defined by

$$
f_\bot(d) = \begin{cases} \bot, & \text{if } d = \bot; \\ f(d), & \text{otherwise,} \end{cases}
$$

where the corresponding projection is

$$
f_\bot^P(e) = \begin{cases} \bot, & \text{if } e = \bot \text{ or } f^P(e) \text{ is undefined;} \\ f^P(e), & \text{otherwise.} \end{cases}
$$

It is easily verified that $f_\bot$ satisfies the requirements for an embedding, and that $(\cdot)_\bot$ satisfies the requirements for a functor on $\mathbf{D}^E$.

For $+$ and $\times$, we define

$$
f + f'\colon D + D' \lhd E + E'
$$

and

$$
f \times f'\colon D \times D' \lhd E \times E'
$$

for embeddings $f: D \lhd E$ and $f': D' \lhd E'$ as follows:

$$(f + f')(i, d) = \begin{cases} (0, f(d)), & \text{if } i = 0; \\ (1, f'(d)), & \text{if } i = 1, \end{cases}$$

and

$$(f \times f')(d, d') = (f(d), f'(d')).$$

These are in fact the sum and product of morphisms in **D** as a whole, and it is easily verified that they yield embeddings for embeddings f and f', where the corresponding projections are $(f + f')^P = f^P + f'^P$ and $(f \times f')^P = f^P \times f'^P$.

Consider now the partial exponentiation $\rightharpoonup$. A first attempt at a definition might be

$$(f \rightharpoonup f')(g) = f \,;\, g \,;\, f'$$

for every $g: D \rightharpoonup D'$. But this does not work because it is *contravariant* in f; to compose functions in this way it is necessary that codom $f = D$ and dom $f' = D'$, whereas we have $f: D \lhd E$ and $f': D' \lhd E'$. To get an embedding

$$f \xrightarrow{E} f': (D \rightharpoonup D') \lhd (E \rightharpoonup E'),$$

we recall that every embedding $f: D \lhd E$ determines a unique projection $f^P: E \rightharpoonup D$, and so we can define

$$(f \xrightarrow{E} f')(g) = f^P \,;\, g \,;\, f' = (f^P \rightharpoonup f')(g)$$

for every $g: D \rightharpoonup D'$.

We can verify that this is an embedding using as the corresponding projection

$$(f \xrightarrow{E} f')^P(h) = f \,;\, h \,;\, f'^P = (f \rightharpoonup f'^P)(h)$$

for every $h: E \rightharpoonup E'$:

$$\begin{aligned} f \,;\, (f^P \,;\, g \,;\, f') \,;\, f'^P &= (f \,;\, f^P) \,;\, g \,;\, (f' \,;\, f'^P) \\ &= \mathrm{id}_D \,;\, g \,;\, \mathrm{id}_{D'} \\ &= g \end{aligned}$$

and

$$\begin{aligned} f^P \,;\, (f \,;\, h \,;\, f'^P) \,;\, f' &= (f^P \,;\, f) \,;\, h \,;\, (f'^P \,;\, f') \\ &\sqsubseteq \mathrm{id}_E \,;\, h \,;\, \mathrm{id}_{E'} \\ &= h. \end{aligned}$$

We verify functoriality as follows:

$$(\mathrm{id}_D \xrightarrow{E} \mathrm{id}_{D'})(g) = \mathrm{id}_D^P \,;\, g \,;\, \mathrm{id}_{D'} = \mathrm{id}_D \,;\, g \,;\, \mathrm{id}_{D'} = g,$$

as required, and, for embeddings $D \stackrel{f_1}{\lhd} E \stackrel{f_2}{\lhd} F$ and $D' \stackrel{f_1'}{\lhd} E' \stackrel{f_2'}{\lhd} F'$, and any $g: D \to D'$,

$$
\begin{aligned}
((f_1 \stackrel{E}{\to} f_1') ; (f_2 \stackrel{E}{\to} f_2'))(g) &= f_2^P ; (f_1^P ; g ; f_1') ; f_2' \\
&= (f_1 ; f_2)^P ; g ; (f_1' ; f_2') \\
&= ((f_1 ; f_2) \stackrel{E}{\to} (f_1' ; f_2'))(g),
\end{aligned}
$$

as required.

We will discuss *total* exponentiation later, but it is now clear how any domain equation $D = \cdots D \cdots$ involving only domain constructions $(\cdot)_\bot, +, \times$, and $\to$ determines a functor on $\mathbf{D}^E$. For example, the equation $D = (T \times D)_\bot$ determines the functor $F: \mathbf{D}^E \to \mathbf{D}^E$ with object part $F(D) = (T \times D)_\bot$ and morphism part $F(f) = (\mathrm{id}_T \times f)_\bot$ for any embedding $f: D \lhd D'$. The following proposition can be used to show that all such functors preserve co-limiting cones.

Proposition 10.7 *The lifting, sum, product, and partial exponentiation functors on $\mathbf{D}^E$ preserve co-limiting cones.*

We discuss only the case of $\stackrel{E}{\to}$. Assume that

$$\{\eta_i: D_i \lhd D \mid i \in \omega\}$$

and

$$\{\eta_i': D_i' \lhd D' \mid i \in \omega\}$$

are co-limiting cones from the ω-sequences of domains and embeddings

$$\{D_i, f_i: D_i \lhd D_{i+1} \mid i \in \omega\}$$

and

$$\{D_i', f_i': D_i' \lhd D_{i+1}' \mid i \in \omega\},$$

respectively. We want to prove that

$$\{\eta_i \stackrel{E}{\to} \eta_i': (D_i \to D_i') \lhd (D \to D') \mid i \in \omega\}$$

is a co-limiting cone from the ω-sequence of domains and embeddings

$$\{D_i \to D_i', (f_i \stackrel{E}{\to} f_i'): (D_i \to D_i') \lhd (D_{i+1} \to D_{i+1}') \mid i \in \omega\}.$$

From Corollary 10.5, it is sufficient to show that

$$\bigsqcup_{i \in \omega} (\eta_i \stackrel{E}{\to} \eta_i')^P ; (\eta_i \stackrel{E}{\to} \eta_i') = \mathrm{id}_{D \to D'}.$$

From the definition of $\xrightarrow{E}$, we get

$$\bigsqcup_{i\in\omega}(\eta_i \xrightarrow{E} \eta_i')^P ; (\eta_i \xrightarrow{E} \eta_i') \;=\; \bigsqcup_{i\in\omega}(\eta_i \rightharpoonup \eta_i'^{\,P}) ; (\eta_i^P \rightharpoonup \eta_i')$$

$$=\; \bigsqcup_{i\in\omega}(\eta_i^P ; \eta_i) \rightharpoonup (\eta_i'^{\,P} ; \eta_i')$$

$$=\; \left(\bigsqcup_{i\in\omega}\eta_i^P ; \eta_i\right) \rightharpoonup \left(\bigsqcup_{i\in\omega}\eta_i'^{\,P} ; \eta_i'\right)$$

$$=\; \mathrm{id}_D \rightharpoonup \mathrm{id}_{D'}$$

$$=\; \mathrm{id}_{D\rightharpoonup D'}. \quad \square$$

Finally, we consider a (total) exponentiation $f \xrightarrow{E} f'$ for $f: D \lhd E$ and $f': D' \lhd E'$. Trying the same approach as for partial exponentiation, we write

$$(f \xrightarrow{E} f')(g) = f^P ; g ; f'$$

for every $g: D \to D'$, and

$$(f \xrightarrow{E} f')^P(h) = f ; h ; f'^P$$

for every $h: E \to E'$, but, as we would expect, this does not work in general. For this to be a proper definition, $f^P ; g ; f'$ and $f ; h ; f'^P$ must be *total* functions but in general the projections f^P and f'^P are *partial*.

We must investigate when the projections corresponding to embeddings are total.

Proposition 10.8

(a) If $f: D \lhd D$ is an identity function, f^P is also an identity function and hence total.

(b) If D and E are domains with least elements and $f: D \lhd E$ is a strict embedding, then f^P is a total function.

(c) For any embedding $f: D \lhd E$, the projection $f_\perp^P$ corresponding to $f_\perp: D_\perp \lhd E_\perp$ is total.

(d) If the projections corresponding to embeddings $f: D \lhd E$ and $f': D' \lhd E'$ are total, so are the projections corresponding to embeddings

- $f \times f': D \times D' \lhd E \times E'$,
- $f + f': D + D' \lhd E + E'$,
- $f \xrightarrow{E} f': D \rightharpoonup D' \lhd E \rightharpoonup E'$, and
- $f \xrightarrow{E} f': D \to D' \lhd E \to E'$.

These results show that the only real difficulty is in *starting* the limit construction: the projection corresponding to an embedding of $\emptyset$ into a non-empty domain is *never* total.

For many equations, it is possible to start the limit construction at some non-empty domain with a least element. For example, consider the equation

$$D = (T \to D)_\perp.$$

We can define $D_0 = \emptyset$ and $D_{i+1} = (T \to D_i)_\perp$ as usual, and there is a unique embedding of D_0 into D_1, but we cannot define an embedding $f_1 : D_1 \lhd D_2$ and corresponding projection $f_1^P : D_2 \to D_1$ as before. Instead, we note that D_1 is a one-element domain and hence has a least element, and that D_2 has the form

We can define the embedding $f_1(\perp) = \perp$ and then $f_{i+1} = (\mathrm{id}_T \xrightarrow{E} f_i)_\perp$ is a good definition for all $i > 0$ because id_T is an identity function and f_i is a strict embedding of domains with least elements. We can then construct the co-limiting cone from the ω-sequence of domains and embeddings

$$D_1 \xleftarrow{f_1} D_2 \xleftarrow{f_2} \cdots \xleftarrow{f_{i-1}} D_i \xleftarrow{f_i} D_{i+1} \xleftarrow{f_{i+1}} \cdots$$

essentially as before and obtain a domain D such that $D \cong (T \to D)_\perp$. However, for an equation such as $D = T + (D \to D)$, no solution is possible.

10.4   Applications

In this section we briefly discuss some typical applications of recursively-defined domains.

10.4.1   Intermediate Output

We can use a recursively-defined domain to describe the semantics of language features that produce "intermediate" output, that is to say, output that is produced by a program *before* it terminates. To illustrate this in the simplest possible way, we add the following form of command:

   Intermediate Output:

$$\overline{\textbf{tick: comm}}$$

The intention is that executing **tick** should have no effect on the computational state, but should append another "tick" to the program output, like a clock. To model this, we assume continuation semantics for commands, as in Section 7.5, and re-define the domain of outputs as a least solution of the following isomorphism:

$$O \cong A + (\{tick\} \times O_\perp) + \{error\}$$

The elements of the resulting domain are essentially the finite sequences of "ticks," terminated by an answer, *error*, or $\perp$, and a limit point, which represents the *infinite* sequence of ticks, modelling the output of non-terminating but "ticking" programs. The ordering on this domain is determined by having a finite sequence of ticks terminated by $\perp$ approximate any sequence obtained from it by replacing the $\perp$ by any output.

The semantic equation for **tick** is then as follows:

$$[\![\mathbf{tick}]\!]uks = \begin{cases} (tick, \perp), & \text{if } k(s) \text{ is undefined} \\ (tick, k(s)), & \text{otherwise,} \end{cases}$$

where we have not bothered to "tag" elements of the domain of outputs.

10.4.2 Lists

Functional languages usually allow data to be organized into *lists* of arbitrary (even infinite) length. Consider adding a new class of phrase types as follows to our Algol-like language:

$$\theta ::= \cdots \mid \mathbf{list}[\theta]$$

We allow the following ways of defining lists:

  Empty List:

$$\overline{\mathbf{nil} \colon \mathbf{list}[0]}$$

  Prefixed List:

$$\frac{X \colon \theta \qquad L \colon \mathbf{list}[\theta]}{X :: L \colon \mathbf{list}[\theta]}$$

If we adopt the coercion $\mathbf{list}[\theta] \vdash \mathbf{list}[\theta']$ whenever $\theta \vdash \theta'$, the constant **nil** coerces into the empty list of *any* list type. The list $X :: L$ has X as its first component and L as the list of remaining components. Finally, we provide the following construct to allow lists to be tested for emptiness and decomposed:

  List Analysis:

$$\begin{bmatrix} \iota_1 \colon \theta \\ \iota_2 \colon \mathbf{list}[\theta] \end{bmatrix}$$
$$\vdots$$

$$\frac{L \colon \mathbf{list}[\theta] \qquad X \colon \theta' \qquad\qquad X' \colon \theta'}{\mathbf{ifnull}\ L\ \mathbf{then}\ X\ \mathbf{else}\ (\iota_1 :: \iota_2).\,X' \colon \theta'}$$

If the list L is empty, the result of evaluating this construct is X; otherwise, the result is X' with ι_1 and ι_2 bound to the first component and the rest of list L, respectively.

As an example of the use of these facilities, the following defines a function that applies its first argument to every component of its second argument:

$$\textbf{letrec } map(f\colon \theta \rightarrow \theta', l\colon \textbf{list}[\theta])\colon \textbf{list}[\theta'] =$$
$$\textbf{ifnull } l \textbf{ then nil else } (hd :: tl).\, f(hd) :: map(f, tl)$$
$$\textbf{in } \cdots$$

Here θ and θ' are arbitrary phrase types.

The semantics of these facilities are as follows. The domain $[\![\textbf{list}[\theta]]\!]$ is to be a least solution of the domain equation

$$D \cong \Big(\{nil\} + \big([\![\theta]\!] \times D\big)\Big)_{\bot} \, ;$$

here, *nil* is the empty list, and the "lifting" gives the domain of lists a least element, so that lists can be recursively-defined. The conversion $[\![\textbf{list}[\theta] \vdash \textbf{list}[\theta']]\!]$ is defined as follows: the least element $\bot$ and the empty list *nil* are preserved, and a pair (v, l) for $v \in [\![\theta]\!]$ and $l \in [\![\textbf{list}[\theta]]\!]$ is converted by applying $[\![\theta \vdash \theta']\!]$ to v and, recursively, $[\![\textbf{list}[\theta] \vdash \textbf{list}[\theta']]\!]$ to l.

The semantic equations are as follows:

$$[\![\textbf{nil}]\!]u = nil$$

$$[\![X :: L]\!]u = ([\![X]\!]u, [\![L]\!]u)$$

$$[\![\textbf{ifnull } L \textbf{ then } X \textbf{ else } (\iota_1 :: \iota_2).\, X']\!]u$$
$$= \begin{cases} [\![X]\!]u, & \text{if } [\![L]\!]u = nil \\ [\![X']\!](u \mid \iota_1 \mapsto v \mid \iota_2 \mapsto l), & \text{if } [\![L]\!]u = (v, l) \\ \bot, & \text{if } [\![L]\!]u = \bot \end{cases}$$

Note that list prefixing is "lazy," in the sense that it is possible to define lists that are conceptually of infinite length; for example,

$$\textbf{letrec } zeroes\colon \textbf{list}[\textbf{val}[\textbf{nat}]] \textbf{ be } 0 :: zeroes \textbf{ in } \cdots$$

defines what can be thought of as an *infinite* list of zeroes. In fact, an implementation would create a finite structure with a "loop." Similarly,

$$\textbf{letrec } numbers\colon \textbf{list}[\textbf{val}[\textbf{nat}]] \textbf{ be } 0 :: map(succ, numbers) \textbf{ in } \cdots$$

defines the list of all natural numbers when $succ = \lambda n\colon \textbf{val}[\textbf{nat}].\, n + 1$ and *map* is as defined above; in this case, an implementation would only need to create as many components as are actually used by the rest of the program.

10.4.3   Untyped Procedures

Some programming languages have type "loopholes" or are deliberately designed to be *untyped* or allow the programmer to define types recursively. In such languages, it may even be possible for a procedure to be applicable to *itself*. For example, the following definition is legal in ALGOL 60:

> **integer procedure** $p(q, n)$;
> **integer procedure** q ; **integer** n;
> $p :=$ **if** $n = 0$ **then** 1 **else** $n \times q(q, n-1)$

A call of the form $p(p, n)$ for $n \geq 0$ returns the factorial of n. Note that the definition is *not* recursive; however, a domain of meanings appropriate for procedures such as p would need to satisfy the following domain equation:

$$D \cong D \times I \to I$$

where I is the domain of meanings of integer-valued expressions or value phrases. In our Algol-like language, an analogous procedure definition could not be written because it would be necessary to specify the *argument* type of parameter q.

As another example, the *untyped* lambda calculus is a language which resembles the *typed* lambda calculus (on which the simple applicative language of Chapter 4 is based), but has no type constraints. There is just a single phrase type, say **term**, and the syntax rules are as follows:

Untyped Application:

$$\frac{P\colon \textbf{term} \quad Q\colon \textbf{term}}{P\,Q\colon \textbf{term}}$$

Untyped Abstraction:

$$[\iota\colon \textbf{term}]$$
$$\vdots$$
$$\frac{P\colon \textbf{term}}{\lambda\iota.\,P\colon \textbf{term}}$$

Note that there is no need to specify the type of the bound identifier in the rule for Untyped Abstraction (because there is only one type), and that the rule for Untyped Application allows *any* term to be applied to *any* term (including itself).

For example, consider the term Y, as follows:

$$\lambda F.\, \big(\lambda x.\, F(x\,x)\big)\big(\lambda x.\, F(x\,x)\big)$$

It is easily verified that Y has the property that, for *any* term F, $Y(F)$ is equivalent to $F\big(Y(F)\big)$ using the untyped analog of the Beta Law. Y is called a *fixed-point combinator*. Essentially, this shows that it is not

necessary to *add* recursion to the *untyped* lambda calculus: recursion is
already defineable in the pure system using Y.

A domain appropriate for this language satisfies the isomorphism

$$D \cong D \to D$$

The non-trivial solution of this domain equation obtained by D. Scott in
1970 was the first natural model of the untyped lambda calculus.

Exercises

10.1 For each of the following domain equations, determine the first few
approximating domains and describe the limit domain:

(a) $D = D$
(b) $D = T$
(c) $D = \{0\} + D$
(d) $D = D_\perp$
(e) $D = (\{nil\} + T \times D)_\perp$

10.2 For each of the equations $D = \{nil\} + T \times D$ and $D = (T \times D)_\perp$,
verify that $\bigcup_{i \in \omega} D_i$ satisfies the relevant equation when the D_i are
the approximating domains defined in Section 10.1.

10.3 Verify that the vertices of the co-limiting cones defined by the general
theory of Sections 10.2 and 10.3 for the equations $D = \{nil\} + T \times D$
and $D = (T \times D)_\perp$ are the expected solution domains.

10.4 Prove that the family of embeddings $\{\eta_i: D_i \lhd D_\infty \mid i \in \omega\}$ defined
in Section 10.2 commutes as follows for every $i \in \omega$:

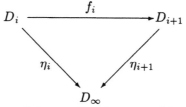

10.5 Prove that if $\psi: \Delta \to D$ is a co-limiting cone, $\bigsqcup_{i \in \omega} \psi_i^P ; \psi_i = \text{id}_D$.

10.6 Verify that the lifting, sum, and product functors on $\mathbf{D}^E$ preserve
co-limiting cones.

Bibliographic Notes

The first important application of recursive domain definitions was to obtain a semantic model of the untyped lambda calculus; this is described

in [Sco70, Sco72b, Wad76, Bar84]. The category-theoretic approach to domain equation solution is discussed in [Wan79, LS81, SP82, Pie91]. The presentation here is similar, but uses *partial* projections, following [Plo85], to allow for possibly "bottom-less" domains.

Bibliography

Let us come now to references to authors. You have nothing else to do but look for a book that quotes them all, from A to Z. Then you put this same alphabet into yours. Perhaps there will even be someone silly enough to believe that you have made use of them all in your simple and straightforward story.

Cervantes, *Don Quixote* (1604)

[AA78]   S. Alagić and M. A. Arbib. *The Design of Well-Structured and Correct Programs.* Springer-Verlag, New York, 1978.

[Abr83a] S. Abramsky. Experiments, powerdomains, and fully abstract models for applicative multiprogramming. In Karpinsky [Kar83], pages 1–13.

[Abr83b] S. Abramsky. On semantic foundations for applicative multiprogramming. In Diaz [Dia83], pages 1–14.

[Abr87]   S. Abramsky. Domain theory in logical form. In *Proceedings, Symposium on Logic in Computer Science*, pages 47–53, Ithaca, N.Y., 1987. IEEE Computer Society Press.

[AGM91] S. Abramsky, D. M. Gabbay, and T. S. E. Maibaum, editors. *Handbook of Logic in Computer Science.* Oxford University Press, Oxford, England, to appear, 1991.

[AL91]   A. Asperti and G. Longo. *Categories, Types, and Structures.* The MIT Press, Cambridge, Mass., 1991.

[AM75]   M. Arbib and E. Manes. *Arrows, Stuctures, and Functors: The Categorical Imperative.* Academic Press, 1975.

[Apt81]   K. R. Apt. Ten years of Hoare's logic: a survey – part I. *Trans. on Programming Languages and Systems*, 3(4):431–483, 1981.

[Bac83]   R. J. Back. A continuous semantics for unbounded nondeterminism. *Theoretical Computer Science*, 23:187–210, 1983.

[Bac86]   R. C. Backhouse. *Program Construction and Verification.* Prentice-Hall International, London, 1986.

[Bar84]   H. P. Barendregt. *The Lambda Calculus: Its Syntax and Semantics*, volume 103 of *Studies in Logic and the Foundations of Mathematics.* North-Holland, Amsterdam (revised edition), 1984.

[Bar91]   H. P. Barendregt. Lambda calculi with types. In Abramsky *et al.* [AGM91].

[BCL85]   G. Berry, P.-L. Curien, and J.-J. Lévy. Full abstraction for sequential languages: the state of the art. In Nivat and Reynolds [NR85], pages 89–132.

[Bek69]   H. Bekič. Definable operations in general algebras and the theory of automata and flowcharts. IBM Laboratory, Vienna, 1969. Also, pages 30–55 in C. B. Jones, editor, *Programming Languages and their Definition*, volume 177 of *Lecture Notes in Computer Science*, Springer-Verlag, Berlin, 1984.

[Ber91]   J. A. Bergstra. Hoare logic. In Abramsky *et al.* [AGM91].

[Bro85]   S. D. Brookes. A fully abstract semantics and a proof system for an ALGOL-like language with sharing. In A. Melton, editor, *Mathematical Foundations of Programming Semantics*, volume 239 of *Lecture Notes in Computer Science*, pages 59–100, Manhattan, Kansas, 1985. Springer-Verlag, Berlin.

[BT82]   J. A. Bergstra and J. V. Tucker. Expressiveness and the completeness of Hoare's logic. *J. Comput. Sys. Sci.*, 25:276–284, 1982.

[BTT82]   J. A. Bergstra, J. Tiuryn, and J. Tucker. Floyd's principle, correctness theories, and program equivalence. *Theoretical Computer Science*, 17:129–147, 1982.

[BW90]   M. Barr and C. Wells. *Category Theory for Computing Science.* Prentice-Hall International, London, 1990.

[Car56]   R. Carnap. *Meaning and Necessity, A Study in Semantics and Modal Logic.* University of Chicago Press, Chicago, 1947; enlarged edition: 1956.

[CD78]   M. Coppo and M. Dezani. A new type assignment for λ-terms. *Archiv. Math. Logik*, 19:139–156, 1978.

[CF58]   H. B. Curry and R. Feys. *Combinatory Logic I.* North-Holland, Amsterdam, 1958.

[CH72]   M. Clint and C. A. R. Hoare. Program proving: jumps and functions. *Acta Informatica*, 1:214–224, 1972.

[Chu40]   A. Church. A formulation of the simple theory of types. *J. Symb. Logic*, 5:56–68, 1940.

[Cla84]   E. M. Clarke, Jr. The characterization problem for Hoare logics. In C. A. R. Hoare and J. C. Shepherdson, editors, *Mathematical Logic and Programming Languages*, pages 89–106. Prentice-Hall International, London, 1984.

[Con90]   R. H. Connelly. *A Comparison of Semantic Domains for Interleaving.* Ph.D. thesis, Syracuse University, Syracuse, 1990. Technical report SU-CIS-90-24, School of Computer and Information Science, Syracuse University.

[Coo78]   S. A. Cook. Soundness and completeness of an axiomatic system for program verification. *SIAM J. on Computing*, 7:70–90, 1978.

[dB⁺80a] J. de Bakker *et al. Mathematical Theory of Program Correctness.* Prentice-Hall International, London, 1980.

[dB80b]   A. de Bruin. Goto statements. In *Mathematical Theory of Program Correctness* [dB⁺80a], pages 401–443.

[dBM75]   J. W. de Bakker and L. G. L. T. Meertens. On the completeness of the inductive assertion method. *J. Comput. Sys. Sci.*, 11:323–357, 1975.

[Dia83]   J. Diaz, editor. *Proc. 10th Int. Colloq. on Automata, Languages and Programming*, volume 154 of *Lecture Notes in Computer Science*. Springer-Verlag, Berlin, 1983.

[Dij76]   E. W. Dijkstra. *A Discipline of Programming*. Prentice-Hall, Englewood Cliffs, N. J., 1976.

[Don77]   J. Donahue. Locations considered unnecessary. *Acta Informatica*, 8:221–242, 1977.

[Dum77]   M. Dummett. *Elements of Intuitionism*. Oxford University Press, 1977.

[EFT84]   H.-D. Ebbinghaus, J. Flum, and W. Thomas. *Mathematical Logic*. Springer, New York, 1984.

[Fel87]   M. Felleisen. *The Calculi of Lambda-v-CS-Conversion*. Ph.D. thesis, Indiana University, 1987.

[FF89]   M. Felleisen and D. P. Friedman. A syntactic theory of sequential state. *Theoretical Computer Science*, 69:243–287, 1989.

[Flo67]   R. W. Floyd. Assigning meanings to programs. In J. T. Schwartz, editor, *Mathematical Aspects of Computer Science*, volume 19 of *Proceedings of Symposia in Applied Mathematics*, pages 19–32. American Mathematical Society, Providence, R.I., 1967.

[Fre92]   G. Frege. Über Sinn und Bedeutung. (On sense and meaning). *Zeitschrift für Philosophie und philosophische Kritik*, 100:25–50,

1892. English translations in *Readings in Philosophical Analysis* (eds., H. Feigl and W. Sellars), pp. 85–102, Appleton-Century-Crofts, New York (1949), and *Translations from the Philosophical Writings of Gottlob Frege* (eds., P. T. Geach and M. Black), pp. 56–78, Blackwell, Oxford (1960).

[Fri75]   H. Friedman. Equality between functionals. In R. Parikh, editor, *Proceedings of the Logic Colloquium '73*, volume 453 of *Lecture Notes in Mathematics*, pages 22–37. Springer-Verlag, Berlin, 1975.

[GM81]   I. Greif and A. R. Meyer. Specifying the semantics of **while** programs: a tutorial and critique of a paper by Hoare and Lauer. *ACM Trans. Programming Languages and Systems*, 3(4):484–507, 1981.

[GMW79] M. Gordon, R. Milner, and C. Wadsworth. *Edinburgh* LCF, *A Mechanized Logic of Computation*, volume 78 of *Lecture Notes in Computer Science*. Springer-Verlag, Berlin, 1979.

[Gol79]   R. Goldblatt. *Topoi, The Categorial Analysis of Logic*. North-Holland, Amsterdam, 1979.

[Gol82]   R. Goldblatt. *Axiomatising the Logic of Computer Programming*, volume 193 of *Lecture Notes in Computer Science*. Springer-Verlag, Berlin, 1982.

[Gor79]   M. J. C. Gordon. *The Denotational Description of Programming Languages*. Springer-Verlag, New York, 1979.

[HG+88] M. T. Hortalá-González *et al.* Some incompleteness results for partial-correctness logics. *Information and Computation*, 79:22–42, 1988.

[HL74]   C. A. R. Hoare and P. E. Lauer. Consistent and complementary formal theories of the semantics of programming languages. *Acta Informatica*, 3(2):135–153, 1974.

[HMT83] J. Y. Halpern, A. R. Meyer, and B. A. Trakhtenbrot. The semantics of local storage, or what makes the free-list free? In *Conf. Record 11th ACM Symp. on Principles of Programming Languages*, pages 245–257, Austin, Texas, 1983. ACM, New York.

[Hoa69]   C. A. R. Hoare. An axiomatic basis for computer programming. *Comm. ACM*, 12(10):576–580 and 583, 1969.

[HP79]   M. Hennessy and G. D. Plotkin. Full abstraction for a simple parallel programming language. In J. Bečvář, editor, *Mathematical Foundations of Computer Science*, volume 74 of *Lecture Notes in Computer Science*, pages 108–120. Springer-Verlag, Berlin, 1979.

[HS79]   H. Herrlich and G. E. Strecker. *Category Theory*. Heldermann Verlag, Berlin, second edition, 1979.

[Jan86] T. M. V. Janssen. *Foundations and Applications of Montague Grammar, part I*, volume 19 of *CWI Tracts*. Center for Mathematics and Computer Science, Amsterdam, 1986.

[Kah88] G. Kahn. Natural semantics. In K. Fuchi and M. Nivat, editors, *Programming of Future-Generation Computers*, pages 237–258. North-Holland, Amsterdam, 1988.

[Kar83] M. Karpinsky, editor. *Foundations of Computation Theory*, volume 158 of *Lecture Notes in Computer Science*. Springer-Verlag, Berlin, 1983.

[Kri65] S. A. Kripke. Semantical analysis of intuitionistic logic I. In J. N. Crossley and M. A. E. Dummett, editors, *Formal Systems and Recursive Functions*, pages 92–130. North-Holland, Amsterdam, 1965.

[Lan64] P. J. Landin. The mechanical evaluation of expressions. *Comput. J.*, 6(4):308–320, 1964.

[Lan66] P. J. Landin. The next 700 programming languages. *Comm. ACM*, 9(3):157–166, 1966.

[Lau71] P. Lauer. Consistent formal theories of the semantics of programming languages. Technical Report TR 25.121, IBM Laboratory, Vienna, Austria, 1971.

[Leh76] D. J. Lehmann. Categories for fixpoint semantics. In *Proc. 17th IEEE Symposium on Foundations of Computer Science*, pages 122–126, 1976.

[Lei85a] D. Leivant. Logical and mathematical reasoning about imperative programs. In *Conf. Record 12th ACM Symp. on Principles of Programming Languages*, pages 132–140, New Orleans, Louisiana, 1985. ACM, New York.

[Lei85b] D. Leivant. Partial-correctness theories as first-order theories. In R. Parikh, editor, *Logics of Programs 1985*, volume 193 of *Lecture Notes in Computer Science*, pages 190–195, Brooklyn, N.Y., 1985. Springer-Verlag, Berlin.

[LF87] D. Leivant and T. Fernando. Skinny and fleshy failures of relative completeness. In *Conf. Record 14th ACM Symp. on Principles of Programming Languages*, pages 246–252, Munich, West Germany, 1987. ACM, New York.

[LS81] D. J. Lehmann and M. B. Smyth. Algebraic specification of data types: a synthetic approach. *Mathematical Systems Theory*, 14:97–139, 1981.

[LS84] J. Loeckx and K. Sieber. *The Foundations of Program Verification*. John Wiley and Sons, and B. G. Teubner, Stuttgart, 1984.

[LW69]   P. Lucas and K. Walk. On the formal description of PL/I. In
          Annual Review in Automatic Programming, vol. 6, pages 105–
          152. Pergammon Press, London, 1969.

[MA86]   E. G. Manes and M. A. Arbib. *Algebraic Approaches to Program
          Semantics*. Springer-Verlag, New York, 1986.

[MC88]   A. R. Meyer and S. S. Cosmadakis. Semantical paradigms: notes
          for an invited lecture. In *Proceedings, 3rd Annual Symposium on
          Logic in Computer Science*, pages 236–253, Edinburgh, Scotland,
          1988. IEEE Computer Society Press.

[McC84]   C. McCarty. Information systems, continuity, and realizability.
          In E. Clarke and D. Kozen, editors, *Logics of Programs, Proceed-
          ings 1983*, volume 164 of *Lecture Notes in Computer Science*,
          pages 341–359, Pittsburgh, PA., 1984. Springer-Verlag, Berlin.

[Mey86]   A. R. Meyer. Floyd-Hoare logic defines semantics: preliminary
          version. In *Proceedings, Symposium on Logic in Computer Sci-
          ence*, pages 44–48, Cambridge, Mass., June 1986. IEEE Com-
          puter Society Press.

[MH82]   A. R. Meyer and J. Y. Halpern. Axiomatic definitions of pro-
          gramming languages: a theoretical assessment. *J. ACM*, 29:555–
          576, 1982.

[Mil72]   R. Milner. Implementation and applications of Scott's logic for
          computable functions. In *Proving Assertions About Programs*,
          pages 1–6, Las Cruces, New Mexico, 1972. ACM, New York.
          SIGPLAN Notices, 7(1), 1972.

[Mil73]   R. Milner. Models of LCF. Technical Report STAN-CS-73-332,
          Dept. of Computer Science, Stanford University, Stanford, Cal-
          ifornia, 1973. Also in K. R. Apt and J. W. de Bakker, editors,
          Foundations of Computer Science II, part 2, pages 49–63, Math-
          ematical Centre Tracts **82**, Mathematical Centre, Amsterdam,
          1976.

[Mil75]   R. Milner. Processes: a mathematical model of computing
          agents. In H. E. Rose and J. C. Shepherdson, editors, *Logic Col-
          loquium '73*, pages 157–174. North-Holland, Amsterdam, 1975.

[Mil76]   R. Milner. Program semantics and mechanized proof. In K. R.
          Apt and J. W. de Bakker, editors, *Foundations of Computer
          Science II, part 2*, pages 3–44. Mathematical Centre Tracts **82**,
          Mathematical Centre, Amsterdam, 1976.

[Mil77]   R. Milner. Fully abstract models of typed λ-calculi. *Theoretical
          Computer Science*, 4:1–22, 1977.

[Mit90]   J. C. Mitchell. Type systems for programming languages. In
          J. van Leeuwen, editor, *Handbook of Theoretical Computer Sci-*

ence, volume B, chapter 8, pages 365–458. Elsevier, Amsterdam, and The MIT Press, Cambridge, Mass., 1990.

[ML71]   S. Mac Lane. *Categories for the Working Mathematician.* Springer-Verlag, New York, 1971.

[MMN75]   R. Milner, L. Morris, and M. Newey. A logic for computable functions with reflexive and polymorphic types. In G. Huet and G. Kahn, editors, *Proving and Improving Programs*, pages 371–394, Arc et Senans, France, 1975. INRIA, Rocquencourt, France.

[Mog88]   E. Moggi. *The Partial Lambda Calculus.* Ph.D. thesis, University of Edinburgh, 1988.

[Mog89]   E. Moggi. Computational lambda-calculus and monads. In *Proceedings, 4th Annual Symposium on Logic in Computer Science*, pages 14–23, Pacific Grove, California, 1989. IEEE Computer Society Press.

[MS76]   R. E. Milne and C. Strachey. *A Theory of Programming Language Semantics.* Chapman and Hall, London, and Wiley, New York, 1976.

[MS88]   A. R. Meyer and K. Sieber. Towards fully abstract semantics for local variables: preliminary report. In *Conf. Record 15th ACM Symp. on Principles of Programming Languages*, pages 191–203, San Diego, California, 1988. ACM, New York.

[Mul87]   K. Mulmuley. *Full Abstraction and Semantic Equivalence.* The MIT Press, Cambridge, Mass., 1987.

[N+63]   P. Naur *et al.* Revised report on the algorithmic language AL-GOL 60. *Comm. ACM*, 6(1):1–17, 1963.

[NR85]   M. Nivat and J. C. Reynolds, editors. *Algebraic Methods in Semantics.* Cambridge University Press, Cambridge, 1985.

[O'H90]   P. W. O'Hearn. *The Semantics of Non-Interference: a Natural Approach.* Ph.D. thesis, Queen's University, Kingston, Canada, 1990.

[Ole82]   F. J. Oles. *A Category-Theoretic Approach to the Semantics of Programming Languages.* Ph.D. thesis, Syracuse University, Syracuse, 1982.

[Ole85]   F. J. Oles. Type algebras, functor categories and block structure. In Nivat and Reynolds [NR85], pages 543–573.

[Ole87]   F. J. Oles. Lambda calculi with implicit type conversions. Technical Report RC 13245, IBM Research, T. J. Watson Research Center, Yorktown Heights, N.Y., 1987.

[OT91]   P. W. O'Hearn and R. D. Tennent. Semantical analysis of specification logic, part 2. Technical Report 91-304, Dept. of Computing and Information Science, Queen's University, 1991.

[Par69]   D. Park. Fixpoint induction and proofs of program properties. In B. Meltzer and D. Michie, editors, *Machine Intelligence*, volume 5, pages 59–78. Edinburgh University Press, 1969.

[Pas86]   A. Pasztor. Non-standard algorithmic and dynamic logic. *J. Symbolic Computation*, 2:59–81, 1986.

[Pau87]   L. C. Paulson. *Logic and Computation, Interactive Proof with Cambridge* LCF, volume 2 of *Cambridge Tracts in Theoretical Computer Science*. Cambridge University Press, Cambridge, 1987.

[Pie91]   B. C. Pierce. *Basic Category Theory for Computer Scientists*. The MIT Press, Cambridge, Mass., to appear, 1991.

[Plo75]   G. D. Plotkin. Call-by-name, call-by-value, and the λ-calculus. *Theoretical Computer Science*, 1:125–159, 1975.

[Plo76]   G. D. Plotkin. A powerdomain construction. *SIAM J. on Computing*, 5:452–487, 1976.

[Plo77]   G. D. Plotkin. LCF considered as a programming language. *Theoretical Computer Science*, 5:223–255, 1977.

[Plo78]   G. D. Plotkin. *The Category of Complete Partial Orders: a Tool for Making Meanings*. Lecture notes for the Summer School on Foundations of Artificial Intelingence and Computer Science, Pisa, June 1978.

[Plo79]   G. D. Plotkin. Dijkstra's predicate transformers and Smyth's powerdomains. In D. Bjørner, editor, *Abstract Software Specifications*, volume 86 of *Lecture Notes in Computer Science*, pages 527–553, Copenhagen, Denmark, 1979. Springer-Verlag, Berlin.

[Plo80]   G. D. Plotkin. Lambda-definability in the full type hierarchy. In J. P. Seldin and J. R. Hindley, editors, *To H. B. Curry: Essays in Combinatory Logic, Lambda Calculus and Formalism*, pages 363–373. Academic Press, 1980.

[Plo81]   G. D. Plotkin. A structural approach to operational semantics. Technical Report DAIMI FN-19, Computer Science Dept., Aarhus University, Aarhus, Denmark, 1981.

[Plo82]   G. D. Plotkin. A powerdomain for countable non-determinism. In *Proc. 9th Int. Colloq. on Automata, Languages and Programming*, volume 140 of *Lecture Notes in Computer Science*, pages 418–428. Springer-Verlag, Berlin, 1982.

[Plo85]   G. D. Plotkin. *Types and Partial Functions*. Lecture notes, Computer Science Department, University of Edinburgh, 1985.

[Pra65]   D. Prawitz. *Natural Deduction: A Proof-Theoretical Study*. Almquist and Wiksell, Stockholm, 1965.

[PY73]   F. P. Preparata and R. T. Yeh. *Introduction to Discrete Struc-tures For Computer Science and Engineering.* Addison-Wesley, 1973.

[RB88]   D. E. Rydeheard and R. M. Burstall. *Computational Category Theory.* Prentice-Hall International, 1988.

[Rey72]   J. C. Reynolds. Definitional interpreters for higher-order pro-gramming languages. In *Proceedings of the 25th ACM National Conference*, pages 717–740, 1972.

[Rey78]   J. C. Reynolds. Syntactic control of interference. In *Conf. Record 5th ACM Symp. on Principles of Programming Languages*, pages 39–46, Tucson, Arizona, 1978. ACM, New York.

[Rey80a]   J. C. Reynolds. Mathematical semantics. In B. W. Arden, editor, *What Can be Automated? The Computer Science and Engineer-ing Research Study*, pages 261–288. The MIT Press, Cambridge, Mass., 1980.

[Rey80b]   J. C. Reynolds. Using category theory to design implicit conver-sions and generic operators. In N. D. Jones, editor, *Semantics-Directed Compiler Generation*, volume 94 of *Lecture Notes in Computer Science*, pages 211–258, Aarhus, Denmark, 1980. Springer-Verlag, Berlin.

[Rey81a]   J. C. Reynolds. *The Craft of Programming.* Prentice-Hall Inter-national, London, 1981.

[Rey81b]   J. C. Reynolds. The essence of Algol. In J. W. de Bakker and J. C. van Vliet, editors, *Algorithmic Languages*, pages 345–372, Amsterdam, 1981. North-Holland, Amsterdam.

[Rey82]   J. C. Reynolds. Idealized Algol and its specification logic. In D. Néel, editor, *Tools and Notions for Program Construction*, pages 121–161. Cambridge University Press, Cambridge, 1982.

[Rey85]   J. C. Reynolds. Three approaches to type structure. In H. Ehrig, C. Floyd, M. Nivat, and J. W. Thatcher, editors, *Mathemati-cal Foundations of Software Development*, volume 185 of *Lec-ture Notes in Computer Science*, pages 97–138, Berlin, 1985. Springer-Verlag, Berlin.

[Rey87]   J. C. Reynolds. Conjunctive types and Algol-like languages (ab-stract of invited lecture). In *Proceedings, Symposium on Logic in Computer Science*, page 119, Ithaca, N.Y., 1987. IEEE Com-puter Society Press.

[Rey88]   J. C. Reynolds. Preliminary design of the programming language Forsythe. Technical Report CMU-CS-88-159, Computer Science, Carnegie Mellon University, Pittsburgh, 1988.

[Rey89]   J. C. Reynolds. Syntactic control of interference control, part 2.
           In G. Ausiello, M. Dezani-Ciancaglini, and S. Ronchi Della
           Rocca, editors, *Automata, Languages and Programming*, vol-
           ume 372 of *Lecture Notes in Computer Science*, pages 704–722,
           Stresa, Italy, 1989. Springer-Verlag, Berlin.

[Rie90]   J. G. Riecke. A complete and decidable proof system for call-
           by-value equalities. In M. S. Paterson, editor, *Proc. 17th Int.
           Colloq. on Automata, Languages and Programming*, volume 443
           of *Lecture Notes in Computer Science*, pages 20–31. Springer-
           Verlag, Berlin, 1990.

[Rob87]   E. P. Robinson. Logical aspects of denotational semantics. In
           D. H. Pitt, A. Poigné, and D. E. Rydeheard, editors, *Category
           Theory and Computer Science*, number 283 in Lecture Notes in
           Computer Science, pages 238–253. Springer-Verlag, 1987.

[Ros86]   G. Rosolini. *Continuity and Effectiveness in Topoi*. D. Phil.
           thesis, Oxford University, 1986.

[RR91]   A. W. Roscoe and G. M. Reed. *Domains for Denotational Se-
           mantics*. Prentice-Hall International, London, 1991.

[Sch24]   M. Schönfinkel. Über die Bausteine der Mathematischen Logik.
           Math. Annalen, 92:305–316, 1924.

[Sch74]   J. S. Schwarz. *Semantics of Partial Correctness Formalisms*.
           Ph.D. thesis, Syracuse University, 1974.

[Sch86]   D. A. Schmidt. *Denotational Semantics, A Methodology for Lan-
           guage Development*. Allyn and Bacon, Newton, Massachusetts,
           1986. Reprinted by W. C. Brown, Dubuque, Iowa (1988).

[Sco69]   D. S. Scott. Privately circulated memo, Oxford University, Oc-
           tober 1969.

[Sco70]   D. S. Scott. Outline of a mathematical theory of computation.
           In *Proc. 4th Annual Princeton Conf. on Information Sciences
           and Systems*, pages 169–176, Princeton, 1970. Also technical
           monograph PRG-2, Programming Research Group, University
           of Oxford, Oxford.

[Sco72a]   D. S. Scott. Mathematical concepts in programming language
           semantics. In *Proc. 1972 Spring Joint Computer Conference*,
           pages 225–234. AFIPS Press, Montvale, N.J., 1972.

[Sco72b]   D. S. Scott. Models for various type-free calculi. In P. Suppes *et
           al*, editor, *Logic, Methodology, and the Philosophy of Science, IV*,
           pages 157–187, Bucharest, 1972. North-Holland, Amsterdam.

[Smy78]   M. B. Smyth. Powerdomains. *J. of Computer and System Sci-
           ences*, 16:23–36, 1978.

[Smy83]   M. B. Smyth. Power domains and predicate transformers: a topological view. In Diaz [Dia83], pages 662–676.

[SP82]   M. B. Smyth and G. D. Plotkin. The category-theoretic solution of recursive domain equations. *SIAM J. on Computing*, 11(4):761–783, 1982.

[SS71]   D. S. Scott and C. Strachey. Towards a mathematical semantics for computer languages. In J. Fox, editor, *Proceedings of the Symposium on Computers and Automata*, pages 19–46. Polytechnic Institute of Brooklyn Press, New York, 1971. Also technical monograph PRG-6, Programming Research Group, University of Oxford, Oxford.

[Sta85]   R. Statman. Logical relations and the typed λ-calculus. *Information and Computation*, 65:85–97, 1985.

[Sta90]   R. Statman. Some models of Scott's theory LCF based on a notion of rate of convergence. In W. Sieg, editor, *Logic and Computation*, volume 106 of *Contemporary Mathematics*, pages 263–280. American Mathematical Society, Providence, Rhode Island, 1990.

[Sto77]   J. E. Stoy. *Denotational Semantics: The Scott-Strachey Approach to Programming Language Theory*. The MIT Press, Cambridge, Massachusetts, and London, England, 1977.

[Sto88a]   A. Stoughton. *Fully Abstract Models of Programming Languages*. Research Notes in Theoretical Computer Science. Pitman, London, and Wiley, New York, 1988.

[Sto88b]   A. Stoughton. Substitution revisited. *Theoretical Computer Science*, 59:317–325, 1988.

[Str67]   C. Strachey. Fundamental concepts in programming languages. Lecture notes, International Summer School in Computer Programming, Copenhagen, 1967.

[Str72]   C. Strachey. The varieties of programming language. In *Proceedings of the International Computing Symposium*, pages 222–233. Cini Foundation, Venice, 1972. Also technical monograph PRG-10, Programming Research Group, University of Oxford, Oxford.

[SW74]   C. Strachey and C. P. Wadsworth. Continuations: a mathematical semantics for handling full jumps. Technical monograph PRG-11, Programming Research Group, University of Oxford, Oxford, 1974.

[Tar56]   A. Tarski. *Logic, Semantics, and Meta-Mathematics*. Oxford University Press, Oxford, 1956.

[Ten81] R. D. Tennent. *Principles of Programming Languages*. International Series in Computer Science. Prentice-Hall International, London, 1981.

[Ten83] R. D. Tennent. Semantics of interference control. *Theoretical Computer Science*, 27:297–310, 1983.

[Ten86] R. D. Tennent. Functor-category semantics of programming languages and logics. In D. Pitt, S. Abramsky, A. Poigné, and D. Rydeheard, editors, *Category Theory and Computer Programming*, volume 240 of *Lecture Notes in Computer Science*, pages 206–224, Guildford, U.K., 1986. Springer-Verlag, Berlin.

[Ten87a] R. D. Tennent. A note on undefined expression values in programming logics. *Inf. Proc. Letters*, 24:331–333, 1987.

[Ten87b] R. D. Tennent. Quantification in Algol-like languages. *Inf. Proc. Letters*, 25:133–137, 1987.

[Ten89] R. D. Tennent. Elementary data structures in Algol-like languages. *Science of Computer Programming*, 13:73–110, 1989.

[Ten91] R. D. Tennent. Denotational semantics. In Abramsky *et al.* [AGM91].

[TT91] R. D. Tennent and J. K. Tobin. Continuations in possible-world semantics. *Theoretical Computer Science*, to appear, 1991.

[TZ88] J. V. Tucker and J. I. Zucker. *Program Correctness over Abstract Data Types, with Error-State Semantics*, volume 6 of *CWI Monographs*. North-Holland, Amsterdam, 1988.

[vD83] D. van Dalen. *Logic and Structure*. Springer, Berlin, second edition, 1983.

[Wad76] C. Wadsworth. The relation between computational and denotational properties for Scott's D_∞ models of the lambda calculus. *SIAM J. on Computing*, 5:488–521, 1976.

[Wad78] C. Wadsworth. *Elementary Domains*. Lecture notes, Dept. of Computer Science, University of Edinburgh, 1978.

[Wan78] M. Wand. A new incompleteness result for Hoare's system. *J. ACM*, 25:168–175, 1978.

[Wan79] M. Wand. Fixed-point constructions in order-enriched categories. *Theoretical Computer Science*, 8:13–30, 1979.

[Win83] G. Winskel. A note on powerdomains and modality. In Karpinsky [Kar83], pages 505–514.

Index

acceptor, 148–51, 159, 182, 187–8
admissible predicate, 102–3, 106–8, 111–12, 132
Algol-like language, xx–xxi, 113–59, 172, 199, 218
ALGOL 60, xviii, 12, 84, 115, 126, 135, 143, 218
ALGOL 68, 67, 126, 135
ALGOL W, 145
aliasing, 129, 134, 191
Alpha law, 81–2, 105, 123
ambiguity, 15, 71, 117, 123, 132, 136, 140, 154
answer-domain adjunction, 196
anti-monotone, 137
applicative language, xix, 12, 59–88, 96–109, 115–21, 123–4, 218
array, 116–17, 130, 147–8
arrow category, 166
assertion formula, 46–52, 126–31, 133, 191–5
assignment command, 34, 36–8, 48, 60, 65, 116–17, 122, 124, 128–30, 134, 148–9, 191
axiomatic semantics, xix–xx, 10–12, 14

Beta law, 81–2, 105, 123, 218
binary relation, 23–4
block expression, 156–7, 196–9

call by name, xxi, 101, 119, 121, 123–4, 217
call by value, xviii, xxi, 101, 124–6, 134
Cartesian-closed category, 171, 181
case selection, 147, 158
category theory, xx, 13, 163–76, 200, 220

Cervantes, 221
chain, 24, 89–103
Church, A., 85
Clarke, E., xxi
co-domain
    of a function, 19
    of a morphism, 164
co-limiting cone, 206
coercion, 117–18, 132, 135–43, 145–6, 148–51, 152, 158–9, 216
Coherence lemma, 71–3
command, 31–57, 115–24, 152–4
commuting diagram, 20
comparable elements, 24
complete partial order, xix, 89 (see also domain, computational)
complete predicate (see admissible predicate)
completeness, xx, 11, 53, 57, 85
completion, 151–7, 182, 197
composition
    of functions, 20, 25, 35, 38, 93, 99
    of functors, 172
    of morphisms, 164, 186, 194
    of natural transformations, 175
compositionality, 7–9, 14, 40, 49
concurrency, xix, 53, 93
conditional, 32–3, 62, 65, 116–18, 121–3, 126, 133, 139, 149–50, 183–4
cone of embeddings, 206
conjunction, 15, 48, 74, 189
conjunctive type, 159
constant function, 20
constant functor, 172
continuation, xviii–xix, 151–7, 182, 185, 216
continuous function, xix, 92, 203

233

continuous functor, 209
contravariance, 173, 176, 181, 186, 212
Cook, S., xx–xxi
Curry, H. B., 75, 85

data structure, 31, 145–8, 216–18
data type, 32
denotational semantics, xix–xx, 9
de-referencing, 117, 122, 136, 148–51
discrete pre-order, 24
disjoint union (*see* sum of sets)
domain
    equation, xix–xx, 200–20
    of interpretation, 4
    computational, xix–xx, 12, 88–96
    of a function, 19
    of a morphism, 164
double chain, 92
dynamically-typed language, xx–xxi,
    216–19

eager evaluation (*see* call by value)
embedding functor, 172
embedding of domains, 204–8
environment, xix, 59, 64–7, 123, 124
equivalence relation, 24
Eta law, 81–2, 105, 123, 190
expansion, 186–7
explicitly-typed language, 70, 138
exponentiation
    of categories, 175
    of domains, 91
    of functors, 180
    of morphisms, 171
    of objects, 170
    of sets, 23
extension of a function, 21
extensionality, 20, 81–2, 106

Feys, R., 75
fixed point
    of a function, xix, 88, 96, 203
    of a functor, 203–15
fixed-point combinator, 218
fixed-point induction, 102, 105–6, 132
flat domain, 90
Floyd-Hoare logic, xx, 46–53, 57, 123,
    127–32, 155–6
forgetful functor, 172
free identifier, 72–3
Frege, G., 7

full abstraction, xx, 9–10, 57, 108–9,
    112
function, 19
functional abstraction, 67
functional language (*see* applicative
    language)
functional type, 60
functor category, 174–5, 177–9
functor, 171–6, 178

good variable, 130, 133, 191, 195, 199
graph of a function, 19

Hasse diagram, 24
higher-order type, 60
Hoare double, 155, 159, 190
Hoare logic (*see* Floyd-Hoare logic)
Hoare triple, 47, 123, 128, 155
Hoare, C. A. R., 46

identity function, 20
identity functor, 172
imperative language, xvii–xviii, xxi,
    12, 31–59, 115
implication, 15, 48–9, 74, 189, 196
incomparable elements, 24
initial object, 168
injection morphism, 169, 196
injective function, 20, 142, 194, 196
input, 41–2
interesting chain, 89, 107
intuitionistic logic, 15, 190–1, 196,
    198–9
invariant assertion, 49–50
isomorphism, 58, 91, 167
iteration, 22, 33–4, 38–41

jump, 31, 41, 151–6, 157, 177, 196

lambda calculus, xvii–xviii, xx, 82, 85,
    126, 171, 218, 220
lambda notation, xxi, 67, 126, 130
Landin, P. J., 68
lazy evaluation (*see* call by name)
LCF (*see* logic for computable
    functions)
least element, 24, 203
least upper bound, 24
Leibnitz, G. W., 188
lifting
    of a domain, 90
    of a functor, 179

limit point, 89, 107, 203, 216
LISP, 67, 126
list, 216–17
local variable, 119, 143–5, 177, 186–8, 192
location, 144–5
logic for computable functions, xx, 105, 111
logical relations, 104

machine configuration, 43
mathematical induction, 22, 39, 44–5
McCarty, C., 191
meta-language, 5, 7, 11
meta-variable, 5
Milner, R., xx
minimal element, 24
ML, xix, 126, 145
MODULA 2, 145
module, 31
monoid, 165, 172
monotonic function, 92, 172

natural deduction, xx, 15–19, 27, 61
natural numbers, 4, 22
natural transformation, 171, 173–6
non-determinism, xxi, 31, 53–5, 57
non-interference, 177, 191–6, 199
non-termination, 38, 42, 47–8, 54, 88, 93, 101, 120, 126, 127, 195, 198
numeral, 4–10, 13

object language, 5, 7
operational semantics, xix–xx, 10–12, 14, 42–6, 56–7, 103–5, 134, 159
opposite category, 165
output, 41–2, 152, 215–16

partial correctness, 47, 54, 198
partial function, xix, 21, 38
partial-order relation, 24
partially-ordered set, xix, 24–5
PASCAL, 68, 116, 144, 145, 148
perturbation of a function, 20
phrase assignment, 76
phrase type, 4
phrase-meaning assignment (*see* environment)
phrase-type assignment, 61
PL/1, 135
Plotkin, G. D., xx–xxi
pointer, 144

poset (*see* partially-ordered set)
possible world, xix, 175, 177–99
post-condition, 47
pre-condition, 47
pre-defined identifier, 61, 105
pre-order relation, 24
pre-ordered set, 26
predicate logic, xix, 9, 48, 69, 74, 79–80
predicate transformer, 57–8
prefix ordering, 202
procedure, 31, 116
product type, 145–7
product
    of categories, 166, 196
    of domains, 89
    of functors, 179
    of morphisms, 169
    of objects, 168
    of sets, 22
program, 41–2, 61, 64, 118, 153, 215
programming logic, 46–53, 73–82, 105–8, 127–32, 155–6, 191–8
projection for an embedding, 204
projection morphism, 168
propositional logic, xix, 15, 17

quantification, 47, 69–70, 74, 79–80, 128, 143, 148, 153–4, 189–91

recursion, 12, 41, 59, 86–8, 97, 99–103, 111–12, 118–19, 132, 200–20
restriction of a function, 20
Reynolds, J. C., xx–xxi, 3, 115, 163

SCHEME, xix, 126
scope of a binding, 61–6, 143
Scott, D. S., xx, 3, 14, 31, 42, 86, 88, 92–3, 204
semantic equation, 6
semantic equivalence, 8
sequencing, 32, 124, 154
sequent, 16, 61, 79
side effect, 126, 157, 177, 196
sieve, 189
SIMULA, 145
soundness, 11, 51–3, 77–8, 80–1
specification formula, 15, 47, 188–96
specification logic, xx, 191–6
state, xix, 31, 37, 120, 124
state-change restriction, 194–5
state-set restriction, 194

static assertion, 48
statically-typed language, xx–xxi
Strachey, C., xx, 3, 14, 31, 36, 53, 59,
    128, 200
strict function, 93
structural induction, 8
Substitution lemma, 78
substitution, 48, 75–80, 146
substitutivity, 8, 10, 81, 123
sum
    of domains, 90, 196
    of morphisms, 170
    of objects, 169
    of sets, 23, 144
surjective function, 20
syntax, 3
    abstract, 15
    concrete, 16
    context-free, xx, 4

terminal object, 167
total function, 21

underlying set, 24
upper bound, 24

validity, 16, 51–3, 77–9, 80–2, 108,
    190, 195
valuation function, 5–6
value phrase, 60
value-like type, 118, 121
variable, 37, 116, 148–50, 186–8
Voltaire, 177